The Globalization of Multinational Enterprise Activity and Economic Development

Edited by

Neil Hood

and

Stephen Young

First published in Great Britain 2000 by
MACMILLAN PRESS LTD
Houndmills, Basingstoke, Hampshire RG21 6XS and London
Companies and representatives throughout the world

A catalogue record for this book is available from the British Library.

ISBN 0–333–74881–6

First published in the United States of America 2000 by
ST. MARTIN'S PRESS, INC.,
Scholarly and Reference Division,
175 Fifth Avenue, New York, N.Y. 10010

ISBN 0–312–22537–7

Library of Congress Cataloging-in-Publication Data
The globalization of multinational enterprise activity and economic development / edited by Neil Hood and Stephen Young.
p. cm.
"This book is based on a workshop which was held at the Strathclyde Graduate Business School in the University of Strathclyde, Glasgow, UK, on 15 and 16 May, 1998"—Pref.
Includes bibliographical references and index.
ISBN 0–312–22537–7 (cloth)
1. International business enterprises Congresses.
2. International trade Congresses. 3. Economic development Congresses. I. Hood, Neil. II. Young, Stephen, 1944– .
HD2755.5.G556 1999
658'.049—dc21 99–26125
CIP

This book is printed on paper suitable for recycling and made from fully managed and sustained forest sources.

10 9 8 7 6 5 4 3
09 08 07 06 05 04 03 02 01

Printed and bound in Great Britain by Antony Rowe Ltd, Chippenham, Wiltshire

Contents

List of Tables

List of Figures

List of Boxes

Preface and Acknowledgements

This book is based on a Workshop which was held at the Strathclyde Graduate Business School in the University of Strathclyde, Glasgow, UK, on 15 and 16 May 1998, on the topic of the *Globalization of Multinational Enterprise Activity and Economic Development*. Through the generosity of a number of sponsors, several of whom have supported our work over a number of years, we were able to invite a distinguished list of authors and discussants to Scotland for this event. For their generous financial contributions we would therefore like to thank Scottish Enterprise, the country's leading economic development agency, Bank of Scotland, Royal Bank of Scotland, Barclay's Bank, Ernst & Young and the Souter Foundation.

We would like to specially thank Irene Hood for making all the arrangements associated with the Workshop and for the superb contribution to its smooth running. We are also indebted to several of our PhD students in Strathclyde International Business Unit who ably assisted during the Workshop. In this regard, therefore, our thanks go to Karl Alorbi, Jürgen Broch, Jaswinder Hayer, Kevin Ibeh, Jeff Johnson and Prathap Oburai.

The production of this volume would not have been possible without the excellent work of Irene Hood as our editorial assistant and we acknowledge her continued outstanding endeavours for us, her diligent coordination of the manuscripts and extensive liaison with all the contributors.

NEIL HOOD
STEPHEN YOUNG

List of Contributors and Discussants

CONTRIBUTORS

Julian Birkinshaw, Stockholm School of Economics, Stockholm, Sweden.

Thomas L. Brewer, Georgetown University, Washington DC, USA.

Peter J. Buckley, University of Leeds, Leeds, UK.

Daniel Chudnovsky, CENIT, Buenos Aires, Argentina.

John H. Dunning, Rutgers University, New Jersey, USA.

Michael J. Enright, University of Hong Kong, HongKong.

Crispian Fuller, University of Wales, Cardiff, UK.

Neil Hood, University of Strathclyde, Glasgow, UK.

Stephen J. Kobrin, University of Pennsylvania, Philadelphia, USA.

Hafiz Mirza, University of Bradford, Bradford, UK.

Kevin Morgan, University of Wales, Cardiff, UK.

Lynn K. Mytelka, UNCTAD, Geneva, Switzerland.

Terutomo Ozawa, Colorado State University, USA.

Ewen Peter, Scottish Enterprise, Glasgow, UK.

Nick Phelps, University of Wales, Cardiff, UK.

Jonathan Slow, Scottish Enterprise, Glasgow, UK.

Stephen Young, University of Strathclyde, Glasgow, UK.

DISCUSSANTS

Ash Amin, University of Durham, Durham, UK.

Julian Birkinshaw, Stockholm School of Economics, Stockholm, Sweden.

Peter J. Buckley, University of Leeds, Leeds, UK.

John H. Dunning, Rutgers University, New Jersey, USA.

Michael J. Enright, University of Hong Kong, Hong Kong.

Neil Hood, University of Strathclyde, Glasgow, UK.

Neil Kay, University of Strathclyde, Glasgow, UK.

Stephen J. Kobrin, University of Pennsylvania, Pennsylvania, USA.

Michael McDermott, University of Strathclyde, Glasgow, UK.

Lynn K. Mytelka, UNCTAD, Geneva, Switzerland.

A. Edward Safarian, University of Toronto, Ontario, Canada.

James H. Taggart, University of Strathclyde, Glasgow, UK.

Part I

Issues and Theory

1 Globalization, Multinational Enterprises and Economic Development

Neil Hood and Stephen Young

INTRODUCTION

This volume has emerged from the long-standing interests of the editors in the interface between corporate strategies of international companies and the economic policies of governments as applied to the attraction and development of foreign direct investment (FDI). In recent years some excellent volumes have emerged dealing with many of the different effects of globalization upon the behaviour of governments (Dunning, 1997); upon the dynamics of the firm (Chandler *et al.*, 1998); upon technology and competitiveness strategies (Casson, 1991); and upon institutional and regional development (Amin and Thrift, 1994). While several of these collections touch on aspects of this volume, the approach here more specifically addresses the globalization of multinational enterprise activity and economic development. The process of globalization has drawn attention to the growing significance of the coordinating and transaction functions of the firm. At the same time it has raised new questions about the role of national and subnational governments as to how (or if) they are able to influence the spatial organization of economic activity in directions consistent with their economic development objectives.

This introductory chapter begins to explore some of these issues. Commencing with a contrasting review of the imperatives which respectively drive companies and countries in their business and economic development, two potential scenarios are suggested for the long-run impact of globalization on economic development. Having thus set the framework for the volume, the final section briefly summarizes the contributions of the authors of each of the chapters.

GLOBALIZATION: COMPANIES AND COUNTRIES

Recognizing that there are many different ways of defining globalization, this volume views it as the process by which the world economy is transformed from a set of national and regional markets into a set of markets that operate without regard to national boundaries. Such an approach removes a number of areas of disagreement which can inhibit the definition of terms for such a volume. By drawing attention to a *process* there is, for example, no impression that this applies only to companies with global reach; or that it is principally to do with the corporate sector; or that it is time-bound with a need to hypothesise precisely when an industry, technology or company became globalized. Equally it is quite clear that this process is far from complete, a point developed by John Dunning in Chapter 2. The direction of the process captured in the definition above has been identified for several decades, and there is some evidence that it has accelerated in the past ten years. Moreover, there are few parts of a country's economic development which are not subject to some influence from the globalization process.

The central thrust of this volume is towards developing a deeper understanding of the ways in which the globalization of business impacts upon economic development. One element of this is therefore about the political economy of globalization. Strange (1997, p. 137) observes that from that perspective globalization means the coincidental effects of three major changes: namely the accelerated internationalization of production; the sharply increased mobility of capital; and the greater mobility of knowledge or information from communication of messages to the transfer of technology. There is little doubt that in various roles the multinational enterprise (MNE) has been a driver, enabler and promoter of these processes. Their strategies have been led by a desire to optimize market, cost and competitive variables within a liberalizing trade and investment environment. The economic development of nation-states has been much influenced as a result. Yet it is evident that the interests of corporate entities and countries are not always the same, and it is possible that globalization processes may serve to highlight the differences between them (Amin and Thrift, 1994; Dicken, 1992, 1994). As part of the setting of the context for this volume, it is therefore necessary to explore the interface between corporate development and economic development in a globalizing world economy. These are considered in Table 1.1 under five headings, namely per-

Table 1.1 Globalization: companies and countries

Corporate imperatives	*Economic development imperatives*
Performance: • Maximize shareholder value and economic value-added • Minimize cost base, consistent with customer needs • Achieve earnings growth targets	• GDP growth, employment quantity and quality enhanced • Create, sustain and develop clusters of related economic activity • Encourage new enterprise development • Effective internationalization of indigenous business and strengthen home base
Responsiveness: • Flexible labour markets with high-quality employees at all levels • Based on supportive hard and soft infrastructure • Ready access to national and international supply chains • Ability to adjust patterns of asset location with predictable costs	• Flexible labour markets with high-quality employees at all levels, but an added desire for higher value-added employment • Support hard and soft infrastructure development • Maximize local supply chain • Pursuit of embeddedness strategies at local level
Networks: • Establish and deploy wide range of business relationships as required, incorporating all relevant stakeholders	• Networks acknowledged and supported but premium placed on the nature of the 'local' dimension
Technology: • Undertake RD&D at whatever locations and by whatever contractual terms are required • Gain access to technology by whatever set of business relationships is required	• Stimulate/develop the local rooting of technology generation and commercialization • Maximize the participation of local technical resources
Higher-order functions: • Optimal location of HQ and divisional functions to match market and customer needs	• Maintenance of indigenous HQs • Growth of 'developmental' subsidiaries of international corporations

formance, responsiveness, networks, technology and higher order functions.

Table 1.1 is based on the premise that it is possible to identify a set of imperatives which *primarily* govern the actions of companies in their business development, and governments in their policies towards economic development. Moreover, in each of the areas selected for consideration, there are grounds for arguing that the process of globalization could lead to a number of situations where both parties will find it more difficult to reconcile these two sets of imperatives. The globalization processes examined in this volume are led by MNEs, and economic development policies are pursued in recognition of where the balance of countervailing power resides.

Taking the area of both performance of corporate and country assets, some of the relative priorities of the two sets of actors are shown in Table 1.1. In an MNE these objectives cannot be pursued irrespective of the geography of markets, but it is for example evident that the maximizing of shareholder value and economic value-added may not coincide with the economic objectives of any given host country. Two of the chapters amply illustrate this. At the level of the enterprise, Julian Birkinshaw (Chapter 3) explores some of the internal resource allocation mechanisms in MNEs which, *inter alia*, determine the location of the various elements of the value chain. While this is not undertaken independent of country characteristics, a country's economic development priorities do not centrally feature within this decision matrix. Equally, Michael Enright in Chapter 13 draws attention to the diverse range of cluster initiatives constructed to meet economic development imperatives in many different countries, but implicitly recognizes that many of the corporate components of such an exercise may only be marginally influenced by such initiatives, especially if they are more to do with aspirations than reality.

Perhaps one of the most evident performance issues in Table 1.1 where globalization causes tensions is that related to the minimization of the cost base, consistent with customer needs. While at one level this can emerge as the constant pursuit of higher productivity by relocating parts of the corporate asset base, it is invariably much more complex than that. For example, the network school of scholars regularly draws attention to the importance of the dynamics of overlapping networks as the valid frame of reference for studying micro/macro interaction. Thus individual firms are more dependent on coordination with specific other firms through exchange relationships (Mattsson, 1998; Lundgren, 1995). One consequence of such corporate interactions is that they are largely immune from most forms of governmental influence, such as might be brought to bear, for example, on a threatened MNE subsidiary closure in a region where there was high unemployment and high social costs of exit.

Before leaving corporate performance dimensions, some comment should be made on the important question of the internationalization of indigenous business as an economic development objective. Many countries would recognize this as a vital element of corporate competitiveness as business more effectively responds to customer needs. Others would regard it as the export of job opportunities. Almost all would acknowledge it is one of the consequences of globalization. A few, such as Australia and Singapore, have actively promoted it as a form of international business development, but most leave it entirely to market mechanisms. Large MNEs can, and do, stimulate this by, for example, requiring their leading international suppliers in a given host country to internationalize in support of their own global strategies. But there are many paradoxes in this area. While it is a tacit economic development objective, there are relatively few countries with measures to realise it; meanwhile on a selective front MNEs stimulate it in pursuit of their broader ends, one of which is not likely to include the strengthening of the home base. A number of issues related to this are touched upon by Stephen Young, Jonathan Slow and Neil Hood in Chapter 5, although the perspective here is more aligned to the corporate strategies of smaller and non-dominant firms as they seek to internationalize.

The question of responsiveness is the second theme emerging in Table 1.1. At the macro-level there is ample evidence that the recent changes in the global economy have affected the geography of foreign direct investment (FDI) and the strategies of MNEs (Dunning, 1998). This section is, however, addressed at the more micro-level. It is evident that a number of the outcomes of globalization require more rapid and flexible responses from corporations. This is, for example, shown in the shortening of product cycles; heightened customer service expectations; the emergence of different business models; the exploitation of many different modes of internationalization; the continued pressures to re-engineer organizations, and so on. Together these aggregate to the types of corporate responsiveness set out in Table 1.1. The country and economic development side of the equation attempts to mirror these demands in this instance as a form of supply-side response. However, the table serves to highlight at least two areas where the country agenda may require more than a demand and supply equilibrium, namely on questions of the locus of higher value-added employment and the embeddedness of the MNE activity. Much has been written elsewhere about these issues. For example, on embeddedness see Grabher (1993) and Harrison (1992); while many aspects of the ways in which the location of value-added activity is addressed within MNEs are covered in Birkinshaw and Hood (1998). The chapter by Ewen Peters (Chapter 14) in this volume gives some invaluable insight into one country's pursuit of value-added activity within the electronics industry, illustrating various initiatives to enhance local clusters.

The responsiveness issue is a complex and controversial one, and it emerges in this volume in a variety of guises. For example, it lies at the heart of the chapter by Peter Buckley and Stephen Young on Egypt (Chapter 7); and there are echoes of it in the Argentinian context in Daniel Chudnovsky's Chapter 8. In part of Lynn Mytelka's work (Chapter 12) there are cautionary notes sounded about what might be a form of over-responsiveness on the part of countries, which is reflected in high degrees of competitive bidding for major inward-investment projects. Equally, the embeddedness and economic contribution aspect of responsiveness is written into Chapter 4, where Neil Hood and Ewen Peters review some of the drivers of the globalization of business services, and hypothesise about the emerging relative importance of different types of location.

Table 1.1 refers to the different dimensions of networks which are associated with globalization and economic development. From the perspective of the MNE these are reflective of more flexible organizational structures and the growing need to deploy a wide range of relationships with different stakeholders across the various countries in which it operates (Staber *et al.*, 1996). One corresponding economic imperative is to ensure that the corporate and country flexibilities match each other in so far as they can, consistent with other aspects of economic policy. Although none of the chapters in this volume is exclusively concerned with network issues, the subject permeates several of them from different perspectives. For example, the historic importance of local networks in the development of smaller and medium-sized MNEs is the theme of Ozawa's Chapter 10. Meanwhile the investment attraction and development implications of these intertwined relationships emerge to some degree in both Phelps, Morgan and Fuller's Chapter 15 with reference to Wales; and in

Mytelka's Chapter 12 with reference to heightened competitive bidding.

Recent years have produced ample evidence of the internationalization of technological activity in large MNEs (Dunning, 1988; Casson, 1991; Cantwell, 1994). Among other outcomes, globalization has involved the establishment of new international structures for technology-creation including tapping into combinations of home and host-country expertise, and providing a means for the outputs of these processes to be speedily exploited on a global scale. Table 1.1 suggests some of the local infrastructural requirements which countries invariably pursue in order to participate in and gain benefit from such developments. In many countries this includes renewed endeavours to enhance linkages between institutes of higher education and MNEs, spurring on the commercialization of locally created intellectual property, and so on. In this volume the policy initiatives considered in Michael Enright's Chapter 13 are much informed by these developments. Equally, the levels of cooperation which have underpinned some of the Asian MNE strategies considered in Hafiz Mirza's Chapter 9 can be viewed as being driven by the nature of technological advantage in these same countries.

The final area touched on in Table 1.1 is that of higher-order functions. While there is much evidence to demonstrate that the shape of the MNE and its relationship to the various environments in which it operates is changing through globalization (Dunning, 1997; Chandler *et al.*, 1998), some core concerns still dominate economic development debates over the location of value-adding activity. Governments therefore seek to attract regional headquarters functions and retain such control centres as indigenous businesses internationalize, recognizing that economic input is likely to be enhanced in the longer term if integrated operations can be maintained. One aspect of this debate which has grown with globalization is the fostering of developmental subsidiaries (Young, Hood and Peters, 1994; Birkinshaw and Hood, 1998). This issue features extensively in this volume in both Chapters 5 and 14.

It will be evident from the preceding paragraphs that there is much scope for research and debate on many of these issues. Globalization does not in itself change the need for corporate and country interests to coexist, but it has already changed the nature of that coexistence. The fact that much of the dynamic for change is on the corporate side has led both country and wider economic region policies to flex in order to gain a growing share in the benefits, without always counting the costs. The reader will encounter many of the ensuing challenges in the chapters which follow. As a consequence, Tom Brewer and Stephen Young's Chapter 11 on global rule-making may be revisited and viewed in a new light.

GLOBALIZATION AND REGIONAL FUTURES

Although it is not possible to predict with any accuracy the outcome of the processes considered in the previous section, it is possible to set out in summary some of the alternative scenarios which might ensue. These are presented here as part of setting the scene for this volume. The authors were not asked to either address or subscribe to them as they constructed their own contributions.

Perspective has a considerable role to play in interpreting Table 1.2. Thus the view from a restructuring economy in Eastern Europe will be rather different from that of Silicon Valley; the expectations of the role of MNEs in economic development will also lead to varying interpretations of a commentator from Singapore as against one from Southern Italy. Equally, some may regard the question of regional futures in the light of globalization as too difficult to call and therefore unworthy of debate in a volume of this type. The authors merely offer their views on alternative outcomes as a stimulus to both analysis and policy formation.

In the positive scenario, the weight of change on the corporate side is towards flexibility of form and strategy, hence more dispersed entities, led by knowledge creation and innovation. This benign and decentralized view of the corporate world creates an abundance of opportunities for regions to benefit. It also signals that the enhancement of education, information exchange, infrastructure and innovation of all kinds is the key to participation for countries and regions. This scenario recognizes that there are different degrees to which these responses will be achieved, but at its core regards it possible for there to be many winners from globalization.

The more negative scenario in Table 1.2 assumes that MNEs take much longer for their globalization strategies to be materially determined by knowledge factors. Moreover, even if they are so determined, the thrust might equally be to centralize that knowledge in key nodes within core regions, defined in terms of markets and technological clusters. In consequence globalization could widen inequality,

Table 1.2 Globalization and regional futures

Regions	*Companies*
Positive Scenario: • Globalization leads to a qualitative shift in the nature of economic competition towards 'knowledge-intensive capitalism' • Peripheral regions gain through creating new forms of high value-added competitive advantage by accessing global networks of productions, consumption and information exchange • 'Learning Regions' and 'Regional Innovation Systems' become a policy focus.	• New, flexible organizational forms, strategies and practices • Geographic dispersal of value-adding activity and regional agglomeration gains increase • Knowledge emerging as more important than 'traditional' factors of production • Cost reduction key to development of sustainable competitive advantage. Companies under pressure to make better use of dispersed activities. • 'Incremental' innovation vital for survival of *all* firms.
Negative Scenario: • Globalization widens inequality between regions as a result of powerful corporate centrifugal forces • The position of core regions is enhanced since these contain most HQ functions and associated clusters • Peripheral regions are further disadvantaged and forced into cost-based competition for economic development	• Relatively slow shift towards being driven by knowledge factors • Globalizing companies become more concerned with collecting and centralizing knowledge to serve their strategic interests • Agglomeration benefits exploited in fewer 'core' locations

further redefining and disadvantaging more peripheral regions which are in turn forced into cost-based competition to sustain economic development. This approach hypothesizes that corporate centrifugal forces (such as shown in Table 1.1), will outweigh economic development forces which are designed to be centripetal, seeking the localization of benefits.

This volume was finally assembled during the autumn of 1998, in a climate of economic uncertainty flowing from cumulative global effects of crises in the Asian and Russian economies, and in the shadow of long-running bull markets in the major stock exchanges. It is possible that a number of these events will result in lower levels of economic growth in the earlier years of the millennium and bring new sharpness to some of these scenarios as MNEs further adjust towards even more integrated strategies on a global basis.

OUTLINE OF THE BOOK

This volume is organized in five parts: Part I, issues and theory; Part II, the corporate perspective; Part III, the country perspective; Part IV, the policy perspective; Part V, conclusions.

Part I: Issues and Theory

In addition to this introductory chapter setting out some of the key issues, this part contains an important contribution from John Dunning, in Chapter 2. He explores whether the received scholarly wisdom regarding the motives, determinants and organizational modes of international business activity still holds in the context of the globalization of economic activity. Dunning identifies three landmarks in theorizing about MNE activity, the first of which was in the first half of the 1960s (Hymer, Vernon, Rugman, Aliber, Knickerbocker and Graham) which witnessed the emergence of partial explanations of FDI and international production. The second half of the 1970s marked the second stage where he records the major advances which were initiated by the paradigms advanced by Kojima and Buckley and Casson, and by his own work in the eclectic theory which, *inter alia*, factored in the spatial aspect of MNE activity. Subsequent theoretical work on the stages of internationalization, resource-based and evolutionary theories of the firm, have led to an increased emphasis on knowledge as a competitive asset. Dunning argues that the events of the 1990s have brought with them challenges to theory-building; especially with respect to asset-augmenting FDI, but he develops his essay to confirm his belief that the eclectic paradigm can accommodate these, albeit with some broadening. He usefully sets out differences in the scenarios of the 1970s and 1990s and concludes that the globalizing economy requires some reconstruction of the theory of internationalization to be more systemic, to give more attention to cross-border transactions, and to revisit the choice of organizational options. The final section of the chapter provides a helpful review of the ways in which globalization is requiring theorists to modify accepted explanations of the geography of FDI.

Part II: The Corporate Perspective

In this section of the volume, the perspective changes. Chapters 3, 4 and 5 examine rather different corporate dimensions of globalization, namely by describing and interpreting changes in the strategy and organization of large MNEs (Julian Birkinshaw); by exploring ways in which the globalization of business service providers impacts upon economic development (Neil Hood and Ewen Peters); and by evaluating the way in which key globalization drivers and determinants have impacted upon the strategies of a sample of small and non-dominant firms (Stephen Young, Jonathan Slow and Neil Hood).

Julian Birkinshaw in Chapter 3 addresses the major issues facing large MNCs in the current economic climate, citing as critical the geographical dispersal of value-adding activities; the competitive pressures pushing companies to make better use of activities so dispersed; and the need to develop more flexible configurations which are responsive to changing market demands. He makes the case for a new model for managing MNCs based on a more micro-level of analysis, namely the subsidiary unit. Moreover, he identifies increasing levels of internal competition between these units in a globalizing world economy. One element of this results in charters being actively competed for by both existing and new locations across the world. These environmental characteristics stimulate Birkinshaw's observations on the emergence of an internal-market model by which activities are increasingly configured and coordinated, specifically in the markets for intermediate products/services, charters and practices. The substance of this argument is that the question of multinationality is still vitally important in structuring MNEs and that globalization tends to make it even more important, hence the need for a conceptual and practical organizational framework within which all appropriate competitive dimensions can be optimized. Birkinshaw demonstrates the richness of this concept, but readily acknowledges the need for both further theoretical reconciliation with other theories and for more empirical testing of the concept.

Chapter 4 turns to a specific sector, as Neil Hood and Ewen Peters examine global trends in professional business services. Set in the context of the literature on the globalization of services, they turn more specifically to explore the key trends and drivers linking service globalization and location. These include the forces leading to both service outsourcing and consolidation, which are then linked to service nodes and customer physical proximity requirements. Explorations of a model for the geographical dispersion of professional business services allows the potential economic development consequences to be woven into the chapter, with different scenarios being set out. The chapter contains a case section which assesses the strategy of three truly global service providers (EDS, FedEx and Andersen Consulting) and matches this by discussing two exemplar regions (Singapore and Phoenix, USA) which have targeted economic development based on attracting global business services. Finally, a tentative model is developed for one of the most ubiquitous business service types, namely the call centre, with some cautionary notes on their longer-term development potential. In the spirit of this volume, this chapter attempts to specifically interlink the corporate and the economic development dimensions emerging from the internationalization and emerging globalization of this sector.

In the final chapter in this part, Stephen Young, Jonathan Slow and Neil Hood report on some exploratory research on small and non-dominant firms headquartered in Scotland. The interest is not only in the response to globalization, but also on the issues for home-country economic development and public policy. Having examined some important criteria for the identification of globalization tendencies, the authors present these in a model which allows companies to be placed on a continuum from domestic to global. This model is then tested using five detailed cases chosen to illustrate the diversity of behaviour of small and non-dominant firms in Scotland. These provide some rich and insightful detail on the evolution of these businesses and the different ways in which they address (and are impacted by) the globalization process. Among the public policy consequences reviewed are whether outward investment should be more actively encouraged by governments and whether the characteristics of developmental headquarters functions are really understood in economic development circles. The authors of this chapter once more acknowledge that their contribution only touches the tip of a very large and rather important iceberg.

Part III: The Country Perspective

Chapters 6 to 10 in this section are all written from a country perspective. Three cover the specific cases of Egypt, Argentina and Japan; while one has a mainly Asian focus and another looks more generally at development post-industrialization but with a specific emphasis on the Indian software industry.

Stephen Kobrin in Chapter 6 recognizes that, while globalization can be defined as broader and deeper economic integration, this process has occurred alongside the increased polarization of wealth and poverty. The chapter goes on to explore the relationship between globalization and development, focusing upon the impact of the information revolution on developing countries. Kobrin believes that late twentieth century globalization does not represent a change in kind from that earlier in the century, but acknowledges the profound impact of deeper integration and the increases in the scale of technology, arguing that the information revolution is the central transformative phenomenon of globalization. The case of the Indian software industry is considered in some depth as one of the foremost examples of the integrating of a developing country into the electronically networked world economy. While recording its success (not least as a means of leapfrogging stages of development), it is argued that the tangible impact on India is modest and it remains an example of dualism in spite of its being globally integrated. The chapter concludes with some keen and considered observations on development in the post-industrial age which are directly addressed to the overall theme of the book.

Chapters 7 and 8 are country cases. Peter Buckley and Stephen Young in Chapter 7 provide a comprehensive review of the role which FDI and MNEs play in the Egyptian economy, a country viewed as characteristic of many of the transitional economies around the world. The authors develop some ideas for policy reform which would *inter alia* create greater integration between the country, MNEs, global and regional economies. The chapter provides a historical perspective on policy formation and assesses Egypt's attractiveness for FDI, illustrating this by some case examples. Buckley and Young set out in some detail a multi-level agenda for policy innovation focusing on FDI attraction, distinguishing between reforms required in legal, institutional, promotional and infrastructural issues. They recognize that the pace of market reform and economic liberalization in Egypt has been slow, yet view the requirement for integration into the world economic system as ever more pressing given local economic conditions. They conclude by observing that at this point Egypt is a country upon which the globalization of MNE activity has scarcely had any economic development impact.

The central concern in Chapter 8 by Daniel Chudnovsky is Argentina, a country which has attracted substantial FDI flows during the 1990s. Setting the role of external investment in its conceptual context, Chudnovsky evaluates recent FDI trends in the country, by motivation, by sector, and by impact on trade and export performance. He reports on survey evidence on the technological and organizational contributions made by inward investors in areas such as productivity, quality and local linkages, concluding that the issue of investment quality remains an important policy question in terms of the more effective integration of Argentina into the world economy.

In Chapter 9, Hafiz Mirza explains how East Asian developing country multinationals have been engendered by globalization and regionalization, assessing their characteristics, strategy and behaviour. The chapter traces the factors which have led to the shift of production to developing countries over the past two decades, evaluating the opportunities which that created for both foreign and local firms and for countries such as South Korea, Taiwan and Singapore. Mirza probes the complex interaction between MNEs, governments and regionalization processes in East Asia, placing this within the broader consideration of developing country MNEs. The latter sections of the chapter examine both the shape of these MNEs and the nature of the FDI patterns which have emerged, as well as commenting on the consequences of these trends. He attributes many of these developments to the simultaneous process of globalization and regionalization, and points the way for further research on developing country multinationals.

The final chapter in this section (Chapter 10) by Terutomo Ozawa is rooted in a historical analysis of small and medium-sized MNCs in Japan. The author regards Japan as a good laboratory in which to study the interactions between the economic phenomenon of industrial clusters and the internationalization processes of SMEs. Ozawa traces the origins of conceptual thinking on clusters back to Adam Smith and uses a framework derived from these origins to chart the structural upgrading of the Japanese economy through four phases over the past five decades. Particular attention is paid to the roles of SMEs as both wealth-creating and business globalizers through this period, and some interesting cases are included. Ozawa concludes that the topic of industrial clusters and international business activities requires much further explanation, but remains confident about the inherent dynamic of Japanese SMEs as active participants in global business.

Part IV: The Policy Perspective

While all of the chapters in this volume give some level of consideration to policy matters, the five chapters in this section do so in a more concentrated way. The coverage is diverse, in that it touches on subjects ranging from global investment rules at the most macro-level to MNE subsidiary development at the more micro-level. Equally, there is an analysis of inter-country competitive bidding for FDI, an exposition of the cluster paradigm as it relates to economic development and globalization, and a small country case on appropriate structures for investment attraction and development. They are united by the common overall theme and serve to remind the reader of the multidimensional levels at which policy issues occur.

Thomas Brewer and Stephen Young start Chapter 11 with the premise that, although there is a long way to go in investment liberalization (especially in some major developing nations and transitional economies), it is essential to lock-in the liberalization which has been achieved to secure the economic development benefits flowing from it. The case for a system of investment rules to complement GATT and WTO rests on this premise. The authors examine the data on both the WTO dispute cases and GATT cases in search of evidence about the implementation of the rules and their economic development consequences. It emerges that while very few of the WTO dispute cases concern investment issues, there is much further work to be done to understand more fully the ways in which trade rules influence the international operations of MNEs. The chapter also covers the future negotiating agenda in areas such as services, intellectual property and government procurement and anticipates that investment issues will become increasingly important in WTO negotiations for a long time ahead. In their concluding section, Brewer and Young note that so far only a very small step has been taken towards multilateral investment liberalization, and anticipate that it may be difficult to achieve much of what is desirable in the medium term due to concerns over national sovereignty. Equally, it is recognized that some better quantification of the effects of liberalization may be necessary in order to show where the economic development gains for globalization may flow.

In Chapter 12, Lynn Mytelka deals with two distinct dimensions of globalization. One concerns the emergence of a global market for investment locations and the locational tournaments which take place across them; the other is the globalization of an innovation-based mode of competition, a process which she argues has been diffused by trade and investment liberalization. The chapter sets the context as one of turbulent learning environments engendered by growing capital mobility and the transference of knowledge at a greater pace. The consequences are then specifically explored in a consideration of locational tournaments in the automobile and electronics industries. The author concludes that the review of the relationship between turbulence generated by accelerated capital mobility and local learning and innovation shows that attracting FDI to a region will not necessarily contribute to greater innovative activity in that region. The perils of intra-country competition are highlighted, although the prospect is that, in spite of mounting criticism of the practice, bidding wars are likely to continue as governments seek to maximize their gains from globalization.

The core of Michael Enright's insightful contribution in Chapter 13 is the argument that the globalization of competition is completely consistent with the localization of competitive advantage in some industries and activities. The chapter sets out the similarities and differences among the cluster-based strategies that have emerged in nations and regions around the world to deal with the globalization–localization nexus. He suggests that, on the basis of the evidence, many such programmes lack a sufficiently rigorous process of cluster identification, characterization and selection and in consequence they may not provide a meaningful basis to inform local economic development strategies. The author remains positive about the role which such a methodology can have when properly formulated and implemented. This chapter is a tour de force for any reader wishing a precise overview of how clusters can and cannot aid governments and others to relate globalization and economic development.

Chapter 14, by Ewen Peters, brings an interesting perspective on some of the processes of plant upgrading in the subsidiaries of leading electronics companies located in Europe and the Far East. It offers some rare insights into the detail of the outworking of MNE globalization strategies in this highly competitive sector. Several important aspects of plant upgrading in manufacturing operations are explained including the co-location of manufacturing and product development; the extent to which the investment which supported upgrading was contestable by alternative locations; the role played by the public sector in stimulating this process in the various locations where it occurred; and the impact which this had on both the subsidiary and the local host economy. The eight cases are evaluated in depth within the chapter and these issues explained for each of them. They are acknowledged to be a relatively rare breed and few appear as open to being contestable as governments would like. As in the Enright chapter, Peters makes a plea for targeted strategies for upgrading, focusing attention on the role played in this by credible clusterings of related activity.

In Chapter 15, Nick Phelps, Kevin Morgan and Crispian Fuller round off the policy perspective by posing the question as to whether constitutional change in a small country with high FDI dependency such as Wales, will exacerbate regional differences in institutional capacities involved with the attraction and support of inward investors in the UK. The chapter reviews the evolution of institutional mechanisms in Wales, emphasising their relative recent origins and relative success in investment attraction but noting that this may be declining. In a globalizing environment, the authors express anxiety that the emergence of an elected Assembly in Wales could be to the detriment of the interface with MNEs, due to a reduction in hierarchical modes of interacting with them and due to the growth of sub-regional competition. It is evident that such tendencies to local fragmentation with not necessarily match with the further corporate integration and co-ordination likely to emerge from the globalization process.

CONCLUDING REMARKS

The chapters in this volume comprise a rich menu of perspectives on globalization and economic development, and many dimensions of the topic are given some consideration. The Workshop on which it was based was designed to strike a balance between the corporate, country and policy components. Issue could readily be taken with the editors that each of these could have filled several volumes on its own. The 17 contributors have brought their distinctive viewpoints to the theme reflecting their training, culture, career track and experience. The editors thank them and hope that the reader will become better informed about some of the many challenges for economic development which lie ahead in the light of the globalization of multinational enterprise activity.

References

AMIN, A. and N. THRIFT (eds) (1994), *Globalization, Institutions and Regional Development in Europe* (Oxford: Oxford University Press).

BIRKINSHAW, J. and N. HOOD (eds) (1998), *Multinational Corporate Evolution and Subsidiary Development* (London: Macmillan).

CANTWELL, J.A. (ed.) (1994), *Transnational Corporations and Innovatory Activities* (London: Routledge).

CASSON, M.C. (ed.) (1991), *Global Research Strategy and International Competitiveness* (Oxford: Basil Blackwell).

CHANDLER, A.D., P. HAGSTRÖM and Ö. SÖLVELL (eds) (1998), *The Dynamic Firm: The Role of Technology, Strategy, Organisation and Regions* (Oxford: Oxford University Press).

DICKEN, P. (1994), 'The Roepke Lecture in Economic Geography: Global–Local Tensions: Firms and States in the Global Space-Economy', *Economic Geography*, vol. 70, pp. 101–2.

DICKEN, P. (1992), *Global Shift*, 2nd edn (New York: Guildford Press).

DUNNING, J.H. (1998), 'Globalization and the New Geography of Foreign Direct Investment', *Oxford Development Studies*, vol. 26, no. 1, pp. 47–69.

DUNNING, J.H. (ed.) (1997), *Governments, Globalization and International Business* (Oxford: Oxford University Press).

DUNNING, J.H. (1988), *Multinationals, Technology and Competitiveness* (London: Unwin Hyman).

GRABHER, G. (ed.) (1993), *The Embedded Firm: On the Socioeconomics of Industrial Networks* (London and Boston: Routledge).

HARRISON, B. (1992), 'Industrial Districts: Old Wine in New Bottles', *Regional Studies*, vol. 26, pp. 469–83.

LUNDGREN, A. (1995), *Technological Innovation and Network Evolution: The Emergence of Industrial Networks* (London: Routledge).

MATTSSON, L.-G. (1998), 'Dynamics of Overlapping Networks and Strategic Actions by the International Firm', in A.D. Chandler, P. Hagström and Ö. Sölvell (eds), *The Dynamic Firm: The Role of Technology, Strategy, Organisation and Regions* (Oxford: Oxford University Press), pp. 242–59.

STABER, U.H., N.V. SCHAEFER and B. SHARMA (eds) (1996), *Business Networks: Prospects for Regional Development* (Berlin and New York: de Gruyter).

STRANGE, S. (1997), 'An International Political Economy Perspective', in J. Dunning (ed.), *Governments, Globalization and International Business* (Oxford: Oxford University Press), pp. 132–45.

YOUNG, S., N. HOOD and E. PETERS (1994), 'Multinational Enterprises and Regional Economic Development', *Regional Studies*, vol. 28, no. 7, pp. 657–77.

2 Globalization and the Theory of MNE Activity

John H. Dunning

INTRODUCTION

This chapter seeks to answer the question 'To what extent, and in what ways, does the globalization of economic activity require a reappraisal of existing paradigms and theories of international production?'[1] More specifically, 'Are the motives, determinants and organizational modes of international business activity, as identified by scholars in the 1960s and 1970s, relevant and applicable to our contemporary world scenario? Are drastic changes called for, or is it simply that our ideas, propositions and paradigms[2] need to be fine-tuned to accommodate the events of the late 1990s?'

The chapter will proceed in the following way. First, it will place the current unease about the state of our theorizing about MNE activity within the context of two previous watersheds in the development of scholarly thinking, viz those of the early 1960s and of the late 1970s; and it will pinpoint such watersheds by both the events of the time and the advent of new analytical insights. Secondly, it will consider how contemporary thinking is affecting our understanding about different types of FDI – and particularly that of Third World MNEs, and that directed to augmenting the competitive advantages of the investing firms; and, thirdly, it will consider how far, and in what ways, economic and behavioural theories of MNE activity need to be integrated if they are to adequately explain the dynamics of international production.

However, three other introductory points should be made at this stage. The first is that globalization is best considered as a *process* towards the deepening of economic interdependence between institutions and/or countries. For the most part, the world economy of the late 1990s is not *globalized*, although some types of value-added activities and corporate functions, some countries and some regions are more globalized than others. What, however, is clear from a plethora of statistics[3] is that economic activity is becoming more globalized –

or at least regionalized[4] – and that the pace and extent of this movement has increased dramatically over the last decade or so.

The second point is that it is difficult to consider the impact of globalization in isolation to the other events which have fashioned the structure of the contemporary world economy. Indeed, there are good reasons for asserting that globalization is not *the* critical parameter encouraging scholars to reappraise the theory of MNE activity. For, while the removal or reduction of cross-border barriers to the movement of goods, services and people has helped facilitate a new international division of labour and new patterns of MNE activity, the engine of that change has been the dramatic technological advances of the last two or three decades. Several scholars, for example Perez (1983) and Lipsey (1997), have argued that we are now witnessing the beginning of a new Kondratieff cycle, which is promoting a new and different kind of cross-border specialization of production both within and between corporations. Though it is difficult to pinpoint a single path-breaking innovation,[5] few would deny that the critical attributes of contemporary technology, viz, its complexity and multiple uses, its cost and its rate of obsolescence, are very different from those of even 20 years ago.

Elsewhere (Dunning, 1998b), the present author has argued that the world is moving into a new phase of market-based capitalism, which is marked by three characteristics. First, the main source of wealth creation has moved from land in the seventeenth century, through machines and finance in the nineteenth and most of the twentieth century, to knowledge as embodied in human beings, in physical hardware and in intangible assets, for example patents, learning capabilities and organizational structures. Second, in the last years of the present millennium, the spatial context of both asset creation[6] and asset usage has widened from the sub-national, through the national to the macroregional[7] and global. Third, the 'typical' organizational form of a firm has progressed from that of the individual entrepreneur or family business, through a managerial hierarchy to a system of corporate governance which, *inter alia*, involves a myriad of inter-firm cooperative agreements.

The late twentieth century capitalism is then knowledge-based, regional or global in its scope, and involves more intra- and interinstitutional alliances than any of its predecessors. It is a combination of these three features which is heralding a new trajectory of economic development and demanding a reappraisal of our theorizing about MNE activity.

Thirdly, it should be recognized that although there are many theories and several paradigms about FDI and MNE activity, the majority are complementary to, rather than substitutable for, each other. This is because they are seeking to explain different aspects of international production, or are based on different units of analysis (the firm, industry or country), or offer a different disciplinary perspective. It can be claimed that globalization is leading to more, rather than less, convergence in the conceptualization and analysis of MNE activity among scholars – especially at a paradigmatic level.[8]

THE THREE LANDMARKS IN THEORIZING ABOUT MNE ACTIVITY

The First Half of the 1960s

Prior to 1960, there was no unique theory or paradigm of the determinants of foreign direct investment (FDI). However, in the 1950s there was a surge of outbound investment by US corporations, especially in Europe.[9] Some of the economic implications of this phenomenon were explored by the present author in his 1958 book (Dunning, 1958), but it was left to Stephen Hymer (1960) of MIT and Ray Vernon of Harvard (1962, 1966) to offer a formal explanation of it.

Neither found the answer in received theory. In his PhD thesis, Hymer, for example, argued that the theory of foreign (portfolio) investment could not explain the territorial expansion of firms, because the essence of this expansion was the transfer of real, not financial, assets; and that it occurred not in perfect, but in imperfect, markets. He used Joe Bain's concept of barriers to entry (Bain, 1956) to explain how a competitive advantage protected by such barriers was a necessary condition for US FDI; and why such FDI was concentrated in certain industries. In a later article, Hymer (1968) more explicitly adopted a Coasian concept of internalization to explain why US firms preferred to engage in FDI rather than cross-border licensing activities.

Quite independently of Hymer, Ray Vernon (1966) was interested in explaining the process, rather than the reason for, the deepening internationalization of US firms. Initially, he turned to trade theory for an explanation, but found it wanting because of its constrained assumptions of perfect competition, immobile factor endowments and product homogeneity. Nevertheless, he did use the tenets of neoclassical economics to explain why, in the 1960s, the US had a comparative advantage in *innovating* particular products; and why other countries had a comparative advantage in *adding value* to these innovations.

In explaining the migration of market-seeking US firms abroad, Vernon used a micro-marketing concept, namely the product cycle. In doing so, he took for granted that US firms possessed some (home) country specific advantages, *vis-à-vis* their foreign competitors, and sought to explain the changing location of their value-added activities as they moved from the product innovation to the product maturation state of the cycle. In retrospect, one of Vernon's critical insights was to distinguish between the asset creation and asset usage functions of firms; and the recognition that each might require a different portfolio of location-specific endowments for their efficient production.

The combined value of Hymer and Vernon's contributions (though not analysed in the literature in this way) was the first major breakthrough in theorizing about MNE activity. Both, however, were scholars of their time, and their explanations were strongly contextual.[10] Both tended to deal with first-time – rather than sequential – *US* direct investment. Both tended to view each act of FDI as a discrete and 'stand-alone' phenomenon. Both assumed that firms ventured abroad to exploit an existing set of monopolistic or competitive advantages. Moreover, both sought to explain foreign-owned production in a world economy in which cross-border trade was substantially restricted by natural and artificial barriers.

The same limitations applied to the other theories of international production which were put forward in this era, though most were directed to explaining particular kinds of FDI and their contexts changed as more countries became outward investors, and as firms became more multinational. Some of the newer explanations came from finance scholars, for example Alan Rugman's (1982) risk-diversification theory and Robert Aliber's (1970) capital-markets imperfections theory.[11] Others, notably Frederick Knickerbocker's (1973) 'follow my leader' theory, Edward Graham's (1978) 'tit for tat' theory, and later work by Ray Vernon (1974) emphasised the importance of firm-specific issues – and especially the strategies of firms engaged in oligopolistic competition.

The 1960s and early 1970s yielded several valuable empirical studies on both the determinants and effects of MNE activity. These, in the main, sought either to establish reasons why US foreign investors tended to favour some sectors rather than others; or why they chose to site their value-added activities in some countries rather than others. Such partial explanations of FDI and international production were exactly that. Compared, for example, to the study of international trade, there was no overarching or unifying paradigm within which the contextually-specific theories could be accommodated.

The Second Half of the 1970s

This second major advance in our understanding about the determinants of MNE activity came in the mid-1970s with the emergence of two closely related (but distinct) paradigms;[12] and also an attempt by the Japanese economist – Kiyoshi Kojima – to formulate a normative theory of FDI to parallel that of trade (Kojima, 1978). Since Kojima's theory was primarily an extension of the extant theory of comparative advantage to embrace the trade in intermediate products (and particularly technology), and took no account of whether the cross-border markets for these products were internalized or not, the author's view is that this was not a paradigm of MNE activity *per se*.[13] Moreover, the application of Kojima's theory was strongly contextual in that it specifically focused on the differences between the structure and determinants of US and Japanese FDI.

Most certainly, the publication of John McManus' classic article on the theory of the multinational firm (1972), and that of Peter Buckley and Mark Casson's monograph *The Future of the Multinational Enterprise* (1976), introduced a new dimension into scholarly thinking; and with the strong, yet for the most part, independent, contributions of Jean Francois Hennart (1982), Alan Rugman (1982) and Birgitta Swedenborg (1979), the focus of attention switched from the foreign value-added production by firms to the very *raison d'être* of the MNE, qua MNE.

The theory of internalization is a simple yet profound one. It avers that firms exist because they can coordinate the deployment of discrete, yet complementary, resources and capabilities at lower costs than can the external market. In a perfectly competitive situation, the transaction costs of using the market to perform this task are zero. Hence production is undertaken either by the owners of the resources themselves or by a firm engaging in a single value-added activity.[14] In an imperfect market, transaction costs are positive. As a consequence, the opportunity for alternative coordinating mechanisms arises. Firms exist and grow where they can undertake the transactional and co-ordinating functions of economic activity more efficiently than can arm's-length markets.

It will be quickly appreciated that this understanding about the nature of the firm is independent of its geography. Certainly, too, most of the market failures initially identified by Buckley and Casson (1976) were not unique to multinational compared to uninational firms. Indeed, as has been argued elsewhere (Dunning, 1998a), internalization economists have in general paid relatively little attention to cross-border market failure *per se*.[15] A recent monograph by Klaus Meyer (1998) does just this.

In retrospect, this author would aver that the major contribution of internalization theory is to offer a formal explanation of why firms internalize the markets for the intermediate products they own, or wish to acquire, rather than choose some other organizational modality. It is acknowledged that some scholars would like to argue that all the monopolistic or competitive advantages of firms derive from the internalization of factor or product markets. We believe that to do so devalues the analytical core of the theory, and that it is not only useful, but essential, to distinguish between the nature and content of the advantages possessed by firms and the way in which these are deployed.

The eclectic paradigm tries to do just this and also to factor in the spatial aspect of MNE activity. When the paradigm was first put forward in 1977 (Dunning, 1977) it was fully recognized that its contents were an amalgam of the partial theories of the MNE and of MNE activity of the previous 15 years. It was also acknowledged that its analytical foundation rested on three sets of economic theory, viz the theory of industrial organization (including market structure), which seeks to explain *how it is possible* for one group of firms to acquire and sustain a competitive advantage (or set of advantages) relative to another group of firms;[16] the theory of the firm, which aims to explain the organizational mode by which firms create, augment or use these advantages; and the theory of location which explains *where* firms choose to locate their value-adding activities.

Like the internalization paradigm, the basic proposition of the OLI paradigm is very simple. It is that, at any given moment of time, the extent, ownership and pattern of MNE activity depends upon the configuration of the competitive (or ownership (O) specific) advantages of MNEs relative to those of non-MNEs, the competitive (or location (L) specific) attractions of one country or region relative to those of another, and the benefits to firms of exploiting these two sets of advantages by internalizing the market for the O-specific advantages (including those arising directly from FDI), that is internalization (I) advantages.

Over the last two decades, the author has made various modifications to the original formulation of the paradigm mainly to accommodate advances in scholarly thinking and to take account of recent economic events.[17] At the same time, there have been several attempts both to test the propositions of the internalization and eclectic paradigms, and to offer alternative explanations of the growth of MNEs or MNE activity. But, as regards the latter, most, like those of the 1970s, continued to address specific issues. Thus the *stages of internationalization* approach, favoured by a group of Swedish and Finnish economists,[18] was primarily a spatially-oriented paradigm. It was also directed at explaining a particular kind of FDI (namely, market-seeking FDI), even though the timing of the transition from exports and/or licensing to foreign production was partly determined by the nature of the competitive advantages of firms in question.

By contrast, both the *resource-based* and the *evolutionary theories* of the firm which were first articulated in the 1980s (the former by management scholars,[19] and the latter by economists[20]), even when discussed within the context of MNE activity,[21] were concerned with identifying and evaluating particular competitive or O-specific advantages of firms, not only at a given moment of time, but over time. Like their industrial organizational colleagues, the resource-based scholars averred that to create and sustain new competitive advantages, markets could not be fully contestable – at least in the short run. However, unlike them they focused more on *firm*-specific competencies and strategies to generate unique and non-imitatible assets, and the capabilities to coordinate these with those of other firms. The evolutionary theorists went a further step and argued that not only was the firm a 'bundle of resources and capabilities', but that bundle represented an accumulation of past created assets which was itself strongly path-dependent.

Though not direct descendants of the eclectic paradigm, both the resource-based and evolutionary theories steered it along a new trajectory. When first put forward, both the eclectic and internalization paradigms were essentially designed to explain the locational and organizational deployment of *existing* competitive advantages – even though it was acknowledged that those advantages had to be created in the first place. The evolutionary theory reoriented the attention of scholars to the upgrading of competitive advantages through innovation; while the resource-based theory emphasised the significance of firm-specific resources, rather than that of country-specific endowments; and of the capabilities of firms to design and implement the strategies which would best advance the competitiveness of these resources.

The emphasis on 'knowledge' as a competitive asset has itself become more pronounced over the last decade; and, as indicated earlier, it is now acknowledged as the principal engine of *increased* wealth of both firms and countries. And, it is the case that most empirical studies have shown that FDI, and particularly that of US MNEs, tends to be concentrated in knowledge-intensive sectors. At the same time, all these studies, including the eclectic paradigm, have tended to presume that firms create (or acquire) their assets in their home countries, *prior* to engaging in FDI, rather than from the countries receiving the investment. This was notwithstanding the findings of several early empirical studies (for example Dunning, 1958; Reddaway, Potter and Taylor, 1968) that the R&D undertaken by the UK affiliates of US firms and the foreign affiliates of UK firms resulted in a valuable feedback of knowledge to their parent companies.

The 1990s

1989 saw the fall of the Berlin Wall. Together with the introduction of more market-oriented policies of the leading industrial nations, the opening up of Chinese economic space, and the transparent economic success of the newly-industrializing Asian countries in upgrading and restructuring their indigenous resources and capabilities to meet the dictates of the international marketplace, these events have combined to deepen the economic interdependence between nations. They are also challenging much of extant thinking about the determinants of MNE activity. In particular, three of these challenges are mentioned here.

The first is that existing theories continue to explain a good deal of contemporary FDI. Take, for example, market-seeking FDI. While the value of some of its determinants – for example investment incentives, labour productivity, communication costs, the physical infrastructure and the presence of related firms influencing (say) US FDI in China and India – may be different than those influencing such investment in Brazil or Germany, for the most part the economic models of the 1970s and 1980s are broadly relevant to explaining such investment in the 1990s. Similarly, most of the OLI variables which have long determined FDI in the natural resource sectors are no less applicable today. Much of the rationale for rationalized or efficiency-seeking FDI prompted, for example, by the completion of the internal market of the European Union, also stems from the work of economists in the 1970s.

But, secondly, it is true that even in these cases the increasing extent and geographical diversity of FDI by many firms is fashioning a new and more integrated international division of labour.[22] At the same time, the technological complexity of many products and production processes, and the changing needs of consumers are reconfiguring locational priorities. In particular, some types of related value-added activities are becoming more spatially interdependent. This especially affects the level and structure of MNE activity designed to augment home-based competitive advantages. In such cases it is fairly obvious that the availability of local technological capability becomes a more important *pull* factor for FDI. This point is subsequently considered further.

The third challenge of the globalizing economy stems from the increasing geographical dispersion of knowledge-intensive assets; and from the need of firms to tap into the core competencies of foreign firms, which are synergistic or complementary to their own. Moreover, in a world of rapidly changing technologies there is increasing pressure on firms to quickly access a variety of tacit intangible assets (for example, ideas and learning experiences) which again are frequently located outside their home countries. Thus, in addition to adding value to their existing O-specific advantages, firms are increasingly engaging in FDI to seek out and harness complementary created assets.

Several scholars have begun to explore the concept of asset-augmenting FDI. In 1993, in *Multinational Enterprises and the Global Economy* (Dunning, 1993), a fourth category was added to the motives of the market, resource and efficiency-seeking FDI traditionally delineated in the literature. This was named strategic-asset-seeking FDI, which it was argued was undertaken to *'add to the acquiring firm's existing portfolio of assets others which they perceive will either sustain or strengthen their overall competitive position, or weaken that of their competitors'* (Dunning, 1993, p. 60). Tom Wesson, in his PhD thesis, developed a model of asset-augmenting FDI (Wesson, 1993, 1997), and this model has been extended by Makino (1998) who also emphasises the need of firms, particularly from developing countries, to gain access to new technologies and organizational capabilities. In his various writings, Teece[23] has also stressed the need of firms to harness and efficiently deploy assets complementary to their own if they are to make the best use of their own core competencies.

There have been several case studies of the growing significance of asset-seeking or asset-complementing FDI. Kuemmerle (1996) found that an increasing proportion of foreign-based research by the leading MNEs in the pharmaceutical and electronics sectors was designed to gain new knowledge rather than to exploit existing knowledge. Almeida, in an analysis of patenting in the US semiconductor industry reported that foreign affiliates tended to use local patents more frequently than did their indigenous competitors (Almeida, 1996); while in a field study of the US biotechnology industry, Shan and Song (1997) showed that the primary purpose of foreign firms investing in this sector was to gain access to advanced technology owned by local firms. In this author's analysis of the sources of competitiveness of 150 of the largest industrial companies listed in *Fortune*, it was not only clear that the executives providing data perceive that a fairly high proportion (between one-third and two-fifths) of their global resources and capabilities were directly derived from their foreign operations, but that this percentage was closely correlated with the degree of a firm's multinationality, and was increasing over time (Dunning, 1996).

All these, and other, studies point to a very different kind of FDI than that traditionally examined in the literature; although there is some parallel with natural resource-seeking FDI, in as much as this, too, is prompted by investors seeking to augment their domestic O-specific advantages. The parallel, however, ceases when one considers that strategic asset-seeking investment is very much a feature of our contemporary globalizing, knowledge-based economy. Moreover, it is part and parcel of the need of firms to sustain and augment their own created assets by acquiring those of other firms; and to tap into the complementary but immobile assets of the host economy.

To what extent can asset-augmenting FDI be explained by existing paradigms or theories of international production? The answer, we believe, is that while new context-specific theories may be required – if for no other reason than the motivation of asset-augmenting FDI is very different from asset-exploiting FDI – the dominant paradigms of international production, and notably the eclectic paradigm, can quite comfortably accommodate it. To explain why this is so, the next section deals very briefly with how each of the components of the paradigm is affected, that is what are the 'add-on' variables. The differences between the scenario of the 1970s and 1990s are summarized in Table 2.1.

Ownership-specific Advantages

- As globalization facilitates, and competitive pressures and technological advances compel, firms to engage in efficiency-seeking FDI, so the unique and sustainable O-specific advantages of such firms are increasingly resting on their capability to manage complex and geographically-dispersed created assets. This is particularly true of MNEs in knowledge-intensive sectors which, according to Doz, Asakawa, Santos and Williamson (1997), is leading to the emergence of the 'metanational' corporation. This they identify as a corporation which is able to 'simultaneously access, meld and leverage locally-bound and context-dependent knowledge from throughout the world.'
- Because of the widening dispersal of knowledge-based assets, and the growing specialization in their asset-enhancing activities, the need of firms to tap into complementary and synergistic assets from outside their national boundaries is growing. The capability to successfully identify the sources of such assets, to acquire them in the most productive way,[24] and to coordinate them with their existing core competencies is becoming a more significant competitive advantage.
- The choice of an optimum portfolio of locations for asset augmentation and asset usage is also becoming a more critical capability, as firms engage in an increasing proportion of value-added activities outside their national boundaries, and/or conclude more alliances with foreign firms.
- With the need to complement their core competencies with those of other firms, the ability of a firm's management to identify and evaluate such partners, to conclude the appropriate collaborative agreements with them, and to ensure that the results of any agreement (be it, for example, a subcontracting, joint research or customer-related design project) is in its best interests, is also becoming more important. To be realized, such advantages require the MNE to learn from, and work effectively with, partner-firms – and, indeed, with other institutions in the foreign country, for example governments, labour unions and consumer

Table 2.1 The changing characteristics of paradigms and theories: some stylized facts

1970s–1980s	*1990s*
• FDI mainly to exploit O-specific advantages of investing firm; one-way flow of resources and capabilities	• Multiple motives for FDI; more global sourcing of assets
• Largely greenfield FDI and sequential FDI financed by reinvested profits	• FDI (particularly in Triad) largely in form of acquisitions and mergers and reinvested profits
• O advantages largely based on privileged possession of (home) country-specific assets (Oa)	• O advantages more firm-specific and related to degree of multinationality and ability to harness and utilize created assets throughout the world
• Clear-cut choice between alternative modalities of exploiting O advantages (licensing compared to FDI, and so on)	• Systemic approach to organization of MNE activities; alternative modalities often complementary to each other; more institutional pluralism
• O-specific advantages (for example unique resources and capabilities) internal to firms	• Recognition of importance of complementary resources and capabilities external to firms (including the quality of institutional and social capital), and how these are coordinated with internally-generated O advantages
• Comparatively little foreign-based innovatory activity; foreign affiliates less embedded in the host countries	• Considerable foreign-based innovatory activity (carried out mainly in advanced industrial countries) and/or via strategic alliances with foreign firms

• Significant inter-country barriers to both trade and FDI	• Reduced barriers to trade and FDI
• Clear-cut international division of labour based on H- and O-type distribution of factor endowments	• International specialization of MNEs based more on Schumpeterian type and FDI
• Locational choices made mainly in respect to asset usage	• Locational choices also made with respect to asset augmentation
• Relatively little attention paid to 'spatial' market failure and location-specific external economies	• More attention paid to gains arising from being part of a complex, or cluster, of firms, and from spatially-linked learning economies
• Static nature of major paradigms	• Better appreciation of need to consider the dynamic nature of OLI variables; and to extend the theory to embrace path-dependent asset-creation and learning capabilities
• Hierarchical organizational structure of MNEs	• Flattened pyramids; more heterarchical structures; more delegation of responsibilities to line managers
• Most strategies towards market failure 'exit' rather than 'voice' strategies	• More voice strategies towards market failure; and particularly towards capturing dynamic externalities of common governance
• Cautious attitudes by many governments to FDI	• Welcoming attitude to FDI by most governments
• Few attempts to integrate interdisciplinary approaches to understand MNE activity	• Recognition of need to draw upon interdisciplinary theories to construct a meaningful and robust systemic paradigm of MNE activity

representatives – in many different cultures, and to gain the maximum benefits from such coalitions.[25]

Location-specific Advantages

Some of the consequences of globalization on the location of economic activity, and particularly that of MNEs, have been articulated in a recent paper by the present author (Dunning, 1998a). Here one or two basic points are made:

- With advances in telecommunications and lowering barriers to trade, the locational options open to firms to engage in both asset-augmenting and asset-exploiting activities have considerably widened. At the same time, the need of countries to attract knowledge-related assets to sustain and upgrade the competitiveness of their own firms and indigenous resources is becoming more acute. Increasingly, as the economic structure of many countries is converging, national governments are seeking to identify and promote the distinctive and non-imitatible immobile resources and capabilities within their midst.[26] Moreover, notwithstanding the lessening of their intervention in the asset-deployment activities of firms, their role as enablers of asset-creating activities is increasing via, for example, the provision of infrastructure and their human-resource development, technology, trade and investment policies.[27]
- Although globalization is widening the options open to MNEs to locate in different countries, *within* countries there is suggestion that at least some kinds of value-added activities – and particularly asset-augmenting activities – are becoming more concentrated, and are favoring sites which have a cluster of related firms. In short, the externalities of spatially-proximate linked activities – first identified by Marshall many years ago[28] (Marshall, 1920) but more recently extended to embrace dynamic learning economics and asset-upgrading activities (Florida, 1995; Krugman, 1995; Storper, 1995; Storper and Scott, 1995) – are becoming a more important locational benefit to firms and, indeed, to microregions as they seek to attract mobile investment to their borders. Examples of such clusters abound.[29] Although by no means confined to high-tech sectors, they are expanding particularly rapidly in these sectors, which are also those in which both FDI and cross-border alliances are assuming greater significance.[30]

- The paradox of 'sticky places within slippery space', as articulated by Markusen (1996), is particularly pertinent to the knowledge-based globalizing economy. Its successful resolution depends on the ways in which both firms and governments react to its challenges. On the part of firms, the gains of efficiency-seeking FDI in multiple locations, and those arising from agglomerative economies, are those most likely to promote competitiveness. On the part of national and subnational governments, the need is to provide and publicize a unique set of immobile assets pertinent to the types of economic certainty they wish to attract and retain, *vis-à-vis* those offered by other countries; and also to promote market facilitating measures which might foster the formation of efficient subnational clusters of related activities. This may require them to reconsider the scope and effectiveness of their fiscal and investment incentive policies (UNCTAD, 1996); and, indeed, for scholars to reappraise the value of these policies as instruments for attracting inbound FDI.

Internalization Advantages

Perhaps, the single most important impact of globalization on the organization of cross-border value-adding activities by firms is that on the costs and benefits of alternative modalities to acquire, create and utilize created assets and intermediate products. More specifically, we believe that the emphasis on the costs of individual transactions as the main determinant of the internalization of intermediate-product markets needs to be broadened to allow for the systemic economies of governance of global operations, and the dynamic coordination costs and benefits arising from the accessing of cross-border assets and learning capabilities. In particular, we would emphasise that four attributes of the globalizing economy are worthy of emphasis:

1. The increasing interaction between related cross-border and intra-border spatial markets. Such externalities suggest that a more holistic approach is needed in analysing the transaction costs of economic activity (both from an intra-firm and an inter-firm perspective), and that more attention should be given to those transactions which are specifically associated with the global division of labour fostered by MNEs.
2. The static and dynamic benefits of alternative organizational modes. Almost, by definition, there are static externalities to be

obtained from the common governance of related activities; and there is little doubt that globalization offers a new range of benefits. But, more than this, in an innovating and alliance-based economy there are likely to be substantial *dynamic* external benefits, for example to do with learning capabilities and the exchange of tacit knowledge. It is at least possible that such economies associated with (say) inter-firm alliances may more than compensate for any static transaction costs associated with such alliances.

3. The increasing significance of distance-related transaction costs in explaining both the international and intra-national distribution of economic activity, and particularly that of knowledge-intensive sectors. The idea of regions as 'loci of untraded interdependencies', and the emergence of new spatial clusters of value-added activities designed to capture the benefits of interrelated trading and learning economies between the clustering firms, has been set out in Storper (1995), Storper and Scott (1995), and more recently by Dunning (1998c).
4. The implications of asset-seeking FDI. When first introduced, the theory of internalization by firms was primarily directed to explaining the modality of cross-border asset deployment. Indeed, it was (and still is) rather better at explaining the existence of firms than their growth. Nor can it comfortably encompass strategy-related issues within its framework; in essence, it is an extension of the neoclassical theory of the firm.

In seeking to identify the optimum transactional vehicle of firms seeking to add to, rather than exploit, their core competencies, a different set of organizational variables needs to be considered. More particularly, the investing firm must believe that the benefits arising from the internalization of the market for the asset(s) it is acquiring, less the transaction costs involved, are greater than those which could have been obtained through some other vehicle of entry. Moreover, even when the market for them is internalized, the benefits arising from the acquired assets are frequently uncertain and likely to be spread over time. The costs, and there must be some costs otherwise all knowledge acquisition would take place through FDI, will be partly the normal costs of governance, and partly those to do with integrating the acquired assets and learning capabilities into the firm's existing portfolio of assets. These, like the costs of any acquisition or technological transfer are unlikely to be negligible, although some at least are common to inter-firm and arm's-length transactions.

In short, then, the globalizing economy requires some reconstruction of the theory of internalization. Partly, this should be in the direction of a more systemic approach which acknowledges that as technology and organization of value-added activities become more complex, the costs and benefits of individual transactions become more interwoven. Partly it should give more attention to the specific features of cross-border transactions – particularly those to do with exchange rate uncertainty and cultural differences. And, partly, it needs to view its choices of organizational options, in terms not only of minimizing its efficiency-related transaction costs, but of upgrading its distinctive wealth-creating capabilities and any future income streams arising from these.

SOME IMPLICATIONS OF THE REVISED PARADIGM OF INTERNATIONAL PRODUCTION

There are implications for scholarly research which can be drawn from the analysis so far presented in this chapter. Two of these are selected for consideration. The first concerns the relevance of, and interface between, some of the leading economic and behavioural theories of the MNE and MNE activity. We shall offer an extremely encapsulated view on this issue. The second relates to the empirical significance of this analysis for explaining FDI between different groups of countries[31] or regions.

Implications for Extant Theories

As one might expect, most of the extant theories require some modification in the light of the kind of revisions to the OLI paradigm which have been suggested. In the case of some, however (for example, the product-cycle model), it is difficult to see how either asset-seeking or efficiency-seeking FDI can be accommodated. In others, for example Knickerbocker's 'follow my leader' hypothesis (Knickerbocker, 1973), the acquisition and merger (A&M) mania of the last decade well illustrates how an asset-seeking FDI by one firm might be followed by others. Graham's 'exchange of threats' thesis (Graham, 1978), similarly stands the test of time well, though less for efficiency-seeking than for asset-seeking FDI. The recent application of signalling theory suggests that where there is imperfect or asymmetrical information, a successful FDI by one firm may act as a signal to other firms to invest[32] (Liu, 1998). At the same time, compared with the early 1970s, there are many more strategic options open to firms in the ways in which they may augment their assets; and what is appropriate to one firm may be inappropriate to another.

What of the contemporary relevance of the exchange and capital imperfections model of Aliber (1970) or the risk-diversification model of Rugman? Since Aliber's theory was originally devised to explain the timing of acquisitions of domestic firms by foreign investors, and why the latter should assign a higher value to the assets of the former than other domestic investors, it might be thought to have some relevance to contemporary asset-seeking FDI. At the same time, it cannot adequately explain why the A&Ms of recent years have been two-way in character, that is the purchases of European assets by US firms have gone side-by-side with the purchases of US assets by European firms. It is difficult, however, to see how the risk-diversification hypothesis can be used to explain such A&M, which are usually firm- rather than country-specific. Perhaps at the margin, where the required assets are broadly similar in (say) a German and US firm, the existing locational portfolio of the assets may be of some relevance. The Rugman hypothesis can, however, be used to explain the distribution of efficiency-seeking FDI within free trade areas and customs unions. One reason given by Japanese manufacturers for targeting France as an investment outlet since the late 1980s is that they believed that their assets were too concentrated in the UK, and that it would be politically judicious for them to spread them more widely.

Turning to two of the leading theories of the firm in the 1980s – the resource-based and evolutionary theories – both can be comfortably accommodated within the revised framework of international production. This is particularly the case with respect to identifying and evaluating the critical O-advantages of knowledge-based firms, and the appropriate modality for exploiting, or adding to, these assets. Together with organizational theories, these strategic-cum-managerial approaches have greatly enhanced our understanding of the endogenous variables affecting MNE activity. In the eclectic paradigm, those specific to individual firms are treated as contextual variables influencing asset-exploiting FDI. Nevertheless, there is no reason to suppose such variables are any the less important in explaining asset-seeking as distinct from asset-exploiting FDI.

In the past decade, the interaction between scholars favouring evolutionary and resource-based theories and those espousing internalization theory has been an uneasy, if not a confrontational, one. To a large extent such uneasiness has been unwarranted, and such confrontation counterproductive. For the most part the authors have been aiming to explain different phenomena, or have offered complementary perspectives on the same phenomena.[33] Moreover, where disagreements have occurred they have been largely of emphasis rather than of substance. One exception is that while internalization theory is geared to identifying the optimum mode for organizing existing assets and capabilities, both the resource and evolutionary theories are focused on ways in which new assets and capabilities are generated, and of how the competitive advantage arising from these may be sustained.[34] However, two of the leading proponents of internalization theory (Casson and Buckley), accept that once one takes on board *dynamic* market failures, the incorporation of *new* O-specific advantages into any theory or paradigm of the MNE becomes appropriate. And, it is the origin and content of these advantages which is the central interest of the evolutionary and resource-based scholars.

The author believes that the current state of our theorizing about MNE activity and the parameters of our contemporary globalizing economy is demanding a reconsideration of the relationship between these three theoretical perspectives, which, between them, embrace the O and I facets of the OLI trilogy. In this chapter it has been suggested that a reconciliation of the approaches is possible if the internalization theory is dynamized and its determinants are widened to embrace the innovatory and developmental benefits of alternative organizational forms, as well as their short-term transactional costs and benefits. If this is done, not only would the distinction between O and I components of the eclectic paradigm become sharper; the I component would also become a more comprehensive explanation of both asset-seeking and asset-exploiting FDI.[35]

The Geography of FDI

The changing motives for, and determinants of, FDI identified in this chapter have not affected all regions or countries alike. More than ever, this author believes models and theories of MNE activity need to be set within a specific geographical context. Let us illustrate by considering how globalization is requiring us to modify our explanations of:

1. FDI by developed-country firms in developing countries;
2. FDI by developed-country firms in other developed countries;
3. FDI by developing-country firms in developed countries; and
4. FDI by developing-country firms in other developing countries.

In making these geographical classifications and the subsequent comments, it is readily conceded that apart from their stages of development[36] there may be as many significant economic differences *within* developed and developing countries as between them.[37]

1. The main impact of globalization on MNE activity from developed to developing countries has been to increase the amount of market-seeking and efficiency-seeking FDI. For the most part, the push factor, viz the exploitation of O-specific advantages of MNEs from the Triad, have been relatively unaffected by recent economic events, save that competitive pressures have forced firms to export some of their more labour-intensive activities to Asian and Latin American locations.[38] However, there remains comparatively little North–South asset-augmenting FDI; and only a small proportion of cross-border strategic alliances or A&Ms have involved developing-country firms.[39] Rather more changes have occurred in the *pull* determinants, as governments from almost all developing countries have adopted more investment-friendly policies, and have sought to develop 'clusters' of related activities based upon their (perceived) comparative advantages.
2. It has been estimated that over the decade 1986–95, three-fifths of the FDI among developed countries took the form of A&M, and that such activities were largely concentrated in the knowledge-intensive manufacturing and service sectors (UNCTAD, 1997). At the same time, four-fifths of the cross-border strategic alliances (and an even higher proportion of those in R&D) have been concluded between firms from the Triad countries. As indicated earlier, there is a general perception among high-tech MNEs that they need to have a substantial presence in each of the major advanced markets of the world, viz the USA, Japan and Western Europe; and while much of FDI by these MNEs continues to be asset-exploiting, an increasing proportion is of an asset-seeking kind. The ability of the investing firms to successfully coordinate their own core competencies with those

of the firms they acquire, or conclude non-equity alliances, is itself one of critical advantages of the contemporary global corporation (Doz, Asakawa, Santos and Williamson, 1997).

The *push* factor driving intra-Triad FDI then needs reappraising, as static theories of MNEs are losing some of their robustness. The *pull* factor also requires reconsideration, as asset-augmenting FDI is increasingly drawn to locations which offer more advanced, or at least similar, created assets to those possessed by the home countries, in contrast to asset-exploiting FDI which tends to seek out a different set of resources and capabilities.

There is, indeed, an interesting parallel here between the rationale for different kinds of FDI and trade. For example, FDI designed to add value to a home-based competitive advantage is likely to parallel inter-industry trade, and be best explained by traditional factor endowment (for example, Heckscher–Ohlin) theory. By contrast, FDI intended to gain access to new created assets is likely to parallel intra-industry trade, which is best explained by scale or neo-technology (for example Schumpterian) theories of trade – or, indeed, strategy-related theories (Krugman, 1986). We have also suggested that knowledge-intensive FDI is likely to favour those locations within host countries which offer not only attractive investment opportunities, but also a cluster of firms engaged in complementary or synergistic activities.

3. The difference between intra-developed country FDI and that by MNEs from developing countries into developed countries lies principally in the O-specific advantages possessed by each; and the relative L-specific advantages of the home, *vis-à-vis* potential host countries. The nature and extent of these differences has led several scholars to question whether traditional theories of FDI based on the comparative advantage of the investing country in asset creation and that of the recipient country on asset usage, hold good in the case of Third World FDI in industrialized countries. This author's view is they can do, but only if the theories are modified. On the one hand, and agreeing with Lall (1983), it is important not to understate the distinctive competencies of Third World MNEs; particularly where part of these competencies are derived from technical and other agreements with First World MNEs. At the same time, it must be accepted that many of the early competitive advantages of Korean, Taiwanese and other

Asian MNEs specifically stemmed from their home-country characteristics and, in particular, their lower real labour costs.

Explaining developing-country FDI in developed countries then rests as much on the *pull* as well as the *push* factors. Some of these can be accommodated within received theory, including the 'stages' of development paradigm of Ozawa (1992).[40] Others – notably the need of investing firms to be in close proximity to their major competitors, and to gain access to European and US intellectual capital and learning experiences (with a view to upgrading their O-specific advantages) – cannot; and it is here where the asset-augmenting theory is again most relevant.[41]

Whether as a result of their FDI in developed countries, MNEs from developing countries can upgrade their O advantages sufficiently to outweigh the increased labour and other costs of producing in the former countries remains to be seen. But certainly, to be successful, such a strategy requires 'a deep pocket' of financial resources. The recent depreciation of Asian currencies looks certain to undermine this strategy, at least for the immediate future. Indeed, this could well mean that for Asian firms the mode of acquiring advanced resources and capabilities will revert back to inbound, rather than outbound, MNE activity.[42]

4. The data (UNCTAD, 1997) show that FDI among developing countries is growing faster than either between developed countries or among developed and developing countries. A major reason for this is, of course, the huge growth in MNE activity between mainland China, Taiwan, Singapore and Hong Kong.[43] At the same time, the share of inbound FDI stock of South, East and Southeast Asia originating from that region rose from 25 per cent of total inward FDI stock in 1980, to nearly 40 per cent in 1995 (UNCTAD, 1997, p. 82). Most certainly, there are very unique ethnic and cultural ties between the countries in Asia (and particularly among the Chinese communities) compared with the rest of the world. At the same time, other kinds of South–South FDI are also growing. There is, for example, a major Indian presence in sub-Saharan Africa; three-fifths of Chilean FDI is located elsewhere in Latin America; while Singapore was the largest foreign investor in Myanmar in 1994.

Much of this FDI can be explained by received theory. It is, for example, entirely consistent with the proposition of the investment-development path (Narula, 1996; Dunning and Narula, 1996) and the notion that FDI tends to be initially directed to countries with the closest psychic, ethic or economic ties. It is, however, worth noting that regional integration schemes are leading to a fall in defensive import-substituting FDI, and an increase in efficiency-seeking FDI. In most main respects, however, the determinants of South–South MNE activity are similar to those of North–South MNE activity. However, one suspects that as the more advanced developing countries upgrade their resources and capabilities, there may be more South–South asset-augmenting FDI. This, indeed, is already occurring in the case of Singaporean MNEs as they seek to develop new clusters of high-value activity in Malaysia.[44]

CONCLUSIONS

The following conclusions of this chapter are highlighted:

1. The characteristics of the globalizing economy of the late 1990s are sufficiently different from those of earlier years to suggest that international business scholars should be prepared to reconsider received paradigms and theories of MNE activity. This suggestion is compounded by the belief that contemporary events are helping to foster the integration of a number of theories from different business disciplines which were first put forward in the 1970s and 1980s.
2. In the past, there have been two major watersheds in the development of international business theory. The first of these, which dominated scholarly thinking between 1960 and the mid-1970s, produced a variety of theories of 'first-time' FDI and international production. Each of these was tailored to explain particular aspects of FDI or types of FDI. The second was the emergence of a general paradigm of MNE activity in the 1970s, and also some new theories designed to explain 'sequential' FDI, the increasing integration of MNE activity, and the sustainability of the competitive advantages arising from such activity.
3. In examining the implications of the globalizing economy for the paradigms and theories of the early 1990s, it has been suggested that both the motives for, and the determinants of, international production have changed – or are in the process of being changed. Foremost among the former has been the increasing significance of asset-augmenting FDI; and among the latter, the rising impor-

tance of a knowledge-supporting human and physical infrastructure as a locational *pull* to mobile investment.

4. The author believes, however, that while new explanations are necessary for some kinds of MNE activity, and other explanations need to be modified as the significance of particular explanatory variables change, the eclectic paradigm of international production remains sufficiently robust and flexible to accommodate most of these changes. Indeed, 22 years after it was first propounded we would like to think of it as a more, rather than less, useful systemic framework for evaluating the kinds of explanations of MNE activity now emerging.[45] However, it is accepted that the paradigm does need to be broadened and dynamized to better take account of current developments in the evolutionary and resource-based theories of the firm; to embrace current thinking on the interface between trade and FDI theory (Markusen, 1995), and on subnational clustering of asset-creating activities; to better acknowledge the role of institutional capital and the social context in influencing the O-unique advantages of firms; and to incorporate the specific characteristics of the emerging metanational corporation as identified by some organizational scholars.

Notes

1. Defined as value-added activity financed by foreign direct investment (FDI) and undertaken or controlled by multinational enterprises (MNEs). We adopt the threshold definition of an MNE as an enterprise which owns or controls value-added activities outside its home country.
2. In this chapter a paradigm is defined as an overarching systemic framework which comprises a set of general assumptions and boundary conditions, and offers some general propositions into which operationally testable theories can be incorporated. As long as new phenomena can be integrated within this framework, without infringing upon the paradigm core assumptions, then they need not threaten its long-term viability (Foss, 1996).
3. Some of which are set out in UNCTAD (1996, 1997) and Dunning (1998a).
4. The issue of whether regionalization is best regarded as a stepping stone towards globalization or a substitute to it is not debated here. For the purposes of this chapter, the word globalization is used to encompass regionalization wherever it is not in direct conflict with the spirit of globalization.

5. Although, generically speaking, the advent of the microchip and biotechnology are two major advances which have given rise to a whole new generation of technological advances.
6. The word asset is used to encompass a stock of resources and capabilities capable of generating a future income stream.
7. A macroregion is defined as a collection of countries in a particular geographical area; and a microregion as a geographical area within a particular country.
8. For example, as between economists and organizational theorists; and as between the explanations of economic geographers and trade economists.
9. The stock of US direct investment in all foreign countries increased by two-and-a-half times in the 1950s; and that in Europe by more than three times.
10. Related to a particular context of, for example, time, place, activity, or type of FDI; and viewed from a particular disciplinary perspective, for example finance, marketing, and so on.
11. For a review of these theories see Rugman (1982, 1996), Dunning (1993) and Caves (1996).
12. Although neither was called a paradigm at the time.
13. Indeed, in the original version of his theory Kojima made no clear distinction between inter-firm and intra-firm trade in technology – the latter being the essence of FDI. Later he incorporated the unique attributes of intermediate trade, undertaken *within* the same firm, in his model (see Kojima, 1992).
14. Since in neo-classical theory firms do exist in perfect markets, yet transaction costs are zero in such markets, it must be presumed that firms either engage in no transactions or do so at no cost. In practice, then, the markets vs firms paradigm relates to the extent to which a firm engages in more than one activity, for example by vertical integration or product diversification.
15. As identified, for example, in Behrman and Grosse (1990).
16. This is the critical reason for distinguishing O from I advantages. O advantages relate to those possessed by one firm relative to another; I advantages refer to those possessed by firms relative to the market.
17. These included the distinction between asset and transaction-cost ownership advantages (Oa and Ot); some suggestions of how strategic variables can be incorporated into a dynamic version of the paradigm; the application of the paradigm to explain the (international) investment development path of countries; the recognition that the O advantages of firms need to incorporate the way in which firms tap into and utilise the O advantages of other firms and the L advantages of countries; and the acceptance that over time the OLI components of the paradigm are all closely interlinked. See especially Dunning (1988, 1993 and 1995).
18. Notably Johanson and Wiedersheim (1975), Johanson and Vahlne (1977, 1990) and Luostarinen (1979).
19. See, especially, the work of Wernerfelt (1995), Conner (1991) and Barney (1991).

20. See, especially, the writings of Nelson and Winter (1982), Dosi, Freeman, Nelson, Silverberg and Soete (1988) and Saviotti and Metcalfe (1991).
21. Most notably by Cantwell (1989, 1991, 1994) and Kogut and Zander (1993).
22. In contrast to a multi-domestic structure in which each affiliate replicates (often in truncated form) the activities of its parent company; and there is relatively little intra-firm trade either between the parent and its affiliates or among the affiliates.
23. See, especially, Teece (1987) and Teece, Pisano and Shuen (1997).
24. This includes achieving a balance between minimizing transaction costs, and ensuring that the dynamic learning capabilities associated with the acquisition are maximized.
25. This choice, of course, depends on the relative costs and benefits of alternative modalities, which are better dealt with under the I component of the eclectic paradigm.
26. Various scholars have written about the increasing parallels between corporations and governments as both seek to evolve their unique competitive advantages – the one ownership, the other locational – in a globalizing economy. The notion of Singapore Inc. explored by Haley, Low and Toh Mun-Heng (1996) is now being extended to other small nation-states, and/or regions within nation states, both large and small. So far, however, the author has not seen any scholarly work on the resource-based theories of the firm as applied to countries.
27. The changing role of national government in the global economy is summarized in Dunning (1998b) and explored in more detail by several authors in Dunning (1997).
28. These included technological spillovers and access to pooled skilled labour, industry-specific inputs and consumers. Much earlier, as Ozawa in his chapter in this volume points out, Adam Smith was also very aware of such external economies.
29. Among those most frequently quoted are Silicon Valley in California, the Bader-Wurttemburg region in Germany, the Solingen Cutlery industry, the cork and port wine industry of Northern Portugal, the watch industry of Geneva, the City of London in the UK, Toyota City in Japan, the Prato wool textile industry and the tomato canning industry of Naples in Southern Italy. For a detailed examination of the *raison d'etre* and effects of these and other clusters see Enright (1993 and 1994), and Chapter 13 in this volume.
30. But mostly it appears in order to gain access to new assets, rather than to exploit existing assets (Birkinshaw and Hood, 1996).
31. Equally this chapter might have examined the implications of the revised paradigm for particular sectors, or particular sizes of firms, or for government policy. There is, indeed, a rich panoply of research waiting to be done!
32. Incidentally, signalling theory may act as a bridge between internalization and strategic oligopolistic behavioural theories.
33. Each, for example, is concerned with different aspects of market failure; and, therefore, it is to be expected each offers different solutions.

34. However, it is true that until recently the resource-based theory has paid little attention to the ways in which the resources and capabilities of a particular firm may be augmented by their association with other firms; or of how they relate to the institutional fabric and social context in which they operate. In a recent paper, Oliver (1997) has explored some of the exogenous factors influencing the sustainable competitiveness of firms (for example incentive systems that nurture competency-sharing, decision-support systems that diffuse resource innovations, training programmes that facilitate resource adoption and learning), and concludes that 'firms need both resource capital and institutional capital for their longer term competitive advantage' (p. 709).
35. At the same time, we have to admit that, generalizing about the behaviour of firms which are pursuing a variety of strategies, and which view a given configuration of OLI variables in a very different light, is much more difficult than under the more constrained contextual assumptions of the internalization economists.
36. Usually measured in terms of gross national product per head. But here the boundary line is sometimes difficult to draw as some rich oil states and Singapore and Hong Kong (usually classified as developing countries) are among the 30 richest countries in the world.
37. With respect, for example, to economic structure, degree of openness, government economic policy, political ideology, culture or ethnic composition, and so on.
38. Not all of these have been low-skill activities, for example office service centres in the Caribbean and computer software in India.
39. According to Narula and Sadowski (1998), only 6.2 per cent of the strategy technology partnering agreements identified by MERIT and concluded between 1980 and 1994 involved firms from developing countries.
40. In which he links the role of inbound and outbound MNE activity to the structural upgrading and economic growth of developing countries. In doing so he identifies three stages of development, which he respectively calls factor-driven, investment-driven and innovation-driven.
41. Although Ozawa (1992) did recognize the 'technology seeking' (his words) motive for FDI in the third phase of his 'stages' paradigm.
42. The optimum way for a firm to acquire created assets – for example by inward or outward FDI, by cross-border alliances, by arm's-length trade in knowledge-intensive products, or by its own innovatory activities – is a subject worthy of more attention by international business scholars.
43. In 1995, such FDIs accounted for over four-fifths of intra-developing-country FDI (UNCTAD, 1995, p64).
44. See, for example, a chapter on Singapore by Chia Siow Yue (1998) in a forthcoming monograph edited by Charles Oman and published by the OECD Development Centre on *Regional Incentives and FDI* (provisional title).
45. The concept of the eclectic paradigm as a systemic framework for accommodating context-specific explanations of MNEs was introduced in the author's original Nobel symposium paper (Dunning, 1977).

References

ALIBER, R.Z. (1970), 'A Theory of Foreign Direct Investment', in C.P. Kindleberger (ed.), *The International Corporation* (Cambridge, Mass.: MIT Press).

ALMEIDA, P. (1996), 'Knowledge Sourcing by Foreign Multinationals: Patent Citation Analysis in the US Semi-conductor Industry', *Strategic Management Journal*, vol. 17 (Winter), pp. 155–65.

BAIN, J. (1956), *Barriers to Competition* (Cambridge, Mass.: Harvard University Press).

BARNEY, J.B. (1991), 'Firm Resources and Sustained Competitive Advantage', *Journal of Management*, vol. 17, pp. 99–120

BARTNESS, A. and K. CERNY (1993), 'Building Competitive Advantage through a Global Network of Capabilities', *California Management Review*, vol. 35 (Winter), pp. 78–103.

BEHRMAN, J.N. and R. GROSSE (1990), *International Business and Governments* (Columbia, South Carolina: University of South Carolina Press).

BIRKINSHAW, J. and N. HOOD (1996), *Foreign Direct Investment and Industry Cluster Development: The Characteristics of Subsidiary Companies in Different Types of Industry Clusters* (Stockholm and Strathclyde: Stockholm School of Economics and University of Strathclyde, mimeo).

BUCKLEY, P.J. and M.C. CASSON (1976), *The Future of the Multinational Enterprise* (London: Macmillan).

CANTWELL, J. (ed.) (1994), 'Transnational Corporations and Innovatory Activities', *United Nations Library on Transnational Corporations*, vol. 17 (London and New York: Routledge).

CANTWELL, J. (1991), 'The Theory of Technological Competence and its Application to International Production', in D.G. McFetridge (ed.), *Foreign Investment, Technology and Economic Growth* (Calgary: University of Calgary Press).

CANTWELL, J. (1989), *Technological Innovation and Multinational Corporations* (Oxford: Basil Blackwell).

CAVES, R. (1982 and 1996), *Multinational Firms and Economic Analysis* 1st and 2nd eds (Cambridge: Cambridge University Press).

CONNER, K. (1991), 'A Historical Comparison of Resource Based Theory and Five Schools of Thought within Industrial Organization Economies. Do We Have a New Theory of the Firm', *Journal of Management*, vol. 17, pp. 121–54.

CONNER, K.R. and C.K. PRAHALAD (1996), 'A Resource Based Theory of the Firm: Knowledge versus Opportunism', *Organizational Science*, vol. 7, no. 5, pp. 477–501.

DOSI G., C. FREEMAN, R. NELSON, G. SILVERBERG and L. SOETE (eds), (1988) *Technical Change and Economic Theory* (London: Pinter).

DOZ, Y.L., K. ASAKAWA, J.F.P. SANTOS and P.J. WILLIAMSON (1997), *The Metanational Corporation*, INSEAD Working Paper 97/60/SM, Fountainebleau, France.

DUNNING, J.H. (1998a), 'Location and the Multinational Enterprise: A Neglected Factor', *Journal of International Business Studies*, vol. 29, no. 1, pp. 45–66.

DUNNING, J.H. (1998b), 'The Changing Nature of Firms and Governments in a Knowledge-Based Globalizing Economy', Discussion Papers on International Investment and Business Studies, no. 250 (Reading: Reading University Department of Economics).

DUNNING, J.H. (1998c), *Regions, Globalization and the Knowledge Based Economy: The Issues Stated* (Reading: Reading University), June, mimeo.

DUNNING, J.H. (ed.) (1997), *Governments, Globalization and International Business* (Oxford: Oxford University Press).

DUNNING, J.H. (1996), 'The Geographical Sources of Competitiveness of Firms: The Results of a New Survey', *Transnational Corporations*, vol. 5, no. 3 (December), pp. 1–30.

DUNNING, J.H. (1995), 'Reappraising the Eclectic Paradigm in the Age of Alliance Capitalism', *Journal of International Business Studies*, vol. 26, pp. 461–91.

DUNNING, J.H. (1993), *Multinational Enterprises and the Global Economy* (Wokingham, England, and Reading, Mass.: Addison Wesley).

DUNNING, J.H. (1988), *Explaining International Production* (London: Unwin Hyman).

DUNNING, J.H. (1977), 'Trade Location of Economic Activity and the Multinational Enterprise: A Search for an Eclectic Approach', in B. Ohlin, P.O. Hesselborn and P.M. Wikman (eds), *The International Allocation of Economic Activity* (London: Macmillan), pp. 359–418.

DUNNING, J.H. (1958), *American Investment in British Manufacturing Industry* (London, George Allen & Unwin). (New, revised and updated edition, London, Routledge, 1998).

DUNNING, J.H. and R. NARULA (eds) (1996), *Foreign Direct Investment and Governments* (London and New York: Routledge).

ENRIGHT, M.J. (1994), 'Regional Clusters and Firm Strategy', paper presented to Prince Bertil Symposium on *The Dynamic Firm, The Role of Regions, Technology, Strategy and Organization*, Stockholm, 12–15 June.

ENRIGHT, M.J. (1993), *Geographic Concentration and Industrial Organization*, PhD dissertation (Cambridge, Mass.: Harvard).

FLORIDA, R. (1995), 'Towards the Learning Region', *Futures*, vol. 27, no. 5, pp. 527–36.

FOSS, N.J. (1996), 'Research in Strategy, Economics and Michael Porter', *Journal of Management Studies*, vol. 1, pp. 1–24.

GRAHAM, E.M. (1978), 'Transatlantic Investment by Multinational Firms: a Rivalistic Phenomenon', *Journal of Post Keynesian Economics*, vol. 1, pp. 82–99.

HALEY, U.C.V., L. LOW and MUN-HENG TOH (1996), 'Singapore Incorporated: Reinterpreting Singapore's Business Environments through a Corporate Metaphor', *Management Decision*, vol. 34, no. 9, pp. 17–28.

HENNART, J.F. (1982), *A Theory of Multinational Enterprise* (Ann Arbor, Mich.: University of Michigan Press).

HYMER, S.H. (1968), 'La Grande Firme Multinationale', *Revue Economique*, vol. 14(b), pp. 949–73.

HYMER, S.H. (1960), *The International Operations of National Firms: A Study of Direct Investment*, PhD thesis (Cambridge, Mass.: MIT Press).

JOHANSON, J. and J.E. VAHLNE (1990), 'The Mechanism of Internationalization', *International Marketing Review*, vol. 7, no. 4, pp. 11–24.

JOHANSON, J. and J.E. VAHLNE (1977), 'The Internationalization Process of the Firm – a Model of Knowledge Development and Increasing Market Commitments', *Journal of International Business Studies*, vol. 8, pp. 23–32.

JOHANSON, J. and P.F. WIEDERSHEIM (1975), 'The Internationalization Process of the Firm – Four Swedish Case Studies', *Journal of Management Studies* (October), pp. 305–22.

KIM, W.S. and E.O. LYN (1990), 'FDI Theories and the Performance of Foreign Multinationals Operating in the US', *Journal of International Business Studies*, vol. 21, no. 1, pp. 41–54.

KNICKERBOCKER, F.T. (1973), *Oligopolistic Reaction and the Multinational Enterprise* (Cambridge, Mass.: Harvard University Press).

KOGUT, B. and I. ZANDER (1993), 'Knowledge of the Firm and the Evolutionary Theory of the Multinational Corporation', *Journal of International Business Studies*, vol. 24 no. 4, pp. 625–45.

KOJIMA, K. (1992), 'Internalization vs. International Business Approach to Foreign Direct Investment', *Hitosubashi Journal of Economics*, vol. 23, pp. 630–40.

KOJIMA, K. (1978), *Direct Foreign Investment: A Japanese Model of Multinational Business Operations* (London, Croom Helm).

KRUGMAN, P. (1995), *Development, Geography and Economic Theory* (Cambridge, Mass.: MIT Press).

KRUGMAN, P. (ed.) (1986), *Strategic Trade Policy and the New International Economics* (Cambridge, Mass.: MIT Press).

KUEMMERLE, W. (1996), *The Drivers of Foreign Direct Investment into Research and Development: An Empirical Investigation*, Working Paper no. 96: 062 (Boston: Harvard Business School).

LALL, S. (1983), *The New Multinationals* (Chichester and New York: Wiley).

LIPSEY, R.G. (1997), 'Globalization and National Government Oolicies: An Economist's View', in J.H. Dunning (ed.), *Governments, Globalization and International Business* (Oxford: Oxford University Press).

LIU, S.X. (1998), *Foreign Direct Investment and the Multinational Enterprise. A Reexamination Using Signaling Theory* (Westport, Conn.: Greenwood Publishing).

LUOSTARINEN, R. (1979) *Internationalization of the Firm* (Helsinki Acta Acadamie Oeconomicae, Helsinki School of Economics).

MAKINO, S. (1998), *Toward a Theory of Asset Seeking Foreign Direct Investment* (Hong Kong: The Chinese University, mimeo).

MARKUSEN, A. (1996), 'Sticky Places in Slippery Space: A Typology of Industrial Districts', *Economic Geography*, vol. 72, no 3, pp. 293–13.

MARKUSEN, J.R. (1995), 'The Boundaries of Multinational Enterprises and the Theory of International Trade', *Journal of Economic Perspectives*, vol. 9, no. 2, pp. 169–89.

MARSHALL, A. (1920), *Principles of Economics*, 8th edn (London: Macmillan).

McMANUS, J.C. (1972), 'The Theory of the Multinational Firm', in G. Paquet (ed.), *The Multinational Firm and the Nation State* (Toronto: Collier Macmillan).

MEYER, K. (1998), *Direct Investment in Economies in Transition* (Cheltenham, UK and Lyme, US.: Edward Elgar).

NARULA, R. (1995), *Multinational Investment and Economic Structure* (London: Routledge).

NARULA, R. and B. SADOWSKI (1998), *Technological Catch-up and Strategic Technological Partnering in Developing Countries*, Occasional Paper 2/98-002 (Maastricht: Maastricht Economic Research Institute on Innovation and Technology MERIT).

NELSON, R. and S. WINTER (1982), *An Evolutionary Theory of Economic Change* (Cambridge, Belknap, Harvard University Press).

OLIVER, C. (1997), 'Sustainable Competitive Advantage: Combining Institutional and Resource Based Views', *Strategic Management Journal*, vol. 18 no. 9, pp. 697–713.

OZAWA, T. (1992), 'Foreign Direct Investment and Economic Development', *Transnational Corporations*, vol. 1, pp. 27–54.

PENROSE, E.T. (1959), *The Theory of the Growth of the Firm* (Oxford: Basil Blackwell).

PEREZ, C. (1983), 'Structural Changes and the Assimilation of New Technologies on the Economic and Social System', *Futures*, vol. 15, pp. 357–75.

PERLMUTTER, H.V. (1969), 'The Tortuous Evolution of the Multinational Corporation', *Columbia Journal of World Business* (January–February), pp. 9–18.

REDDAWAY, N.B., S.T. POTTER and C.T. TAYLOR (1968), *The Effects of UK Direct Investment Overseas* (Cambridge, Mass.: Cambridge University Press).

RUGMAN, A.M. (1996), *The Theory of Multinational Enterprise*, vol. 1 (Cheltenham, Glos.: Edward Elgar).

RUGMAN, A.M. (ed.) (1982), *New Theories of the Multinational Enterprise* (London: Croom Helm).

SAVIOTTI, P.P. and J.S. METCALFE (eds) (1991), *Evolutionary Theories of Economic and Technological Change – Present Statistics and Future Prospects* (Chur: Harwood Academic Publishers).

SCHUMPETER, J.A. (1934), *The Theory of Economic Development* (Cambridge, Mass.: Harvard University Press), originally published in German in 1911.

SHAN, W. and J. SONG (1997), 'Foreign Direct Investment and the Sourcing of Technological Advantage: Evidence from the Biotechnology Industry', *Journal of International Business Studies*, vol. 28, no. 2, pp. 267–84.

STORPER, M. (1995), 'The Resurgence of Region Economies: Ten Years Later: The Region as a Nexus of Untraded Interdependencies', *European Urban and Regional Studies*, vol. 2, no. 3, pp. 191–221.

STORPER, M. and A.J. SCOTT (1995), 'The Wealth of Regions', *Futures*, vol. 27, no. 5, pp. 505–26.

SWEDENBORG, B. (1979), *The Multinational Operations of Swedish Firms: An Analysis of Determinants and Effects* (Stockholm: Industriens Utredningsinstitut).

TEECE, D. (1987), 'Profiting from Technological Innovation: Implications for Integration Collaboration, Licensing and Public Policy', in D. Teece (ed.); *The Competitive Challenge* (Cambridge, Mass.: Ballinger Publishing).

TEECE, D.J., G. PISANO and J. SHUEN (1997), 'Dynamic Capabilities and Strategic Management', *Strategic Management Journal*, vol. 18, no. 7, pp. 509–33.

UNCTAD (1997), *World Investment Report 1997, Transnational Corporations, Market Structure and Competition Policy* (Geneva and New York, UN).

UNCTAD (1996), *Investment Incentives* (New York and Geneva: UN).

UNCTAD (1995), *World Investment Report 1995: Transnational Corporations and Competitiveness* (New York and Geneva: UN).

VERNON, R. (1974), 'The Location of Economic Activity', in J.H. Dunning (ed.), *Economic Analysis and the Multinational Enterprise* (London: Allen & Unwin).

VERNON, R. (1966), 'International Investment and International Trade in the Product Cycle', *Quarterly Journal of Economics*, vol. 80, pp. 190–207.

VERNON, R. (1962), 'The Trade Expansion Act in perspective', in *Emerging Concepts in Marketing*, American Marketing Association, pp. 384–9.

WERNERFELT, B. (1995), 'The Resource Based View of the Firm: Ten Years After', *Strategic Management Journal*, vol. 16, pp. 171–4.

WESSON, T. (1997), 'A Model of Asset Seeking Foreign Direct Investment', Proceedings International Business Division, *The Administrative Sciences Association of Canada*, vol. 18, no. 8, pp. 110–20.

WESSON, T.J. (1993), *An Alternative Motivation for Foreign Direct Investment*, PhD dissertation (Cambridge, Mass.: Harvard University).

YUE, C.S. (1998), 'Singapore', in C. Oman (ed.), *Regional Incentives and Foreign Direct Investment* (Paris: OECD Development Center).

Part II
The Corporate Perspective

3 Multinational Corporate Strategy and Organization: An Internal Market Perspective

Julian Birkinshaw

INTRODUCTION

The objective of this chapter is to describe and interpret some of the recent changes observed in the strategy and organization of large multinational corporations (MNCs). The argument is that there have been a number of important but subtle changes over the last decade, including an increasing emphasis on the *geographical* location of value-adding activities, an increasing disaggregation of value-chain activities, and increasing competition between subsidiary units. Together, these changes indicate the need for new conceptual models. In the second half of the chapter one such model is proposed based on the concept of 'Internal Markets'. Three different types of internal market are described, and their implications for subsidiary strategy and corporate strategy are discussed.

CONTEXT

When reviewing the literature on multinational corporations, it is customary to identify two distinct but interrelated schools of thought – the transaction-cost/internalization approach, started by Hymer (1960) and brought to prominence through the work of Buckley and Casson (1976), Dunning (1980), Rugman (1981) and others; and the multinational management approach put forward by Prahalad and Doz (1987), Bartlett and Ghoshal (1989), Hedlund (1986) and others. The two schools of thought vary on a number of important dimensions – the former is rooted in economics, the latter in organization theory and general management; the former is concerned primarily with *why* multinational corporations exist, the latter with *how* they function; the former uses the acronym MNE, the latter MNC; and so on. But, of course, the core phenomenon that both schools of thought are studying – the large multinational corporation – is the same, and as a result it seems to be possible to discern a gradual convergence between them, or at least an increasing level of cross-fertilization. Thus, for example, the observation that subsidiary companies were taking on increasingly strategic roles was first brought to light by multinational management researchers (Bartlett and Ghoshal, 1986; Hedlund, 1986), but was subsequently incorporated into and reconciled with the transaction-cost approach (Dunning, 1993; Rugman and Verbeke, 1992).

But there is one further observation that should be made about these two schools of thought, which is in many ways rather curious. When the luminaries in each camp are considered, it is fair to say that the transaction-cost school (Buckley, Casson, Dunning, Hennart, Rugman and others) is still vitally concerned with issues of multinationality, internalization, economic impact on host and home countries, and so on; whereas the multinational management group – notably Bartlett, Doz, Ghoshal, Hamel, Hedlund, Kogut and Prahalad – moved on to other research agendas around the beginning of this decade, essentially abandoning the question of multinationality *per se*.[1] It is, however, important not to paint too stark a picture here, because all of the individuals in question are clearly still interested in multinational corporations. However, when one looks at the focus of their research, it is more about corporate renewal, knowledge management and core competence development, all of which are generic concerns of large firms; and less about geographical dispersal, environmental heterogeneity, or the management of foreign subsidiaries, which are the issues that are specific to *multinational* corporations.

Why has the focus of management research on large multinational corporations swung away from the multinational-specific issues? In part, it reflects the growing maturity of many multinational corporations, in that they perhaps feel they have worked out how to manage their network of foreign subsidiaries, and are now moving on to other questions. But it seems likely that this shift owes more to the changing interests of this small number of academics, and their ability to define the research agenda. Issues of knowledge management, competency development, networks, and alliances are alluring for managers and researchers alike, but it is important to recognize that they do not address the unique concerns of multinational corporations.

The purpose of this chapter, then, is to look carefully at the major issues facing large multinational corporations in the 1990s and beyond, and to describe some of the strategic and organizational responses that are emerging. While a complete rethinking of the issues facing large MNCs is probably not necessary, there have been some qualitative shifts over the last decade that need analysing and explaining. Concepts like the *Transnational* and the *Heterarchy* were leading-edge in the late 1980s, but are now standard parts of the MNC's repertoire. The objective in this chapter is to move beyond such concepts, and to propose a new way of modelling the MNC which takes into account some of the recent changes that have occurred.

One additional point should be made at this stage. The author comes at these issues with a background in research on MNC subsidiaries, so not surprisingly this chapter ends up focusing on a 'bottom-up' approach to MNC management that differs significantly from the 'top-down' models that currently dominate.[2] Whether this is right or wrong is for others to judge, but it is argued that a subsidiary-based perspective allows one to look with fresh eyes on the challenges facing corporate managers in large multinational corporations, and hopefully to come up with some new insights.

The chapter is in four parts. The first will briefly describe some of the major issues facing large MNCs in the current economic climate. In the second some of the emerging responses will be set out, both in terms of organizational mechanisms and overall firm strategy. In the third part the various ideas will be drawn together, resulting in an 'internal market' model that many MNCs appear to be gravitating towards. And finally, in the fourth section some of the implications will be discussed.

ISSUES FACING LARGE MULTINATIONAL CORPORATIONS

While large multinational corporations face a variety of strategic issues, the focus in this chapter is on those that are a direct consequence of globalization. This is not the setting in which to enter into a detailed discussion of the drivers of globalization, but in brief they include:

1. economic change, specifically increasing free trade within and between trading blocks, increasing mobility of capital, and increasing openness to inward investment;
2. technological change, especially the rapidly-increasing ability to coordinate international activities such as product development through electronic media; and
3. global competition, driven by the growth ambitions of firms in both developed and developing nations, and the never-ending search for economies of scale and scope.

Expressed in a slightly different way, Dunning (1998) has argued that the world is in the midst of transition into a new phase of market-based capitalism, marked by (1) a shift in the source of wealth-creation from land, labour and finance to knowledge; (2) a broadening spatial context of asset-creation and usage from local to national to global; and (3) an evolution in organization form from the individual entrepreneur through the managerial hierarchy to an alliance-based form of capitalism. Taken together, these trends are having a significant impact on the strategies and structures of individual multinational corporations. Three sets of changes, in particular, appear to be critical.

First, *there is a de facto increase in the geographical dispersal of value-adding activities in most large MNCs.*[3] The term *de facto* is used to indicate that this dispersal is not always planned. There is a strong 'push' component driven by the efforts of MNC managers to build their presence in major overseas markets, to counter the threats of competitors, and to get access to leading-edge ideas or low-cost factors of production. There is also a strong 'pull' component that is driven by the efforts of host-country governments to bring in additional inward investment, and by the initiative of subsidiary managers who are attempting to develop their own operations. Finally, some geographical dispersal is an unintended consequence of other strategic actions, such as international acquisitions or strategic alliances.

The net result of these factors is that by accident *and* design most large firms are undertaking ever-larger amounts of their value-adding activity outside the home country. Consider the case of Swedish multinationals, which are already among the most geographically dispersed corporations on the planet. Between 1986 and 1996 the top 20 Swedish MNCs saw an average increase in foreign employees of 159 per cent (that is, people working outside Sweden), while the number of domestic employees decreased by 3 per cent (Affärs Världen, 1998). The key point here is not that this increased dispersal is occurring, but that it is making the job of managing large multinational corporations much harder.

Second, *competitive pressures are pushing MNCs to make better use of their geographically dispersed activities* – to make them more efficient and to coordinate them more effectively. Nowhere is this more clear than in formerly polycentric firms like Philips, Electrolux, Johnson & Johnson and Shell, all of which have understood that they can no longer justify the cost of standalone country operations. These firms have all rationalized their manufacturing and R&D activities, but typically by assigning 'world mandates' to subsidiary companies rather than by recentralizing them in the home country. A related trend is the emergence of 'centres of excellence' in subsidiary companies, which are typically pockets of expertise that the firm wants to disseminate to other operations around the world.

A key driver of these changes is benchmarking, which enables firms to quantify their relative efficiency in any given process or activity. Its ubiquitous use is having a major impact on the configuration and coordination of firms' global operations. *Internal* benchmarking allows firms to compare related operations in different locations, resulting in performance league tables, best-practice transfers, and the emergence of centres of excellence. It also stimulates internal competition between operations for future investment. *External* benchmarking helps firms to identify which of their activities or practices are substandard, which in turn drives performance improvement programmes, decisions to relocate to lower-cost locations, or decisions to outsource activities to specialized suppliers. Again, this change is a gradual one that has been going on for decades, but its net effect is to further emphasise the relative locational advantages of certain countries (low cost labour, tax breaks, presence of key competitors, and so on) and to push geographical dispersal yet further.

Third, *MNCs are recognizing the need to develop more flexible configurations to make them more responsive to changing market demands*. This issue is somewhat more sector specific than the first two, but in industries as different as automobiles, telecommunications, pharmaceuticals and insurance managers have been heard to emphasise the need to become better at developing new technologies, identifying emerging market needs, cannibalizing existing products, and so on. Of course this is not a new issue, and neither is it unique to multinational corporations, but it is mentioned here because the *response* that many MNCs are experimenting with is to push their foreign subsidiaries to be far more entrepreneurial, and this obviously is a multinational-specific issue.

It should be clear that this list of issues is broadly consistent with similar lists written in the 1980s and indeed even earlier. Most of the challenges have not changed, but the ongoing process of globalization has probably made them more acute, and the responses that are beginning to emerge *are* substantially different from those seen in earlier decades. The key concepts to highlight are the increased level of internal competition between subsidiaries, the disaggregation of value chains, and the increasing demand being placed on leading-edge capabilities. Together, as the next section will show, they provide a foundation for a significantly different organizational model.

ELEMENTS OF A NEW MODEL

Why a New Model?

This section will present the elements that make up the 'new model' that can be discerned in some firms. It should be clear that the ideas presented here are based on what the author has observed happening in certain large MNCs. They are not necessarily representative of all firms, or indeed better practices than those occurring in other firms. But hopefully the reader will agree that there is internal consistency and face validity to the logic put forward, and that it therefore represents a useful hypothesis about how future MNCs will look.

The first point to make is that *our discussion of strategy, organization, and competitive advantage needs to be framed at a lower level of analysis* – perhaps the subsidiary unit, possibly the value-adding activity or process. There are several reasons for this:

- Benchmarking leads to an evaluation of competitiveness at the level of the activity or process, because that is the level where comparison can accurately be made. Once this has been done, all subsequent related action such as the transfer of best practice, identification of centre of excellence, outsourcing, and so on, must also take place at the activity or process level.
- Greater geographical dispersal makes it very hard to pretend that the MNC is a monolithic entity. Each subsidiary unit, by virtue of its geographical location, has a unique set of network relationships, and to some extent also has its own unique history. Even if that

subsidiary is bundled organizationally with other units in different countries, it is likely to retain a unique identity.

- Building on the last two points, capabilities[4] are in large part built at the unit level. Of course capabilities are built at multiple layers in the corporation, and some (for example, an innovative culture) are corporate-wide. But the proven value of benchmarking attests to the existence of important capabilities that emerge in certain locations. And research into knowledge management (Szulanski, 1996; Zander, 1991) shows how hard it can be to effectively transfer such capabilities to other locations.
- The demands for greater efficiency are pushing consolidation at the activity level. On the R&D side, rather than create a single worldwide R&D operation, firms are more likely to end up with three or four operations, each with a specific technology mandate. In manufacturing, firms are moving to focused factories that have global responsibility for a single product-line or family of products. Dedicated distribution or logistics centres are being created. Treasury management, call centres, human-resource (HR) training, and a host of other support activities are being pulled out of the existing infrastructure, and set up as standalone Europe-wide operations.

For the sake of simplicity, the term *subsidiary unit* will be used to signify the appropriate lower level of analysis, but it should be clear that a lower level of analysis such as an activity or process may be equally valid – indeed many companies are downsizing their profit centres to this lower level of analysis as a way to better understand their competitiveness. The critical point is that we cannot make progress in understanding the strategy and organization of the MNC by treating it as a monolithic entity. As Hedlund (1994) pointed out, the M-form organization worked on the basis of division, which created order and efficiency but drove out creativity and flexibility. Instead, he advocated an N-form based on novelty and recombination. The point here is essentially the same; namely that competitive advantage is ultimately built at the corporate level, but it is achieved through the effective bringing together of capabilities and market relationships built at the subsidiary level.

The second point is that it is evident that there are *increasing levels of internal competition between subsidiary units* (and indeed between other entities such as product divisions, R&D centres and factories). Internal competition is an awkward term. Many managers dislike it, because it has some rather negative connotations; and academics also have some problems with it because competition is seen as a 'market' activity, not one that is undertaken within an organizational 'hierarchy'. But the fact of the matter is that internal competition *does* occur, and it is fairly easy to make the conceptual argument that large firms attempt to create market-like mechanisms within their boundaries as a way of realising some of the benefits of market systems, while not sacrificing the benefits of corporate membership, such as cooperation.

Two major species of internal competition can be identified:

- Internal competition for a 'charter' (Galunic and Eisenhardt, 1996) which is a responsibility to perform certain activities for the corporation as a whole. For example, Volkswagen recently awarded the global charter for New Beetle production to its Mexican subsidiary, after considering competing bids from other plants around the world.
- Internal competition for a 'customer' (in the next stage of the value chain). This involves two units undertaking parallel development or production work, with the decision about which is preferred only being taken once that stage is completed. Tracy Kidder's book *The Soul of a New Machine*, for example, documented the internal competition between development groups in Data General. Such an approach seems enormously wasteful, because of the duplication of effort, but it can be valuable if speed to market is critical. Thus, Hewlett-Packard reputedly encourages its product divisions to actively cannibalize one another's products, rather than wait for a competitor to do it.

Both these forms of competition, it should be noted here, are 'bounded', that is, they take place according to certain corporate-defined rules. More will be said about this later. On the basis of anecdotal evidence, internal competition for charters appears to be increasing, whereas internal competition for customers is on the wane because the costs of parallel development are so great. But even if the discussion stays with internal competition for charters, there is another complication. Consider the case of IBM in Greenock, Scotland. In 1991 this plant was the European assembly operation for PCs. In an effort to 'extend the value chain' in Greenock, and thereby strengthen their position, management identified a monitor development activity currently being undertaken near London as a complementary activity that they could potentially take responsibility for. They put together a proposal explaining why the monitor development work should be relocated to Greenock, and this was duly accepted.

The reasons for relocating the monitor development activity to Greenock are probably many, but the point of this vignette is that it represented a case of internal competition for an existing activity. Charters, in other words, are open to competition when they are first established (the New Beetle in Mexico), but they are also potentially *contestable* at any time in the future as well, as IBM's Greenock management proved. The term contestability is used in a specific way here. In economics, a contestable market is one which has little or no actual competition, but one in which the costs of entry are so small that a competitor could potentially enter at any time. As a result, the incumbent may actually be in a monopoly position, but its ability to extract monopoly profits is severely attenuated because of the market's inherent contestability (Baumol, Panzer and Willig, 1982).

So it is with internal competition. As long as the subsidiary unit or division recognizes that its charter is contestable, it is likely to behave more-or-less as if it were in a market system. When charters are 'stolen' or 'transferred' the benefits are usually quite substantial because the challenger typically has to make an extraordinarily good case before the change is made. More importantly, occasional cases of charter changes provide the proof of contestability, which encourages other units to keep their own charters competitive. As one Honeywell manager interviewed in Canada observed, 'the corporate philosophy at the time was: You could have done a better job, so you should have done before somebody took the work [the charter] off you. And that's what kept us competitive.'

At what level does the internal competition for charters occur? New charters often stimulate competition on a global basis. One corporate investment, for example, had a Canadian, an Australian, and a US site on its shortlist. Obviously the selection criteria are critical here – if low cost is a priority, the firm may consider options as dispersed as Southeast Asia, India, South America and Eastern Europe; but if proximity to a certain market is key, the choice will be limited in spatial terms. Competition for existing charters seems to occur on a regional or sub-regional basis. Most examples familiar to the author occurred within a single country or between adjacent countries. Only in the case of Ericsson, where there are some 40 software development centres around the world, have incidences of charters changing hands on a global basis been observed, and even here the preference is to avoid such drastic shifts.

The third point to make is that *charters are being actively sought by existing and new locations around the world*. Again, the underlying concepts here are well-established – countries differ in their attractiveness for undertaking certain value-adding activities; industry clusters make agglomeration economies and learning opportunities available to investing firms; and certain markets have strategic significance to MNCs participating in global competition (Kogut, 1985; Porter, 1990; Prahalad and Hamel, 1985; Vernon, 1979). All these factors would predict greater dispersal of the MNC's activities around the world, and indeed all have had considerable impact in recent decades. But the interesting shift is the shift from HQ-led *push* to host-country led *pull*. Two factors are at work:

- Host-country economies, and cities or regions within countries, are becoming very aggressive in their pursuit of inward investment. For example, there are around 55 separate investment promotion agencies in Tokyo, each one trying to persuade Japanese MNCs to invest in their country or region. Moreover, these agencies are not simply providing information about their region – they are actively looking for ways to differentiate their 'offering' from that of their competitors, by focusing on certain industry segments, by seeking only certain types of investment, and by offering whatever hard and soft incentives they are allowed to. What is emerging, as a result, is even greater regional specialization than economic models might predict. If you want to build a European headquarters, go to Belgium; a semiconductor plant, consider Scotland and Ireland; a pharmaceutical R&D investment, New Jersey, and so on. Such investments are easy to promote by inward-investment agencies because that is where their comparative advantage lies, and they are easy to justify for the MNC.
- Subsidiary managers are increasingly seeking out incremental investments from their parent companies that build on their existing capabilities. This has been written about elsewhere (Birkinshaw and Hood, 1997, 1998) in terms of the development trajectory seen in many foreign subsidiaries, and the important role of subsidiary initiative as a driver of the process. What is particularly relevant here is that such efforts by subsidiary managers are driven in large part by the pressures of outsourcing and benchmarking.

The net effect of these two factors is an increasing level of 'specialization' of value-adding activities according to the relative strengths and weaknesses of different regions and subsidiary units around the world. Obviously there are other factors at play and strong inertial forces that limit the speed of change, but the overall impression one gets is that the impact of differential comparative advantage and industrial clusters on the spatial configuration of MNCs is only increasing.

A Model of the MNC Subsidiary

Taken together, these three points have some interesting implications for the way that we make sense of the modern MNC. The remainder of this chapter will spell out a few of these implications, but this section will be concluded by suggesting a richer conceptualization of the subsidiary[5] on the basis of the foregoing argument. Figure 3.1 depicts this conceptualization in terms of three elements, namely, the subsidiary's charter, its resources and capabilities, and its local context (see Birkinshaw and Hood, 1998, and Galunic, 1996 for related ideas). The charter is defined as the business, or elements of a business, that the subsidiary undertakes on behalf of the MNC and for which it has responsibility (Galunic and Eisenhardt, 1996). A charter is essentially a licence, a franchise or a mandate, which the MNC parent grants to the subsidiary because it believes the subsidiary can manage the charter effectively. But such a charter is not granted in perpetuity. As the IBM Greenock case showed, charters can and do change locations, and as such they do not *define* the subsidiary. They are merely an expression of what the subsidiary is doing at any given time.

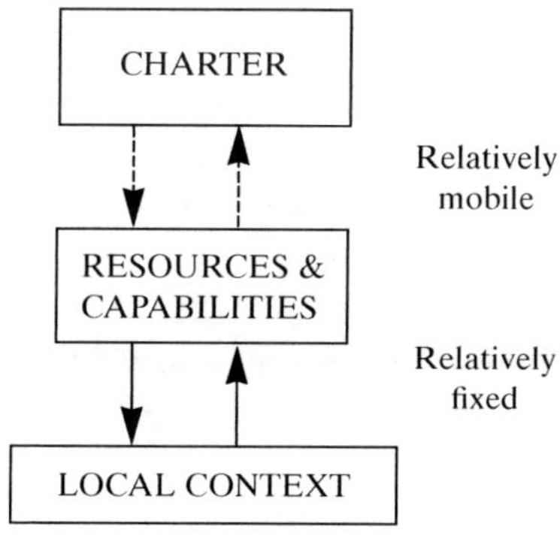

Figure 3.1 A model of the MNC subsidiary

The heart of the subsidiary is its resources and capabilities. By resources is meant the stocks of available factors that are owned or controlled by the firm which consist, *inter alia*, of physical, human and technological assets. By capabilities is meant the firm's capacity to deploy resources using organizational practices and routines (Amit and Schoemaker, 1993, p. 35). Such practices and routines develop over time as a function of the resource base of the subsidiary (and its local context – see below), and as a function of the activities it undertakes in the fulfilment of its charter. But while capabilities tend to be a reflection of the subsidiary's charter, they are unlikely to map exactly onto it because both are continuously evolving. Instead, capabilities evolve both in anticipation of and in reaction to changes in the subsidiary's charter (Birkinshaw and Hood, 1998).

Finally, the subsidiary's resources and capabilities are physically located in a local context, from which they draw and to which they contribute. In comparison to the charter–resources interface, which is relatively fluid, the resources–context interface is extremely 'sticky', though perhaps becoming less sticky over time through the globalization process. Most subsidiary units have a clear physical location that does not change. There are clearly some cases where this is not the case – Honeywell moved a production line from Minneapolis to Toronto in 1986 for example, and Pharmacia & Upjohn is moving its head office from Windsor to New Jersey – but these are very much exceptions. As a general rule, physical and human resources are either too expensive or too reluctant to move, and the associated capabilities are so intertwined with the existing resources that they cannot be moved either. Moreover, the capabilities of the subsidiary are often very much a function of the relationships its people have with the local milieu. The latter include formal supplier and customer relationships, and informal ties connecting individual employees to the local social network.

This model provides the foundation for the next section of this chapter. It emphasises three points:

1. that the basic building block is the subsidiary unit, which is defined in terms of its resources and capabilities;
2. that geographical location matters, as the soil in which the subsidiary's root system is established; and
3. that charters are mobile, and can potentially flow from subsidiary to subsidiary (or indeed to external entities).

How this subsidiary-level model ties back to the changing nature of the MNC as a whole and to questions of HQ-level strategy and organization, will be considered next.

THE INTERNAL MARKET MODEL

In considering the changes underway in many MNCs, it seems that a combination of changes in the business environment and experimentation on the part of some leading firms is resulting in a shift towards an 'internal-market' model. By internal market is simply meant that activities are configured and coordinated through a give-and-take process of mutual adjustment between units, rather than 'centrally planned' and dictated by headquarters.

Before examining the specifics of the internal-market model, it is important to be clear that it applies only to a subset of the population of MNCs. To generalize enormously, three archetypal organizational forms appear to exist among large firms – the 'traditional' manufacturing firm like GM, that coordinates both its own operations and its suppliers on a central basis; the 'virtual' firm like Nike or Dell that outsources large parts of its business system; and the 'internal-market' firm like ABB that continues to own most of its business system but coordinates it through a more bottom-up process (cf. Snow, Miles and Coleman, 1990). The expectation here is that the 'traditional' model still works reasonably well in global industries with high economies of scale, but that it is gradually being eclipsed by the 'virtual' and the 'internal-market' models, both of which are better suited to the dynamic business environment encountered today. The choice between the virtual and the internal-market models, however, is not simple. In some respects they are quite similar, because both involve the use of market systems to facilitate coordination; but they differ in one critical respect, namely that the virtual model involves the coordination of multiple independent firms whereas the internal model involves coordination within a single legal entity. There is not space here to evaluate the pros and cons of these two models, but that clearly needs to be done in subsequent work. The focus for the remainder of this chapter is on the internal-market model, and the implications for firms that wish to go down that road.

The internal-market concept is reasonably well-established in the academic literature. A book by Halal *et al.* (1994) is the most comprehensive overview of the concept, but it should also be noted that many of the ideas behind the internal-market model can also be found in other frameworks – notably the interorganizational network of Ghoshal and Bartlett (1990); the business networks perspective (Forsgren and Johanson, 1992); Hedlund's (1986) heterarchy; and indeed the literatures on empowerment, corporate entrepreneurship, intra-organization ecology and self-organizing systems. However, far from just being another label for the same phenomenon, the internal-market approach appears to reflect some of the actual changes that are underway in large MNCs at the moment, and as such it offers an important new perspective on their emerging strategies and structures.

Before getting to the key question of a 'market for what?' a few of the basic principles of the internal market approach need to be laid out. This is probably not a comprehensive list, but the following should be acknowledged as critical principles:

1. Internal markets allow individual units to make choices in what activities they undertake, the source of their inputs and the destination of their outputs, through the availability of alternative suppliers and customers.
2. Every internal market is embedded in an external market (that is, the market economy), from which it draws and to which it contributes. The 'porosity' of this boundary is critical, because one of the key choices a unit can make is whether to sell to or source from external units.
3. Markets work in large part because of the existence of high-powered incentives (Williamson, 1991). Thus, for the internal market model to work well, top management has to give extraordinary attention to the incentive system – both the 'hard' and the 'soft' components.
4. The responsibility of subsidiary managers in the internal market is to maximize the performance of the subsidiary, according to the defined incentives.
5. Internal markets are very good at enhancing efficiency, but not so good at enhancing effectiveness. Efficiency thus becomes the responsibility of subsidiary managers who are responding to the 'market' incentives; while effectiveness becomes the responsibility of top management, who define the appropriate incentive system and the 'rules of the game'.
6. The internal-market system is a theoretical lens not a normative model. Thus, the approach is relevant even in MNCs that still

> prefer a centrally-planned structure. It may indeed be in top management's interest to *restrict* the internal market in certain cases, and certainly there is plenty of evidence of subsidiaries that rarely if ever experience the workings of the internal market.

It should also be noted at this point that the internal market model under discussion here assumes that the value-adding unit is the relevant level of analysis. The ideas could easily be taken down to the level of the individual – by looking at the internal labour market, how specific projects compete for key individuals, and so on – but for the sake of clarity the focus here is at the unit and organization levels.

Types of Internal Market

While the idea of internal markets has been around for some time, the key insight here is that *subsidiary units in the MNC are participating simultaneously in three different internal markets*. These are the markets for intermediate products/services, charters, and practices (Table 3.1).[6] The argument is that to understand how the large MNC really works we have to consider all three markets together. Only then can sense be made of concepts like 'subsidiary strategy' and 'corporate strategy'. Each of these markets is now considered in turn.

The Market for Intermediate Products and Services

This is the form of internal market that is the focus of Halal *et al.*'s (1994) book. In 'traditional' MNCs, the value-adding system is broken into steps, and the unit responsible for each step supplies its intermediate product to the next unit in the chain. Using an internal-market approach, this chain is broken up into discrete value-adding units,[7] and for each unit one asks: how much choice of suppliers/customers should this unit have, either inside or outside the firm? Using a traditional vertically-integrated model there would be no choice at any stage, and transfer prices would essentially be mandated from above or calculated on a cost-plus basis (Eccles, 1985). Under an internal-market model, there might be two or more internal suppliers or customers, and there might be several external suppliers or customers as well. ABB, for example, has moved to an internal-market approach in which each business unit has more-or-less complete freedom about who it sells to and who it buys from. Obviously in such a system the transfer price internally has to be at or close to the external market price.

Table 3.1 Types of internal markets and their characteristics

	Market for:		
	Intermediate product or service	*Charter*	*Capability or practice*
Competition between:	Value-adding activities (regardless of where performed)	Value-adding units (the physical entities)	Value-adding units (the physical entities)
Customer:	Next stage in value chain	Resource allocator, HQ or divisional decision-maker	Other value-adding units
Driving question in the establishment of this market:	To what extent does the MNC want to internalize the existing market system?	Where (physically) do we want each specific value-adding activity to take place?	How can leading-edge capabilities or practices be efficiently identified and transferred?
Role of subsidiary unit:	Compete with internal and external competitors in delivery of product or service to customer	Compete with internal and external competitors for new and existing charters	Actively seek out 'suppliers' of practices, and make available practices to other units
Role of HQ:	Define extent to which each stage of value chain will be internalized, and customer's freedom in selecting among competing alternatives	Define extent to which new and existing charters will be competed for, and extent to which external bids will be accepted	Define systems that help to maximize flow of practices inward and internally, but which limit the flow of practices outward (to external entities)

The extent to which an internal market for intermediate products and services is created is very much a strategic issue that top management must decide on. There are two separate questions. First, should external customers and suppliers be used in competition with internal ones? As a general rule, such external relationships are valuable as a means of enhancing efficiency, but there are times when they can be contrary to strategic interests as, for example, when a new component ends up getting sold into competing products. The second question is should the MNC itself maintain two or more value-adding activities acting in parallel? The costs of such duplication are of course high, but they can be beneficial, both as a means of enhancing time to market and as a means of trying out different approaches. The sense one gets, as noted earlier, is that this form of internal market is on the wane, but cases of it are still seen, particularly in the very early stages of the value chain (in research labs) and in the final marketplace (for example, the launch of Internet or telephone-based banking services which compete for existing customers through a new channel).

Of the three internal markets, this one has least specific relevance to the MNC because it is concerned with the 'value-adding activity' not the physical unit. Thus, the discussion above gives no explicit attention to where the activity is located, it is just concerned with the extent to which multiple paths will be followed. Having said that, this form of internal market is still of critical concern to large MNCs because the size and dispersal of units around the world makes the opportunity for multiple internal sources and customers much greater. ABB, again, is a classic example of this.

The Market for Charters

The internal market for charters is most visible[8] in cases of new investments – a new production plant, an R&D centre, or a logistics centre. In such cases, as indicated earlier, there are likely to be multiple subsidiary units and inward-investment bodies clamouring for the opportunity to receive that investment. Here, the strategic decision by top management is twofold. One part is the definition of the criteria by which the investment decision will be made. The second part, which is more relevant here, is how 'open' to make the competition for the charter. On this issue, MNCs today run the full spectrum from no choice at all ('we need to make a strategic investment in China'), to the identification of a small number of candidate locations that are then evaluated, through to a very open competition that is broadcast to all subsidiary units around the world. External competitors, again, are often considered, depending on how strategic is the investment in question.

While new investments are almost always actively competed for, it was argued earlier that *existing* charters are increasingly deemed to be mobile and therefore open to competition. This may be the most interesting element of the internal-market model, because it represents a much more fundamental shift in how activities within the MNC are allocated. New investments have always been competed-for, but the idea that a subsidiary could lose a charter for failing to perform, just as weak companies go bankrupt in the open market, is a relatively new one to most MNCs.

What are the costs and benefits of internal-market competition for charters? The benefits are, as indicated, increased efficiency in operations, and an increased level of self-sufficiency on the part of subsidiary units. The costs are of two types. First, making this form of market work is quite expensive, because proposals have to be evaluated. Unlike the first type of internal market which operates through a form of invisible hand, charter decisions have to be judged by top management or by some form of review board. The second cost is analogous to structural employment in the market system. If a unit loses its charter, its employees are essentially out of work, and it is therefore in the MNC's interests to find a way of relocating them, to find them a new charter, or perhaps even to outplace them. All of which are costly options.

The internal market for charters is central to the working of the modern MNC. As the subsidiary model in Figure 3.1 indicated, charters are mobile and competed-for, while the subsidiary's resources, capabilities and local context are the differentiating factors by which it competes for charters. Subsidiary strategy, as the next section will explain, is therefore about building a sustainable position *vis-à-vis* both internal and external competitors.

The Market for Capabilities and Practices

The third type of internal market is for capabilities and practices, and it is most visible in cases of best-practice transfer between sites (for example, Arvidsson, 1997; Szulanski, 1996; Zander, 1991). But this market differs on one important dimension from the other two, namely that the competitive element is missing. 'Buying' units are those in search of a new practice, and they can potentially access that practice from any other internal unit as well as from countless external operations. But of course the 'selling' unit, the one transferring its best-practice, typically does not get any material reward for that service, and as a result the market for practices does not work at all efficiently. The challenge, which many MNCs are experimenting with, is to provide the appropriate incentives to encourage best-practice transfers between units. These can include structural approaches such as the creation of centres of excellence, and softer approaches such as evaluating individuals' propensity to cooperate with individuals in other units.[9] A complementary approach which can be seen in some firms is the emergence of 'brokers' in the market for practices, who specific role is to link up 'buyers' and 'sellers'.

The internal market for practices, then, is rather different from the other two but is no less important because it helps to make all units more efficient. Internal benchmarking, as noted earlier, is one manifestation of a more active internal market for best practices, and the interest among scholars in knowledge transfers is also testament to the growing importance of this phenomenon.

Two more points are also very relevant in the discussion of internal markets for practices. First, the efficiency of the internal market is important as a means of ensuring that best practices get spread around, but perhaps even more important is the links with the external market in which the MNC is embedded. External benchmarking studies, imitation of competitors, diffusion of practices from customers, links to consulting companies, and so on, are all mechanisms for facilitating the inward flow of practices into the internal market. But at the same time as inward flows are essential, it is equally important for the MNC that outward flows are *restricted*, lest proprietary practices are given away to competitors. The internal market for practices, in other words, should be ideally designed such that it is permeable in one direction only.

The other point to make about the internal market for practices is that it is not readily compatible with the other two internal markets. Both the first two internal markets require sister units to compete with one another whether for margins, or for charters. The market for practices requires them to cooperate and to share freely with one another. Interestingly, this form of schizophrenia that requires units to cooperate and compete at the same time seems to work quite well in practice. HP and Ericsson, for example, both seem to do a good job of managing the balance, perhaps because of the strong corporate culture in both cases, and perhaps because the incentives systems are well designed to reward both types of behaviour.

DISCUSSION AND CONCLUSIONS

The internal-market model suggests a number of different implications for both theory and practice. If we take practice first, the key insight is that two distinct levels of strategy emerge. The lower level is the subsidiary unit, or perhaps the factory, the R&D centre or the division. Such units become semi-autonomous entities *responsible for their own destiny*. They remain as members of the internal market in which practices are shared and various corporate assets such as technology are commonly owned, but they also actively compete with various internal and external units. Viewed in this way, the concept of a subsidiary 'strategy' becomes much more real. Subsidiary entrepreneurship, which has been looked at in detail in earlier studies (Birkinshaw, 1995, 1997), is simply the actions of a responsible subsidiary manager who is looking for ways of enhancing the competitiveness of his or her operation. And certain strategic actions, such as developing a unique technology, or being the highest-quality plant in the MNC, begin to make sense as analogs to Porter's (1980) generic strategies.

The higher level of strategy is at the corporate level. In terms of the internal-market model corporate management's job is to define the 'rules of the game', including how much internal competition will be allowed, the criteria for awarding charters, defining appropriate incentive systems to make the markets function, and so on. But as noted earlier, internal-markets are primarily designed for enhancing efficiency, so an equally or more important part of corporate management's role is to steer the MNC's effectiveness. This means, amongst other things, defining which markets and technologies to enter, defining the MNC's competitive positioning, and creating an ability to adapt to changing environmental conditions. All of these can *to some degree* be achieved through the definition of the internal-markets, for example, by allowing internal competition in the consumer marketplace, the MNC becomes flexible to changes in customer tastes; and by tilting the criteria for awarding charters towards quality and service metrics, the MNC defines its overall competitive positioning. But eventually there are probably some aspects of the corporate strategy that may end up being the sole responsibility of corporate management, rather than something that is facilitated through the internal market.

The theoretical implications of the internal-market model are also quite significant. By adopting the market metaphor, there is obviously a wealth of theoretical ideas that apply to the market economy that could potentially be applied to the internal workings of the MNC. The concept of contestability, for example, was invoked earlier as a way of explaining how existing charters might be challenged by other subsidiary units. Equally, it should be clear that the internal market is *not* the same thing as an external market, and as such some concepts will not adapt well to the internal market setting – high-powered incentives, for example, exist in the external marketplace, but can only be proxied in the internal market.

There appears to be a lot of potential in exploring the internal-market metaphor in the context of large MNCs. Other theoretical approaches, such as network theory, the intra-organization ecology perspective, and the resource-based view of the firm, need to be reconciled with the internal-market model, and of course there is a need to think through what transaction cost theory would say about all the above.

The Question of Multinationality

We should now come back full-circle to the issue with which the chapter began. It was observed that researchers from the 'multinational management' school had begun to move away from the multinational-specific questions, leaving it open to debate whether the issue of multinationality *per se* really mattered any more. In response to that rhetorical question, this essay has sketched out the elements of a new model of the MNC based around the idea of internal markets. In doing this, it took a 'bottom-up' perspective, that started with the subsidiary unit *in its local context* as the basic building block. The MNC, in other words, can be modelled as a federation or a network of interdependent subsidiary units, whose geographical location matters because it is the link to the local context, and the development of location-specific capabilities, that provides the basis for the subsidiaries' competitiveness.

The argument, in other words, is that the question of multinationality *per se* is still vitally important. Indeed, the process of globalization is making it even more important because the geographical dispersal of value-adding activities in firms continues to increase. It is also quite neat to bring the idea of internal markets into the management literature. The well-established theory explaining why MNCs exist is of course built on the idea that MNCs internalize the market for intermediate products. Here, the idea of an internal market is being broadened to include not just the market for intermediate products but the market for charters and practices as well.

Finally, if the reader is not yet convinced of the importance of the internal-market model, it is relevant to note that many MNCs are actively embracing the terminology and some of the ideas set out here. Skandia AFS, for example, talks about its internal-market system; and ABB and Ericsson have both refined elements of the internal-market model (the intermediate market type for ABB, the charter type for Ericsson). Of course this does not 'prove' the validity of the model, but it does suggest that there is an important line of inquiry that is worth pursuing. While this chapter has put together some of the elements of the new model, much remains to be done, both in playing out the ideas alluded to here and in reconciling the internal-market model with existing theories.

Notes

1. This is a generalization, of course. Exceptions are Yves Doz (Doz and Santos, 1997), who is now studying the implications of geographically dispersed knowledge, and Bruce Kogut, who has played out his thinking on the theory of the firm for multinational corporations in particular (Kogut and Zander, 1995).
2. To be clear, the Transnational, Heterarchy, and Network models all give explicit and genuine attention to the changing roles of foreign subsidiaries, but they do so from the perspective of head-office management. Nowhere is this clearer than in the definition of subsidiary roles – in the Transnational model, roles are 'assigned' by head-office managers (Bartlett and Ghoshal, 1986); using the bottom-up perspective, subsidiary roles (or strategies) are 'assumed' (cf. Hagström, 1994).
3. The high-level environmental drivers of this shift have been discussed countless times and in far greater detail than could possibly be achieved here. However, to ensure that the reader understands the author's own perspective on what the important drivers are, one should simply acknowledge the following: (a) economic change, specifically increasing free trade within and between trading blocks, increasing mobility of capital, and increasing openness to inward investment; (b) technological change, especially the rapidly-increasing ability to coordinate international activities such as product development through electronic media;

and (c) global competition, driven by the growth ambitions of firms in both developed and developing nations, and the never-ending search for economies of scale and scope.

4. Capabilities are defined as 'the capacity to deploy resources, usually in combination, using organizational processes to effect a desired end', Amit and Schoemaker (1993).
5. As an aside, the term *subsidiary* is increasingly inappropriate for business entities that have significant value-adding activities of their own and considerable degrees of freedom to enact their own strategy. The term is retained here, for the sake of consistency, but other terms such as affiliate and auxiliary may be rather more appropriate.
6. Other internal markets can also be identified. One might be the market for capital expenditure, which overlaps significantly with the market for charters. Another might be the market for corporate attention or reputation, which in some ways transcends all three. Clearly there is scope for additional conceptualization here.
7. Note that the value-adding unit can be very small, and certainly well below the subsidiary as a unit. Examples include the manufacture of a component, a call centre, a research centre and a sales team.
8. Though probably most common at a lower level of analysis as, for example, in the allocation of research project charters to different R&D groups.
9. Interestingly, though, it is hard to find any firms that use monetary incentives. Presumably the concern with such a system is that the true 'value' of practices is hard to measure, so all sorts of suboptimal behaviours would emerge, such as less-capable units trying to sell their practices to others in the hope of reward.

References

AFFÄRS VÄRLDEN (1998), 'De nya utvandrarna', 14 January, pp. 26–31.

AMIT, R. and P. SCHOEMAKER (1993), 'Strategic Assets and Organizational Rent', *Strategic Management Journal*, vol. 14, pp. 33–46.

ARVIDSSON, N. (1997), *Intra-firm Geographical Transfer of Capabilities. Obstructed by Perceptions Gaps? – The Case of Marketing and Sales Activities*, paper presented at the AIB Conference, Monterrey, Mexico, 8–12 October.

BARTLETT, C.A. and S. GHOSHAL (1989), *Managing across Borders: The Transnational Solution* (Cambridge, Mass.: Harvard Business School Press).

BARTLETT, C.A. and S. GHOSHAL (1986), 'Tap your Subsidiaries for Global Reach', *Harvard Business Review*, vol. 64, no. 6, pp. 87–94.

BAUMOL, W.J., J. PANZER and R. WILLIG (1982), *Contestable Markets and the Theory of Industry Structure* (New York: Harcourt Brace Jovanovich).

BIRKINSHAW, J.M. (1997), 'Entrepreneurship in Multinational Corporations: The Characteristics of Subsidiary Initiatives', *Strategic Management Journal*, vol. 18, no. 3, pp. 207–29.

BIRKINSHAW, J.M. (1995), 'Entrepreneurship in Multinational Corporations: The Initiative Process in Canadian Subsidiaries', unpublished doctoral dissertation, Western Business School.

BIRKINSHAW, J.M. and N. HOOD (1998), 'Multinational Subsidiary Development: Capability Evolution and Charter Change in Foreign-owned Subsidiary Companies', *Academy of Management Review*, vol. 23, no. 4, pp. 773–95.

BIRKINSHAW, J.M. and N. HOOD (1997), 'An Empirical Study of Development Processes in Foreign-wned Subsidiaries in Canada and Scotland', *Management International Review*, vol. 37, no. 4, pp. 339–64.

BUCKLEY, P.J. and M.C. CASSON (1976), *The Future of the Multinational Enterprise* (London: Macmillan).

DUNNING, J.H. (1998), *The Changing Nature of Firms and Governments in a Knowledge-based Globalizing Economy*, University of Reading Department of Economics, Discussion papers on international investment and business studies, Paper no. 250, March.

DUNNING, J.H. (1993), *Multinational Enterprises and the Global Economy* (Wokingham: Addison-Wesley).

DUNNING, J.H. (1980), 'Towards an Eclectic Theory of International Production: Some Empirical Tests', *Journal of International Business Studies*, vol. 11, pp. 9–31.

DOZ, Y.L. and J.F.P. SANTOS (1997), *On the Management of Knowledge: From the Transparency of Collocation and Co-setting to the Quandary of Dispersion and Differentiation*, paper presented at the EIBA meeting, Stockholm, December 1996.

ECCLES (1985), *The Transfer Pricing Problem: A Theory for Practise* (Lexington, Mass.: D.C. Heath & Co.).

FORSGREN, M. and J. JOHANSON (1992), *Managing Networks in International Business* (Philadelphia: Gordon & Breach).

GALUNIC, D.C. and K.M. EISENHARDT (1996), 'The Evolution of Intracorporate Domains: Divisional Charter Losses in High-technology, Multidivisional Corporations', *Organization Science*, vol. 7, no. 3, pp. 255–82.

GALUNIC, D.C. (1996), 'Recreating Divisional Domains: Intracorporate Evolution and the Multibusiness Firm', in B. Keys and L.N. Dosier (eds), *Proceedings of the Academy of Management Conference 1996*, pp. 219–24.

GHOSHAL, S. and C.A. BARTLETT (1990), 'The Multinational Corporation as an Interorganizational Network', *Academy of Management Review*, vol. 15, no. 4, pp. 603–25.

HAGSTRÖM, P. (1994), *The 'Wired' MNC* (Stockholm: Institute of International Business).

HALAL, W.E., A. GERANMAYEH and J. POURDEHNAD (1994), *Internal Markets: Bringing the Power of Free Enterprise Inside your Organization* (New York: John Wiley).

HAMEL, G. and C.K. PRAHALAD (1985), 'Do You Really Have a Global Strategy?', *Harvard Business Review*, vol. 63, no. 4, pp. 139–45.

HEDLUND, G. (1994), 'A Model of Knowledge Management and the N-form Corporation', *Strategic Management Journal*, vol. 15, pp. 73–90.

HEDLUND, G. (1986), 'The Hypermodern MNC: A Heterarchy?', *Human Resource Management*, vol. 25, pp. 9–36.

HYMER, S. (1960/1976), *The International Operations of National Firms: A Study of Foreign Direct Investment*, PhD dissertation, Massachusetts Institute of Technology (Boston: MIT Press).

KIDDER, T. (1971), *The Soul of a New Machine* (Baston, Mass.: Little, Brown & Co.).

KOGUT, B. (1995), 'Designing Global Strategies: Comparative and Competitive Value-added Chains', *Sloan Management Review*, Summer 1995, pp. 15–27.

KOGUT, B. and U. ZANDER (1995), 'Knowledge of the Firm and the Evolutionary Theory of the Multinational Corporation', *Journal of International Business Studies*, vol. 25, no. 4, pp. 625–46.

PORTER, M.E. (1990), *The Competitive Advantage of Nations* (New York: The Free Press).

PORTER, M.E. (1980), *Competitive Strategy* (New York: The Free Press).

PRAHALAD, C.K. and Y.L. DOZ (1987), *The Multinational Mission* (New York: The Free Press).

RUGMAN, A.M. (1981), *Inside the Multinationals: The Economics of Internal Markets* (London: Croom Helm).

RUGMAN, A. and A. VERBEKE (1992), 'A Note on the Transnational Solution and the Transaction Cost Theory of Multinational Strategic Management', *Journal of International Business Studies*, vol. 23, no. 4, pp. 761–72.

SNOW, C.C., R.E. MILES and H.J. COLEMAN (1992), 'Managing 21st Century Network Organizations', *Organizational Dynamics*, Winter, pp. 4–20.

SZULANSKI, G. (1996), 'Exploring Internal Stickiness: Impediments to the Transfer of Best Practises within the Firm', *Strategic Management Journal*, vol. 17 (special issue), pp. 27–44.

VERNON, R. (1979), 'The Product Cycle in the New International Environment', *The Oxford Bulletin of Economics and Statistics*, vol. 41, pp. 255–67.

WILLIAMSON, O.E. (1991), 'Comparative Economic Organization: The Analysis of Discrete Structural Alternatives', *Administrative Science Quarterly*, vol. 36, pp. 269–96.

ZANDER, U. (1991), 'Exploiting a Technological Edge – Voluntary and Involuntary Dissemination of Technology', Doctoral Dissertation, Stockholm School of Economics.

4 Globalization, Corporate Strategies and Business Services

Neil Hood and Ewen Peters

INTRODUCTION

While it is possible to debate the scale, pace and degree to which globalization is occurring in the world economy, there is little doubt that a transformation is underway in both countries and companies. It is being driven by three mutually reinforcing factors, namely the growing scale, mobility and integration of the world's capital markets; the diminishing significance of national boundaries as deregulation accelerates and as barriers to trade are reduced; and by the ability to use technology to exploit knowledge on a worldwide basis. These factors impact equally upon goods and services, although the latter is the concern of this chapter.

In recent years there has been considerable academic interest in the globalization of service industries. Much of this literature has considered the motivation and modality of the internationalization of service firms (Dunning, 1989; Mathe and Perras, 1994; Vandermerwe and Chadwick, 1989); others have focused more on the ways in which globalization drivers and global strategies impact various types of services (Lovelock and Yip, 1996; Campbell and Verbecke, 1994); while some have compared service and manufacturing internationalization (Buckley *et al.*, 1992). All of these insights are of relevance for this chapter, but its specific interest is in the ways in which the trend towards the globalization of professional business service providers exerts an influence upon economic development at a national or regional level. This particular topic has received much less attention in the literature. Central to this type of concern are the corporate strategies of those service providers as they come to terms with both the globalization and the regionalization of services.[1]

The chapter is shaped as follows. It commences with a brief overview of some of the relevant academic literature on the globalization of services. The second section is largely conceptual in that it explores some ways of identifying the key trends relating to service globalization and location. The third section is more empirical and provides illustrations, both of the strategies of corporate service entities and of geographic regions with service clusters in different parts of the world. These are designed to amplify the conceptual material and are examined within the parameters of the frameworks established. The final section presents the conclusions emerging from the analysis and considers the policy implications for economic development in successful clusters. Many aspects of the chapter are exploratory as befits a difficult and under-researched topic. Its contribution is to specify a rich research agenda and to point to some areas where that agenda could be usefully focused.

THE GLOBALIZATION OF SERVICE INDUSTRIES

The purpose of this section is to highlight the important global trends in the development of services foreign direct investment (FDI) over the past two decades. The growth in services FDI has been such that towards the late 1980s and early 1990s, it became more important as a source of outward FDI than the primary and manufacturing sectors. By 1990, tertiary sector FDI across the key developed countries was already around 50 per cent of both the inward and outward investment stock. It would appear that the growth in both stocks and flows of services FDI will continue, but it is unlikely to replace industrial FDI. Indeed its very growth is indicative of the emergence of a more integrated global economy, and there are evident symbiotic relationships between the integration of service and industrial activity (Sauvant and Zimny, 1988; Dicken, 1992; Aharoni, 1993).

As regards the sectoral patterns within these growth trends, finance and insurance were the largest service sectors expanding abroad accounting for between 30 per cent and 80 per cent of the FDI stock in services in selected OECD countries by 1990, with Japan and the USA being the main source nations. The next largest sector was trade-related services, such as wholesale and retail trade and marketing. During the 1990s there has been much evidence of growth in other sectors as a result of liberalization and deregulation policies applied in many OECD countries in sectors such as telecommunications and financial services. GATT estimates for 1993 suggest that some 21 per cent of global trade consisted of cross-border trade in services.

It is important to emphasise that not all FDI in services is undertaken by enterprises which are themselves service specialists. However, a considerable number of multinational enterprises (MNEs) recognize that their competitive advantage depends on the effective combination of manufacturing and services (O'Farrell, 1995). Thus the oil majors operate tanker fleets and petrol stations; automobile producers have finance affiliates; while computer manufacturers have extensive service affiliates to proffer advice and consulting to their installed base. There are, of course, large numbers of service MNEs, but on the whole a relatively small number of firms account for the bulk of MNE activities in most service sectors. Moreover, there has been a tendency for a number of the largest service MNEs to diversify into related service sectors, with clusters forming. This is evident in finance-related services, data services, tourism and travel, as well as in some professional services like accounting and advertising. Such trends can often be attributed to the use of common information technology systems, customer bases and channels to market, as well as to economies of scale in production and delivery. In terms of modality, it is evident that non-equity organizational forms are prevalent in international services, not least because of different regulatory regimes and the nature of competitive advantage enjoyed by an international, as distinct from a national, provider. For example, in accounting and audit, international operations are often organized as loose collections of largely autonomous partnerships; while franchising and management contracts are widely used in industries such as hotels, car rentals and fast foods.

Turning now to the drivers of FDI in services which have led to these developments. A number of these can be readily identified as flowing from major innovations in information and communications technologies; increasing specialization and differentiation in products; and government policies of deregulation and privatization, together with the unilateral liberalization in investment and trade regimes (Sauvé, 1995). In addition, countries have adopted new strategies to attract services FDI, not least by innovation in both skills development and property provision. To these factors has to be added the impact of the growing demand for services as a large proportion of product offerings require service support (for example, in information technology); increasingly complex and internationally-integrated financial, production and distribution environments requiring similar support (for example, in the auto industry); and the need for services to handle the management and administration for the growing numbers of transnational corporations. Multinational service corporations have in turn expanded to meet these demands and have themselves become increasingly global, often initially in support of their industrial MNE customers.

From a conceptual perspective, a number of studies have examined the determinants of FDI in services. Orthodox theory has been deployed to explain the activities of MNEs in the various service sectors (Dunning, 1989). In particular, quality (product differentiation), economies of scale and scope, firm size and growth, technology and information, and favoured access to inputs or markets have been suggested as the main *ownership specific advantages*. In terms of *locational variables*, suggested factors include input prices, quality and productivity, international transport and communications costs, investment incentives and disincentives and other government regulations, infrastructure, psychic distance, global oligopolistic reaction, industry concentration, tradability of service industries, and the economics of centralization of knowledge-intensive activities.

Studies at the micro-level give greater insight into the importance of some of these variables. For example, Segal-Horn (1993) has presented a dynamic model of growth and competition for international service businesses. In studying the globalization of service MNEs, other authors have indicated the importance of strategic variables such as centralized innovation versus high national responsiveness; high or low networking capabilities (Campbell and Verbecke, 1994); and the importance of customer focus and competitive positioning (Sarathy, 1994). A number of these issues are further developed in the next section.

CONCEPTUAL CONSIDERATIONS

This section sets out to construct and develop some models and frameworks which inform the policy issues considered later. Before so doing it is necessary to establish some boundaries for the discussion. The analysis is in three stages. The first of these concerns the scale of globalization and the degree to which it can be claimed to exist; the second examines the demand for and supply of business services; and the third considers some of the economic development implications of the patterns identified.

The Scale and Pace of Globalization

Relatively few companies are able to pursue truly global strategies which involve the worldwide integration of both the formulation and implementation of strategy. Multidomestic (or multilocal) approaches which provide for the independent development and implementation of strategies by country or regional units are more common (Hout *et al.*, 1982; Prahalad and Doz, 1987). It is evident, for example, that globalization potential in a corporation depends on industry characteristics and on the strength of globalization drivers in areas such as markets, costs, government policies and competitive behaviour. Moreover, the use made of global strategies within any given business or sector differs depending upon the various elements of the value-adding chain (Kogut, 1985; Prahalad and Doz, 1987).

Some aspects of these observations can be related to the perspective on globalization shown in Table 4.1. Those estimates suggest that some 23 per cent of world GDP might consist of industries which are globalized in most aspects of their strategic behaviour. This categorization emphasises commodities and scale at this end of the spectrum. Meanwhile, at the lower end, some 50 per cent of world GDP is regarded as in the early stages of globalization, and essentially still local in its focus. Here the emphasis is strongly placed on branding, although it could be debated whether this is both a necessary and sufficient condition for a company to be able to pursue a global strategy. By this measure some 25 per cent of world GDP, but a much higher proportion of employment, has low prospects of globalization. More relevant for this chapter is the middle category where globalization is accelerating at a rapid pace, since this 15 per cent includes professional business services, and a variety of consumer goods. Within this broad category there are of course many existing global companies such as Coca-Cola, McDonald's, Microsoft, Nike, Andersen Consulting and so on. In summary, Figure 4.1 provides a broad backcloth to the degree to which this phenomenon is represented in world business, but it is not robust enough for detailed scrutiny at corporate level. However, it serves another purpose in that it places professional business services[2] into context. Later observations will be advanced on the more detailed categorization of business services, linked to the work of Lovelock and Yip (1996).

Demand and Supply Trends

The second stage of this analysis requires the identification of the directions of change in both the demand and supply side of business services. This is a difficult and speculative exercise, but it is necessary to attempt to identify the drivers of the globalization of services.

Table 4.1 A perspective on globalization

Category – Industries	*Size of industry based on world GDP, 1995, US$ trillion*		
1. *Physical commodities* Petroleum, mineral ores, timber	2.0	23%	Globalized
2. *Scale-driven business goods and services* Aircraft engines, construction equipment, semiconductors, airframes, shipping, refineries, machine tools	1.0		
3. *Manufactured commodities* Refined petroleum products, aluminium, specialty steel, bulk pharmceuticals, pulp, speciality chemicals	2.8		
4. *Labour skill-/productivity-driven consumer goods* Consumer electronics, personal computers, cameras, automobiles, televisions	0.9	15%	Accelerating globalization
5. *'Brandable', largely deregulated consumer goods* Soft drinks, shoes, luxury goods, pharmaceuticals, movie production	0.5*		
6. *Professional business services* Investment banking, legal services, accounting services, consulting services	2.5		
7. *'Hard to brand' globally, largely regulated consumer goods and services* Food, personal financial services, television production, retail distribution channels	6.3	50%	Early globalization, still local
8. *Local (unbranded) goods and services* Construction materials, real estate, funeral homes, education, household services, medical care, utilities	6.4		
Total	$25.3		

* Provisional

Note: There are some limitations to this table including, for example, the fact that the 'software and related services' sector straddles several of the segments shown above and is a $ multi-billion global business.

Source: *World Development Report* (World Bank); McGraw-Hill/DRI *World Economic Outlook 1996*; United Nations, 1995, National Income Accounts; McKinsey analysis. Reported in Fraser and Oppenheim (1997).

Starting with the demand side, Figure 4.1 suggests that, based on the example of many large manufacturing corporations, the two dominant changes in their demand for external service provision are those for outsourcing and consolidation. The former trend is well-established and stems from the progressive redefinition of core competencies as sets of interwoven skills that are strategically critical to the company's current and future performance (Collis and Montgomery, 1995; Grant, 1991). The resultant outsourcing of non-core activities to specialist third-party providers is often driven by capital requirements, competitive focus, relative competencies, economies of scale, and so on. In others the primary motivation is the pace of change where external service providers are an important catalyst for change-management programmes. Many of those activities cited at the three different corporate levels in Figure 4.1 have long been outsourced in whole or part; others such as local accounting, management information systems, research, design and development, more recently feature as outsourced revenues. For other corporations outsourcing in such areas remains 'a step too far'. However, the principle is clear, namely that substantial global markets exist in outsourced services emerging from corporations that are themselves widely dispersed in geographical terms. This international demand calls for matching, homogeneous and quality supply responses, thereby creating opportunities for the globalization of service provision. Some of the best examples of this are to be found in the software and computer services sectors.[3]

Consolidation, as shown in Figure 4.1, may have similar effects, and take many forms. At one level this may be purely internal to the corporation, as for example in shared service,[4] data-processing,[5] or value-added logistics centres[6] providing services to a large corporate network. A number of these develop expertise which is traded in the open market. Others arrive at the same position by alliances, while still more contract out total corporate services in areas such as facilities management and customer services. It is evident that these trends towards consolidation go far beyond the historic ebb and flow of centralization/decentralization which has characterized control procedures in international corporations for several decades. The opportunities it has generated for global service providers are illustrated by such diverse cases as Cadence (US) undertaking shared research and training for the semiconductor industry, and TeleTech (US) in the provision of multi-client customer services centres in many different countries.

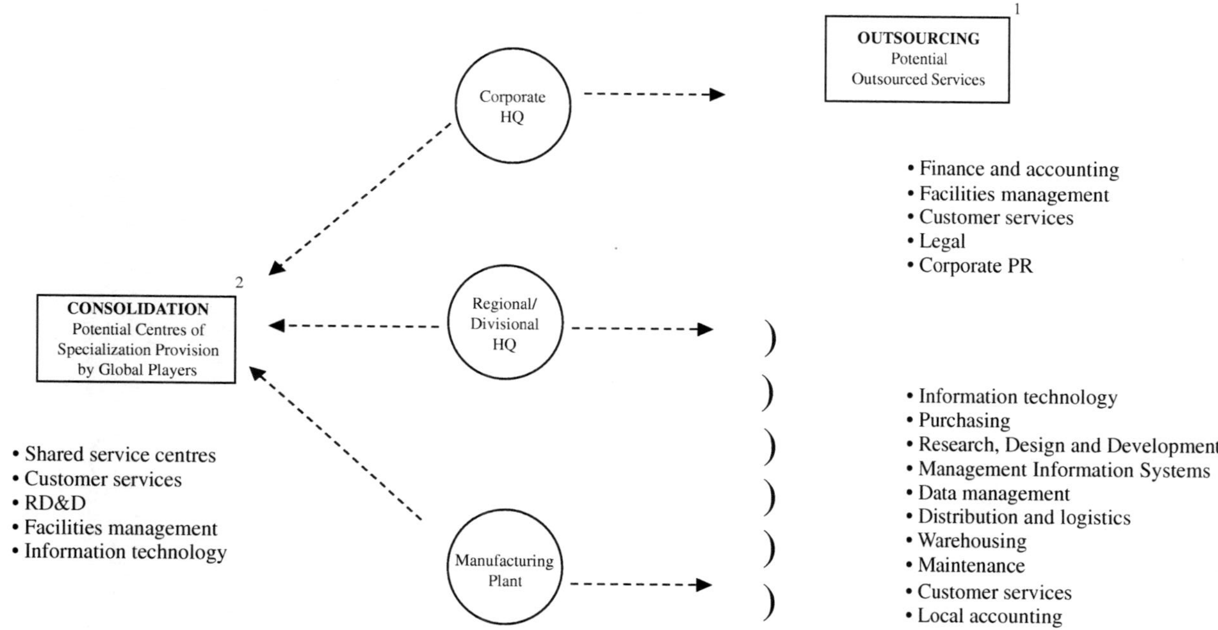

Notes:

1. Key drivers are the redefinition of core competencies and the outsourcing of non-core activities to specialist third-party providers for reasons of investment demands; competitive focus; relative competencies; and economies of scale.
2. The trend towards a 'consolidation' of certain types of activity (across all the 'levels' of a business) and the development of partnerships with those having centres of specialization in service provision. Drivers include customer service improvements; exploitation of brand advantage; costs; cycle and process times; flexibility, and so on.

Figure 4.1 Trends in the provision of services to large corporations

Figure 4.2 introduces both the locational dimension and the supply side of the equation. Based on an established classification of service types (Lovelock and Yip, 1996), it explores the relationship between customer physical proximity and the location of service nodes, namely the point at which the service is delivered to the customer. The crucial distinction is perhaps in the relationship between the front and back office elements of the delivery of different types of service. As the figure suggests, there are detectable trends for the latter to be less

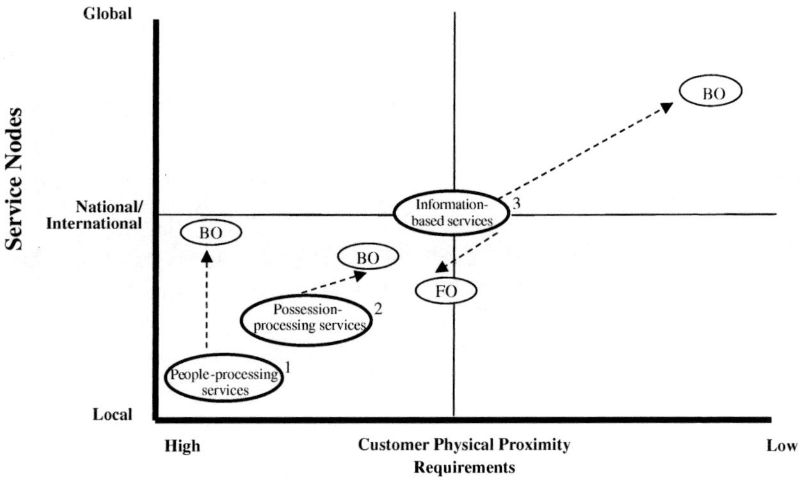

Notes:
Service production and delivery systems are divided into back office (BO) and front office (FO), the latter being the part of the 'service factory' encountered by customers. The arrows denote directional trends that are already evident in these different types of services.

1. People-processing services involving tangible actions to customers in person (for example, passenger transport, healthcare, airlines).
2. Possession-processing services involving tangible actions to physical objects to improve their value to customers (for example, freight transport, warehousing, equipment installation and maintenance). Local presence required but service processes can often be administered from a distance.
3. Information-based services (IBS), dependent on collecting, manipulating, interpreting and transmitting data to create value (for example, banking, consulting, insurance, legal services). Potentially able to be delivered from a single 'hub', with local presence limited to a terminal.

Figure 4.2 Service types, customer proximity and service nodes

proximate to any given customer group, while the front office is still subject to pressure for customer proximity – although this could diminish in some business services. Information-based services offer the best opportunities to split these two functions, with the growing prospect of centralizing back-office functions on a regional or global basis. In effect, Figure 4.2 highlights one of the inherent economic development challenges arising from the growth of services, namely whether the location of the type of value-adding services which contribute most to cluster formation and development are more or less likely to be local, international or global. We will return later to consider this matter in greater detail. Meanwhile, from the corporate perspective, Figure 4.2 points to the scope for providing many different business services on a national/international basis.

Before proceeding it is worth reviewing the demand, supply and locational trends suggested by Figures 4.1 and 4.2. Figure 4.1 illustrated the shape of demand through two related corporate processes which are driven by the desire to improve competitiveness and enhance shareholder value in many large corporations. Figure 4.2 suggested that while the supply response differed by service type, there was a tendency for proximity to diminish in importance, at least for back-office functions. At a minimum, the two figures together point to dynamic demand and flexible supply options within each of which companies have to balance the demands of both localization and globalization.

Economic Development Dimensions

It is evident that globalization is radically changing the environment within which corporate competition and economic development occurs (Dunning, 1997). Some regard it as giving signs of a purposeful functional integration of the world economy (Asheim and Dunford, 1997), and there are clearly many processes at work at the interface of corporate and economic development imperatives (Amin and Thrift, 1994). The third stage of this analysis explores the locational and economic development consequences of the discussion so far.[7] Figure 4.3 gives a rather stylized view of the way in which the business service provision may be related to the geographical location of service nodes. Its central thrust is to presume that most major international corporations in any given country will have their

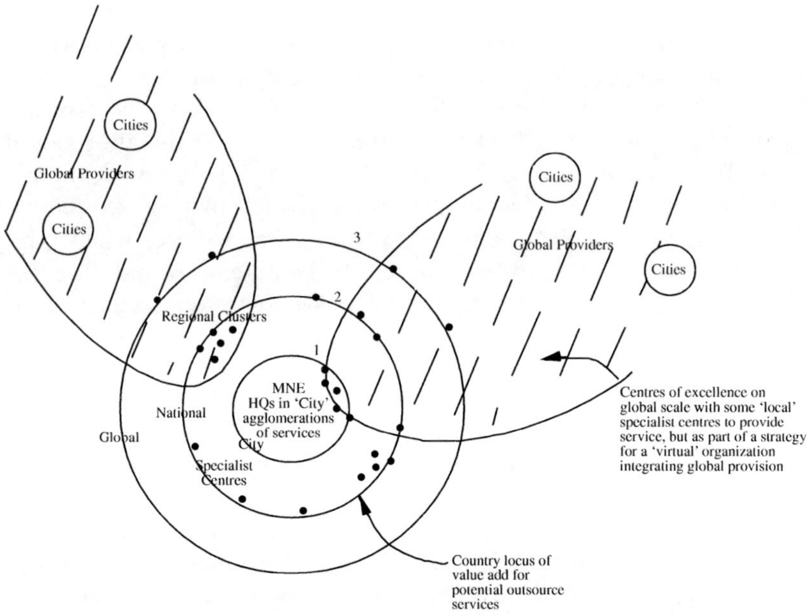

Notes:
1. Assumption of most MNE HQs having a location in or near an agglomeration of business services, invariably in a large city. These providers able to meet outsourcing and consolidation demands.
2. Characterizes a series of single or clustered providers within a given nation who can provide outsourced services as set out in Figure 4.1. These may be internationally-owned and may or may not exist in a cluster in a smaller city or region within a country. The clusters could range from 'R&D centres' around key universities, to 'call centres' tapping into local labour markets in secondary cities.
3. The third concentric ring characterizes global players operating centres of excellence. They will also have operations (as depicted) in both the city and national clusterings, but will operate on global source points for reasons of costs, logistics, flexibility and so on.

Figure 4.3 A stylized geography of the trends in proximity of the provision of business services

headquarters within a city or city region in which there is an agglomeration of business services.

In various locations at the wider national level, there emerge a variety of specialist service centres or groups of centres within sub-regional clusters. Whether singly or in groups, these centres stand to benefit from the outsourcing and consolidation trends noted in Figure 4.1, and become locations in which value-adding activity takes place. The premise is that they are not substitutes for the 'city' agglomerations but complementary to them by, for example, allowing lower cost service provision. However, to think on a national basis alone is clearly inadequate given the importance of regional strategies (for example, at EU level), the diverse ownership of service companies, and the growing strength of global providers. As Figure 4.3 suggests, these global service businesses may have front or back offices in the cities or sub-regions, but increasingly think in terms of integrating service offerings on a pan-national scale. Moreover their size, reach and economies of scale and scope, enable them to offer very specialist services and establish themselves as having centres of specialization beyond the capability of the city or national provider. On the demand side outsourcing, consolidation, business re-engineering, privatization and deregulation have been among the many drivers creating new opportunities for global providers.

Figure 4.4 pursues some of the potential consequences of the trends suggested in Figure 4.3. The background to it is the level of expectations which surround both the rapid growth in business services and the pace of change in information and communications technologies (ICT). In economic development circles, this is often viewed as likely to lead to a widespread dispersion of high value-added business services and to a consequent enhancement of employment opportunities at sub-regional level. As Figure 4.4 indicates, it is possible to develop quite different scenarios when evaluating these trends, in this case one being 'vicious' and the one 'virtuous'. The analysis in this chapter would point to the former, with the 'sub-regional' growth being in lower value-added services aided by trends in ICT. These same trends can enable better integration of highly specialist expertise in existing 'city' locations and contribute towards virtual and global service structures.

CASE EXAMPLES

This section introduces some practical illustrations of both companies and regions flowing from the analysis and propositions set out above. Recognizing that there are relatively few truly global business service providers, three brief cases are examined from information technol-

A Vicious Circle

→ More diverse business ownership at all scales of organization
→ Fewer HQs located in regions as a probable consequence
→ Less prospect of maximizing 'local' service purchases
  (i) Ownership changes bring an existing network of suppliers
  (ii) Service purchase decisions are centralized at HQs
→ Process reinforces existing service hierarchies in terms of
  (i) Locus of high value-added services and corporate command functions at points of critical mass in major cities and their hinterland
  (ii) Expanding lower value-added services disperse to the periphery on grounds of cost, labour availability, telecoms infrastructure, and so on. At best these would be
    - around industry clusters
    - export-led service complexes

B Virtuous Circle

→ Replacement of rigid hierarchical organizational forms by leaner flexible forms: more SMEs, and so on.
→ More vertical disintegration and contracting out of services
→ Information and communications technologies (ICT) change requirements for proximity to customers
  (i) Evident in development of back-office functions and tele-services in provincial cities
  (ii) Less certain for advanced business services or product design, R&D where ICT may better integrate dispersed expertise in existing locations
  (iii) Emergence of cluster effects through infrastructural investment (for example, Malaysia) or skill specialization, as in Indian software industry
→ Some regions will have specialist centres which are part of global/international service providers

Figure 4.4 Business services and sub-regional economic development: vicious and virtuous circles

ogy (EDS), express transport (FedEx) and management and technology consulting (Andersen Consulting). These are three of the main activities where globalization is evident. All three cases highlight scale, speed of growth and global reach. As observed, however, there are debates about the consequences of those trends for nations, and especially for regions within nations. In pursuit of the latter, two sharply contrasting examples (Singapore and Phoenix, Arizona) are briefly reviewed in order to examine the types of strategies being pursued to maximize the economic gains from these trends. Finally, and with a degree of speculation, the issue of call centres is addressed as one of the most widespread illustrations of the dispersal of business services, and one of the most appealing from the perspective of national and sub-regional development.

Companies

Box 4.1
EDS

Electronic Data Systems Corporation (now EDS) was founded in 1962 in Dallas, Texas, by Ross Perot. The company is now a leader in the global information technology services industry with around 100 000 employees in over 40 countries. In the year ending 31 December 1997, its total revenues were $15.2bn, with a net income of $730.6m. It was floated on the New York Stock Exchange in 1968, but was purchased by General Motors in 1984, subsequently splitting off from GM in 1996. The EDS activities span many aspects of the public and private sectors and include systems development, integration and management, process management and a range of other innovative service offerings.

The international development of EDS commenced at an early stage by winning its first contracts in Europe in 1973. During the 1990s it has been increasingly active in acquisitions, including the purchase of the management consultants, A.T. Kearney, in 1995. The company has many major global contracts, one of the earliest of which was Xerox Corporation in 1993. Some of its expansion has involved the transfer of clients' staff to EDS as part of outsourcing or co-sourcing contracts. In the UK, for example, staff from over 30 public and private organizations are now on the EDS payroll.

Companies such as EDS display (with reference to Figure 4.3) many different ways of addressing the balance between global resource integration and localization. For example, in the UK the company has on average around 9000 staff at 90 sites in mixes of different contractual relationships, including those with the Inland Revenue and Department of Social Security. Yet at the same time the company has a global reach able to serve the needs of the same client wherever their networks are located, as evidenced, for example, in their aerospace and defence, communications and health-care practices. While the question of the locus of higher or lower value-added services is inevitably more determined by fulfilling client needs than any imperatives of economic development, the various specialist centres are potentially enhanced by the global scope of EDS as, for example, in the Rolls-Royce Aerospace Group and its co-sourcing contract with the Swedish retailer, Koperativa Förbundet.

Box 4.2
FedEx

Federal Express (since 1994 FedEx) was set up in 1973 in Memphis, Tennessee, based on the pioneering hub-and-spoke concept of transportation management. The company is now the largest express transport company in the world with some 140 000 employees, serving over 200 countries from over 300 airports. It operates over 600 aircraft (plus 40 000 vehicles), placing it among the world's leading airlines in its own right. In the year ending 31 May 1997, the total revenues of the company were $11.5bn, with a net income of $361m.

The strategic vision of FedEx has been to drive for fast, time-definite, reliable distribution through its integrated, all-cargo express network. The core elements of its competitiveness lie both in transport infrastructure and information technology, given that some 60% of all FedEx packages are generated by electronic links with clients. Although its first intercontinental service (between New York and London) only dates from 1985, the company now claims to be able to offer its standard service to markets representing 90 per cent of world GDP. The growth in the demand for its services has been driven by the internationalization of its clients and by the competitive forces calling for reduced inventories and precise distribution times over both short and long-haul distances. Competition for international express cargo is based on air routes and market access. On both counts FedEx has considerable advantages including access to many restricted markets, including China.

Although dramatically successful in its global expansion, FedEx has not been highly profitable. Its 1997 acquisition of Caliber System, a major US trucking company and leading competitor to United Parcel Service, is thought likely to enhance its profit performance. Ground fleets are much cheaper to operate than the combined FedEx air, IT and vehicle systems which span the globe. However, FedEx operates in a market which is expected to grow from $12bn in 1997 to $150bn in the next ten years and should be in an excellent position to exploit this.

In terms of Figure 4.3 Fedex locations and clusters of activity are distinctly transport-led in number – some 1400 world service centres being reported in recent company reports. Clearly these will vary dramatically in terms of economic development potential, although all will be determined by ways in which value can be added to customers.

Box 4.3
Andersen Consulting

This company, a subsidiary of Andersen Worldwide, which now accounts for 50 per cent of its revenues, was established in 1989 with revenues of $1bn as a split-off from the original AA accounting business. In the space of eight years it has established itself as a global player in management and technology consulting, with revenues of $6bn (50 per cent in the Americas), 51 000 employees, and offices in 47 countries across six continents. The core strategy of the group is business integration, namely the alignment of an enterprise's people, processes and technology with its strategy. To achieve this the firm is organized in a tripartite structure for each of the staff. They primarily belong to a 'competency group' (change management, process, technology) as well as to a 'business organization', which refines the type of service delivered. They may also belong to a specialist industry practice which covers six main sectors. The company spends almost 6.5 per cent of annual revenues in educating its staff, with an a additional 12 per cent in R&D. In a recent annual report AC claimed to have worked with two-thirds of the world's 100 largest public companies in a single year.

In a business of this scale and complexity it is difficult to illustrate the wide diversity of its services. In the context of this chapter its joint venture with BP is interesting. Developing from the position where AC took over the running of the finance and administration services of its European-based exploration division, AC expanded its business process management relationship to undertake the same services for BP throughout the US. Late in 1996 a joint venture was formed in Europe between BP and Mobil, whereby BP operated fuels and Mobil the lubricants business. A key to this is the sharing of support services, hence AC was given a seven-year contract for finance, administrative services and procurement for this joint venture. More characteristically, AC would be employed in high-level strategy development and implementation. More visible examples of this in recent years include managing parts of JP Morgan's global technology infrastructure; bringing new drugs to market at a faster pace with Hoechst; restructuring Chase Manhattan Bank, and so on.

AC could be regarded as both a facilitator and a byproduct of the globalization of business. Its product offerings and skill-base are highly relevant in providing solutions to complex, high impact and very visible business problems. The consulting teams are regarded as regional/international assets and are called together on a project basis. In terms of Figure 4.3, the national level is the only one at which resources cluster, and there are few substantial resource groupings at sub-regional level. This is as a result of the cost and senior level of the advisory service plus the limited size of the client base which can afford these highly specialized services. In every sense they are global players whose contribution to economic development flows through the services offered to clients on the assumption that it aids business development or improves economic efficiency.

Regions

Singapore

In some ways this is a unique example of a national economic development strategy directed over recent years towards the internationalization of services. From the 1960s, the country has had highly favourable tax policies towards MNEs and has invested heavily in infrastructure. From a trading base, manufacturing (especially electronics) had become more significant to the economy than trade by the 1970s. Starting from the mid-1980s, the focus of policy was placed on higher value-added manufacturing and expanding the concept of Singapore as a 'total business centre' – with manufacturing and services both being engines for growth. Among the policy instruments adopted was a new operational headquarters tax incentive in 1986 and the setting up of a Services Promotion Division within the Economic Development Board (EDB). The latter gave particular attention to engineering services, IT and telecoms, leisure, medical and educational services, and computer services.

The 1990/91 strategic economic plan was a watershed in terms of setting a strategy for service-related activities. It recognized the rapid rise in real wages, land and labour constraints, together with the need to 'upgrade' economic activity. One aspect of this was the desire to encourage MNCs to have an increased local presence, treat Singapore as a home base, and develop greater technological capability. This led to a series of initiatives to stimulate investment in soft infrastructure and to the pursuit of an industrial strategy based on reinforcing selected niches. Among these were the development and implementation of integrated strategies for headquarters functions; for R&D with the establishment of the National Science and Technology Board (NSTB) in 1991; for publishing and multimedia industries; logistics, insurance and banking. The Porterian cluster approach has been applied throughout this period and in the business service context this has been particularly evident in the strategies towards building international hubs, information technology, R&D centres and finance, each of which is led by a branch of government. Moreover there has been a vigorous pursuit of the key linkages between critical activities in order to create a more fully integrated local economic system, and services have been a vital part of this.

Reviewing the Singapore experience in the light of Tables 4.3 and 4.4, its distinctive locational advantages and aggressive and integrated policy environment must be acknowledged. It is a city-state which has developed competitive advantage in a very focused manner over an extended period with the same party in power since independence. Its policy stance has consistently placed it in a position to benefit from its strategic location and, more recently, from the trends in the globalization of services. Among the many examples of this is the building of R&D to 2 per cent of GDP and the operation of Asia's largest (and reputedly one of the world's best) international airport with a capacity for 24 million passengers.

Phoenix, USA

In sharp contrast, Phoenix (Arizona) is an example of a US city which, like many others which are not major national centres, has attempted to pursue a strategy to attract business services in recent years. From the 1950s, where copper, cotton and cattle were major employers, this city grew rapidly until the late 1980s aided by the growth in defence spending, construction and tourism. Thereafter growth started to decline and concern was consistently expressed about the absence of HQs, low job quality and the absence of growth clusters. The state of Arizona had also suffered from the boom and bust cycle of real-estate development and the savings loan crash, while others were competing for FDI on a more active basis.

During the 1990s the city has attracted a number of data-processing centres for the credit-card industry, aided by a change in state law regarding interest rates which the card companies could levy. This was subsequently followed by a large influx of customer service centres for all the normal reasons of labour and property-associated costs. Thus companies such as Chase Manhattan, Excel Multimedia, Bank of America and AT&T all have major operations in the Phoenix area. The city is the main centre for AMEX worldwide operations for processing and customer services. This campus employs over 7000 people and has been in Phoenix since 1968, but it has continued to flourish in a context of dramatic corporate change. In the early 1990s, AMEX had 48 financial resource centres and planned to reduce this to three, all of which would be identical and provide complete back-up for each other. The three are Phoenix, Brighton and New Delhi.

In many ways Phoenix represents the phenomenon of the secondary city/region striving to develop a series of public and private initiatives to gain a share of business service growth. The Arizona

Department of Commerce has led much of this and it has a National Marketing Office to attract inward investment. The first economic development plan was launched in 1991 and involved an attempt to integrate several city bodies in the region and was led by a team from SRI International. Relatively speaking, Phoenix is at an early stage of its strategy towards services, with the results still pointing to the lower end of the value-added scale. Indeed, it is not clear whether any distinctive city/regional specialisms in business services will emerge in this case. In fact, research in the US has suggested a 3-tier city system of national, regional and sub-regional nodal centres (Daniels, 1991; Enderwick, 1989). While all have significant concentrations of national and regional HQs of manufacturing and service corporations, a diverse set of service firms and good infrastructure are often foci for wholesale distribution functions. However, only the national nodal centres (such as New York, Los Angeles and Chicago) are part of the 'world city' system where the major service MNEs cluster.

Call Centres

In some economic development contexts the growth in call centres is regarded as the most visible evidence of the expansion of business services, and one which has the potential to benefit from the internationalization of services, if not from their globalization.

The growth of tele-services based in call centres has been driven by factors such as the high telephone penetration in OECD countries, falling real costs of usage, rapid developments in communications software, and so on. These centres have proved to be the most mobile of business services over the past decade and are found at all the levels depicted in Figure 4.3. Their activity range is highly diverse but spans external services such as sales and customer support in sectors such as retail financial services; travel, hotel and other forms of reservation; catalogue-based selling; technical support for installed equipment, and so on. For reasons associated with advanced communications, labour quality and costs, and financial incentives in some contexts, these centres are in diverse locations including provincial cities and smaller towns in rural areas. In some instances there are significant agglomerations of call centres as, for example, in the UK in Manchester, Leeds, Newcastle and Glasgow. Invariably they are seen as evidence of the potential for economic development in business services and often come with high expectations. Some UK estimates suggest that around 1 per cent of the UK workforce will be in call centres within the next 5–7 years.

While in no way minimizing the substantial benefits brought to local employment by call centres, it is not unreasonable to ask how they will develop and whether they will be national or international in their scope. Figure 4.5 introduces that topic and suggests three potential development trajectories, while recognizing a spectrum of call-centre activity in value-adding terms. The commentary suggests the need for a degree of caution about placing too much emphasis on a service industry economic development strategy based in this type of FDI, or of expecting call centres alone to contribute too much to the virtuous circle scenario suggested in Figure 4.4. However, call centres are a recent phenomenon and it is not easy to predict exactly how they are likely to develop. What is clear is that nations and sub-regions will continue to compete for higher value-adding centres (types 2 and 3 in figure 4.5) and perhaps do so on an increasingly global basis in order to tap into the gains from the globalization of business services.

CONCLUSIONS AND POLICY IMPLICATIONS

This chapter has charted a number of the drivers of both the demand for, and supply of, business services on an international and global scale. Outsourcing and consolidation are considered to be dominant elements of the demand side, and they have generated a wide variety of supply responses. As regards the shape of the supply equation, it was shown to be useful to distinguish between people-processing, possession-processing, and information-based services. It was suggested that the relationship between customer physical proximity and the location of service nodes was changing, especially with regard to back-office functions and call centres which could increasingly be managed on a pan-national or global basis.

The analysis then sought to link these corporate dimensions to locational and economic development consequences. The evidence suggests that although many business services are mobile, they are highly spatially concentrated in a small number of agglomerations in large cities or their hinterland. While there are diseconomies of urban concentrations which partially offset agglomeration, many of the decentralized activities have few local concentrations in their host regions and often involve routine activity which scarcely requires any. The

Category	Type of Centre		
	1 'One of many'	*2 Value-added provider*	*3 'Developmental' centre*
Activity	Minimum advice content National focus English language Single product	Technical advice/consulting International Multilingual Multi-product	Varied prospects – shared services; IT development for call centres; call-centre management; targeting capturing and leveraging high-value information internationally. Could have global focus
Labour	Low skill base and job-related training: many part-time	High proportion of graduates and high technical skills	Multi-skilled and high-level
Trading base	Single client, in-house facility	Multi-client, third parties	Multi-client
Ownership	Subsidiary	Subsidiary	Subsidiary/new business
Employment size	100–2000 per centre	100–500 per centre	50–200 per centre

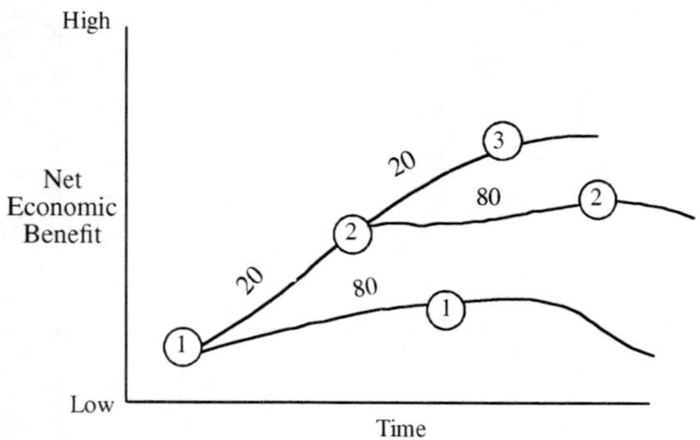

Notes:
(a) Figure suggests little economic impact-enhancement as Type 1 grow larger over time. The expectation is that only 20% will grow from 1 to 2, with 80% having little development potential beyond large-scale job generation. A similar effect is posited for the centres which start as Type 2. Few would be expected to start as Type 3 and most are likely to be set up as 'developmental' centres rather than go through the first two stages.
(b) While Type 1 are expanding rapidly, they face medium-term (5–7 years) threats from a number of directions. These include the exclusion of intermediaries by use of the Internet; productivity gains as technology is enhanced; and the bundling of services direct to a 'customer segment of one' based on effective data capture, warehousing and mining.

Figure 4.5 Call centres: potential development trajectories

absence of senior jobs, the presence of external control and low local multipliers raise questions about the sustainability and durability of some provincial service centres. In short, the thrust of corporate demands may continue to pull towards the international or global integration of high-level business services, with some opportunities for specialist centres at regional level, but with little prospect of high value-added, self-sustaining business service clusters.

From an economic development perspective, the discussion on the locus of business services was regarded as crucial. In the interests of relating assumptions to consequences, two different scenarios were offered involving a virtuous and a vicious circle of development. While the jury must be out on these, and further empirical work would have to be undertaken to verify them, the thrust of this analysis was towards a vicious process which reinforced existing service hierarchies, albeit with wider dispersion of lower value-added service activities, such as call centres. It is, however, evident that not all business service centres share the same qualities. For example, within Europe some have groupings of corporate headquarters and resultant high-level networks (for example, London); others have a network of specialist services supporting a sector such as electronics (for example, Central Scotland); while others have export-led services in sectors such as wholesale banking and finance (for example, Dublin). Perhaps a key economic policy lesson from this analysis is to identify an appropriate and realistic niche and consistently reinforce the infrastructure which is capable of supporting it.

The penultimate section of the chapter presented some case examples, initially of three of the world's major global providers of business services. While these cannot be claimed to be representative of the present shape of business services, they serve to illustrate the global reach of those rapidly expanding sectors and the emergence of businesses whose strategies combine 'local for local' with 'global for global'. To some extent these global providers may progressively concentrate on the world's major business and governments as their client base. Recent accounting and banking mergers would suggest that. Such a scenario could leave space for new national providers to emerge. On balance this is rather unlikely given the scale, depth of talent and ability to mobilize resources for major clients which are part of the competitive advantage of global players. Their major economic development contribution at national level may therefore be to economic efficiency rather than to service-cluster development.

The country/region policy cases cited are a reminder that government and industry groups are cognizant of the challenges and opportunities which these trends bring to local environments. The two cases considered are deliberately very different, one long-term and national; the other recent and sub-regional. Either way they point to 'fitness for purpose' strategies over an extended period, setting policy sights at realisable goals wherever they rest in the hierarchy of business service centres. The call-centre development case was introduced to strike a note of caution. In some ways it is too early to say what these might lead to in any given provincial location, many of which in different parts of the world are encouraged by their emergence over the past decade. While it is relatively easy to differentiate between different types of centre and predict different prospects for these, it is much more difficult to predict what they could emerge into in the longer term. There are several reasons for this growth in telephone-mediated services including cost, technology and the acceptance of a telephone culture. Each of these variables could be subject to change and in turn rapidly reshape this sector which grew rapidly in the US in the 1980s and has spread to other OECD countries in the 1990s.

Although the tone of this chapter has been cautious and the approach to the analysis at times speculative, there is much yet to happen on the question of FDI in business services. This could in turn lead to different prospects for emerging service centres. The international deregulation of services in general has some way to go and inspection of the General Agreement on Trade in Services (GATS) shows that it is only a first step in the direction of trade and investment liberalization in services, and does not imply moves to free trade in services in the near future (Sauvé, 1995; OECD, 1996). However, on the basis of this analysis, policy-makers would be advised to look carefully at the types of business service centres their cities/regions were attracting, examine how they might develop and invest for the longer term in the hard and soft infrastructure to aid their future development.

Notes

1. Some parts of this chapter draw upon work undertaken by Scottish Enterprise in a project on *FDI in Services* undertaken in 1995/96.
2. Business services are conventionally defined in eight sub-sectors, viz., computer and related; professional services (legal, tax, audit, etc.); marketing; technical; renting and leasing; recruitment; operational services (security, cleaning, transport); others (packaging, bill collection, etc.).
3. In the professional services sub-section of the software industry, Gemini, Andersen Consulting and EDS have truly global structures to meet these demands. In computer services outsourcing there have been some very large-scale and innovative deals in recent years, and these are provided on a global scale by companies such as CSC, EDS, IBM, GE and Andersen. For example, EDS has a $2bn contract with the Inland Revenue; and a $3.2bn contract with Xerox; while SHC Systemhouse has $10bn and $550m outsourcing contracts with Canada Post and the Mexican Finance Ministry respectively.
4. *Shared service centres* have been common in US companies, but have only emerged in Europe over the past 5–7 years. Their scope usually covers finance, administration, and some aspects of operations (such as procurement, information technology and internal consulting) for the groups' network of businesses in a region. They are driven by the desire to reduce and manage costs, but also by the need to standardize procedures and response times across a range of different country environments. American Express, Eaton Corporation, Intel and Unisys are among the US companies to have opened such centres in Europe in recent years.
5. *Data processing centres* involve the transfer and processing of information from different mediums at a single point for onward transmission by disc or by electronic transfer. They have, for example, been extensively used by airlines such as British Airways (in New Delhi), Swissair (in Bombay) and Cathay Pacific (in Guangdong Province). Examples of those developing for third-party trade include the Caribbean Data Services subsidiary of American Airlines in Barbados and the Dominican Republic.
6. *Value added logistics centres* usually combine some manufacturing/assembly with distribution in industries where transit times are vital and where the products are non-standard with an important element of customization. In Europe they are invariably located in Netherlands, Belgium or Northern France for reasons of infrastructure and ready market access throughout the EU.
7. For the purposes of this chapter and in the interests of clarity, geographical terms are understood as follows:

global	(multi-country, many continents)
regional	(groupings of countries, as in EU)
national	(one country)
sub-regional	(part of a nation)
city	(a single large connurbation)

References

AHARONI, Y. (ed.) (1993), *Coalition and Competition: The Globalization of Professional Services* (New York and London: Routledge).

AMIN, A. and N. THRIFT (eds) (1994), *Globalization, Institutions and Regional Development in Europe* (Oxford: Oxford University Press).

ASHEIM, B.T.M. and M. DUNFORD (1997), 'Regional Futures', *Regional Studies*, vol. 31, no. 5, pp. 445–57.

BUCKLEY, P.J., C.L. PASS and K. PRESCOTT (1992), 'The Internationalization of Service Firms: A Comparison with the Manufacturing Sector', *Scandinavian International Business Review*, vol. 1, no. 1, pp. 39–56.

CAMPBELL, A.J.A. and A. VERBECKE (1994), 'The Globalization of Service Multinationals', *Long Range Planning*, vol. 27, no. 2, pp. 95–102.

COLLS, D. and C. MONTGOMERY (1995), 'Competing on Resources: Strategy in the 1990s', *Harvard Business Review*, July/August, pp. 118–28.

DANIELS, P.W. (1991), *Services and Metropolitan Development: International Perspectives* (London and New York: Routledge).

DICKEN, P. (1992), *Global Shift: The Internationalization of Economic Activity*, 2nd edn (London. Paul Chapman).

DUNNING, J. (ed.) (1997), *Governments, Globalization and International Business* (Oxford: Oxford University Press).

DUNNING, J. (1989), 'Transnational Corporations and the Growth of Services: Some Conceptual and Theoretical Issues', *UNCTC Current Studies*, no. 9, series A (New York: UN).

ENDERWICK, P. (ed.) (1989), *Multinational Service Firms* (London and New York: Routledge).

FRASER, J. and J. OPPENHEIM (1997), 'What's New about Globalization?', *The McKinsey Quarterly*, no. 2, pp. 168–80.

GRANT, R. (1991), 'The Resource-based theory of Competitive Advantage: Implications for Strategy Formulation', *California Management Review*, Spring, pp. 114–35.

HOUT, T., M.E. PORTER and E. RUDDEN (1982), 'How Global Companies Win Out', *Harvard Business Review*, September/October, pp. 98–108.

KOGUT, B. (1985), 'Designing Global Strategies: Comparative and Competitive Value-Added Chains', *Sloan Management Review*, Summer, pp. 27–38.

LOVELOCK, C.H. and G.H. YIP (1996), 'Developing Global Strategies for Service Businesses', *California Management Review*, vol. 38, no. 2 (Winter), pp. 64–86.

MATHE, H. and C. PERRAS (1994), 'Successful Global Strategies for Service Companies', *Long Range Planning*, vol. 7/1, pp. 36–49.

OECD (1996), 'International Trade in Professional Services: Assessing Barriers and Encouraging Reforms' (Paris: OECD).

O'FARRELL, P.N. (1995), 'Manufacturing Demand for Business Services', *Cambridge Journal of Economics*, vol. 19, pp. 523–43.

PRAHALAD, C.K. and Y.L. DOZ (1987), *The Multinational Mission: Balancing Local Demands and Global Vision* (New York: Free Press).

SARATHY, R. (1994), 'Global Strategy in Service Industries', *Long Range Planning*, vol. 27, no. 6, pp. 115–24.

SAUVANT, K.P. and Z. ZIMNY (1988), 'Services: Their Ascendency and Impact', *The CTC Reporter,* no. 26 (Autumn), pp. 26–32.

SAUVÉ, P. (1995), 'Assessing the General Agreement on Trade in Services', *Journal of World Trade*, vol. 29, no. 4, pp. 125–45.

SEGAL-HORN, S. (1993), 'The Internationalization of Service Firms', in *Advances in Strategic Management*, vol. 9 (New York: JAI Press), pp. 31–55.

VANDERMERWE, S. and M. CHAWICK (1989), 'The Internationalization of Services', *The Services Industry Journal*, pp. 79–93.

5 Globalization and the Growth of Small and Non-dominant Firms: Case Evidence from Scotland[1]

Stephen Young, Jonathan Slow and Neil Hood

INTRODUCTION

Although there is much debate as to the precise characteristics of a 'global company', it is generally accepted that there are relatively few truly global enterprises. Despite this fact, globalization can be regarded as a ubiquitous process which will impact virtually all firms, which require in turn strategic transformation in order to ensure survival and growth (Fraser and Oppenheim, 1997). Thus, it is necessary to differentiate between global competition and global firms: a firm can face global competition without being a multinational or global enterprise. Research on this subject, involving a wider range of firms than hitherto, is, therefore, undoubtedly necessary. In a similar way, most of the research and writing from an economic development perspective has related to host as opposed to home-country interests. But concerns about how to grow global companies and what their economic development impact will be are beginning to figure on the policy agendas of some countries.

The purpose of this chapter is to undertake exploratory research using illustrations of a limited number of small, emerging and mature businesses headquartered in Scotland (UK). Investigation focuses upon the key globalization drivers and determinants, and their importance in influencing corporate strategy; the main directions of company policy in response; and the issues which arise for home-country development, and public policy.

ISSUES FROM THE LITERATURE

Definitions.[2] No general agreement exists on the definition of terms such as global industry, global company or global strategy. A number of the broadly accepted concepts in the strategy field stem from Porter (1986), Prahalad and Doz (1987), Doz (1986) and Bartlett and Ghoshal (1989). These scholars presented a global strategy as one which involved a coordinated and/or integrated approach to operating multinationally, and contrast this to multi-domestic or local responsiveness strategies; but such distinctions, at least in the stark way in which they were presented, probably no longer apply. Recent work has stressed more strongly that the extent of globalization may vary widely among constituent parts of the value chain according to differences in the globalization potential of the industry and firm strategy. Moreover, the notion of globalization as a continuum (Porter, 1986) is more generally accepted (OECD, 1997; Makhija *et al.*, 1997). The measures used to identify the degree of internationalisation or globalization of the industry or the firm are also attracting increasing attention (see, for example, Shanks, 1985; Kobrin, 1991; Morrison and Roth, 1992; Sullivan, 1994; Makhija *et al.*, 1997), although to date there has been little attempt to differentiate internationalization from globalization.

The exploratory approach taken in this chapter and the focus upon small and non-dominant firms suggests a broad approach to these definitional questions, with the aim of identifying globalization tendencies. Arguably, the following criteria should be included:

- Geographical spread of sales and sourcing activities. On the marketing side, higher levels of globalization would be evidenced by a sales presence on a number of continents, including, therefore, countries/markets where the degree of psychic distance is high. Globalization of sourcing would be indicated by a similar pattern of dispersion.
- For export-based companies, overseas sales would be supported by sales subsidiaries in a number of markets. Larger-scale activities and greater commitment would be reflected in a variety of market servicing methods, including licensing, joint ventures and strategic alliances, and so on.
- A range of value activities outside the home country.
- The coordination and/or integration of geographically dispersed value activities.

- Global vision and perspective, which would be evidenced by a variety of factors, including a proactive search process for global opportunities; a worldwide view of customers, suppliers and competitors; the use of global performance measures, for example, market share; evolving geocentricism in HRM policies; and a global corporate culture (see Kobrin, 1994; *Financial Times*, 1998).

Clearly, if a larger-scale study was to be undertaken, consideration would need to be given to weighting the above criteria; and the dimensions cannot be considered in isolation. For example, a global spread of sales *per se* would not portray a global firm. More questionable is whether a global spread of sales supported by sales subsidiaries in major markets would be indicative of globalization. Past research would suggest an emphasis on the range of value activities internationally and the extent of their coordination and integration; while recently more attention has been paid to managerial vision and mind-sets (Maignan and Lukas, 1997).

Figure 5.1 presents the globalization indicators along a continuum from domestic to global. Different companies will, of course, be at different points on the continuum implied by these criteria. This will depend partly upon the underlying globalization characteristics of the industries and/or clusters in which they operate, corporate strategy and the size and age of the firm.

Drivers and Determinants of Global Strategy

Taking an industrial organisation perspective, Porter (1986) and Yip (1989) developed a contingency approach linking industry conditions to the appropriateness of global strategy. The industry globalization conditions identified (Yip, 1989) were market drivers, cost drivers, governmental drivers and competitive drivers. And there have been a number of empirical studies testing such variables on an industry and cross-industry basis (for example, Kobrin, 1991; Johansson and Yip, 1994). In a more recent review of the literature, Yip (1997) added organization factors, for example organization structure, management structure, people and culture as important influences on strategy (see also Weinzimmer, 1996).

There is a close relationship between strategy determinants and the competitive advantages believed to accrue from globalization. Issues

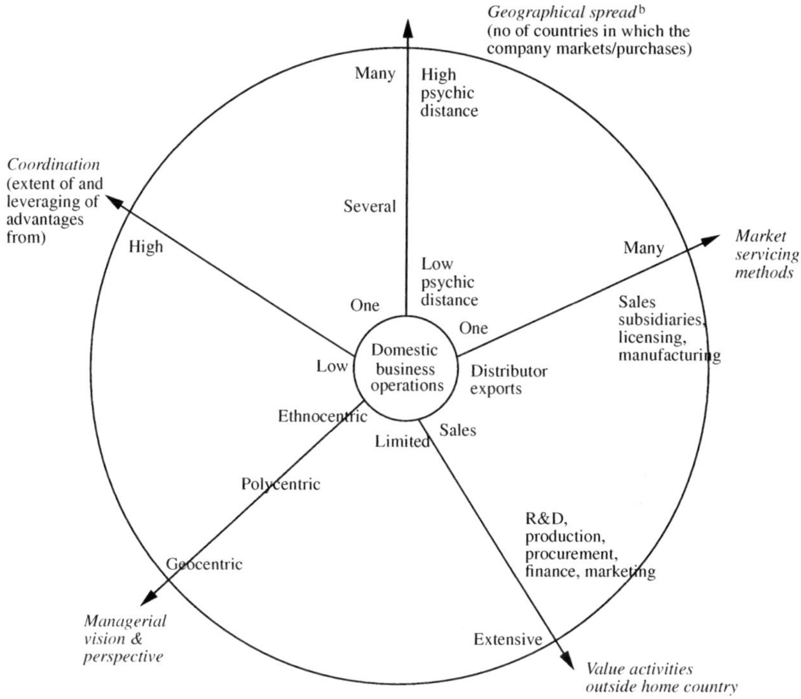

Note:

[a] The dimension of configuration of activities (concentrated/dispersed) has been omitted from this figure (see chapter end-note 4).

[b] It is questionable whether psychic distance is an indicator of globalization, since in high-tech industries, for example, markets will be in industrialized countries where psychic distance is relatively low.

Source: Authors, developed from Scottish Enterprise/Synthesis Consulting, 1998.

Figure 5.1 Indicators of globalization[a]

such as cost reduction, improved quality of products and programmes, enhanced customer preferences and increased competitive leverage have been suggested. Kogut (1985) focused upon operational flexibility in terms of arbitrage opportunities and leverage opportunities (see also Mitchell *et al.*, 1992). Among such factors, perhaps most interest attaches to the related issues of global scanning, the creation of a global intelligence system and the maximization of knowledge transfer. Potential disadvantages also exist in the form of higher coordination costs, management problems and the sacrificing of local competitiveness. To date there have been few empirical studies showing the effects of global strategy on performance.

The emerging literature on 'global start-ups' or 'born globals' (Oviatt and McDougall, 1994; Madsen and Servais, 1997) is also relevant: these are firms which aim at international markets or even the global market right from their birth. Influencing factors include new market conditions, such as the emergence of niche markets as a consequence of large firm globalization and other factors; the growth of global sourcing and cross-border networks; and the globalization of financial markets. Technological change has also facilitated new production process technology for small-scale operations, as well as lowering the costs of cross-border transactions. Finally, emphasis is placed upon human resource factors and the emergence of a breed of entrepreneurs with global vision, international business competence and established international networks (McDougall *et al.*, 1994).

Corporate Strategies for Globalization

Industry globalization drivers do not dictate one formula for success. The pioneering work of Porter (1986), Prahalad and Doz (1987) and Bartlett and Ghoshal (1989) focused upon a number of strategy dimensions around the themes of globalization/localization and configuration/coordination. When such frameworks are applied across the value chain, many options are feasible.

In respect of empirical studies, Morrison and Roth (1992) identified four broad strategies being pursued by US operating units in global industries: domestic product niche, exporting high-quality offerings, international product innovations and quasi-global combination. Roth (1992) studied the basis configuration and coordination patterns for medium-sized US based firms competing in global industries. Five archetypes were identified, viz., concentrated hub, local innovator, transnational innovator, regional federation and primary global. The authors concluded that selective globalization, in which a firm defines its global strategy around a narrow subset of the value chain, could lead to the most effective outcome. Other relevant studies include those of Leong and Tan (1993); and Taggart (1997).

Such work, while valuable, does not capture the full range of strategic options available to the globalizing enterprise (a good illustration of strategy variety in the white goods industry is shown in

Baden-Fuller and Stopford, 1991). Little attention has been paid to corporate-level as opposed to business-level strategies, and to patterns of global expansion associated with acquisition as opposed to organic growth.

Empirical research on the strategies of global start-ups is quite limited. Jolly *et al.* (1992) highlighted a combination of policies based around a number of features: global vision; a high quality, innovative product that redefines the product area; a standardized product with success in niche markets; broad and rapid market access, frequently using alliances; selective, functionally specialized investments abroad; early emphasis on follow-on products and breadth of competence; and a tightly networked global organization. Weaknesses identified included dependence on a single product and a limited breadth of competences. A review of various studies is contained in Madsen and Servais (1997; see also Jones, 1998).

CASE ILLUSTRATIONS

With the aim of this chapter being to explore the impacts of globalization on the firm (and thereafter on the country), case selection was designed to provide widely differing illustrations. The sample cases were chosen partly on the basis of access to the companies and to company information, and partly to ensure a range of size, age and sectoral experiences. Company names have been changed to help preserve anonymity.[3]

Linked closely to the literature review, questions investigated in the cases of small and non-dominant firms were as follows:

- How have companies evolved over time, particularly in respect of their international business development?
- What have been the main drivers and determinants of strategy, including the influence of specific globalization factors?
- What broad strategic directions can be identified? And what has been the relative importance of organic growth and acquisition in domestic and international development?
- What globalization indicators (derived from Figure 5.1) can be identified in respect of geographical spread of sales and sourcing activities; market servicing methods; value activities outside the home base and their coordination/integration; and global vision and perspective?

Box 5.1
'Assynt Group'

Background and Evolution

This company was formed by two marine engine consultants in 1871, based around a patented boiler feed pump. Despite various metamorphoses in its long history, Assynt has remained an important producer of pumps for marine and land use. Ranked number 6 in the world in the manufacture of pumps, this product area still represented 50 per cent of turnover in 1996. After a traumatic period in the 1970s and 1980s, Assynt's strategy was redefined in terms of the manufacture of engineered (as opposed to standard) products for niche markets. In 1994, the acquisition of a major pump manufacturer in the USA provided Assynt with overseas manufacturing capacity in a range of countries, but the need for a stronger production presence outside the UK is still recognized. Competitors' perceptions of the company are that it is small albeit strong and profitable, with quality products.

Company Profile, 1996

Sector	Mechanical engineering products and services
Total turnover	£620m (of which UK £187m, 30.2 per cent of total)
Profits	£49m (7.9 per cent of turnover)
Total employment	8200 (of which Scottish employment 1250, 15.2 per cent of total)

Geographical markets	UK	Americas	Europe
(percentage of turnover)	29.0	32.0	10.5

Geographical markets	Middle East & Africa	Australia	Pacific Rim
(percentage of turnover)	11.2	5.7	11.6

The basic management model is that of overarching strategy and decentralized control. Companies in the group devise and implement their own development plans, and acquired firms are permitted significant autonomy. Assynt operates a matrix structure comprising products and divisions with area managers within divisions. A small group-operations team has the responsibility for coordination across the company.

International Business Activities

- Assynt has manufacturing operations in 18 countries, mainly wholly-owned subsidiaries but also joint ventures in Chile and China for local content reasons. Much of this overseas manufacturing capacity came with Assynt's 1994 US acquisition. Poor experience in the past, especially in terms of lack of control, has led to withdrawal from a number of joint ventures. Specialist design and manufacturing represents a very high proportion of tender costs, and these activities will remain in the flagship operations in the UK and USA. Maintenance is mainly undertaken on site via a number of associate companies in the Americas, the Middle East and Australia.

- Companies currently make their own sourcing decisions, although a trend towards global sourcing is regarded as inevitable.
- Intra-group trading involves a number of divisions and international operations, but accounts for only a small proportion of turnover.
- R&D and technology transfer. R&D is undertaken at subsidiary level, where the focus is on product development and applications' problems; typical spend is roughly in line with the UK average for the sector. Licensing agreements operate in China, India, Czech Republic and South Africa, although technology is carefully protected.
- Marketing is decentralized through an international sales and marketing network.

Globalization Drivers and Determinants

Probably because of the company's long international experience, Assynt did not identify specifically global influences on its strategy, although it regards itself as a global player. It is, however, accepted that privatization policies have opened up markets and generated business domestically and internationally.

The policies pursued by UK governments in the 1980s were considered to have provided the greatest fillip to the company, as productivity was raised to levels comparable with those in Germany and the USA. While the Scottish end of Assynt was weakened in the early 1980s with the transfer of some operations to southern England, under current management there is a strong commitment to Scotland.

Directions of Corporate Strategy, and Indicators of Globalization

Assynt's stated objective is 'to concentrate ourselves in specialist niches in the market where the mastery of more difficult technology – be it manufacturing technology or design – can give us a competitive edge internationally'. At the next level is a strategy of concentric diversification in product and geographical markets. Geographically, Assynt is seeking to grow organically or through acquisitions in North and South America, Europe, the Middle East and Africa. The USA in particular is regarded as the major market and operations have been restructured in readiness for growth there. Manufacturing capabilities need to be expanded, especially in developing countries, in order to win government orders, but the company is withdrawing from low-margin business everywhere. The

Continued

international sales and marketing network of the company is also to be developed as a means of getting closer to the customer.

To date, Assynt is still a classic UK-centred, international company operating in a series of multi-domestic industry sectors worldwide. Despite its apparent longevity, Assynt has been rebuilt as a company in the last 15 years, a period which has seen the enterprise (in common with many other UK MNEs) reorient its activities from developing to

Box 5.2
'Hope Group'

Background and Evolution

This family-owned company has its origins in fishing and ship repairing and in the provision of support services to other traditional industries. In 1970 the company had about 600 employees in these activities with a turnover of £4m. A visit to a Houston oil exhibition in 1972 was the catalyst for a fundamental change of direction towards oil-related services and international business. By 1975, employment had increased to 1350 and turnover to £16m, including onshore and offshore logistic services to the North Sea oil industry as well as off-shore engineering services. The traditional industry activities were demerged into a separate parent company in 1982, and diversification continued into other oil and increasingly non-oil operations around the world. Two key related decision events were firstly, from the early 1980s, to use the acquisition route to overcome the company's relative inexperience in oil industry technology, after experimenting with the recruitment of experienced but expensive offshore oil managers and joint ventures with technologically experienced firms. Secondly, in 1995 the decision was taken at a group conference to create a global as opposed to simply international company to exploit the worldwide human resources expertise of the enterprise.

Company Profile, 1996

Sector	Energy and oil engineering services
Total turnover	£440m (of which UK £297m, 67.5 per cent of total)
Profits	£24m (5.5 per cent of turnover)
Total employment	4514 (of which Scottish employment 1599, 35.4 per cent of total)

Divisional operations are highly decentralized with strategic business units (SBUs) pursuing their own profits, growth and strategy, the aim of which is to maintain short decision-making lines and avoid over-bureaucracy. Schlumberger and ABB have been used as role models.

developed-country markets. Local responsiveness strategies are reflected in Assynt's small headquarters management team. To date there has been only limited coordination or integration of effort across the company's worldwide spread of businesses. Significant opportunities would seem to be available, however, in exploiting the globalization potential of the group, and, conversely, threats to this relatively small player from not doing so.

International Business Activities

- Over 50 subsidiary companies operating in the majority of the world's major oil provinces. The bulk of these were derived from small, strategic acquisitions. The international business experience of the Hope Group has been stimulated by such acquisitions, especially in the USA where a number of acquirees already had international operations. A recent proposal to float on the NYSE was put on hold.
- Company has experienced both successes and failures with international joint ventures (JVs). Involved in both inward and outward (for example, Malaysia and Thailand) licensing, primarily for repair and maintenance of gas turbines.
- Extensive international sourcing patterns involving companies throughout the group.
- Research and development. Most companies have their own development units. R&D departments exist in Scotland, England, the USA and Asia, with annual expenditure of approximately £10m. The company has a number of research projects with UK universities and research institutes.
- Marketing operations are located throughout the world.

Globalization Drivers and Determinants

A number of features of the international policy environment have had an important influence. For example, the Montreal Protocol which led to the phasing out of halon gas products worldwide has created significant opportunities for alternatives. Similarly countries' privatization programmes have generated substantial outsourcing opportunities, for example, outsourcing of military engine repairs in the USA. OPEC decisions on the oil price have a major impact on the level of production activity. However, UK government factors have been influential too, including privatization but also the transfer of Department of Trade and Industry functions to Scotland which in turn attracted the major oil companies and helped create a critical mass.

Continued

Despite the above, the major driving forces have undoubtedly been internal, with the group Chief Executive being responsible for the succession of key decisions, including, currently, globalization intent.

Directions of Corporate Strategy, and Indicators of Globalization

With the decision at the start of the 1980s to focus upon the oil and gas industries, the Hope Group's goal was to consolidate its status as an international energy industries' manufacturing and service enterprise. As at the late 1990s, the corporate vision had become: 'the achievement of global recognition as a leading contracting and service company in energy-related markets worldwide'.

Aside from global intent, there are also illustrations within the Hope Group's activities of globally-integrated operations. For example, for electric submersible pumps and valves, and well-head products, research,

Box 5.3
'Teallach Group'

Background and Evolution

This long established Scottish-based banking group has undergone radical change in the past fifteen years or so. From the mid-1980s onwards, it diversified its income base both within the UK and by purchasing a relatively small bank in the USA. Further evidence of early internationalization and preparation for the Single European Market was apparent in its alliance with, and minority stake in, a Spanish bank. At this stage one of its most successful innovations was to develop a major direct motor insurance business, which gave a separately branded route to market for many of its parent's core products. A profits collapse in 1991/92 was associated with the selling-off of non-core businesses. Subsequently the group launched on the radical re-engineering of the core UK bank over a five-year period which focused on business segmentation by customers; job redefinitions; better controls of credit, costs and revenues; as well as a major technology update. These changes, and an improved business climate, resulted in a good profits and enhanced shareholder value throughout the latter half of the 1990s.

Company Profile, 1997

Sector	Banking and financial services
Total assets	£72.6bn
Capital resources	£5.7bn
Operating profit	£760m
Total employment	30 900 (of which Scottish employment 11 500, 37.2 per cent of total)

design and marketing activities are based in the USA. Manufacturing is undertaken in various overseas countries, including China, India, Taiwan and Thailand, with the manufactured parts being assembled in Argentina, Venezuela, the Middle East and Asia-Pacific as well as at the main facility in the USA. Apart from cost factors, the influences on this manufacturing strategy have been the need to generate value-added in national markets and the provision of a 'local shop window' for customers.

In general, the industries in which the company competes have a fairly high local responsiveness requirement at the level of marketing and supply/service to the customer and mostly involve mature technologies. However, there are clearly areas where integration/coordination could further improve competitiveness, for example, research and development and the generation of new, innovative services which may be offered worldwide; and, more generally, worldwide know-how interchange and international human resource management policies, and so on.

International Business Activities

- As evident from the above, Teallach has few direct international interests and globalization has been a relatively unimportant dimension of corporate strategy. The US venture is not regarded as a precursor to extensive acquisitions in that market, but as a regional project which requires investment and has expanded to ensure that economies of scale are achieved. The ten-year-old relationship with a Spanish bank is a formal one with a small equity stake. In addition to providing European support for UK corporate and commercial customers, it has involved the sharing of strategy, operational practices and technology. Again it has not been recognized as necessary to follow the costly and relatively unsuccessful route of other EU banks towards mergers and acquisitions. Customers are being served throughout the EU by an international banking system developed jointly by Teallach and the Spanish partner.
- In assessing its response to globalization, the company views its strategy as being very open to ideas and products from global markets and its priority has been to internalize these within its UK franchises. Examples of this in operation include the deployment of US technology and cost-control techniques; the existence of outsourced contracts, initially in cheque clearing and several joint ventures. One of the latter is with a US bank which concentrates on credit cards in its home market and has novel approaches to marketing: it is run as a virtual company with a very small core team and had some 350 000 customers by the end of 1997. In a similar vein, Teallach has a direct insurance

Continued

business in Spain with another partner which is designed to build on its extensive UK experience.

- In evaluating the Teallach perspective on its non-core business, it would regard its direct international involvement as largely in that category, principally for reasons of shareholder value. Currently some 20 per cent of pre-tax profits are earned from overseas operations, mainly in the USA.

Globalization Drivers and Determinants

Teallach is a company which has had an international dimension for the past decade, but where there are relatively few direct global influences on its strategy. However, it clearly operates in a sector with numerous global players and within which there have been many large acquisitions and mergers in the past decade. One explanation for its position lies in the fact that it is not oriented round large global corporate customers, its UK corporate business being rooted in the middle to upper size range. There is a recognition that as a result of some of the recent banking divestments and take-overs, UK competition could become more severe. In effect, substantial global restructuring could change the shape of national

Box 5.4
'Wyvis plc'

Background and Evolution

Established in 1982 by microbiologists from a Scottish university. Backed by substantial venture-capital funding, professional management were brought in and employment increased rapidly from 10 in 1986 to 80 a year or two later. The basic medical test product, however, flopped, and a new managing director was recruited to build product revenues which by 1990 were effectively zero. The acquisition route was chosen as the mechanism to do this (six full or partial acquisitions taking place between 1992 and 1997), while new products were being developed internally, with funding being assisted by a stockmarket listing in 1993. Employment at this time was 36, a figure which had grown to 110 (50 per cent graduates, including 11 PhDs) by spring 1998.

Wyvis is an in-vitro diagnostics (IVD) company which manufactures medical diagnostic kits for disease risk assessment. The IVD industry is considered to be global and the main target markets are continental Europe and North America: developing country markets lack the resources to fund test technology; and the same comment applies to the UK National Health Service which is regarded as being cost- not value-driven. Consequently, Wyvis has exported since 1991 and obtained the

competition. Clearly there is scope for further UK bank rationalization and cost improvements.

Directions of Strategy

Teallach has a well-articulated strategy for its future development which views the UK bank and its joint-venture assurance operations as its core business areas. It continues to be active in the development of joint ventures in its retail and direct marketing businesses in order to capitalize on its infrastructure, product quality and to gain access to additional groups of UK customers, mainly in the UK. At any period in time the company is in the process of creating new businesses, especially in retail, several of which are joint ventures with international partners either for the UK or other European markets. Given the present configuration of its assets, UK GDP and the related credit cycle remains a key determinant of its performance. As regards international influences, these are mainly at the European level in that the advent of the euro and the scale of the European market could lead to a considerable degree of product convergence and heightened competition over time. For Teallach these are both potential opportunities and threats if it can continue to develop its product, brand and routes to market options from a strong UK base.

Queen's Award for Export Achievement in 1995 and again in 1997. Two acquisitions in 1996 have provided products suitable for developing country markets.

Company Profile, 1996/97

Sector	Biotechnology (in-vitro diagnostics)
Total turnover	£5.8m (of which UK £1.8m, 31 per cent of total)
Profits	–£1.3m
Total employment*	99 (of which Scottish employment 96, 97 per cent of total)

* March 1998 figure was 110.

Geographical markets (percentage of turnover)	UK	Rest of Europe	North America	Rest of world
	31.4	39.9	14.3	14.3

In total the company exports to about 60 countries.

Continued

International Business Activities

- The main vehicle chosen for international business has been OEM agreements, of which around 12 account for two-thirds of total sales. Agreements take the form of rolling contracts for the supply of complementary products to the top IVD companies in the world. The aim has thus been to utilize the worldwide distribution networks of these OEMs.
- To complement OEM deals, agents and distributors have been used, and over 60 such contracts account for 25 per cent of sales. The signing up of this large network of distributors reflected a desperation for revenues some years ago. Selection was made through previous industry contacts and knowledge of the main players.
- The company has no out-licensing arrangements, because of a preference to manufacture in-house and retain more of the value chain. A related arrangement has involved Wyvis in the development and manufacture of a product specifically for the number-2 IVD company in the world for which royalties are paid. There has been some in-licensing from UK universities and research centres.
- As part of the Wyvis strategy to increase sales into the Asia-Pacific area, a regional Business Development Executive was recruited in October 1997 based in Kuala Lumpur. The aim is to aid the marketing efforts of the company's current distributors and recruit new distributors, and thereby raise sales from the current level of £250 000 to £1m over a three-year period.
- International sourcing. The principle is to buy from wherever is most competitive.

Globalization Drivers and Determinants

The IVD industry is dominated by a few large global players. There are thus huge barriers to entry, the principal one being instrumentation (Wyvis

Box 5.5
'Conival Ltd'

Background and Evolution

Conival was founded in 1987 by two partners who had worked in marketing and engineering respectively for the UK subsidiary of a large American multinational. The product idea was a portable instrument for noise and vibration analysis, a smaller version of equipment manufactured by the partners' former employers. Supported by equity finance from the Scottish Development Agency and 3i and advised by Ernst & Young, the first year of operation was spent researching the market, developing

test equipment is used on the instrumentation of these global MNEs), and this driver, together with that of competition, effectively requires a global response from a company such as Wyvis.

Revenue generation is also a determinant of globalization, with rising global healthcare costs and attempts by governments around the world to cap these increases. Regulatory issues are important in the USA and Japan, although not to date in Europe: the company perspective is that regulation is beneficial in the sense that it constrains competition.

Directions of Corporate Strategy and Indicators of Globalization

The goal of Wyvis is to become a leading international IVD company and, more specifically, 'to be recognized as an innovator and developer of new products which meet the needs of intermediate and final customers'. Following the period of acquisitions, the focus has turned to organic growth. R&D spending, which represented £1.1m in 1996/97 (19 per cent of turnover, and up from 11 per cent a year earlier), is being pushed up substantially to £2m for 1997/98 (29 per cent of sales). Essentially, the core competences of the company are regarded as development and manufacturing. The company has decided that it could not replicate the global distribution of the big MNEs, although the OEM approach has the disadvantages of lack of control over end-user markets and to some extent limited market feedback. Nevertheless, Wyvis scans information on a worldwide basis. And, reflecting the nature of the industry, Wyvis looks to set global revenues by product area; thinking is not constrained in any way by a domestic/overseas market distinction.

A location in Scotland (or elsewhere in the UK) was not viewed as optimal because of the non-commercial thinking in universities. The company is constantly searching for new product ideas, and feels that the home area should provide a support base that allows the commercialization of new ideas.

the product and identifying distributors in Europe. The product was launched at an exhibition in the Netherlands in May 1988. As a niche player, Conival's aim was to internationalize rapidly, albeit on a phased basis, establishing a distributor network in Europe initially and then launching in the USA within a year and subsequently in the Asia-Pacific region. While the company has been consistently profitable, its growth has been well behind its business plan targets. Explanations for this range from over-reliance on and difficulties of supporting a worldwide distributor network, and the very small size of the target market, to a legal problem

Continued

in the USA which cost £250000 in legal fees (essentially Conival's exclusive US distributor was sued by a competitor manufacturer for patent infringement).

Company Profile, 1997

Sector	Electronic instrumentation
Total turnover	£3m (of which UK £1.2m, 40 per cent of total)
Profits	n.a.
Total employment*	31 (of which Scottish employment 31)

* 70 per cent of employees are HNC/degree-level engineers. In addition as at Spring 1998, Conival was negotiating two small acquisitions, one in Scotland and one in mid-west USA.

Geographical markets	UK	USA	Korea
(percentage of turnover approx.)	40.0	20.0	5.0

Other significant markets include France, Germany, S. Africa and Australia, out of the total 30–40 overseas markets. The company's export share has declined from 70 per cent to 60 per cent, consequent on growing sales to the UK auto industry.

International Business Activities

- Conival has 30 distributors worldwide, almost all exclusive to national markets. There has been a significant turnover of distributors since inception, with only one of the original 12 in Europeremaining. In 1998, two-thirds of the distributors were 'not very active'. At time of start-up, Conival had considered the option of contracting a large multinational with global distribution, but this was rejected because the companies approached did not understand the market.
- As part of distributor research in the USA, Conival entered into negotiations with Hewlett-Packard (H-P) which agreed to fund the development costs for a new high performance analyser; this was subsequently manufactured under licence by H-P for the US market. Conival had two other licensing agreements, the first with a state-owned Chinese enterprise, and the second with a UK software company.

DISCUSSION OF CASES

Globalization Drivers and Determinants

The case companies were selected to highlight a variety of experiences and their very different industry contexts have had an important influence on the firms. Thus the extent of industry globalization and both global competition and global customers were significant factors,

- International sourcing. Conival subcontracts all manufacture to another Scottish producer, and in a recent development most procurement is also subcontracted.

Globalization Drivers and Determinants

The business of 'condition monitoring' within which Conival's instrumentation competes is considered to be global and dominated by US companies. The major influences have been market factors and the drive for improved efficiency in process industries: condition monitoring enables companies, as, for example, in paper, to plan for replacement and avoid shutdowns. In the automotive industry, global competition has led to increasing efforts to reduce noise levels, hence presenting opportunities in the areas of noise and vibration analysis. The opening up of markets, as in Russia, has also generated business opportunities.

Despite the relatively slow growth of this company, there is little question that the 'global intent' of one of the founders was instrumental in the 'export from day one' strategy. This was partly derived from his previous experience, allied to a family background of self-employment and a desire to build a company.

Directions of Corporate Strategy, and Indicators of Globalization

Conival had reached a position at the end of 1996 where its strategy of global spread required to be supported by new products/services and/or new market segments. Research has led to the targeting of the automotive and food industries. Contacts from some years previously and market investigation in the mid-west USA identified a small company (six employees) producing complementary software for the auto sector, and a deal has been reached to acquire this firm. Similar research in food uncovered a small, insolvent Scottish producer of portable food-analysis instrumentation. A substantial hike in business activity was thus imminent in Spring 1998.

Although all the direct employees of Conival are still based in Scotland, the mindset of this company is unquestionably global. All employees interact with non-UK distributors and customers, and both engineering and sales and service personnel provide client support on the spot.

alongside privatization policies, deregulation, market opening and legislative change. Given the industry context, these are market, cost and competitive drivers, but mainly governmental drivers in Yip's (1989) terms. Two of the sample enterprises did not recognize specifically global influences on strategy, either because the industry was still multi-domestic or deregulation was at an early stage.

The external environment does, nevertheless, need to be considered alongside the internal, organizational environment, and in two or three cases the global vision, intent or understanding of the CEOs was a major influence on corporate behaviour. This latter issue is beginning to emerge in the literature and clearly requires further investigation; but in the cases this entrepreneurship factor seemed to be highly significant in determining whether or not companies actively sought to exploit globalization potential (even when the industry might appear to be multi-domestic in character).

Strategic Directions

Geographical expansion has undoubtedly been a key strategy for all companies except Teallach, with little distinction apparent between domestic and international business. Growth revolved around takeovers in the main, with the US acquisition having a key role in some cases. The US focus can be assumed to be linked to low psychic distance, including similarities in business practices, large internal market size and technological sophistication.

The strategy of Teallach, by contrast, has emphasised product development, product extension and market penetration within the domestic UK market. The success raises questions about the inevitability of internationalization, let alone globalization. To some extent the relatively slow advent of globalization in the industry has permitted this domestically-based strategy; the rapid changes taking place in a European context mean that it is more questionable longer term. There is little comparative work against which to review these findings. Roth (1992) suggested that the most effective global strategy involved a narrow subset of the value chain, but only Wyvis had defined its core competences and strategy in this way. Both Wyvis and Conival possessed some of the characteristics of 'global start-ups', although they are still at an early stage of corporate development.

Globalization Indicators

In respect of the extent of globalization in the case enterprises, Figure 5.2 positions the companies against the proposed criteria. The diagram does not fully distinguish between global and multi-domestic or local responsiveness strategies. As suggested earlier, excessive attention has been paid to this distinction, especially in terms of the benefits which are presumed to accrue from globalization.

The case companies have developed furthest along the global spread dimension, but only the two largest international companies employ a range of market-servicing methods and have a number of

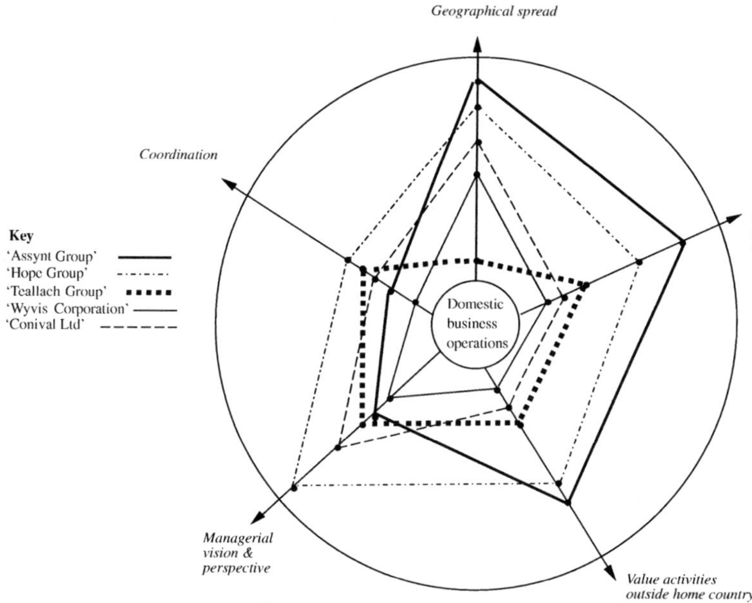

Figure 5.2 Globalization of case companies

value activities outside the home country. The two most significant measures of globalization are management vision and coordination. The former is an important attribute of the small firms and the Hope Group. On the other hand, whether the industries in which they operate are global or multi-local, all currently rank fairly low on the coordination continuum, even though there would seem to be significant potential benefits from closer coordination of their international operations. According to Porter (1986, p. 30) 'coordination allows the sharing and accumulation of know-how and expertise among dispersed activities', and thereby represents a potential source of competitive advantage. The transfer of firm-specific advantages from parent to subsidiary, of course, provides the basis for initial local competitiveness (Hu, 1995); but coordination focuses upon the sharing of know-how designed to enhance the firm-specific advantages of the group as a whole.

The coordination benefits may apply to all the firm's value activities, as represented by the ability to gain scale, scope or learning and knowledge-management advantages as well as the potential benefits from flexibility and leverage opportunities. As the case data show, the

Hope Group in particular has begun to recognize and act upon such potential, although its decentralized management style and quasi-autonomous subsidiaries may be barriers to wider group learning. Assynt is probably a vicim of its history and still behaves as a classic multi-domestic MNE. The opportunities to date are more limited in Conival since it currently has had no value activities outside its home base. The company did not, however, seem to exploit its worldwide distributor network. Teallach, the most domestic of the case enterprises by most criteria, is, nevertheless, one of the most advanced in terms of its openness to ideas and products from global markets.

Relative to the major corporate players in the world, the case enterprises are all fairly small and for such firms the transaction costs of coordination may be high. With the prerequisite of a global market, nevertheless, significant coordination benefits may be achievable through the mechanism of technology management (for example, use of the Internet), people management (for example, international recruitment, group conferences) and organizational management (for example, a structure which builds trust and exchange while stimulating internal competition and coordination and managing knowledge and intellectual capital).

A conscious effort to exploit coordination benefits is especially important when international expansion has commonly taken the form of acquisitions as opposed to organic growth. The pursuit of local responsiveness strategies reduces the incentive to capitalize upon potential synergies in acquisitions.

ISSUES FOR ECONOMIC DEVELOPMENT AND PUBLIC POLICY

The development and policy dimensions are dealt with fully in other chapters of this volume, but some comment is necessary at this point because of the home-country focus of the present work. The debates of the 1960s (for example, the Hufbauer and Adler, 1968, and Reddaway *et al.*, 1968 reports) concerning the displacement effects of outward foreign direct investment have largely been forgotten. With a recognition that internationalization/globalization is necessary and desirable, then the policy issues concern the encouragement of outward expansion and enhancing the home country benefits from this expansion. In the former category are issues concerning ways of improving the home nation's ability to act as a successful global platform for MNEs, policies for generating cluster formation and the generation of agglomeration economies and so on, as well as strategies for stimulating entrepreneurship. In the latter category are policies to improve managerial performance, linked to the exploitation of globalization potential as a mechanism for enhancing competitiveness. Of course, MNEs design their strategies and structures with the aim of maximizing the economic value of their enterprise to shareholders. There will only be a coincidence of interests between the enterprise and its home nation when spatial competitiveness decisions favour a home-country location.

Among the case enterprises, such a coincidence of interest has, generally, existed to date. For example, in Assynt the concentration of specialist design and specialist manufacturing in Scotland provides a major economic advantage for the economy. Conversely, there was little evidence of a coordination of decentralized R&D activities which would benefit the home base. In the Hope Group, company discussions emphasised the benefits to the country from international expansion, derived from higher output levels, the launch of new services, the maintenance of core capabilities in Scotland, the development of international networks and the provision of worldwide legal and financial services from the home country. On the other hand, weaknesses in the economic base in Scotland, both in the level of R&D and in the commercialization of research, were highlighted by Wyvis.

There has been considerable interest of late in the developmental MNE subsidiary. Attention now needs to be given to the characteristics of the equivalent developmental headquarters (HQ) corporation. Among such characteristics might be the following: overall company growth, linked in turn to export growth and the extent of geographic scope in export operations; the range of HQ decision-making activities; the extent of value activities at HQ; and the scanning, networking, acquiring and diffusing capabilities for all value activities globally and domestically, coordinated at HQ.

Can public policy help? Within the free market model pursued by the UK, critical importance attaches to policies designed to ensure macroeconomic growth and stability and related measures which can help provide a supportive local environment. In the context of inward investment, there is a history of attraction policies and growing interest in after-care policies of both an operational and strategic nature. But curiously there has been very little attention paid to parallel measures for outward investors. While there are a (confusing) plethora of schemes for exporters, there is scant evidence of firm-level support of a strategic or holistic nature for international business more generally defined. And it might seem that radical culture change would be necessary in many UK enterprises before such support (whether provided by the public or private sectors) would be accepted. In young, small high-technology firms some opportunities do exist, especially where, say, venture-capital support is being provided and international business expertise is regarded as deficient. As with many of the other issues raised in this chapter, further inquiry is both necessary and important.

Notes

1. At the time of undertaking this study, a 'Global Companies Enquiry' was also underway within Scottish Enterprise (the development agency for Scotland). It was addressing questions such as: what is Scotland's comparative position in the area?; what is Scotland's potential for creating future global businesses?; what barriers need to be addressed? While this chapter has benefited from access to material in the 'Global Companies Enquiry', its approach is quite different and is not designed to be 'Scotland-specific', albeit using case evidence from Scotland. It is not a study of global companies, but rather of global focus and corporate responses.

   The term 'non-dominant firms' is used in the title of the chapter. Following Mascarenhas (1986), non-dominant firms are those firms which are smaller than the largest firms in their industry on a worldwide basis, and which do not have the typical advantages of leaders. Some of the sample companies are among the largest and best-known indigenous firms in Scotland, but even they are non-dominant in global terms.
2. The authors are grateful for the contributions of colleagues in a discussion of definitions of globalization at a SIBU Research Workshop on 4 March 1998. More generally, the observations of Stephen Kobrin, the discussant for this chapter when it was originally presented on 15 May 1998, have proved very helpful.
3. Information collection: interviews were undertaken with 'Conival Ltd' on 16 October 1996 and 19 March 1998; interviews were undertaken with 'Wyvis Corporation' on 31 March 1998 and with 'Teallach Group' on 6 April 1998; data for the 'Assynt Group 'and 'Hope Group' cases were derived from Hood and Young, 1984 and Synthesis Consulting, 1998 – the assistance of Scottish Enterprise in permitting access to the latter report is gratefully acknowledged. The case names are the names of some of the highest mountains in northern Scotland.
4. The view of the present authors is that configuration of activities (see Porter, 1986) does not provide a measure of globalization. Thus both concentration and dispersion are compatible with global strategies.

References

BADEN-FULLER, C.W.F. and J.M. STOPFORD (1991), 'Globalization Frustrated: The Case of White Goods', *Strategic Management Journal*, vol. 12, pp. 493–507.

BARTLETT, C.A. and S. GHOSHAL (1989), *Managing Across Borders: The Transnational Solution* (Boston, Mass.: Harvard Business School Press).

DOZ, Y. (1986), *Strategic Management in Multinational Companies* (Oxford: Pergamon).

FINANCIAL TIMES (1998), 'Managing Global Business', Part 1, London.

FRASER, J. and J. OPPENHEIM (1997), 'What's New About Globalization?', *The McKinsey Quarterly*, no. 2, pp. 168–79.

HOOD, N. and S. YOUNG (1984), *Industry, Policy and the Scottish Economy* (Edinburgh: Edinburgh University Press).

HU, Y.-S. (1995), 'The International Transferability of the Firm's Advantages', *California Management Review*, vol. 37, no. 4, pp. 23–88.

JOHANSSON, J.K. and G.S. YIP (1994), 'Exploiting Globalization Potential: US and Japanese Strategies', *Strategic Management Journal*, vol. 15, no. 8, pp. 579–601.

JOLLY, V.K., M. ALAHUHTA and J-P. JEANNET (1992), 'Challenging the Incumbents: How High Technology Start-ups Compete Globally', *Journal of Strategic Change*, vol. 1, pp. 71–82.

JONES, M. (1998), 'International Expansion of Small High Technology Based Firms: The Role of External Linkages in International Growth and Development', PhD thesis (Glasgow: University of Strathclyde).

KOBRIN, S.J. (1994), 'Is There a Relationship Between a Geocentric Mindset and Multinational Strategy?', *Journal of International Business Studies*, vol. 25, no. 3, pp. 493–511.

KOBRIN, S.J. (1991), 'An Empirical Analysis of the Determinants of Global Integration', *Strategic Management Journal*, vol. 12, pp. 17–31.

KOGUT, B. (1985), 'Designing Global Strategies: Profiting from Operational Flexibility', *Sloan Management Review*, vol. 27, no. 3, pp. 27–38.

LEONG, S.M. and C.T. TAN (1993), 'Managing Across Borders: An Empirical Test of the Bartlett and Ghoshal (1989) Organizational Typology', *Journal of International Business Studies*, vol. 24, no. 3, pp. 449–64.

McDOUGALL, P.P., S. SHANE and B.M. OVIATT (1994), 'Explaining the Formation of International New Ventures: The Limits of Theories from International Business Research', *Journal of Business Venturing*, vol. 9, pp. 469–87.

MADSEN, T.K. and P. SERVAIS (1997), 'The Internationalization of Born Globals: An Evolutionary Process', *International Business Review*, vol. 6, no. 6, pp. 561–83.

MAIGNAN, I. and B.A. LUKAS (1997), 'Entry Mode Decisions: The Role of Managers' Mental Models', *Journal of Global Marketing*, vol. 10, no. 4, pp. 7–22.

MAKHIJA, M.V., K. KIM and S.D. WILLIAMSON (1997), 'Measuring Globalization of Industries Using a National Industry Approach: Empirical Evidence Across Five Countries and Over Time', *Journal of International Business Studies*, vol. 28, no. 4, pp. 679–710.

MASCARENHAS, B. (1986), 'International Strategies of Non-Dominant Firms', *Journal of International Business Studies*, vol. 17, no. 1, pp. 1–25.

MITCHELL, W., J.M. SHAVER and B. YEUNG (1992), 'Getting There in a Global Industry: Impacts on Performance of Changing International Presence', *Strategic Management Journal*, vol. 13, pp. 419–32.

MORRISON, A.J. and K. ROTH (1992), 'A Taxonomy of Business-Level Strategies in Global Industries', *Strategic Management Journal*, vol. 13, pp. 399–418.

OECD (1997), *Globalisation and Small and Medium Enterprises*, vol. 1, Synthesis Report (Paris: OECD).

OVIATT, B.M. and P.P. MCDOUGALL (1994), 'Toward a Theory of International New Ventures', *Journal of International New Ventures*, vol. 25, no. 1, pp. 45–64.

PORTER, M.E. (1986), 'Changing Patterns of International Competition', *Californian Management Review*, vol. 28, no. 2, pp. 9–40.

PRAHALAD, C.K. and Y.L. DOZ (1987), *The Multinational Mission: Balancing Local Demands and Global Vision* (New York: Free Press).

ROTH, K. (1992), 'International Configuration and Co-ordination Archetypes for Medium-Sized Firms in Global Industries', *Journal of International Business Studies*, vol. 23, no. 3, pp. 533–49.

SCOTTISH ENTERPRISE/SYNTHESIS CONSULTING (1998), *The Impact of Scottish Global Companies: Company Profiles for Scottish Enterprise*, Glasgow, March.

SHANKS, D.C. (1985), 'Strategic Planning for Global Competition', *Journal of Business Strategy*, Winter, pp. 80–9.

SULLIVAN, D. (1994), 'Measuring the Degree of Internationalization of a Firm', *Journal of International Business Studies*, vol. 25, no. 2, pp. 325–42.

TAGGART, J.H. (1997), 'An Evaluation of the Integration-Responsiveness Framework: MNC Manufacturing Subsidiaries in the UK', *Management International Review*, vol. 37, no. 4, pp. 295–318.

TAYLOR, W. (1991), 'The Logic of Global Business: An Interview with ABB's Percy Barnevik', *Harvard Business Review*, March–April, pp. 91–105.

YIP, G.S. (1997), 'A "Borderless" World: Issues and Evidence', in I. Islam and W. Shepherd (eds), *Current Issues in International Business* (Cheltenham, UK and Lyme, USA: Edward Elgar), pp. 87–107.

YIP, G.S. (1989), 'Global Strategy In a World of Nations?', *Sloan Management Review*, vol. 31, no. 1, pp. 29–41.

UNCTAD (1993), *World Investment Report 1993: Transnational Corporations and Integrated International Production* (New York: UN).

WEINZIMMER, L.G. (1996), 'Identifying Management Factors that Motivate Domestic Companies to Pursue International Activities', *Multinational Business Review*, Fall, pp. 94–103.

Part III
The Country Perspective

6 Development after Industrialization: Poor Countries in an Electronically Integrated Global Economy

Stephen J. Kobrin

INTRODUCTION

The International Monetary Fund (IMF) defines *globalization* as broader and deeper integration,

> . . . the growing economic interdependence of countries worldwide through the increasing volume and variety of cross-border transactions in goods and services and of international capital flows, and also through the more rapid and widespread diffusion of technology.
>
> (IMF, 1997, p. 45)

While there have been dramatic increases in international economic integration during last 30 years, change has been particularly intense over the last decade. During this period (roughly the mid-1980s to the mid-1990s) trade grew twice as fast as world output, foreign direct investment three times as fast, and cross-border trade in shares ten times as fast (*The Economist*, 1997, p. 79).

Integration of markets has expanded opportunities for developing countries. Participation in international trade '. . . improves resource allocation, enhances efficiency by increasing competition among firms, and induces learning and technology transfer, thus facilitating growth' (World Bank, 1996, pp. 3, 4). One cannot, however, consider the developing world as a coherent whole. While many countries have experienced considerable economic growth and development over the past three decades – indeed several are now 'newly industrialized' – large numbers have grown relatively and absolutely poorer. While many have been further integrated into the world economy, others have been marginalized.

The IMF presents some striking and disturbing data, in a recent *World Economic Outlook* (IMF, 1997). Using GNP/capita, 108 non-oil-producing developing countries were arrayed across five income brackets or quintiles. In 1965, 52 fell in the lowest quintile. Three decades later, that number had *increased* to 84. The IMF concludes:

> [S]imply put, over the past thirty years the vast majority of the developing countries . . . have either stayed in the lowest-income quintile or fallen into that quintile from a relatively higher position. Moreover, there are now fewer middle-income developing countries and upward mobility of countries seems to have fallen over time.
>
> (IMF, 1997, pp. 77–8)

While the IMF data show relative rather than absolute increases in poverty, increased polarization of wealth and poverty and increased global economic integration have occurred concurrently. There is some indication that the growth of poverty is actually accelerating over time. The UNDP reports that while 200 million people saw their per capita incomes fall from 1965–80, over one billion did so from 1980–93. In 70 developing countries, average incomes are less than they were in 1980 (quoted in Castells, 1998, p. 81).

Many developing countries became less integrated into the world economy over the last decade. The ratio of trade to GDP fell in 44 of 93 countries in a World Bank sample and, despite dramatic overall gains, the ratio of foreign direct investment (FDI) to GDP fell in over one-third (World Bank, 1996, p. 20).

While correlation certainly does not imply causality, large parts of the developing world are not benefiting from increased economic integration and globalization. The past three decades have seen dramatic increases in both globalization and polarization, in economic integration and an increasing maldistribution of income and wealth.

This chapter will explore the relationship between globalization and development, focusing on the impact of the information revolution on developing countries. While electronic integration and digitalization of the world economy is but one aspect of globalization, it may well be the most significant: in large part it is what differentiates the late twentieth century global economy from international world economies of the past (Kobrin, 1997, 1998). The chapter begins by briefly discussing globalization in general and then examining its impact, and particularly the impact of the emergence of an electronically integrated world economy on development and developing countries. It then turns to the software industry in India as a case example and concludes by attempting to generalize by placing globalization and development within a larger contextual framework.

GLOBALIZATION OR GLOBAL BALONEY?

Many authors note that there was a 'first global economy', and that on any number of metrics the world economy at the end of the nineteenth century was as, if not more, international than that at the end of the twentieth century. Given the levels of trade relative to GDP, capital flows and currency convertibility, the period from 1870 through 1914 has been called 'the golden age' of economic integration (see Dunning, 1993; Kobrin, 1997; Krugman, 1992; and Williamson, 1996, for example). The implication is that the dramatic increases in internationalization experienced over the postwar period are no more than a return to the norm, to the levels of integration experienced in 1914.

The author believes firmly that late twentieth century globalization does represent a change in kind; a qualitative change in the structure and functioning of cross-border economic (and political) relations compared with the world economy of a century ago. While globalization can convey an almost endless variety of meaning, six components are suggested that comprise – if not exhaustively – economic globalization:

- deeper and wider integration of national economies through trade, direct investment and other capital flows;
- increased autonomy, scale and velocity of international capital markets;
- the enormous cost, risk and complexity of technology in many strategic or leading sectors;
- the blurring of the distinction between manufacturing and services as a result of the core importance of information processing, combined with the electronic integration of individuals, firms and markets;
- and, relatedly, the digitalization of the economy: the shift from 'trade in atoms to trade in bits' (Negroponte, 1995) combined with the movement of markets from geographic space to cyberspace.

- space–time compression; simultaneous awareness in every part of the globe of events, trends and ideas, at least among elites. The CNN world.

Two aspects of globalization will be discussed briefly, namely deeper integration and increases in the scale of technology, before turning to the information revolution. One significant difference between the first and second global economies is that production, rather than trade, has become internationalized. Deep integration implies much more than cross-border flows of goods, it entails production organized through hierarchically integrated multinational firms. One symptom is the rising relative importance of intra-firm and intra-industry trade.

At the end of the nineteenth century, cross-border flows were primarily of goods – in the main, raw materials and finished goods. At the end of the twentieth century, cross-border flows entail some goods, especially intermediate products, but also technology, managerial skills and information in many other forms. Globalization has entailed a shift from market to hierarchy as a primary mode of integration of the world economy.

Of more importance is the dramatic increase in the scale of technology – its cost, risk and complexity – in industries such as semiconductors, aerospace, telecommunications and pharmaceuticals. At this point, even industry leaders from the advanced industrial countries may not have the resources to mount a competitive R&D effort, given the enormous costs involved, the uncertainty of outcomes, shortened product life cycles and the complexity of technology (see Kobrin, 1997, for further discussion). This dramatic increase in the scale of technology has two important implications for globalization. First, in combination with the growth of electronic networks it helps explain the increase in cross-border inter-firm alliances over the last decade, especially in high technology industries. Second, even the largest national markets are now too small to allow recovery of R&D expenses in many of these industries. Put differently, given the cost, risk and complexity of technology in these leading-edge industries, national markets may no longer be large enough to serve as viable units of the world economy.

This chapter argues that the information revolution is the central transformative phenomenon of globalization; it *is* the change in quality compared with previous international world economies. As this subject has been discussed in depth in earlier papers (Kobrin, 1997, 1998), only a summary is necessary here. Electronic information technology has reduced the importance of physical proximity as a factor in management and organization. It facilitates the integration of geographically dispersed operations and allows networked coordination to replace ownership and hierarchy as the primary mode of control (Dicken, 1994). One result is the rise of networked integration, the disintegration of value chains organized through hierarchies, and their reintegration within electronically enabled – often dense, complex and transborder – networks; the replacement of vertically integrated hierarchical firms with flexible alliances. 'Capitalism today thus entails the detailed disaggregation of stages of production and consumption across national boundaries, under the organisational structure of densely networked firms' (Gereffi, Korzeniewicz and Korzeniewicz, 1994, p. 1).

Perhaps most important, the information revolution has transformed both the means and products of production; it entails an alchemic-like transformation from atoms to bits; from tangible, physical objects to digital zeros and ones, from material to information, from products to services. We now download rather than ship. This includes, or will include, everything from software to music, movies, all kinds of visual images, newsletters, reports, and perhaps 'books'.

Markets are moving, albeit slowly, from geographic space to cyberspace. International financial markets are constructed in electronic space; they are comprised of hundreds of thousands of screens linked globally through electronic networks. As electronic commerce gains in importance, other markets will follow. Markets will exist as complex electronic networks where information (for example, a downloaded symphony) is exchanged for information in the form of electronic cash. Geography, including borders and territorial jurisdiction will become increasing irrelevant.

DEVELOPMENT AND GLOBALIZATION

In the post-World War II era the transactional mode of integration of the international economy has evolved from trade (markets) to the internationalization of production through MNEs (hierarchy), to alliances (networks). To a large extent, conceptualization of the means and ends of 'economic development' has correspondingly evolved.

'Economic development' first attracted serious attention in the late 1950s and 1960s, partially as a result of Cold War tensions. In an era when trade still dominated the international economy – the term multinational enterprise (MNE) was first used in 1960 – development revolved about industrialization and modernization of a *national* economy and *national* society or polity. Until the 1970s, it was seen as a process of economic and social transformation, organized nationally, that is within the context of a territorially defined national market and nation-state (McMichael, 1996). Development focused on industrialization, economic growth (Rostow's 'Takeoff') and modernization; on development of the national economy as a defined unit. This was the era of import substitution – especially in Latin America under the influence of Raul Prebish and ECLA – the development of indigenous industries to generate rearward and forward linkages to stimulate broadscale industrial development.

During the 1970s, the primary mode of organization of the international economy evolved from market to hierarchy, from trade to the organization of production internationally within the organizational hierarchy of the MNE. In a sense an epitome of this era was Ford Europe which produced components in a number of European countries and then assembled the vehicles in Germany, the UK and Spain. The internationalization of production internationalized Fordist organization, vertical integration across distances and across national borders.

One result of the internationalization of production was a polarization of development theory into two diametrically opposed streams. Both were linked by a marked transformation from a focus on the national economy in *relative* isolation to a concern with the mode of attachment to the emerging global economy; to participation in a globally organized process of economic growth (McMichael, 1996). As the IMF put it more recently, '. . . the world economy is becoming, more and more, the relevant context for economic decisions' (1997, p. 46).

Mainstream analysis turned from import substitution, and a focus on development within the national economy, to export promotion and integration into the world economy. The World Bank's *World Development Report 1980*, for example, argued for a shift to export promotion, to 'Reducing the general bias towards import substitution . . .'. It explicitly endorsed the recommendations of the Brandt Commission calling for 'emphasis on the interdependence – through trade, energy and capital flows – of all countries . . .' (World Bank, 1980, pp. 13, 22). The Asian NICs came to be seen as exemplars of development through integration into the global system of production. Export industries were seen as an 'engine of growth' in that linkages to the rest of the national economy resulted in growth and development.

In contrast, the vast literature of Neo-imperialism and *Dependencia* argued that integration into the world economy was the problem rather than the solution. In Frank's (1969) view, development and underdevelopment were opposite sides of the same coin; wealth and poverty were created simultaneously. Underdevelopment was seen as a result of the dependence – economic, technological and cultural – of the Third World upon the First. While the dependency literature focused on analysis rather than policy prescription, the assumption was that true 'development' required breaking the bonds of dependency, the links to the international capitalist system.

The emergence of an electronically networked economy has increased the emphasis on the importance of integration into the international economy for development. However, as will be discussed in detail below, it raises serious questions about the meaning of the term *development* in a postindustrial world. It raises questions about exactly who and what is integrated into the world economy. Integration in the 1990s takes place increasingly within global electronic networks rather than through trade and investment. The information revolution renders physical proximity and distance irrelevant. It has shifted emphasis from linkages within territorially defined national economies to relations between nodes in an 'a-geographic' network; a network which can exist within cyber- rather than physical space. The information revolution raises fundamental questions about the meaning of a national market (Kobrin, 1997).

There is no question that globalization has expanded opportunities for developing countries. Regardless of the current Asian crisis, the performance of countries such as South Korea, Thailand, Malaysia, to say nothing of Hong Kong and Korea, over the past two decades must be deemed a 'miracle'. While they are certainly feeling the backlash from globalization at present, integration into the world economy – albeit controlled integration in some cases – has resulted in substantial progress in each instance.

The information revolution facilitates integration by removing, or limiting, the barriers posed by physical distance and geography. It reduces the importance of the location of resources and factors of production in the international division of labour, and increases the importance of the capacity to create new knowledge and apply it rapidly across space and time (Carnoy *et al.*, 1993). An information-based international economy also facilitates the globalization of services. Digitalization has made many services 'tradable' that were not in the past. For the first time it allows the provision and consumption of services to take place at different points in space and in time.

As Primo (1996) notes, this provides another source of opportunity for less-developed countries (LDCs). It allows services to be provided in developing countries and consumed in the advanced industrial countries. It provides an opportunity for LDCs to move into increasing value-added activities, from data entry to programming for example. Digital networks also facilitate the transfer of technology and learning to the developed countries. Globalization also provides potential pitfalls for LDCs. It puts a premium on competition and on an appropriate policy framework. While the digital economy may compress space and time, it also increases the ante for participation in terms of both social and physical infrastructure: education and training, communications networks and the like. As noted above, it also raises very real questions about what is meant by an LDC or a national economy. About where transactions take place and what development and growth mean.

To examine these questions, the next section now turns to what may be the foremost case example of integration of a developing country into the electronically networked world economy: the Indian software industry.

THE INDIAN SOFTWARE INDUSTRY

In an article titled 'Bangalore Bytes,' *The Economist* (1996, p. 67) argued that '. . . parts of the Indian economy . . . are skipping right over the "second" industrial age, and straight into the information era'. By any measure, the Indian software industry appears to be an outstanding success story, a headlong leap into the postindustrial digital global economy.

In 1997/98, the 'turnover' of the Indian software industry reached an estimated $2.70 billion versus a mere $10 million a decade ago. The compound annual growth rate for the last five years exceeds 52 per cent. The industry is export-driven: 1997/98 exports ($1.75 billion) accounted for 65 per cent of total turnover, and the export CAGR for the last five years was 55 per cent. Exports for 1998/99 are expected to grow by another 54 per cent to $2.7 billion (Nicholson, 1998 and NASSCOM, 1997).

The industry's primary advantage is India's relatively large number of well-trained software professionals – drawing from the second largest English speaking pool of scientific and technical people in the world – who do world-class work at very competitive rates compared to their counterparts in Europe or the USA. In 1996, the industry employed 160 000 software professionals, a increase of 20 000 over the previous year, and estimates indicate a demand for another 55 000 professionals per year over the next three years.

Origins and Development

The software industry developed originally in Bangalore, a large Southern Indian city, and over 20 per cent of the largest firms are still headquartered there. While early industrialization involved traditional textile manufacturing, after independence the new government made a decision to locate strategic and defence-related industry in Bangalore, which is well-removed from borders and the sea coast (Madon, 1997). This in turn resulted in the development of a number of scientific and technically oriented universities and institutions, which led to the development of high-technology industries such as electronics, telecommunications and information technology. By 1995, the city accounted for almost 40 per cent of Indian high-technology industrial production (Madon, 1997).

Indian economic policy, which can be described as statist, restrictive (especially with regard to FDI) and protectionist certainly played a role in the development of the industry. As Heeks (1996, p. 51) notes in his comprehensive study of the industry, Indian software policy can be described '. . . only in loose terms of a broad trend of liberalisation rather than the reverse, because the trend has been patchy and has progressed quite far in some areas, yet hardly at all in others'. It can be described as *liberal* only within the Indian context.

Perhaps most important here, from the 1970s onward, Indian policy tied importing hardware to exports of software. While policy was liberalized over time, it continued to reinforce an export orientation. In 1986, for example, importing hardware and software became easier and restrictions on the domestic use of imported hardware were dropped. However, at the same time, software export obligations (produced from imported hardware) were strengthened (Heeks, 1996). The Indian domestic market for software development grew in the 1970s when firms using computers began to 'outsource' software development. Tata Consultancy Services was the first firm to export software in return for permission to import hardware in 1974, an event Heeks (1996) describes as marking the birth of the Indian software export industry.

Several factors led to the growth of the industry over the 1980s. First, with standardization and the phenomenal growth of the PC, a world software market developed rapidly during that decade. Second, hardware import policy was liberalized in 1984 and the introduction of PCs into India resulted in the emergence of a domestic software industry comprised of large numbers of small firms (Heeks, 1996). Furthermore, towards the end of the decade, multinational firms such as Citicorp began to invest in software development subsidiaries and joint ventures in India.

While statistics on the Indian software industry are of varying accuracy, there is no question that it has grown exponentially over the last two decades. The membership of India's National Association of Software and Service Companies (NASSCOM) grew from just 38 firms in 1988/89, to 430 in 1996/7 (NASSCOM, 1997). Heeks (1996) estimates that software-related employment in India grew tenfold between 1986 and 1995.

Export Orientation

The industry is export-dominated and has become more so over time. Heeks (1996) argues that domestic production has a lower priority than export, and that the relative importance of exports grew from about half of overall production in the mid-1980s to roughly three-quarters in the mid-1990s. NASSCOM data (1997) indicates that the domestic share of total output has been declining, albeit slowly, from 41 per cent in 1994/5 to 40 per cent in 1995/6 to 38 per cent in 1996/7 to 35 per cent in 1997/98. It is acknowledged that these figures may understate domestic production as they do not include in-house development.

Indian software exports are dominated by professional services (47 per cent) and consultancy and training (27 per cent); products and packages account for only 11 per cent of total exports. The USA is the dominant export market (58 per cent in 1996/7), with Europe a second destination (21 per cent). While there are more than 550 companies exporting software, the top 20 exporters account for almost 60 per cent of the market (NASSCOM, 1996, p. 7). The main sectors serviced by Indian firms are financial services, insurance and 'certain segments of manufacturing' (Balasubramanyam and Balasubramanyam, 1997).

If virtually all Indian software exports take the form of services rather than products, how are they delivered? The answer is one of two ways: either through on-site services where Indian programmers actually travel to the client's offices and work there for a given period of time (known as 'body shopping'), or off-shore where programmers in India work on computers in the USA or Europe directly via satellite or other communications links. The latter is growing in importance each year; in 1988, 90 per cent of exports took the form of on-site services while currently that has been reduced to 59 per cent (NASSCOM, 1997). Given increasing visa restrictions in the USA and in Europe, one would expect a continued shift to off-shore services in the future.

Increasingly, Indian software exports are a result of outsourcing by American and European firms; they represent the Indian firm working for a single client or collaborator. For example, NASSCOM (1997, p. 54) estimates that about half of *all* exports in 1996/97 were US software development work outsourced to India. In his survey of the industry, Heeks (1996, p. 84) found that the vast majority of exports of all but seven of the top 25 Indian exporters were sales to a single foreign company and that, on average, 65–75 per cent of their exports went 'to or through' a single foreign company. Thus, the vast majority of software exports involve an Indian programmer working on a client's computer – and problems – either physically or virtually. Well over half of exports involve 'body shopping', an Indian programmer actually travelling to New York or London and working in the client's office. In an increasing number of cases, however, a programmer sitting in Bangalore or New Delhi works directly on a client's computer via satellite or other data network.

The Industry in Perspective: Benefits and Costs

The Indian software industry is an unquestionable success story. There are a large number of firms, many of them indigenously-owned and managed, developing and exporting software services to world market standards. Indian programmers do have a significant cost advantage: one recent comparison estimated that an engineering graduate in the USA could cost as much as $60 000 per year with benefits compared with $15 000 in Bangalore (Landers, 1995). However, Indian programmers are productive; the quality of their work is competitive on the world market.

Hardware aside, the industry is not import-dependent – most of the value added is 'labour' – and it adds to India's balance of payments. It provides interesting and relatively well-remunerated employment to Indian engineering graduates who might otherwise emigrate in search of jobs. In fact, more than one of the leading Indian software firms have been founded by emigrants who returned home. Furthermore, the industry provides technological training for its personnel who are working on current problems all over the world, often in collaboration with firms from the developed countries. It also provides an important and visible demonstration of the return to entrepreneurship and innovation, and a motivating 'case study' of what can be done in the Indian context. It clearly represents a return to liberalization of import regulations, a lesson one hopes will not be lost on Indian policy-makers.

As a World Bank report notes, the industry has had an impact well beyond the software and IT sectors:

> It has been a source of dynamism and technological innovation. It has provided demonstration effects for other industries, in terms of export orientation, strategic alliances and foreign investment. It has been building India's image abroad in terms of entrepreneural and technological capabilities. It has been India's window on the global technology revolution. It continues to provide a strong domestic voice for liberalisation and competition.
>
> (Hanna, 1994, p. xii)

While the success of the industry in terms of its growth and competence is beyond question, its tangible impact on India is not. Although the comparison is not fair, its 1996/97 turnover of $1.75 billion is almost inconsequential relative to Indian GDP. More important, while NASSCOM's estimate of total professional employment of 160 000 in the most recent year is impressive in absolute terms, as Heeks notes (1996, p. 93) the software industry cannot be described as a significant employer in more general terms. It accounts for no more than 5 per cent of employment in the electronics industry, and 0.5 per cent of total manufacturing employment in India. The context has, however, to be borne in mind. India's size is overwhelming: the population of Bangalore alone approaches five million.

The excessive export orientation of the industry is problematic. '(I)t is clear that the domestic market has been neglected by the mainstream software industry in comparison to exports . . . that a lower priority has been afforded to the domestic market' (Heeks, 1996, p. 72).

Exports accounted for approximately 65 per cent of turnover in 1997/98 and their share is growing, albeit slowly.

As noted above, the vast majority (close to 90 per cent) of exports are services, and primarily support services rather than products. While a number of Indian companies would like to move up the value chain, they have not as yet been able to do so. To date, no Indian company has produced a software product that has succeeded in developed-country markets (Guha, 1998). As will be recalled, body shopping still accounts for well over half of exports; that implies that much of the actual development is taking place outside of India. Furthermore, contract work for American and European firms is increasing in importance.

Whether the export mode is body shopping or off-shore, programmers are working on their clients' problems (and computers). They are not working on problems relevant to India and development of the Indian economy. Areas such as rural health care, rural development, education, public management and small business applications are much in need of locally-relevant IT and software solutions.

A number of authors argue that there are limited links between the export and domestic markets, and that the links which do exist tend to flow from the latter to the former. Professionals tend to move from domestic development to the export sector, rather than the other way around. There is little in the way of transfers of skills, knowledge or standards gained in export work to domestic development. Despite the rapid growth of opportunities for software professionals in India, emigration is still a problem, exacerbated by the export orientation and the opportunities for migration that arise as a result of body shopping (Hanna, 1994; Heeks, 1996).

The Indian software industry is a clear example of dualism in development, which certainly is not a new phenomenon. Even in Bangalore's state of Karnataka, polarization is severe. The software firms in their modern offices, often in industrial parks, exist as islands in a sea of poverty. More directly relevant to the arguments here, dualism and polarization can be observed within the information-technology sector in India. There is a stark difference between the development of infrastructure and facilities for the export industry and Indian IT development more generally.

While numbers are hard to come by and generally suspect, there is a very clear and dramatic underdevelopment of the Indian IT industry. For example, while the Asian region is experiencing the fastest growth of internet-related activities in the world (Valigra, 1997), access to the internet is still 'woefully inadequate' in India, due in some part to policy restrictions (Chowdary, 1997). While all estimates of internet usage are outdated before the 'ink' is dry, in 1997 there were an estimated total of 50000 internet users in India compared with half a million in Malaysia and Thailand which are much smaller countries (Chowdary, 1997). Recent data (January 1998) shows 7175 internet hosts in India, compared with 32269 in Malaysia, 14378 in Thailand, and (an admitted unfair comparison) 176836 in Taiwan (Internet Domain Survey, 1998).

The limited internet penetration in India is due, in part, to the immense size and overall poverty of the country and correspondingly low overall educational levels. However, the Indian middle class is huge in absolute numbers and has been compared to the population of Germany. The Indian higher education system is superb and, as noted above, manages to produce relatively large numbers of scientific and technical personnel. Furthermore, access to English, the language of the net, is less of a barrier in India than many other Asian countries. Indian government policy which has limited access-providers for a number of reasons and still maintains relatively high tariffs on networking IT products, is certainly important here (India Not Yet Wired, 1997).

All of that being said, the external focus of the software industry is certainly part of the problem. Development of the external market is, at least in part, responsible for underdevelopment of the domestic market. In discussing the limited internet penetration in India, the executive director of NASSCOM noted that the Indian software industry seemed to be 'mesmerised by revenue-generation from the year 2000 problem', and ignoring other critical issues (India Not Yet Wired, 1997).

Dualism certainly extends to infrastructure development. Since Texas Instruments pioneered direct satellite links between its subsidiary in Bangalore and its mainframe computer in Dallas in 1986 (Landers, 1995), the practice has become relatively widespread. Indian software firms, often located in modern technology parks, have well-developed external electronic linkages with Europe and the USA; they exist in an international work environment (Madon, 1997). At the same time, domestic technical infrastructure in terms of access to computers and the internet is woefully underdeveloped.

Despite the very real, and very important, gains from the development and rapid growth of the industry, there are serious questions about its local impact. While not directly analogous, it may be useful to think about the impact of the Indian software industry in terms of the concepts of 'export enclaves' and 'growth poles' from the development literature. Albert Hirschman argued that the critical factor in economic development 'was calling forth and enlisting for development purposes resources and abilities that are hidden scattered, or badly utilised' (1958, p. 5). The development impact of a foreign investment, or any investment for that matter, depends to a large extent on its *linkages* with the rest of the economy. Backward linkages involve the supply of raw materials, intermediate goods, supplies, machinery, technology and the like; forward linkages entail the use of an investment's output as input into another enterprise.

An investment, or an industry, that establishes linkages to the local economy stimulates further investment and development, it serves as a 'growth pole'. In contrast, an 'enclave' has only the most limited linkages to the local economy and its impact on development is basically its fiscal contribution. The classic example of an enclave is a geographically isolated natural resource export operation where capital, technology and management are imported and unprocessed raw materials are exported. Linkages are limited to some very basic supplies and some local labour.

The Indian software industry obviously differs qualitatively from the traditional export enclave. It is largely an indigenous phenomenon with firms owned, managed and staffed by Indian nationals. On the other hand, the analogy is useful: an Indian resource, productive and competitive technological 'labour' is exported, directly in the case of body shopping. The extent and strength of backward and forward linkages with the Indian domestic economy are questionable. And last, one has to ask what geographic isolation means in an electronically networked, virtual world economy.

As noted above, the domestic software market is very underdeveloped, the industry focuses on services rather than product development, and technological capability (at both the individual and the firm level) tends to flow from the domestic to the export market, rather than the reverse. The critical question is whether the industry is stimulating increased software (or hardware) development by contractors and suppliers, or whether backward linkages are limited to increased demand for technologically trained graduates. And has the development of the industry affected the quality of information-technology-related education? Forward linkages do appear to be quite limited; there is little evidence of a range of end-users developing in India.

The export focus of the industry and relative underdevelopment of the domestic sector means that the problems dealt with are those of clients in developed countries which may not be relevant to India. India is a country beset with problems which require systems analysis and software solutions. However, Indian software companies and Indian programmers' attention is directed elsewhere, such as to the year-two-thousand (Y2K) problem, or a glitch in a New York bank's operating system. The industry's attention is diverted from India's development needs. Furthermore, there may well be an internal brain drain of qualified and well-educated Indians into jobs in the software industry, which are relatively well-paying, rather than others which may better meet the country's development needs. Balasubramanyam and Balasubramanyam (1997) argue that the industry 'creams off' the best and the brightest who may actually be overqualified for software development. They end up working to solve problems of the industrialized countries which may be irrelevant to India's development needs.

It is far from clear what 'geographic isolation' means as we enter the digital world. Indian software firms are far from an isolated 'oil patch', they are typically located in major metropolitan areas. On the other hand, the export-oriented Indian software industry is an 'enclave' in India that is more of the developed than the underdeveloped world. Programmers who engage in body shopping, working on clients' problems at clients' computers, are physically in the industrialized world much of the time.

Perhaps more important, given trends, the 'location' of programmers who work on clients' computers via satellite links is problematic. Physically, they are in India; however, they are working in cyberspace and in a part of cyberspace that is very much part of the industrialized world. They spend much of their days 'in' New York or London. Even their offices are removed from the Indian context: they could as well be in Silicon Valley as Bangalore. It is reasonable to ask whether a programmer 'in' Bangalore working via satellite on the year-two-thousand problem (Y2K) on a bank's computer in New York is really 'in' India, at least during his or her working hours. It is far from clear where the transaction takes place, and if the question is even relevant. This results in what Heeks (1997, p. 270) calls a 'shearing' of Indian society. A group of highly educated individuals who spend much of their time 'in' other places. Their reality is not India: they tend towards use of American English and 'joke' that their capital is New York, not New Delhi (Heeks, 1997).

The purpose of this chapter is not to minimize the very real achievements of the Indian software industry in a relatively short period of time. It is an amazing story of innovation, talent, entrepreneurship and effort. Furthermore, the companies or individuals in the industry cannot be held responsible for the development of the Indian economy. Many of them have returned to India from the USA and Europe and have been extremely successful, providing income, exports and employment. Their story is truly admirable.

However, in the context of this chapter, the Indian software industry serves as a basis for speculation on the opportunities and problems the information revolution presents for developing countries and on the meaning of development in the digital age. The Indian software industry is clearly a metaphor for what is possible in the information age. It does demonstrate that the opportunity exists to 'leapfrog' over several stages of economic development, directly into a postindustrial economy and to compete globally. But the industry also raises some very troubling questions. Given the underdevelopment of the domestic sector and the lack of linkages to the Indian economy in general, can it be described as a growth pole or a leading sector? Or does it exist in Balasubramanyam and Balasubramanyam's terms (1997, p. 837) as a small island of affluence in a vast sea of poverty and backwardness?

DEVELOPMENT IN THE POSTINDUSTRIAL AGE

In the modern era, and especially during the industrial age, terms such as *nation-state* and *national market* were not abstractions: they described tangible, physical reality. The modern state, and the modern state system, which are conventionally dated from the Treaty of Westphalia (1648) organize politics and economics geographically in terms of mutually-exclusive territorial sovereignty. A national market can be described precisely in terms of political-economic control over geographic territory surrounded by discrete borders.

In that context, terms such as national economic development and less-developed countries made perfect sense. Development and modernization involved industrialization of a geographically-defined national economy and economic growth, and could be measured in terms of GDP/capita – geographically measured income per head. Development was a national project. Even after the internationalization of production, the organization of international transactions within the hierarchies of MNEs, one could still talk meaningfully about linking a national economy to the global economy.

That certainly is not to say that development and economic growth were evenly distributed within a market; that all boats rose with the incoming tide. Dualism, enclaves, centres and peripheries were all issues widely discussed during this period. Large segments of the population in all developing countries were marginalized and left out of the process. However, at the end of the day it still made sense to talk about national economic development and economic growth. National markets were a phenomenon which could be described precisely in both qualitative and quantitative terms.

In the emerging postmodern electronically networked world economy the very idea of territoriality is losing meaning. The international financial market may well be a metaphor; it is organized electronically in cyberspace. Geography is increasingly irrelevant as a basis for the definition of markets and the organization of economic activity. Fragmentation is a primary attribute of the postmodern era. Geographically-defined markets (and states) are disintegrating and the world economy is reintegrating in a very different 'a-spatial' form through electronic networks; fragments, of individuals, groups and organizations are reassembled electronically in cyberspace.

Castells (1996) notes that, in the past, time and space were linked. Processes that required simultaneity in time also required spatial proximity: economic activity was organized in terms of a 'space of places'. The information revolution has broken this time–space connection: spatial proximity is no longer a requisite for simultaneous processing – as demonstrated, for example, in a programmer in Bangalore working on a computer in New York. He argues that in our emerging networked society, the space of places is being replaced by a space of flows. 'Thus, the network of communication is the fundamental spatial configuration: places do not disappear, but their logic and their meaning become absorbed in the network' (1996, p. 412). This argument does not apply to all economic activity; space, territory and geographic markets retain meaning in many sectors. In others, space is losing importance and transactions and markets are moving to cyberspace. This is particularly true in economic activity which is information-driven.

Given that caveat, it is reasonable to ask whether the idea of national economic development, indeed of a national economy, still retains meaning. Economic units become nodes in a global network, often with only the most tenuous linkages to their own *economy*. 'We certainly still have spatial forms, since societies and economies develop on a given territory . . . yet the logic and dynamics of territorial development are increasingly placeless from the point of view of the dominant organisations and their social interests' (Castells and Henderson, 1987, p. 7).

Concepts such as dualism, enclaves and core–periphery relations have been part of the development literature for decades. For example, in 1971 Galtung argued that both developing and developed nations had centres and peripheries and that there were linkages, a harmony of interests, between the centres; that the 'developed' elites in a developing country might have more in common, and more readily identify, with the metropolitan centre than with their own periphery; that dependent development led to a process which focused on the needs (and material culture) of the first world rather than the third, especially in the more advanced sectors in Third World countries.

The debate over enclaves, centre and periphery, and dualism takes on new meaning in the postindustrial era. As in the case of the Indian software industry, in the information age linkages to the national economy may be more tenuous. Economic fragments in developing countries have become part of a global electronic network. Participants are located in a part of cyberspace defined by a relational network and not in the national territory. Programmers are absorbed into the global network and to some extent, at least during working hours, the physical world becomes irrelevant. While a programmer in Bangalore is not in New York, she is not really in Bangalore either. She is 'in' a network constructed in cyberspace. Again, at least during her working hours, she is transported, and this is not meant metaphorically, to another 'place' and is concerned with the problems, culture, language and mores of that 'place'. The fact that the place exists in an electronic rather than a physical reality is not critical.

Fragmentation and reintegration through electronic networks has its advantages. It greatly facilitates integration into the world economy for individuals and firms in the developing countries. It allows for the development of industries that one could not have imagined in India or Malaysia even a decade ago. It provides middle-class status and economic security to large numbers of individuals. It allows segments of every economy to 'leap-frog' into the digital age. However, there is a cost:

> Greater openness has made small parts of the developing world fully fledged members of the global village. But in many developing nations, globalised islands of prosperity are thriving along-side vast and growing expanses of economic stagnation and human deprivation.
>
> (Heredia, 1997)

This chapter began with a discussion of the increasing polarization of wealth and income among developing countries. The information revolution is likely to exacerbate that trend. It can result in simultaneous inclusion and marginalization: it can link up 'valuable people and activities from all over the world, while switching off from the networks of power and wealth, people and territories dubbed as irrelevant . . .' (Castells, 1998, p. 1).

The information revolution puts a premium on education and access to computers and communications networks. Given the requisite social and physical infrastructure, it provides unparalleled opportunities, regardless of one's location. However, the opposite is also true. Without the requisite education and access, one is simply left out of the global network, 'switched off' or, more likely, never connected in the first place. One can live anywhere and be part of the networked global economy. One can also live anywhere and not be connected; consigned to live on, at or beyond the margins of meaningful economic activity.

While this chapter has focused on developing countries, it should be clear that one does not have to go to India to see extremes of wealth and poverty, to see populations switched off and disconnected. Indeed, one has to go less than a mile from the author's house in Centre City Philadelphia.

Solutions are not easily at hand. They do, however, have to be found. A system in which large segments of the population are marginalized is not stable, and this holds both within and across countries. Extremes of poverty and wealth cannot coexist. Social unrest, disease and human degradation cannot be contained. The networks are bidirectional. There is a backlash to globalization which could well snap back upon us all.

References

BALASUBRAMANYAM, V.N. and A. BALASUBRAMANYAM (1997), 'International Trade in Services: The Case of India's Computer Software', *World Economy*, vol. 20, no. 6, pp. 829–43.

CARNOY, M., M. CASTELLS, S.S. COHEN and F.H. CARDOSO (1993), *The New Global Economy in the Information Age* (University Park, Penn.: The Pennsylvania State University Press).

CASTELLS, M. (1998), *The End of the Millennium. The Information Age: Economy, Society and Culture*, Vol. III (Malden, Mass.: Blackwell).

CASTELLS, M. (1996), *The Rise of the Networked Society. The Information Age: Economy, Society and Culture*, Vol. I, (Malden, Mass.: Blackwell).

CASTELLS, M. and J. HENDERSON (1987), 'Techno-economic Restructuring, Socio-political Processes and Spatial Transformation: A Global Perspective', in J. Henderson and M. Castells (eds), *Global Restructuring and Territorial Development* (London: Sage), pp. 1–17.

CHOWDARY, T.H. (1997), 'The Internet Divide', *Telecommunications*, international edition, vol. 31, no. 9 (September), pp. 95–6.

DICKEN, P. (1994), 'The Ropke Lecture in Economic Geography: Global–Local Tensions: Firms and States in the Global Space Economy', *Economic Geography*, vol. 70, pp. 101–20.

DUNNING, J.H. (1993), *Multinational Enterprises and the Global Economy* (Reading, Mass.: Addison-Wesley).

THE ECONOMIST (1997), 'Schools Brief: One World?, 18 October, pp. 79–80.

THE ECONOMIST (1996), 'Software in India: Bangalore Bytes', 23 March, p. 67.

FRANK, A.G. (1969), *Capitalism and Underdevelopment in Latin America* (New York: Monthly Review Press).

GALTUNG, J. (1971), 'A Structural Theory of Imperialism', *Journal of Peace Research*, vol. 2, pp. 81–117.

GEREFFI, G., M. KORZENIEWICZ and R.P. KORZENIEWICZ (1994), 'Introduction: Global Commodity Chains', in G. Gereffi and M. Korzeniewicz (eds), *Commodity Chains and Global Capitalism* (Westport, Conn.: Praeger), pp. 1–14.

GUHA, K. (1998), 'Booming Indian Software Sector is Facing a Challenge', *Financial Times*, 13 August, p. 13.

HANNA, N. (1994), 'Exploiting Information Technology for Development: A Case Study of India', Washington, World Bank Discussion Paper no. 246.

HEEKS, R. (1996), *India's Software Industry: State Policy, Liberalization and Industrial Development* (New Delhi: Sage).

HEREDIA, B. (1997), 'Prosper or Perish: Development in the Age of Global Capital', *Current History*, vol. 96, no. 613 (November), pp. 383–88.

HIRSCHMAN, A.O. (1958), *The Strategy of Economic Development* (New Haven: Yale University Press).

INTERNATIONAL MONETARY FUND (1997), *World Economic Outlook, May 1997* (Washington, IMF).

'India Not Yet Wired' (1997), 20 August, http://www.nb-pacifica.com/headline/indianotyetwired08201054.html

'Internet Domain Survey' (1998), January, http://www.nw.com/zone/WWW/report.html.
KOBRIN, S.J. (1998), 'Back to the Future: Neomedievalism and the Post-modern Digital World Economy', *Journal of International Affairs*, vol. 51. no. 2 (Spring), pp. 361–86.
KOBRIN, S.J. (1997), 'The Architecture of Globalization: State Sovereignty in a Networked Global Economy', in J.H. Dunning (ed.), *Governments, Globalization and International Business* (Oxford: Oxford University Press), pp. 146–71.
KRUGMAN, P. (1992), 'A Global Economy is not the Wave of the Future', *Financial Executive*, March–April, pp. 10–13.
LANDERS, J. (1995), 'Engineer Surplus in Bangalore Lures U.S. Firms to India's High Tech Capital', *Dallas Morning News*, 18 December.
MADON, S. (1997), 'Information-Based Global Economy and Socioeconomic Development: The Case of Bangalore', *The Information Society*, vol. 13, pp. 227–43.
McMICHAEL, P. (1996), *Development and Social Change: A Global Perspective* (Thousand Oaks, Cal.: Pine Forge Press).
NASSCOM (1997), *The Software Industry in India: 1997–98* (New Delhi: National Association of Software and Service Companies).
NASSCOM (1995), *The Software Industry in India: 1995* (New Delhi: National Association of Software and Service Companies).
NEGROPONTE, N. (1995), *Being Digital* (New York: Alfred A. Knopf).
NICHOLSON, M. (1998), 'Exports Grow Strongly: By Phone', *Financial Times*, 10 July, p. 7.
PRIMO, B.C. (1996), 'The Impact of the Internationalization of Services on Developing Countries', *Finance and Development*, vol. 33, no. 1, pp. 34–8.
VALIGRA, L. (1997), 'Intemet Fever Hits Asia', Telephony (Intemet Edge Supplement), October 6, pp. 30–35.
WILLIAMSON, J.G. (1996), 'Globalization, Convergence and History', The Journal of Economic History, 50, 2, pp. 277–306.
WORLD BANK (1996), Global *Economic Prospects and the Developing Countries* (Washington: International Bank for Reconstruction and Development).
WORLD BANK (1997), *World Development Report, 1997* (New York: Oxford University Press).
WORLD BANK (1980), *World Development Report, 1980* (New York: Oxford University Press).

7 Egypt at a Crossroads: MNEs and Economic Development in a Global Environment

Peter J. Buckley and Stephen Young

INTRODUCTION

A study of Egypt is appropriately included in this volume because it is genuinely at a crossroads, facing the same dilemmas as many of the transition economies around the world. Egypt is positioned at a strategic crossroads within the North African, Middle East and West Asian regions and has substantial opportunities to influence and to exploit the regional economic potential of the area. At the same time, the country is at a critical crossroads in its own economic strategy: thus it is seeking to switch from inward-oriented economic development to an outward-looking, export-oriented policy, in which multinational enterprises (MNEs) will inevitably have a focal role. But this is against the backdrop of fears of social and political unrest stemming from job losses associated with market reforms and privatization; and a lack of understanding of the potential benefits of foreign direct investment (FDI) and, indeed, fears of MNE domination. The aim of this chapter is to highlight the role which FDI and MNEs currently play in the Egyptian economy, and to discuss some ideas for policy reform which would *inter alia* create greater integration between Egypt, MNEs and the global and regional economies.

In 1914, Egypt was a totally open economy, with trade, finance and industry overwhelmingly concentrated in foreign – mainly French, British and Belgian – hands. In 1958, however, the open door closed, and in the following years all joint stock companies were nationalized and state control was extended throughout the economy. With the ending of the Nasser regime in 1973, a more liberal system of trade, investment and pricing was reintroduced and many restrictive legislative rules were abandoned. State ownership is still overwhelming, nevertheless, and the legacy of state intervention in terms of institutional rigidity, centralization and public-sector domination has remained.

Following the adoption of Sadat's open-door policies, Egypt achieved rapid economic growth in the period up to 1985 aided by significant increases in foreign assistance, workers' remittances and FDI. This period of growth ended in 1986, partly as a consequence of the decline in oil prices and partly due to the maintenance of an inward-oriented growth strategy. Severe macroeconomic imbalances developed subsequently, causing unemployment and increased poverty. After this period of stagnation, the immediate goal set by the new government in 1991 was to achieve rapid private-sector-led outward-oriented economic growth. It introduced and implemented successfully the Economic Reform and Structural Adjustment Programme (ERSAP I) with the support of the IMF and the World Bank. A further programme of structural reforms (ERSAP II) designed to reduce the public sector concentration of the Egyptian economy and to foster growth was introduced in 1996.

Policy objectives identified by these reform programmes were as follows:

- Maintain a stable macro-economic environment and increase the rate of economic growth. Improved macro-economic stability has been achieved by ensuring fiscal and monetary discipline and by strengthening monetary policy tools. However, GDP per capita remains low because of population growth, and the Government of Egypt has set a target of over 7 per cent GDP growth by the year 2000. This objective is believed to be attainable, despite the risks associated with it, but structural reforms are essential.
- Open the economy. The government has recognized the need to remove obstacles to trade, promote exports and develop new export markets to invigorate the outward-oriented growth strategy. However, the process of trade liberalization needs to be deepened and accelerated. Necessary reforms include actions to improve trade transportation, to simplify customs procedures, and to improve national quality control systems and standards. Actions to forge buyer–seller links and to foster an export mentality are also important.
- Privatize and enhance competitiveness. Privatization has been identified as one of the main elements of the economic reform programme. At the macro-level, privatization provides substantially

increased government resources and reduces the government's financing requirements. At the micro-level, it improves the performance of enterprises both directly and indirectly. Privatization also improves the business climate by sending a signal of confidence to both domestic and foreign investors.

- Create a business-friendly environment through establishing a comprehensive and transparent set of business regulations, including the judicial, legislative and regulatory environment for investment.
- Develop capital markets. The government has identified the need to increase competition in the financial sector and to strengthen financial market institutions and the Capital Market Authority.
- Enhancing government support for the market economy, where needs have been identified in a wide range of areas including: improvement and development of infrastructure; human resource development; and improvements in the legal system, in the commercial judicial system, and in tax administration.

This list represents a formidable range of challenges for Egyptian policy-makers, and progress to date has been mixed. At the macro-level, Egypt's performance has been impressive, whereas the extent of privatization has been limited (recognizing that it only began in 1996) and bureaucratic obstacles remain strong. Included within the list of policy objectives is the attraction of FDI which is viewed as important in increasing the level of private capital inflows in total domestic capital formation, in providing technology and improving management and marketing techniques, and in increasing and diversifying manufacturing exports.

EGYPT'S FOREIGN DIRECT INVESTMENT POSITION

With a population of 60 million, stable macro-economic conditions and a wide industrial base, Egypt has considerable potential as a location for FDI. Yet during the 1990s when the developing world as a whole was attracting much higher inflows, FDI into Egypt lacked a significant upward momentum (see Table 7.1). Historically, the bulk of FDI has been in extractive industries, particularly energy, with relatively few instances of downstream processing. Data for 1996/97 on approved projects show a shift to manufacturing which represented 45 per cent of total value, although much of this is likely to represent

Table 7.1 World foreign direct investment inflows in Egypt and other developing economies, 1990–96 (US$ billions)

Rank/Country	*Average 1990–96*	*1996*
More than 10 billion		
1. China	22.6	42.3
More than 5 billion		
2. Brazil	3.2	9.5
3. Singapore	5.6	9.4
4. Indonesia	2.9	7.9
5. Mexico	5.9	7.5
6. Malaysia	4.3	5.3
More than 3 billion		
7. Argentina	2.3	4.2
8. Peru	1.3	3.5
9. Chile	1.3	3.1
10. Colombia	1.4	3.0
More than 1 billion		
11. India	1.0	2.6
12. Hong Kong	1.8	2.5
13. Thailand	1.8	2.5
14. Korea, Republic of	1.2	2.3
15. Vietnam	0.8	2.1
17. Nigeria	1.2	1.7
18. Philippines	1.0	1.4
19. Taiwan, Province of China	1.2	1.4
20. Venezuela	0.9	1.3
More than 0.5 billion		
21. Egypt	0.6	0.7
22. Pakistan	0.4	0.6
Total developing countries	73.4	128.7

Source: UNCTAD, 1999.

assembly or packaging for the domestic market; followed by tourism (27 per cent); services, including petroleum (18 per cent); and finance (8 per cent).

The US has the largest share of FDI stock in Egypt, with the UK, Germany and Italy having significant, albeit much smaller, shares. Middle Eastern investors are very prominent, especially in construction. Most FDI has taken the form of joint ventures, the level of foreign equity participation in all projects approved up to 1997 being about 30 per cent. Recent statistics suggest that both domestic and foreign investors have responded very positively to improvements in economic performance and in the business climate, with investment projects approved for 1995/96 and 1996/97 being larger in number than total approvals for the previous two decades. The investment potential, therefore, appears very favourable.

As indicated above, much FDI is domestic market-oriented reflecting the legacy of import substitution strategies at country level. Because of this, Egypt's exports reveal a dependence on agricultural commodities, minerals and metals, with a relatively low representation of manufactured exports. Among FDI sectors, only the chemical industry is a significant exporter. The patterns and performance of FDI in Egypt thus reflect history, economic strategy and, until recently, relatively low business attractiveness. In the context of this volume, Egypt has been a bystander on the world stage, as globalization pressures have led to increasing integration of both companies and countries elsewhere in the world.

ANALYZING EGYPT'S ATTRACTIVENESS FOR FDI

Conceptual Framework

A starting point for assessing Egypt's attractiveness for FDI is an analysis of the strategies of MNEs. On the basis of a comparison of Egypt's attributes with the determinants of FDI, it could be possible to find appropriate niches which Egypt may exploit. Only a limited amount of conceptual work has been undertaken to identify the links between MNEs' strategies and export-oriented development in host nations. Following Casson (1986), who draws on Vernon (1966, 1979) and Wells (1983), five separate structures of industry, trade and FDI can usefully be identified, namely, new product manufacturing industry; maturing product manufacturing industry; rationalized product manufacturing industry; resource-based industry; and trading services industry.

It is unlikely at this stage that Egypt can find a niche in new product manufacturing industries (Type 1) where production and consumption takes place in the advanced, high-income economies. Trade and the world market is confined to developed countries and is supplied by exports from the innovating source country.

In maturing product manufacturing industries (Type 2), production costs fall and the mass market increases. Technology is more easily codified and can be transferred internationally to foreign affiliates. Import-substituting production begins in other countries and exports of finished products from the source country declines. However, MNEs begin the outward FDI process and export specialized capital equipment to foreign affiliates which may be complemented by exports of key components. Markets may be serviced from foreign affiliates which are closer to these markets than is the parent country, and so 'regional product mandates' may be conferred on particular subsidiaries. There may be possibilities for Egypt to develop a niche in these industries, but the crucial issue is that of moving beyond import substitution into exporting.

Within rationalized product industries (Type 3), MNEs exploit the economies available from redesigning the product for assembly from standardized and versatile components. These components are designed to be transported at low cost. The location of production of each component is specialized, in order to exploit both increasing returns and differences in comparative advantage between locations. Individual affiliates may be mandated to product particular 'components', with MNE divisions in less-developed countries producing labour-intensive components and undertaking assembly (and possibly distribution activities). There would appear to be significant opportunities for Egypt in rationalized product industries: outward processing activities in textiles are a primary example; other industries include jewellery manufacturing.

In resource-based industries (Type 4), the major source countries for raw materials produce output which moves through a vertical sequence of extraction, purification, refining or processing and then fabrication or compounding. At some stage, this intermediate product is exported. Tourism, whose primary activity is locationally fixed, can be analysed as a resource-based industry.

Finally, trade in services (Type 5 industries) is a growing part of the global economy and Egypt has opportunities here. Suez Canal fees provide service income, and financial services is one area of services among many which are capable of MNE involvement to a far greater extent than currently achieved levels. In seeking niches in export-oriented industries, one consequence is much greater competition from other potential locations around the Mediterranean. For domestic-market-oriented FDI, internal market size and growth is the major investment determinant (Guisinger, 1985).

Opportunities and Illustrations

Table 7.2 translates the discussion above into specific opportunities for attracting FDI to Egypt. The evidence available (see Box 7.1 on Glaxo Egypt) suggests that MNEs in Type 2 industries will only evolve into exporting over time. An interview with the Swiss MNE Nestlé confirmed this view, commenting that MNEs 'should not set up a manufacturing operation with an export orientation initially because it is too risky'. Opportunities also seem to exist for labour-intensive, export-oriented FDI (Type 3 industries), associated with low labour costs and Free Zone incentives. In Egypt, most Free Zone investment to date has been in the textile sector, with only a limited presence in electronics (semiconductor assembly); the latter is particularly important because it represents an access point into the fastest growing industry in the world.

The framework presented above perhaps gives insufficient attention to the role which Egyptian partners may have in FDI attraction, and the issue of partnerships is important in the final two opportunity sectors shown in Table 7.2 (see also Boxes 7.2 and 7.3). There is substantial potential for tourism projects in Egypt and Box 7.2 presents the case of Accor Hotels S.A.E. which is a joint-venture involving the French Accor Group. Despite the joint venture relationship, the continued involvement of the foreign partner is crucial in terms of brand name, ensuring quality of service and quality of physical infrastructure. It should be noted that joint ventures are less common in the international hotel industry than management contracts, where the foreign partner provides the management expertise and quality assurance. Software development is a further potential source of FDI: the large number of university graduates in Egypt, along with the fact that all the main international computer software companies are already active in the country, suggest a very positive outlook for this sector.

A final category concerns the potentially important area of partnerships. While a number of Egyptian private sector enterprises have developed a strong competitive position based upon dominance of the domestic market, their future expansion requires the technological upgrading of processes and products, and eventually support for their own internationalization. Partnership arrangements with overseas-owned MNEs offer opportunities for mutual benefit: Box 7.3 presents the example of the Ezz Group which took the initiative in establishing a joint venture with the Italian corporation Danieli; while Box 7.4

Table 7.2 Opportunities for FDI in Egypt

Domestic market-oriented manufacturing FDI	*Labour-intensive export-oriented FDI*	*Resource-based and services FDI*	*Partnerships*
Key FDI determinants:			
• Domestic market size and growth • Import barriers	• International market size and growth • Access to regional and global markets	• Domestic market size and growth • Access to regional markets	• Resources and know-how of domestic enterprises
• Consumer preferences • Incentives	• Labour and other costs • Export transaction costs • Free Zone incentives	• Natural and human resources • Physical infrastructure	• Domestic market size and growth • Foreign enterprises' international networks
Examples:			
Pharmaceuticals, food, automobiles, consumer electronics	Clothing, leather, PCB assembly, construction materials	Hotels, tour operators, software development, financial services	Metals, software development, food and confectionery, pharmaceuticals

Source: Adapted from UNCTAD, 1999.

Box 7.1
Glaxo Egypt S.A.E.

- The British pharmaceutical MNE Glaxo Wellcome exported to Egypt via agents from 1928 until the industry was nationalized in the 1950s. The US MNE Squibb re-entered the market in 1980 with Sadat's Open Door Policy, but it was not until 1990 that Glaxo acquired a minority shareholding in a local pharmaceutical company; the Glaxo equity stake has subsequently been increased to 90 per cent through capital investment and is valued at £140 million. The significant investment in Egypt reflects the Glaxo view that entry into an emerging market is a long-term commitment and needs substantial support to overcome problems of infrastructure, distribution and suppliers.
- Glaxo's early years in Egypt involved substantial restructuring as well as investment. The employment in the company at entry was 741, but the public sector, 'jobs for life' culture proved highly problematic. Thus, although employment has subsequently been increased to 1000, 380 workers have been made redundant and 700 hired. A large scale programme to retrain and reorient existing workers and to enable them to assimilate the technology was instituted, with a major shift of emphasis from assembly to other operations. Both manufacturing facilities and the distribution system have been totally rebuilt.
- Development of the Glaxo Egypt operation has had three major components. First, efforts to achieve a total quality management system. Second, the company established a development laboratory in 1995 with the principal objective of developing products off-patent. Four people are presently involved in development and 40 in quality assurance and control. Third, the company has taken its initial steps into exporting and is the first pharmaceutical MNE in Egypt to market outside the country. Approval has been given to supply Qatar, Yemen and Nigeria. There are hopes that Glaxo Egypt will be granted the regional mandate to become one of two supply sources for Glaxo Wellcome for the Middle East and African market. However, while Egypt is the largest supply source in the region, the company also has facilities in South Africa, Kenya and Saudi Arabia. No decisions have yet been taken on any reallocation of market and product franchises to individual countries; and the operations are strongly country-centred at present. In the short term, exports from Egypt will focus on markets which are small or fragmented, where the maintenance of one manual production line in the factory facilitates short production runs. Some bureaucratic obstacles have been faced in export procedures.
- Glaxo is still in the early stages of a large development programme in Egypt, and its strategic plan envisages continual upgrading of existing facilities and capacity expansion. The labour force in Egypt

Continued

is regarded as loyal, inexpensive and productive and there is a ready source of graduates – for example, all 350 Glaxo reps are pharmacy graduates. Problem issues for the company and the pharmaceutical industry as a whole concern rigid government pricing policies; patent protection which relates only to the process; and weak laws on intellectual property.

Source: Adapted from UNCTAD, 1999.

Box 7.2
Accor Hotels S.A.E.

- In 1992, Accor Group of France took over the Wagon-Lit Group and its business in Egypt. Established in August 1980 under Investment Law number 43, 1974, and known as Compagnie Internationale Des Wagons-Lits et Tourism – Egypt, its business in Egypt was comprised of management contracts for a number of hotels and the onboard catering and sleeper-car services provided for the Egyptian railway network. To develop and expand its operations in Egypt, the Accor Group invited collaboration and active investment from the Egyptian private sector. The El Maghraby Group joined forces with Accor and in July 1994 Accor Hotels S.A.E. was launched as a joint-stock venture specialized in the field of hotels management and tourist development.
- The company currently has capital employed of US$ 9 million. The tourist group manages 22 hotels, owns 3 hotels and is part shareholder in 4 hotels under construction. They have a 300-bed medical (mainly optical) hotel and a chain of opticians.
- The company employs 4755 employees and their sales have reached a value of US$ 74 million, which was expected to increase to US$ 86 million in 1998. They have also allocated substantial investments reaching LE 90 million to a number of projects including building a 120-room extension to the existing Winter Palace Hotel in Luxor and to renovating the Sofitel Old Winter Palace Hotel and its gardens. They also plan to build a 152-room extension to the Novotel Sharm El Sheikh Hotel and to renovate the Novotel Dahab Hotel and other projects.
- In October 1997 Accor Group of France and Accor Hotels S.A.E. signed a Master Franchise Agreement for a further 30 years, extending Accor Hotels S.A.E.'s entitlement to operate all the hotel management brand names owned by Accor Group of France: these are Sofitel, Novotel – Ibis and Mercure. It also entitles them to the establishment of a joint investment fund between the two groups and other international and Egyptian private-sector investors. The input from the French partner is largely in the form of hotel

executive human resources training, as well as access to the brand names.

- The management believes that FDI flows into Egypt are likely to grow significantly over the coming five years from a tourism perspective. The key issue is the quality of services and this depends upon the quality of training of the service personnel. It is believed that the way forward is to develop two-centre holidays with cultural tourism mixed with resort tourism, to develop resort areas, and encourage business travel with conference business and golfing holidays.

Source: Adapted from UNCTAD, 1999.

Box 7.3
The Ezz Group

- The Ezz Group has been the leading private Egyptian company in the iron and steel sector for the last two generations and is probably the largest private steel producer in the Arab world. The company's primary activity of steel rolling is complemented by commerce and transport, and by ceramic tile production. The latter together with the company's new steel-rolling plant are located in Sadat City, 100 km away from Cairo.
- The company started in the 1920s and operated as a supply, contracting and shipping enterprise until the 1980s. With strong import and export links to Eastern Europe, at one time the Ezz Group shipped around 1 million tons of steel locally and internationally on an annual basis. This business stagnated but was reactivated with the establishment of a steel-rolling mill in Ramadan City in 1991, and a further facility in Sadat City in 1996. Employment in the sector now totals 1300 people.
- The first ceramic tile line went into production in the late 1980s and rapid expansion led to a growth in production capacity from 1–12.5 million square metres over a six-year period; employment expanded from 100 to 1200 in the same period.
- The Ezz Group has a commitment both to the use of state-of-the-art technology and to best business practices. The company has been reorganized twice using Arthur Andersen and Booz-Allen consultancy firms. There is also a strong commitment to training: 200 personnel are fully funded for two-year training programmes; the company has established its own training institute in collaboration with an overseas university; and 13 people are on full-time sabbaticals studying MBAs in the USA and Europe.
- An interesting recent feature of the group's expansion has been the establishment of a joint venture with the Italian company Danieli.

Continued

The two private enterprises had worked together over a ten-year period on three projects involving technology and equipment importation from Italy. Through this collaboration, both firms were able to understand each other: for Danielli, it meant an understanding of the quality of Ezz Group personnel and of the ethics of the company, as well as knowledge of the Egyptian environment. The joint venture involved a steel project which was too large and technologically sophisticated for Ezz to handle on its own. It is regarded as the first of a series of such ventures to assist the technological upgrading of the Ezz Group and its expansion both in Egypt and overseas.

Source: Adapted from UNCTAD, 1999.

Box 7.4
R.P. Scherer Egypt

- R.P. Scherer is an American pharmaceutical company which has a dominant share of the world soft gels production. Scherer had a long export relationship with Egypt which ended when the Socialist period prevented importation, but began again in the early 1970s. The current company is a joint venture with 10 per cent US ownership and 90 per cent Egyptian ownership (this changed from 40 per cent/60 per cent). Scherer has 12 factories worldwide and its Egyptian partner, Pharco, has other pharmaceutical interests, notably in anti-tropical disease drugs.
- Scherer's contribution was to bring in the technology, brand names and training methods. Many of the employees have been seconded for training to the UK and French plants of Scherer for 3 months and Scherer personnel have visited Egypt for training purposes. The sophisticated machinery employed produces very low reject rates and the plant currently operates 7 days per week, 24 hours per day. The Egyptian plant exports 15 per cent of its output to some 35 markets. The major export market is Romania (where there are 25 sales representatives) with Yemen, Saudi Arabia and Uruguay featuring strongly.
- The Egyptian parent, Pharco, aims largely to satisfy the domestic market and part of its mission is to specialize in tropical diseases such as bilharzia. The future investment plans of the Egyptian company include an entry into biotechnology – some work has begun and the company hopes to begin patenting. Expansion of the company is greatly facilitated by workers and middle managers remaining loyal to the company and 'growing up with it'. Staff turnover is not a problem and recruitment can go forward on this firm base.

- Managers within the company see Egypt as having a comparative advantage 'if a good foreign partner can be found who can run the company to international standards'. Major assets include the price of land, manpower and electricity. Running costs are thus low and these can be combined with machinery and raw materials 'whose price is the same all over the world'.
- This case illustrates inward technology transfer to an Egyptian plant given a *de facto* regional product mandate (Middle East, Africa and part of Eastern Europe). The domestically-oriented part of the company has the opportunity to expand, building from a strong and growing domestic market to develop export potential.

Source: Adapted from UNCTAD, 1999.

shows a different illustration from the pharmaceutical industry, where, unusually, the US partner reduced its stake in the Egyptian operation from 40 per cent to 10 per cent.

Egypt's Attractiveness

There have been numerous reports on Egypt's attractiveness as an investment location, particularly comparing it with Turkey, Israel, Morocco and Tunisia, which are assumed to be its major regional rivals. Such studies are very specific to a particular point in time and the (often subjective) rankings can change quickly. For example, the World Economic Forum's World Competitiveness Report for 1997, ranked Egypt 28 out of 53 countries. On the positive side, the country ranked highly in terms of the investment protection schemes that are available to investors, its geographic location, exchange stability and labour costs. Problems identified, however, concerned the size and efficiency of government, the country's openness to trade, a lack of management skills, an inflexible labour market and poor quality institutions supporting commercial activity. In an additional survey within the Global Competitiveness Report, international business executives were asked whether changes to government policies in a country had improved competitiveness in the preceding year; Egypt was ranked first in the 58 nations included.

UNCTAD's survey of business executives (UNCTAD, 1999) highlighted favourable expectations by foreign investors of potential market growth in Egypt. Factors linked to cost, availability, skills and productivity of labour and capital costs also received positive ratings. However, other business transaction costs were identified as disincentives to FDI. Considering Egypt's potential attractiveness over the next five years, factors believed to be important included a continuance of political stability, the availability of skilled labour at competitive wage rates, and the signing of trade agreements with the EU and the USA which would enhance opportunities to expand markets, particularly abroad.

Egypt's attractiveness to incoming FDI is damaged by the high level of transaction costs which were frequently referred to by company executives there. High levels of transaction costs inhibit effective supply-chain management when an Egyptian unit is part of the chain. This results from unreliability in delivery, quality and cost performance, as for example in some areas of textiles and in fabrication. Long lead times and a lack of flexibility (high adjustment costs) are also features of indigenous Egyptian operations. The business culture of Egypt can be extremely clannish and this tribal attitude to business operations can present serious obstacles to the foreign investor or to the principal firm in subcontracting or other contractual arrangements. Institutional and transport barriers compound these difficulties.

POLICY ANALYSIS AND RECOMMENDATIONS

It is apparent from the discussion above that multinationals could have a central role to play in integrating Egypt into the global economy and in supporting the country's export-oriented development efforts. Improving the attractiveness of the economy for FDI is, however, integrally bound up with the wider process of market reform and privatization, and the all-embracing nature of the required reform would seem to provide a daunting prospect for policy-makers. On the optimistic side, Egypt has many common characteristics with other emerging economies around the world, and the large MNEs, at least, have experience in operating in numerous such environments. Observations by MNE executives in Egypt interviewed as part of this project stress the necessity of strong financial support from parents when entering emerging markets; the danger of expecting too much too quickly; the lengthy time to achieve profitable business; and, overall, therefore, the requirement for a long-term commitment. But there are big opportunities in Egypt and committed MNEs have generated significantly profitable businesses.

For a policy perspective an emphasis on FDI and specifically MNEs has two advantages. First, it requires and encourages a holistic view of public policy because of the links to investment flows, trade, technological development and technology transfer, and managerial innovation. Second, it necessitates a focus on the corporation as a mechanism for achieving economic benefits in each of these areas. It should, therefore, be possible to use multinationals as a driver of reform in Egypt. Table 7.3 sets out an agenda for policy innovation in Egypt focusing upon FDI attraction. Policy reforms are required at different levels. At the international level are issues relating to support for organizations like the WTO, and adherence to the principles of international trade and investment rules. At the regional level, progress with the development of a free zone within the Middle East is important if MNE activity is to be encouraged: even more significant is the signing of the European–Mediterranean Partnership with the EU, which is designed to create a free trade area and build economic and financial cooperation among the 27 countries by the year 2010. This was under negotiation in mid-1998. Within Egypt itself, required policy reforms are identified at the macro, macro-organizational and micro levels.

The distinction is also made in Table 7.3 between policy areas, namely, legal, institutional, promotional and infrastructural issues. There is in fact a further overriding dimension which concerns attitudinal factors and bureaucratic behaviour: the mentality of state-ownership and control and suspicion of foreign multinationals will be a fundamental barrier to change. Such problems are recognized in the context of privatization in Egypt, where programmes have been undertaken to prepare the public and workforces for change; the slow pace of privatization to some extent reflects the need to overcome public resistance. In a similar vein, the World Bank (1997) has recommended actions to educate the public and create an 'export mentality'. To date, however, there have been no such programmes to educate the electorate and state officials on the merits of FDI: attitudes to MNEs are ambiguous at best. Welcoming attitudes could create a much greater tolerance of regulatory and institutional barriers at least in the short to medium term.

With such a wide agenda, there is a danger of trying to do too much too quickly and in the process, for example, introducing new laws which are unsatisfactory and create further uncertainties; or making legislative change without adequate consultation and with short timescales for its introduction; or failing to coordinate policy reforms across different government departments and between different objectives. The way ahead suggested here is, firstly, to focus on institutional reform, on the grounds that a strong body supporting FDI

Table 7.3 Policy reform for FDI attraction in Egypt

Policy level	Policy area			
	Legal	*Institutional*	*Promotional*	*Infra structural*
International	• Support for WTO and key principles of national treatment, MFN and non-discriminatory treatment		• Targeted international marketing by country, sector, company	
Regional	• European–Mediterranean Partnership agreement • Arab Free Trade Zone	• Collaboration with foreign investment agencies in EU • Accelerating technology transfer through cooperation with MNEs and international cooperation agreements	• Targeted regional marketing by country, sector, company	
National				
Macro	• Maintenance of stable economic environment • Opening the economy and promoting privatization			

Macro-organisational	• Competition policy • IPR laws and action against counterfeiters • Improvements in company law • Improvements in incentive systems, and evaluation of tax holidays	• Creation of attraction-oriented foreign investment agency, with general authority and/or general coordinating authority		• Education and training focusing on investor needs • Transport and communications; for example, ports road and rail, telecommunications • Science and technology – to enhance commercialization
Micro	• Improvements in judicial system and in litigation • Removal of key blockages; for example, company incorporation and registration, land allocation, building permits, and operating licences	• Support for investors to overcome bureaucracy and red-tape • Action-oriented MNE forum	• Marketing inside country to prospective investors • Use of existing successful MNEs in demonstration role • After-care services • Internal marketing – educating the public and policy-makers	

may be a driver for change in other areas; secondly, to prioritize reform measures linked to the targets for FDI attraction proposed earlier.

Institutional and Promotional Dimensions

A major problem for investors in Egypt historically has derived from the number of governmental authorities responsible for issuing certificates, licenses, authorizations and incentives, employing large numbers of employees and overlapping with other similar authorities. Procedures for establishing investment projects in Egypt have been extensive and time-consuming: in terms of time-cost, it can take up to three months for investment proposals to go through the approval and establishment phase in Egypt; other countries in the region take as little as a few days to grant approval, and at most six weeks.

A large number of regulatory agencies in Egypt have had an involvement in investment projects. The principal ones are the General Authority for Investment and the Free Zones (GAFI) and the General Organization for Industrialization (GOFI). In the past the activity of GOFI was mainly that of granting business licences, registering and monitoring industrial investment in Egypt. Approval and monitoring by GOFI was a cumbersome, time-consuming and inefficient procedure. At present, the mandate of GOFI is in the process or being reoriented towards identification of projects and opportunities, enhancing the Cupertino between technical institutes and industry. Until 1996, GAFI was a regulatory body reflecting the inward-looking industrial policy orientation of the country. Its size – GAFI has approximately 1400 employees with branch offices throughout Egypt – emanates from this regulatory role. Recently, attempts have been made to reform GAFI into a facilitating and promoting body for FDI rather than a regulating and controlling one as in the past.

Investment Law Number 8 of 1997 is the key legal instrument governing investment, enacted to replace a plethora of earlier rules. For companies registered under Law Number 8, the official view is that there is no approval process *per se* for foreign direct investment, with only notification being required; tax exemptions are provided automatically; inputs can be imported without registration; capital inflows and profit remittances are not monitored; and permission for new projects is no longer required. Similarly, the previous vetting and authorization process no longer exists for expansion of existing projects, increases in capital, changes in product mix or the start-up of a new production line. The role of the GAFI Board of Directors is to discuss policy.

The reality of this apparent openness is untested. And despite the redefinition and restatement of GAFI's role, Egypt's Civil Service Reform Secretariat is working on plans for a new body and structure which could involve investment service offices ('one-stop-shops') at the regional level. These would be staffed by project officers with responsibility for pre-establishment information and contacts, the facilitation of permits and clearances, and post-establishment information and contacts. Key blockages (including company incorporation and registration, land allocation, building permits and operating licences) have been identified, together with possible solutions.

Accepting that decisions have not yet been taken on institutional reform, Table 7.4 highlights the broad functions of a foreign direct investment agency as operated in other parts of the world (Young and Hood, 1994; Young, Hood and Wilson, 1994); and shows the necessary changes in orientation and activity to move from a regulatory to an attraction orientation in Egypt in the new era of export-oriented development. Screening and approval procedures would basically be abandoned, with the core functions emphasising investment promotion and attraction, the granting of incentives (as an attraction mechanism) and after care services. The type of body necessary to undertake these new functions is fundamentally different to the GAFI it would replace in respect of the following characteristics:

Organization of Egyptian foreign direct investment policy

Organization	*Governmental*	*Quasi-governmental*
Size (number of professionals)	1400	50–100
Educational/professional background of employees	Administration, law, economics	Marketing, business administration
Previous experience of employees	Government sector	Private sector
Performance evaluation	Time-span for project approval	Effectiveness of marketing programmes; for example, number of enquiries, number of site visits, number of new projects, jobs created, level of financial assistance per job created, and so on

Table 7.4 Functions of foreign direct investment agency in Egypt

Key issues	*Regulatory orientation*	*Attraction orientation*
• Role of agency	– Central body, but extensive independent involvement of other ministries, organizations, etc.	– Central body, with general authority for FDI and/or general coordinating authority
• Policy formulation	– Strategies for regulation and control within inward-oriented development strategy	– Strategies for attraction within export-oriented development strategy
• Investment promotion and attraction	– Limited to some missions and exhibitions – No marketing inside the country	– Marketing information and intelligence – Marketing planning and targeting – Marketing and promotion programmes abroad – Marketing inside the country
• Investment screening and approval	– Ownership conditions – Sectoral conditions – Operational conditions	– None or limited to informal commitments on employment, foreign exchange, etc., linked to granting of incentives
• Incentives and assistance	– Extensive but regulatory orientation and bureaucratic implementation	– Extensive. Designed to attract investment
• After-care services	– None or limited to approval processes for new projects etc.	– Significant. Designed to encourage expansion projects and plant upgrading

To effectively fulfil the basic marketing and promotion function, the new body must have a strong private-sector orientation, that is the professional staff should be able to talk to MNE executives in terms they understand and appreciate. If not a private sector organization, therefore, the new agency should at least be quasi-governmental; namely, established outside the normal civil service rules and practices. With screening procedures removed, staffing levels would be substantially reduced. Similarly, the educational background and professional experience of the agency staff would be very different, as indicated above. Finally, performance measures would change from timescales for project approval (since no approval would be necessary) to the effectiveness of marketing programmes. To ensure that this organization is a driver for reform, it would need to be headed up by a senior director with access to and support at Cabinet level in the government.

A Phased Approach to Policy Reform

The policy agenda set out in Table 7.4 encompasses three broad areas, namely, the investment framework, private sector development and regional cooperation. Although the government has accepted the challenge to take actions in these areas, the timescales will inevitably be lengthy. There is a case, therefore, for short-term actions, such as those cited below, to try to make an immediate impact on Egypt's attractiveness for FDI.

- *Internal marketing.* Educating the public and policy-makers and changing the mindset of state bureaucrats is not a short-term task; and reorienting attitudes towards MNEs must be part of a wider programme of promoting the market economy and private sector development. Nevertheless, the task of retraining and reorientation is highly important and possible priority actions include the following:
  - A media campaign to explain the contribution of MNEs to economic development in Egypt. This should be encompassed within an informational and publicity framework supporting the private sector and export orientation more generally. Support may be available from some MNEs themselves which are portrayed as successful models.
  - Short, intensive training programmes for politicians and policy-makers – beginning at the highest level – to demonstrate the

economic benefits of MNE-led development. Case studies of successful MNEs in Egypt and successful policies in neighbouring competitive countries will prove valuable.

– Public seminars on the attraction of FDI and its economic contribution. These should be oriented towards positive aspects rather than impediments to FDI in Egypt, with contributions from Egyptian nationals and developing-country-focused organizations.

- *Investor support at the firm level.* Given the numbers still employed in the public sector, attitudinal change among mid- to low-level state officials is an enormous task. In the short to medium term, circumventing and overriding bureaucratic procedures is a necessary way ahead. In other work (World Bank, 1997) recommendations have been made for simplifying customs procedures, by, for example, establishing a 'green channel' for imports to allow exporters to import raw materials and capital goods. Issues of wider institutional reform for FDI attraction are discussed above, but even this is going to take time to implement. To reduce bureaucratic discretion and the costs of bureaucracy, early consideration might be given to the appointment of a cadre of executives (who will become employees of the proposed new FDI agency) with the authority to ensure fast-track approvals for MNEs at time of entry and establishment and for up to two years after start-up. Given the size of the problem, it is doubtful if each executive could be responsible for more than a few multinationals on a continuing basis; it would be sensible if they were based in the company premises. There would have to be some restrictions on the nature and size of investment for which his support would be available.
- *International marketing.* Research has shown that developing countries of the Mediterranean basin tended not to be included in prospective investors' lists of possible investment sites because they were considered to be too risky; and that in terms of business climate rating Egypt was at the lower end of countries in the region. Along with other actions to improve the business climate, 'image-building activity' (Wells and Wint, 1990), designed to improve the image of Egypt as a place to invest is clearly necessary. Probably the bulk of international marketing expenditures should be focused on image building given the negative perceptions, especially in the West, of the Arab world as a whole. Suc-

cessful foreign investors can have a very positive demonstration effect in this regard; conversely action is necessary to reduce the perceived harassment which tourists receive from street vendors in Egypt, since tourist attitudes work through to business attitudes. However, some initiatives should also be launched in 'investment-generating and targeting activity'. Because of their lengthy international experience and ability to take the long view, there is a significant group of MNEs which would tend to have an FDI presence in most countries of any size. This group is an obvious first target for marketing activity. Related activity could entail targeting those large MNEs with a presence in neighbouring countries but not in Egypt: the intention would be to encourage the corporations to set up in Egypt with a product line not yet manufactured in the region. Thereafter there is scope for well-planned initiatives in targeting sectors and companies as discussed previously. Part of this international marketing should entail marketing Egypt to Arab investors as a location for manufacturing or service investment as opposed to investment in real estate.

- *Liberalization measures.* Within a planned programme of reform for the longer term, there is a case for undertaking a series of bold, high-profile (even if limited in scope) liberalization measures which are well publicized internally and externally. This recognizes the need to take action in respect of liberalization but also the problems of poorly drafted legislation. Liberalization measures which may be targets for action include: clarification of land ownership rights; elimination of apparent discrimination in favour of domestic and Arab investors over non-Arab investors; improvements in the judicial system and in litigation, to eliminate the situation whereby companies include arbitration clauses in contracts but then find that, for example, traffic offences are covered by Egyptian law; and the creation of an action-oriented MNE forum which guarantees foreign investors direct access to a senior politician.

CONCLUSIONS

This volume has shown very different experiences among developing countries in respect of their interactions with MNEs and the global economy. The pace of market reform and economic liberalization in Egypt has been much slower than in the other countries studied. Yet the requirement for integration into the world economic system is extremely pressing given the low levels of income per head in the country and rapid population growth. At the micro-level, the economy requires the capital investment, the stimuli to managerial efficiency and worker productivity, the technology transfer and the trade links to the regional and global economies which MNEs can bring. And although the policy agenda to achieve these economic benefits is an extensive one, even modest reforms along the lines outlined earlier could enable the country to attract substantially higher inflows of FDI. This optimistic scenario, of course, assumes political stability within the Middle East and internal security within Egypt.

There is also a need to overcome the legacy of suspicion of foreigners and fears of MNE domination and exploitation, and the tradition of a highly-centralized and authoritarian state which work through into high transaction costs for business. But both issues are integrally bound up with market reform, privatization and FDI liberalization. The crucial question concerns the relative merits of a 'gradualist' versus 'big bang' approach to reform. Egypt has chosen the former route. This recognizes the social and political problems of large-scale redundancies in a country which lacks a proper social security system, and where unemployment and poverty can be exploited by Islamic radicals.

The case of GAFI provides an illustrative microcosm of the Egyptian economy as a whole. The World Bank (1997) recommended privatizing the entire FDI business by giving it to a small group of experienced sales professionals who worked to specific and agreed targets. And the chairman of the General Authority for Investment has stated that 'if I were to start up this office, I would need about 50 or 60 people to run it efficiently. But I have 1400' (*Financial Times*, 12 May, 1998). A ' big-bang' approach is probably not realistic for GAFI, nor is it for the economy as a whole. Nevertheless, ways have to be found to improve the efficiency of the inward investment attraction effort (and economic efficiency for the country as a whole) within a framework of gradualism. At the moment, at least, the globalization of MNE activity has scarcely impacted upon economic development in Egypt.

References

CASSON, M. (1986), *Multinationals and World Trade* (London: George Allen & Unwin).

GUISINGER, S.E. and ASSOCIATES (1985), *Investment Incentives and Performance Requirements* (New York: Praeger).

UNCTAD (1999), *Investment Policy Review of Egypt* (Geneva: UNCTAD).

VERNON, R. (1979), 'The Product Cycle Hypothesis in a New International Environment', *Oxford Bulletin of Economics and Statistics*, vol. 41, pp. 255–67.

VERNON, R. (1966), 'International Investment and International Trade in the Product Cycle', *Quarterly Journal of Economics*, vol. 80, pp. 190–207.

WELLS, L.T. Jr. (1983), *Third World Multinationals: Rise of Foreign Investment from Developing Countries* (Cambridge, Mass.: MIT Press).

WELLS, L.T. Jr. and A.G. WINT (1990), *Marketing a Country. Promotion as a Tool for Attracting Foreign Investment* (Washington DC: World Bank).

WORLD BANK (1997), *Egypt: Issues in Sustaining Economic Growth*, 4 vols, 15 March, Washington DC.

YOUNG, S. and N. HOOD (1994), 'Designing Developmental After-care Programmes for Foreign Direct Investment in the European Union', *Transnational Corporations*, vol. 3, no. 2, pp. 45–72.

YOUNG, S., N. HOOD, and A. WILSON (1994), 'Targeting Policy as a Competitive Strategy for European Inward Investment Agencies', *European Urban and Regional Studies*, vol. 1, no. 2, pp. 143–59.

8 MNEs, Globalization and Economic Development: The Case of Argentina in the 1990s

Daniel Chudnovsky[1]

INTRODUCTION

Foreign direct investment (FDI) is generally regarded as a driving force for integrating developing countries into the globalization process that characterizes the world economy, and the capacity to attract growing FDI inflows is often taken as a key indicator of success in their development record.

In this connection, Argentina is a very good case. The country has re-emerged as a leading recipient of FDI flows among the relatively few developing countries in Latin America and Asia that attract such investments. From about US$650m on average in 1984–89, annual FDI inflows to Argentina reached $2.1bn in 1990–91, $3.3bn in 1992–93, $4.3bn in 1994–96 and in 1997 a record of $6.3bn was registered.[2] The latter represents 2 per cent of GDP. Between 1990–93 most FDI inflows were channelled into the privatization of State enterprises, but since 1994 manufacturing, oil, mining and some services like supermarkets and especially banks have attracted significant investment. The fact that FDI has continued flowing into the country beyond the privatization of the state enterprises and despite the deep recession of 1995 does not support the idea of lumpy FDI flows as suggested in UNCTAD (1996).

It is tempting to see the phenomenal growth in FDI as a positive response to the structural reforms undertaken since 1990 and to the creation of Mercosur in 1995. Unilateral trade liberalization jointly with subregional integration, privatization of state enterprises and further liberalization of FDI regulations may be seen as the main forces behind the FDI boom. In turn, the growing volume of FDI may be taken as a vital contribution to the development process in Argentina. This is indeed the interpretation of the mainstream in the economic profession. However, the contribution of FDI to the economic development of the host country depends not only on its volume but also on its 'quality' and on the conditions under which it operates. The type of investment, the kind of assets brought by the multinational enterprises (MNEs) and the access to their international networks, as well as the locational advantages and the present and past policies implemented by the host country, are most important determinants (Chudnovsky, 1993).

It is useful to classify FDI into four main types: resource-seeking, market-seeking, efficiency-seeking and strategic asset-seeking. The taxonomy proposed by Dunning is certainly useful to distinguish the main motivation of a foreign investor, though the different motivations are often combined.

Whereas resource and market seeking investments are generally made by standalone subsidiaries, efficiency-seeking (or rationalized) FDI allows the subsidiary to participate in the MNE system through simple integration strategies (for example, as supplier of components for the parent company or other affiliates). More complex integration strategies in which various functional activities, such as production, research and development and training, are located wherever they can be done best to fulfil the MNE overall strategy usually require strategic asset-seeking investments (United Nations, 1993).

As a host country Argentina has important locational advantages that have attracted both resource and internal market-seeking FDI since the beginning of the century. It is a resource-rich developing country with a significant domestic market, fairly high wages and a large base of skills. Despite its long history of macroeconomic and political instability, the country received substantial FDI inflows, especially during the phase of the import substitution industrialization (ISI) process which lasted from the late 1950s to the late 1970s. In the stagnant and highly inflationary economy of the 1980s, with sharply reduced domestic investments in human and physical capital, FDI inflows became less significant and more erratic. Whereas in the ISI period, MNEs mainly did business in Argentina through market-seeking investments by standalone subsidiaries operating in heavily protected markets, some efficiency-seeking investments were made to be able to cope with the trade liberalization experience that took place in 1978–81 and later with the difficult macroeconomic conditions of the past decade.

With the implementation of the structural reforms in the 1990s, and especially with the emergence of Mercosur as a customs union, the received eclectic FDI theory would predict that efficiency and eventually strategic asset-seeking investments would become increasingly important as time passes, as structural reforms are consolidated and as foreign affiliates become part of regional or global networks of activities. As regards its impact, it would predict that

> in the right circumstances, efficiency-seeking FDI can assist host countries to restructure their economic activities more in line with their dynamic comparative advantages, reduce the costs of structural adjustment; and foster more demanding purchasing standards by firms and consumers. Strategic asset-seeking investment may help integrate the competitive advantages of the acquired firm with those of the acquiring firm and increase competition between domestic firms.
>
> (Dunning, 1994, p. 38)

However, efficiency-seeking or strategic asset-seeking investments are not necessarily made with the purpose of integrating the subsidiary more into the MNE system as suggested by Dunning. Rationalized investments may also be made by standalone foreign firms in response to greater competition or other pressures. The market share of the acquired firm may constitute the main reason for a strategic asset-seeking investment by the MNE, and the acquired firm may become a standalone subsidiary.

In order to discuss the FDI impact in Argentina, it is important to bear in mind some key policy aspects. Price stabilization was achieved through a currency board scheme which pegged the Argentine peso to the US dollar (the so called Convertibility Plan) from April 1991. Structural reforms were carried out in a quick and generalized way[3] completely opening the trade and capital accounts, liberalizing the financial system and privatizing most state-owned firms. At the same time, Argentina has one of the most liberal FDI regimes in the world.[4] None-the-less, some specific policies have been implemented in automobiles and autoparts, where trade has not been fully liberalized, and some sectoral regulations are in force in privatized natural monopolies for example telecommunications and energy.

Whereas price inflation has been practically non-existent since 1994, the GDP grew more than 6 per cent per year in 1990–97, and

GDP per capita is now US$9000. However, the growth process has been very unequal: income distribution has worsened and unemployment reached record levels in 1995–96 (18 per cent) before being slowly reduced to 14 per cent in 1997. Imports have grown in a significant manner since 1991 while exports started to increase in 1994, reaching record levels in 1996 and 1997. As result of the growth in trade flows, Argentina is a much more open economy than in the past, though imports and exports respectively accounted for 9.4 and 7.8 per cent of the GDP in 1997. The availability of foreign savings made it possible to finance the higher trade and current account deficits. In this connection portfolio foreign investment has grown even more than FDI and was estimated in the balance of payments figures to be around 3.4 per cent of the GDP in 1997.

Taking into account these considerations, the objective of the present chapter is to shed light on the basic features, main motives and the microeconomic impact of recent FDI in Argentina by addressing the following issues:

1. Which are the activities attracting most FDI inflows; which is the country of origin of the main investors and how important are foreign firms in production and trade?
2. How important is Mercosur as a factor of attraction? Is FDI internal market-seeking and/or export-promoting?
3. Have trade liberalization, deregulation and entry of newcomers, combined with performance requirements in the regulated sectors, led to greater efficiency? To what extent has FDI contributed to this development? Has FDI also led to the enhancement of local capabilities and to beneficial spillovers?

In addition to the author's studies on the effects of trade liberalization upon business strategies in the Argentine manufacturing sector (Chudnovsky *et al.*, 1996) and secondary sources, the main information for the analysis comes from the responses collected in two surveys of 50 and 31 leading foreign enterprises[5] carried out in 1993–94 and in 1996–97, respectively. The results of the first are analysed in Chudnovsky *et al.* (1997) – and reproduced when required here – and those of the second are examined in Porta (1997).

The following sections briefly examine the relevant information on each issue. Thereafter the overall contribution of recent FDI to Argentine economic development and some policy implications are discussed in the final section.

DESTINATION, ORIGIN, CHARACTERISTICS AND MOTIVATION

Main Overall Features

As shown in Table 8.1, without taking into account the investments made after privatization by the new owners, the share of FDI into privatized enterprises relative to total flows was 47 per cent in 1992–93. On the basis of our own estimates it was over 60 per cent in 1990–93. Later on its importance is reduced, to some 12 per cent in 1994–97. Besides privatization, FDI through takeovers have become increasingly important since 1994; this form of FDI accounted for 38 per cent of total FDI flows in 1994–97. Whereas profit reinvestment does not show a clear trend, FDI as such became important from 1994 and has a similar share in total flows as does takeovers in 1994–97. The share of greenfield investment has also been growing: from 10.3 per cent in 1990–96 to 45.4 per cent in 1997–2000 according to other official estimates (CEP, 1997a).

As regards sectoral focus, electricity, gas, water and telecommunications, namely the sectors in which the bulk of the privatization process was concentrated, attracted the largest FDI inflows in 1992 and 1993. No official information is available for 1990 and 1991. FDI in manufacturing industry increased its share in total flows from 19 per cent in 1992–93 to 40 per cent in 1994–96. Food processing, chemicals and petrochemicals (where an important privatization took place in 1995) and transport equipment accounted for the majority of the flows into manufacturing industry. In addition to important inward investment in oil,[6] mining has attracted growing FDI flows in 1995 and 1996. FDI in banking and commerce (mostly supermarkets) has also increased its importance in recent years. In 1997 there were significant takeovers of domestic banks by foreign investors.

Whereas in 1990–93, FDI inflows were largely policy-driven, namely in activities in which specific investment incentives were in place such as privatized services and automobiles, this has not been the case since 1994. Most recent FDI flows can be characterized as spontaneous. They have been channelled into both manufacturing activities and services whose internal demand has been dynamic and in which oligopolistic competition through branded goods and services is the rule of the game.

As shown in Table 8.1, the United States has been the leading foreign investor followed by Spain. Chile became a very important

Table 8.1 FDI inflows to Argentina

Year	*1992*	*1993*	*92/93*	*1994*	*1995*	*1996*	*1997*	*1994/96*
Total (US$ millon)	4014	2515	3265	3116	4783	5090	6327	4330
By type (in%)								
Profits reinvestment	20.3	34.6	27.4	26.9	12.7	11.1	12.5	16.9
Investment	11.8	25.0	18.4	41.3	34.5	32.8	33.3	36.2
Take overs	9.6	4.0	6.8	27.9	30.4	47.5	42.3	35.2
Privatizations	58.3	36.4	47.4	3.9	22.4	8.6	11.9	11.6
By main sector (in %)								
Oil	25.2	9.5	17.4	14.0	6.6	13.8	n.a.	11.4
Mining	0.0	–0.2	–0.1	0.5	2.9	6.1	n.a.	3.2
Manufacturing industry	10.9	26.9	18.9	51.4	37.2	30.2	n.a.	39.6
– food	8.6	7.9	8.3	25.8	14.2	–0.3	n.a.	13.2
– chemical	0.0	0.0	0.0	0.4	1.1	0.4	n.a.	0.6
– transport equipment	2.6	3.3	3.0	6.6	7.8	3.9	n.a.	6.1
Electricity, gas, water	52.4	41.7	47.1	5.3	20.0	13.5	n.a.	12.9
Commerce	2.2	1.2	1.7	6.6	5.5	11.0	n.a.	7.7
Communications	1.6	–1.8	–0.1	10.7	13.0	1.6	n.a.	8.5
Banks	4.8	16.6	10.7	3.3	10.0	15.4	n.a.	9.5
By main country of origin (in %)								
USA	16.0	48.2	32.1	44.3	37.9	26.9	n.a.	36.4
Spain	4.3	2.5	3.4	–6.4	4.6	13.7	n.a.	4.0
Chile		11.6	5.8	3.8	12.2	12.8	n.a.	9.6
France	4.5	1.8	3.2	14.8	2.7	6.4	n.a.	8.0
United Kingdom	5.5	11.1	8.3	3.6	–0.2	4.7	n.a.	2.7
Netherlands	4.4	3.7	4.0	8.3	4.1	4.2	n.a.	5.6
Italy	12.4	–9.0	1.7	2.4	3.1	2.4	n.a.	2.6
Germany	3.2	6.5	4.9	6.2	1.0	0.9	n.a.	2.7

Source: Author's elaboration from Ministerio de Economia (1998).

investor in Argentina (especially in electricity and commerce); France, the United Kingdom, Italy, Germany and Netherlands are also significant investors. Brazilian investment is not reported separately in the available information but it has been estimated to be the second Latin American investor. In contrast, neither Japan nor other East Asian countries registered significant investments into Argentina. Hence, extraregional investments from North America and Europe have characterized the current boom. Except for Chile, regional investments have been relatively unimportant.

In consequence of the FDI boom, foreign firms[7] increased their share in the sales of the 500 largest industrial firms from 33.6 per cent in 1990 to 51 per cent in 1995. Among the 500, there were 116 foreign firms in 1990 and 212 in 1995. In all manufacturing branches except steel and leather, foreign firms accounted for more than 40 per cent of each branch total sales in 1995 (Porta, 1997). Contrary to what happened in the 1960s and 1970s when a similar process took place and greatly contributed to the dependency debates, the current denationalization process has not been subject to serious criticism. Nonetheless, the role played by domestic entrepreneurship in the Argentine development process may become an important policy issue.

FDI in Privatized Enterprises

In contrast to Mexico and Chile, FDI in Argentina in the early 1990s was dominated by privatization. In addition to North American companies, European and Chilean investors have taken significant shares, and many of these were newcomers. Investment in Argentina has been the first foreign operation for several firms, and for most their first investment in Latin America. Though there was no legal impediment to establish wholly foreign-owned firms, in most privatized enterprises the new owners are joint ventures involving foreign firms, local conglomerates and international banks. Foreign operators are in charge of the technical and operational aspects of the business, while domestic partners take charge of the administrative and financial aspects, with the international banks providing financial resources.

In collecting data on these investment decisions, the various factors motivating the investment decision were stated in a form where the surveyed firms had to rank their importance. Fairly obviously the existence of a privatization scheme was regarded as a decisive element, though the stability of economic policy and the prospects of a growing market in a virtual monopoly situation also influenced investment decisions. The possibility of acquiring state firms, as allowed in the revised FDI legislation was also acknowledged as an important factor. In contrast, the availability of natural or human resources did not play any role in investment decisions by these corporations. Furthermore, the size, knowledge of the local environment, and especially lobbying skills, of the domestic partners were acknowledged as more important than their technical skills.

The government considered the participation of foreign investors in the privatization programme important in order to reduce 'country risk'. For the international banks that were very active in the design and implementation of the privatization programme, the presence of foreign operators in the new ventures was essential to reduce the 'enterprise risk'. Besides this *external* legitimization, the government was eager to show a quick improvement in the efficiency of the privatized services to obtain an *internal* legitimization of the programme. The privatization rules stated that firms with proven previous experience in the same activity should take care of the technical operation and have an equity participation in the new venture. As the government considered that the technical staffs of the enterprises to be privatized were not reliable, and since there were no private domestic firms with previous experience as service operators, it was implicitly assumed that foreign firms should be in charge of the technical operation. Thus for both *external* and *internal* legitimization reasons, foreign firms became indispensable partners.

The privatization programme was strongly influenced by the evolving macroeconomic situation. The telephone company provides an example of earlier difficulties. With modest mandatory investments, a loosely defined regulatory framework, a sharp increase in telephone charges and preservation of the monopoly character of the service, privatization was completed in 1990. Despite the telecommunications business potential but taking into account the high level of country risk, only three consortia led respectively by Telefonica of Spain, Telecom and STET from France and Italy, and Bell from the United States, submitted their offers and the first two were chosen by the government.

Most remaining state firms were sold in 1992–93, at a time when the economy was growing and inflation registered a sharp fall. In gas and electricity, the privatization mechanism and regulatory bodies were better designed and the tariffs fixed in a more reasonable manner. Even so, significant incentives had to be maintained to attract investors. Most companies were transferred without any liabilities and with valuable physical assets. The rate system ensured reasonable profitability, and geographical monopolies were assigned to all relevant public services operators. Furthermore, some power generating companies were sold with contracts with distributing firms, thus guaranteeing the selling price of their outputs.

Whereas Chilean firms obtained most power-generating companies and one large distribution company, the other electricity distribution company was sold to a consortium led by Electricité de France. The Buenos Aires gas distribution company was sold to a consortium led by British Gas; while the gas transportation companies were transferred to consortia led by Enron and Nova from the United States and Canada, respectively.

FDI into Manufacturing and Mining

As in privatization, the prospects of growth of the internal market was a key determinant of the investment decisions by manufacturing firms, especially in consumer goods where demand increased substantially with the reduction in inflation and the reappearance of consumer credit. Although, as shown below, the Mercosur became a key destination market for their exports, foreign manufacturing firms interviewed both in 1993–94 and in 1996–97 ranked domestic market perspectives as the most important factor in motivating their investments.[8]

The strategies of MNEs already operating in Argentina had to be redefined by trade liberalization and changes in the competition regime. On the one hand, the production structure of the affiliates was often modified; more imported inputs and components were used and finished imported goods became a much larger part of domestic sales. On the other hand, intrafirm trade rose in both imports and exports and the Mercosur has increased its importance *vis-à-vis* other markets. Some globalization/regionalization strategies gained in importance, especially in the automobiles and autoparts sector. Affiliates of several MNEs reoriented their production patterns to be able to export parts, components and some finished goods to other affiliates of the same parent corporation within an international trading network.

Automobile Sector

These emerging specialization patterns have been reinforced by the regulatory framework governing production and trade in the automobile and autoparts sector. Since 1991, local production of vehicles has been protected from imports through quotas and established automakers can import vehicles at a reduced tariff within the quota. In exchange, these firms have to generate exports – in which final vehicles have a higher premium than autoparts – to be able to compensate for the imports; to undertake investments to modernize their facilities; and to reduce the range of vehicles produced in the country. Originally planned to run until the end of 1994, the regime has been extended to 2000 when the WTO rules should be applied. At the same time, in 1995, the Brazilian government established a sectoral regime even more comprehensive than that in force in Argentina.

This set of policies stimulated a strong growth in car production (from less than 100000 units in 1990 to more than 445000 units in 1997) and a corresponding investment response. Until 1994, existing automakers[9] had slowly increased their investments in their old facilities in Argentina, and Toyota decided to make a greenfield investment to make commercial vehicles. In 1995, the decisions by Fiat and General Motors to build new wholly-owned facilities and integrate their production lines with those of their Brazilian affiliates have led to a new investment phase. Renault has also regained the control of its Argentine operation and is building a new plant in Brazil. In this way, the MNEs are wholly controlling a sector of the economy that was until the early 1990s mainly in the hands of domestic firms producing under licence agreements and with minority equity shares from the MNEs.

It is only in this regulated sector where efficiency-seeking investments aimed at complementing and specializing manufacturing plants within Mercosur are taking place in the way suggested by the literature. The Mercosur regime (or more precisely the managed trade agreement in force for this sector) is crucial to specialization patterns of Argentine vehicles and auto-parts makers. The specialization criterion is to make expensive models in Argentina, since they are not highly penalized by the lack of scale, whereas the Brazilian production would continue for the mass market where scale economies are crucial.

Food Sector

In the food industry, which is relatively well-developed, MNEs like Cargill used to predominate in the production and export of agricultural commodities with national firms in making branded goods for the domestic market. Since 1992, MNEs such as Philip Morris, Parmalat, Nabisco, Cadbury and Danone have entered this industry, mostly through takeovers of large national firms with both well-known trade marks and established distribution systems. These were precisely the strategic assets MNEs were looking for. MNEs preferred to pay large sums for such market share rather than to start with greenfield investments and develop their own marketing channels.

At the same time, rapid import expansion of final goods was a distinctive feature of the food firms surveyed. By importing relatively small quantities from other affiliates, the firms test the domestic market. Those goods with better marketing and production possibilities are then locally manufactured. As compared with the importers of food items, the domestic distribution networks are the main advantage of the MNEs affiliates in the relevant market segment. The possibility of combining imports, local production and exports are their key advantages *vis-à-vis* Argentine food producers.

Among the 500 largest firms of the country, the number of foreign enterprises in food, beverages and tobacco increased from 25 in 1990 to 49 in 1995, and their share of sectoral sales rose from 37.3 to 50.8 per cent in the same period. For surveyed food firms, the prospects of the domestic market and the stability of economic policy were even more important factors than the availability of natural resources. The need to be present in the main markets and the possibility of linking their subsidiaries to corporate globalization/regionalization strategies were also an important factor for them.

In contrast to the motor vehicles industry, no switching of activities or product lines within affiliates of the same corporation in the Mercosur countries has taken place in the food processing sector. However, a 'loose' integration process seems to be in force. MNEs with affiliates in several countries of the region seem to fully utilize their different production capacities and to take immediate advantage of the internal demand cycles in each of the countries. In this framework, intrafirm exports and imports flows are adjusted to the demand conditions and facilitate the full utilization of the installed capacity without leading to major investments.

Mining Sector

Resource-seeking investments by leading MNEs have been quite significant in the production and commercialization of agricultural commodities.[10] They have also gained momentum in the mining sector. A new policy was launched in 1993 to promote mining investments, which had been a very underdeveloped sector in Argentina compared to Chile. The new legislation ensures fixed tax rates for 30 years, 3 per cent maximum royalty on the 'mine-head' value of the mineral extracted, and increases the size of the areas allocated for geological surveying to 100 000 hectares per company and per province.

Since 1993, some 100 foreign mining firms have established offices in Argentina and half of them submitted projects, all geared to export markets. According to official sources, investment in exploration rose from US$15m in 1993 to $130m in 1997, and FDI in mining production amounted to $453m in 1995–96. For mining investors, not only the availability of natural resources but also the stability of economic policy and the sectoral regulations were decisive factors for deciding their investments. Legal security and the foreign investment policy were also ranked high among mining investors.

INTERNATIONAL TRADE BY FOREIGN FIRMS

Taking into consideration the exports of the largest 1000 exporters of the country (accounting for 92 per cent of total exports), Chudnovsky & López (1998) estimated that whereas Argentine total exports were augmented by more than 80 per cent between 1993 and 1996, exports by foreign firms grew 105 per cent in the same period. In exports destined to the Mercosur countries, those originating in foreign firms grew nearly half as much again as those from domestic firms.

The share of foreign firms in the external sales of the leading 1000 exporters increased from 33.7 per cent in 1993 to 37.8 per cent in 1996. In the case of exports to the Mercosur, the respective share increased from 42.3 to 50.2 per cent in the same period. Hence, foreign firms have certainly taken more advantage of the opportunities created by subregional integration. Foreign firms also had a higher share in the imports of the 1000 leading exporters[11] in 1996 (58 per cent as against 38 per cent)[12] and their imports grew more than those by local firms in 1993–96. Whereas foreign firms registered a positive trade balance in 1996, it is important to take into account that this was mostly due to the fact that some foreign firms are leading exporters of commodities. Exports by the automobile industry (though very significant) and other manufacturing industries (except food processing) were far lower than imports.

This estimated greater contribution of foreign firms to imports than to exports is in line with the information collected among surveyed firms. In the 1990–94 period, imports increased (from US$264 to 2102m) much faster than exports (from US$796m to 1978m). Final goods registered the largest increase, though inputs also grew rapidly. Whereas all surveyed firms increased their imports, exports were mostly from foreign firms producing agricultural commodities and from the auto-makers. The remaining firms had low export coefficients. Intrafirm trade by the surveyed firms accounted for 83 per cent of exports and for 92 per cent of imports in 1994, and such trade increased most within the Mercosur.

The sharp increase in imports was due to both trade liberalization and higher economic activity. Affiliates complemented local production with imports from the parent company or from other affiliates. Imported final goods, which generally require more advanced technologies for their manufacture, were aimed at more wealthy consumers and/or were intended to replace local goods whose production has been discontinued. The increase in imported inputs was a consequence of both the reduced domestic content and the growth in local production. The reduced domestic content in automobiles was explicitly allowed by the regulatory framework. Greenfield investments and rationalization activities have led to growing imports of capital goods.

On the other hand, the allocation of one model to the Argentine plant to be exported to regional or world markets has been a key factor to allow some scale economies and hence make exports of vehicles more feasible. In fact, exports of vehicles have grown in a significant manner, largely to the Brazilian market.

With the exception of traditional resource-seeking investments geared to the world market, such as agricultural commodities, and to the efficiency-seeking investments in automobile and autoparts production that are leading to both higher exports and imports in such a branch, for the remaining foreign firms both the imports of final goods and inputs are generally far more significant than exports. Mercosur is important for their exports but export coefficients are not yet significant. This situation may change in the future. Once the ongoing investments are made and efficiency gains are consolidated, foreign firms may be in a better position to increase their exports, especially if a more favourable macro-environment for export growth is developed in the country. However, greater export coefficients by Argentine subsidiaries and higher integration to the MNE system not only depend on the local conditions, they are also influenced by global and regional decisions of the MNEs to which they belong.

Finally, though no study is yet available on the balance-of-payments effects of FDI, it may be that if FDI flows are not going to be so significant in the near future, the growing trend in dividends to the parent companies may become a policy issue.

TECHNOLOGICAL AND ORGANIZATIONAL CONTRIBUTIONS

Management, Productivity and Quality

Significant management changes have been implemented in the privatized companies. With the purpose of developing a new organizational culture at all personnel levels, new management methods have been introduced along with computerization. Procurement and subcontracting policies have been modified to reduce costs and delivery times, and a better registry of clients and the quick improvement in collection methods have been priorities for distribution companies.

As result of the large initial lay-offs and the application of new management methods, labour productivity and, in some cases, quality standards have increased. The lines in service per employee have been sharply augmented in telephone companies, and quality indicators such as uncleared faults, average repair time and percentage of lines out of service have improved and new services have been incorporated. None-the-less, the gaps in data productivity, density and quality indicators *vis-à-vis* the parent companies of foreign operators and other countries are wide and the differences in the service charges are quite significant. In the remaining surveyed privatized services some quality improvements were visible, though more modest than in the telephone area. However, large fines on operators have been levied by the gas and electricity regulatory bodies for non-compliance with the targeted quality standards.

The specific contribution of foreign investors to these organizational improvements is not easy to assess. In telecommunications, where technological change has been significant, foreign operators have played an important role in diffusing the latest technologies mainly through the expertise of their personnel. In other privatized services like gas, power or water where technological change is slow, the contribution of the foreign operators has been mostly concentrated on the design of the investment plan, automation and efficiency improvements. In electricity, and especially in gas, foreign operators have contributed by organizing independent business operations and transactions in services that were previously carried out internally by state enterprises. Most quality improvements are due to explicit requirements in the privatization schemes and supervisory action by the regulatory bodies; the effect of regulation seems more significant than the 'FDI effect' in explaining the better performance of privatized enterprises.

To cope with trade liberalization and greater competition, most manufacturing enterprises operating in Argentina have been implementing rationalization strategies to reduce costs and increase efficiency (Chudnovsky *et al.*, 1996). This is clearly reflected in the significant growth in labour productivity[13] in the manufacturing sector and in the increase from only three firms in 1993 to 310 firms with ISO 9000 certificates in 1997. One-third of these firms are foreign-owned. In this context, it is not surprising that foreign manufacturing enterprises have been very active in undertaking efficiency-seeking activities, especially when the demand for their products has grown faster than the average. In comparison with national firms, foreign firms have a quicker access to product, processes and organizational innovations, and can rely on intrafirm trade to get inputs and final products from other subsidiaries of the MNE system.

Productivity and efficiency gains were obtained at the beginning through better utilization of existing capacity and by the introduction of modern management and organizational methods. Later on, the adoption of these methods has been a more generalized and significant phenomenon in surveyed firms. In those projects in which capacity expansion and greenfield investments have taken place, the technological contribution of foreign investors has been much greater and the productivity gap with plants in industrialized countries has been sharply reduced (Porta, 1997).

New product technology is the main foreign contribution in all manufacturing firms. Marketing and packaging techniques and sometimes quality standards are the key input from the parent companies in food processing and other branded goods sectors. In processes and organizational technologies the foreign contribution is uneven. While in established firms they are generally introduced by the local management, in the case of newcomers instructions from parent companies seem to have played a greater role.

Personnel Training

The availability of relatively cheap and skilled manpower was not considered an important factor in motivating investment in Argentina by foreign firms. Labour costs are high in dollar terms due to the current exchange rate. Due to the backward production methods, insufficient training on the job and the crisis in the educational system, the quality of labour has also deteriorated. In view of this situation, surveyed manufacturing firms, especially in automobiles, auto-parts and telecommunications equipment assigned significant resources to training in 1993–94. In some exceptional cases this was 1 per cent of their turnover. To be able to implement the described organizational changes and new production processes which are based on the concepts of polyvalence and multifunctionality of the staff, foreign firms have had to further increase their training efforts. These efforts ranged from 20 to 200 hours/man/year among surveyed firms. The greater efforts were made by newcomers and in greenfield investments (Porta, 1997).

The automobile makers, which already had their own technical schools, have also developed training programmes jointly with the Labour Ministry. However, training on the job remains their priority. Newcomers are far more ambitious in their training programmes, and General Motors was clearly ahead in this field. A new labour agreement has been negotiated with the union in which, among other things, training and team work are crucial items.

Excess personnel, corruption, uneven technical formation and bad working habits have been the problems facing the new management of privatized enterprises, and personnel training has been one of the means to modify the inherited situation. Furthermore, new technicians and professionals have been incorporated, thus increasing their share in total employment. Due to technological requirements, these efforts and changes have been more significant in telecommunications than in the other privatized enterprises.

Foreign personnel have been used in the privatized firms for some key management positions and for short-term consultancy assignments. The remaining high-level managerial and technical positions have been provided by the local partners or recruited in the Argentine market. Few foreign managers are employed in manufacturing firms, and this is mostly by newcomers.

Linkages with Local Suppliers and R&D Activities

The easy access to imported parts and components and to capital goods has sharply reduced the possibilities of developing backward linkages. Hence the impact of FDI into local suppliers has been very limited except in the automobile sector. To comply with sectoral regulations the domestic content of automobile production is 60 per cent and, for this reason, the development of reliable auto-parts makers has became a priority in this sector and has contributed to the modernization process in this sub-sector.

However, MNEs are following international trends towards concentrating their purchases in a small group of first-tier suppliers. These international suppliers have been in turn taking over existing auto-parts makers both in Argentina and Brazil, leading to a growing denationalization of this important activity.

In contrast to efforts made to improve productivity and quality, R&D received little if any attention in both surveys.[14] Among privatized enterprises, only one telephone company has a R&D unit to deal with domestic operations and has no link with R&D activities in the parent company. Within manufacturing firms, the strongest R&D efforts are made by telecommunications equipment manufacturers. In one case they accounted for 1 per cent of total sales. In food processing, the export-oriented firms have been more active in R&D than the remaining ones, though their efforts are very modest. Whereas in the Brazilian affiliates some R&D activity is taking place among automakers, the main technological activity in Argentine affiliates is to adapt the models brought from the parent companies or Brazilian affiliates to local conditions, relying on a relatively small staff.

CONCLUDING REMARKS

The recent boom in FDI in Argentina has certainly been motivated by a favourable macroeconomic framework. In an international context in which MNEs have increasingly paid more attention to business opportunities in some key developing countries, the stabilization and structural reforms programme has led to a reduction in country-risk as perceived by foreign investors. Whereas FDI deregulation has played a significant role only for investments into privatized firms, the growth of the domestic economy, price stabilization and, to some extent, the Mercosur have been decisive factors in the investment decisions by MNEs.

However, neither the volume nor the sectoral composition of the recent FDI flows can be explained by these general factors. Most FDI flows in 1990–93 were not merely market but also policy-driven. Both the privatization schemes, in which the participation of foreign enterprises and banks have been implicitly encouraged, and the regulatory framework for the automobile and auto-parts branch, protecting the wider Mercosur market and providing preferential means to finance the sectoral restructuring process, have been the leading policy initiatives to make Argentina more attractive for foreign investors. Spontaneous FDI flows have became increasingly important as time passes and the economy continues growing. These flows have been attracted by activities where internal demand has been very dynamic and in which oligopolistic competition through branded goods and services is the rule of the game. This is clearly the case of the food industry and is probably applicable to services like banking, hotels, supermarkets, and so on.

The growth in internal demand has been the main locational advantage to induce recent FDI in Argentina both in non-tradables and in tradables. However, in contrast to what happened in the ISI, most recent investments have been not only internal market-seeking but also efficiency-seeking.

The impact of the Convertibility Plan upon demand growth in an open economy, together with the entry of new competitors and the requirements of the sectoral regulatory frameworks, have forced most foreign firms to apply their human and physical resources in a more efficient way. While for manufacturing firms this development can mainly be attributed to greater actual and potential competition, in privatized firms it has largely depended on how well the regulatory bodies have performed their functions. In this context, the good performance of the surveyed firms cannot be attributed only to the influence of FDI. Although such an influence cannot easily be separated from the other factors mentioned, some specific contributions from foreign investors to such performance have been highlighted by the survey findings.

Though in varying levels and according to each case, foreign operators in privatized ventures have provided their knowledge and capabilities on technological issues, commercial management and investment planning. In this way, an incipient technology-transfer process has been taking place mainly through the training of local personnel and higher requirements to suppliers operating in the country. At the same time, the presence of foreign operators in key management positions may have contributed to reduce the cost of external borrowing for these companies. Personnel training, modern organizational techniques and product technology are the most significant foreign contribution in most manufacturing firms, though also in varying degrees. In greenfield investments their contribution towards reducing the productivity and quality gap with plants in industrialized countries seem more significant than in existing undertakings.

In so far as the MNEs have more appropriate assets and financial resources than domestic firms to undertake efficiency-seeking investments to compete in open economies, their contribution in this connection seems to be greater than that of domestic investors, especially in greenfield investments. It is plausible to think that the lack of such assets has been one of the reasons motivating domestic entrepreneurs to sell their enterprises to foreign investors, though no evidence is available to support this hypothesis. Furthermore, beyond the figures on the growing share of foreign firms, no information is available on what the domestic entrepreneurs have done with the funds received from foreign investors. The whole issue certainly deserves further research.

Most FDI has a significant import content, besides large exports in resource-based activities. But so far only in the auto industry (and geared to the Mercosur) has FDI led to significant export growth. At the same time, the integration of Argentine operations into wider MNEs systems suggested in the literature is taking place only in this sector. In the remaining activities, most foreign-owned (or with foreign presence) firms operating in Argentina are, as yet, following mainly standalone strategies. It is also clear that most manufacturing surveyed firms have not yet defined explicit strategies of integration with world or regional markets. Therefore, access to intrafirm international trading networks for export promotion is a potential rather than an actual advantage of the MNE presence in the country.

While the sectoral policies applied in Argentina have been effective in attracting substantial FDI flows and in fostering some positive externalities to the host economy, they have been less successful in generating technological spillovers. The evidence available on research and development efforts and spillover effects clearly suggests a lack of technological deepening. This may be attributed to several factors: the previous lack of design and development capabilities in the affiliates, the weaknesses of local supply linkages and institutions, explicit policies of the MNEs regarding the role to be played by the Argentine affiliates and/or the inexistence of explicit technology policies in the host country. Unfortunately, the surveys did not provide enough information to shed light on the relative importance of these factors. Whereas the continuation of the economic growth process would probably be enough to ensure more FDI, higher 'quality' FDI would require more proactive public policies.

Trade and FDI liberalization, effective regulatory policies in protected sectors and competition policies are necessary but not sufficient conditions. New policies to foster endogenous technological, managerial and organizational capabilities and local supply linkages and institutions are called for to obtain, among other objectives, far more spillovers from FDI and to aim at participating in the MNEs' more complex integration strategies in the world economy.

Development of clusters at regional and local levels, enterprise incubators, science and technology parks, encouragement of intramural R&D activities, and linkages between private firms and public research laboratories and universities have hardly been applied in the country. To be able to benefit more from the globalization process and foster economic development, Argentina should attempt to catch up with the international best practices (as examined in several chapters of this book) in this area, and take advantage of the potentialities of the Mercosur in such an attempt.

Notes

1. The comments and suggestions from John H. Dunning and Stephen Young on a previous draft are gratefully acknowledged. The usual caveats apply.
2. The FDI figures for Argentina since 1992 are those estimated by the Ministry of Economics in the balance-of-payments information and reproduced in Table 8.1. Except for 1996, they differ from those reported in UNCTAD (1997). The FDI figures until 1991 calculated by the Central Bank have not been revised by the Ministry of Economics; although not strictly comparable with the information since 1992 they are the only available official source.
3. An examination of this crucial issue is obviously beyond the scope of the present chapter. Frenkel (1995) provides a critical assessment while Cavallo and Mondino (1995) give the official view.
4. The already liberal Foreign Investment Law of 1976 underwent some revisions in 1989 and 1993. No approvals, formalities and registry of

any kind are required. The few sectoral restrictions were practically eliminated in 1993. There are neither discriminatory withholding taxes towards income, nor taxes applied to the remission of profits and dividends emanating from FDI.

5. Although not based on statistically random samples, the surveyed firms are representative of the activities where the majority of FDI flows were channelled (namely, privatized services, food processing, automobiles and auto-parts and other manufacturing sectors).
6. It is important to bear in mind that YPF, Argentina's largest corporation with activities in oil and gas exploration and development both upstream and downstream, was privatized in 1993 in a different form. This was carried out through the sale of shares in small blocks on domestic and international markets. A total of shares representing 58 per cent of the company's capital stock were placed in this way. An unknown proportion of the stock is owned by foreign investors but they are considered in the official balance-of-payment figures as portfolio investments. The national government and several provincial administrations retain a minority interest in the company and a share ownership programme has been implemented covering 10 per cent of the capital stock.
7. Foreign firms were considered as those controlled by non-residents. The privatized oil firm (YPF) was considered as nationally-controlled. Though most foreign firms are affiliates of MNEs, a number of them belong to international investment funds (such as Exxel and Soros) or to foreign investors that have not yet become MNEs, such as some Chilean and Brazilian firms.
8. The prospects for the domestic market was also considered as the main factor of attraction for foreign firms investing in Brazil. For them Mercosur was seen as an extension of the large domestic market (Laplane and Sarti, 1997).
9. They were Ford with a wholly-owned subsidiary; a local firm making Fiat and Peugeot cars under licence; and Renault that sold the controlling share of its subsidiary to a group of local businessmen in 1992 to continue making the cars under licence.
10. Though no official information is available, it is known that FDI in agriculture has been very significant. As result of such investments, George Soros – through a controlled firm – became the largest landowner of the country and Benetton a very important one.
11. These imports accounted for only 28 per cent of Argentine total imports. However, while exports of foreign firms among the largest 1000 exporters amounted to US$8300m, their imports were US$8800m in 1996.
12. In the imports by the largest 1000 importers – that accounted for 65 per cent or Argentine total imports – the participation of foreign firms was 57 per cent.
13. According to official information, labour productivity in manufacturing from 1990 to the first half of 1997 grew 6.8 per cent per year, whereas in the 1980s it grew only 0.8 per cent per year (CEP, 1997b).

14. Private firms (both foreign and domestic) invest little in R&D. As a percentage of GDP total R&D in the private sector was only 0.13 per cent of the GDP in 1996, a coefficient much lower than in Brazil and Chile.

References

CAVALLO, D. and G. MONDINO (1995), 'Argentina's Miracle? From Hyperinflation to Sustained Growth', in M. Bruno and B. Pleskovic (eds), *Annual World Bank Conference on Development Economics 1995* (Washington DC: The World Bank).

CENTRO DE ESTUDIOS PARA LA PRODUCCIÓN (CEP) (1997a), 'Síntesis de la Economía Real', vol. 10, Buenos Aires, Secretaría de Industria, Comercio y Minería.

CENTRO DE ESTUDIOS PARA LA PRODUCCIÓN (CEP) (1997b), 'Notas de la Economía Real', 4, Buenos Aires, Secretaría de Industria, Comercio y Minería.

CHUDNOVSKY, D. (1993), 'Introduction' to TNCs and Industrialisation', *United Nations Library on TNCs*, Vol. 11 (London: Routledge), pp. 1–24.

CHUDNOVSKY, D. and A. LÓPEZ (1998), *La inversión extranjera directa en la Argentina en los años 1990: tendencias, determinantes y modalidades, Argentina de Cara al Mundo* (Buenos Aires: Ministerio de Relaciones Exteriores y Comercio Internacional).

CHUDNOVSKY, D., F. PORTA, A. LÓPEZ and M. CHIDIAK (1996), *Los límites de la apertura. Liberalización, reestructuración productiva y medio ambiente* (Buenos Aires: Alianza Editorial).

CHUDNOVSKY, D., A. LÓPEZ and F. PORTA (1997), 'Market or Policy Driven? The Foreign Direct Investment Boom in Argentina', *Oxford Development Studies*, vol. 25, no. 2, pp. 173–88.

DUNNING, J. (1994), 'Re-evaluating the Benefits of Foreign Direct Investment', *Transnational Corporations*, vol. 3, no. 1 (February), pp. 23–51.

FRENKEL, R. (1995), 'Macroeconomic Sustainability and Development Prospects: Latin American Performance in the 1990s', *UNCTAD Discussion Paper*, no. 100, Geneva.

LAPLANE, M.F. and F. SARTI (1997), *Internacionalização Produtiva no Mercosul: o caso do Brasil* (mimeo), Universidade de Campinas.

Ministerio de Economía (1998), *Inversión Extranjera Directa en Argentina. 1992–1997*, Buenos Aires.

PORTA, F. (1997), *La Inversión Extranjera Directa en la Argentina en los Años '90. Factores de Atracción y Estrategias Empresarias* (mimeo) (Buenos Aires: CENIT).

UNCTAD (1997), *World Investment Report 1997. Transnational Corporations, Market Structure and Competition Policy* (Geneva: UNCTAD).

UNCTAD (1996), *World Investment Report 1996. Investment, Trade and International Policy Arrangements* (Geneva: UNCTAD).

UNITED NATIONS (1993), *World Investment Report. Transnational Corporations and Integrated International Production* (New York: UN).

9 The Globalization of Business and East Asian Developing-Country Multinationals

Hafiz Mirza

INTRODUCTION

The current global political economy can trace its origins back to the world economic crisis of the 1970s and a number of consequent 'corporate survival strategies'. As the discussion below will show, these strategies have, both intentionally and unintentionally, transformed the world economy to such an extent that it is now possible to glean the preliminary structures of a global, but regionalized world system of the twenty-first century.[1] A specific manifestation of this process has been the 'rise' of East Asia. Despite the recent Asian financial crisis, this region will continue to constitute a significant and growing component of the world economic system. Moreover, in consequence, East Asian developing-country multinationals (EA-DCMs) will figure as a formidable force in the future, both regionally and – increasingly – globally. This chapter aims firstly to explain how EA-DCMs have been engendered[2] by globalization (and its handmaiden regionalization; Mirza, 1998); secondly, to describe their principal dimensions and characteristics; thirdly, to analyse their strategy and behaviour, especially in a regional context; and, finally, suggest some further avenues for research and investigation.

FROM GLOBAL CRISIS TO GLOBALIZATION: A WALK THROUGH HISTORY

The world economic crisis of the 1970s and onwards cannot be discussed fully here, but suffice it to say that its genesis was a heady mix of declining global growth rates (perhaps a downturn in the

Kondratieff long-wave), a heavily overburdened post-Vietnam war United States economy (which resulted in an end to the dollar hegemony in the cross-border system of payments and a move to a flexible exchange rate system), and the oil crisis (an eight-fold increase in oil prices within a decade put paid to the hitherto unchallenged notion of cheap energy underwriting the international economy). At the corporate level its essence was that firms, primarily in Western industrialized countries, found themselves faced with slow-growth markets, declining profits and intensifying competition. In response, they were forced to take a number of exigent measures and, at an international level, three strategies stand out as being significant: namely, the use of cheap labour, the search for new markets and strategic alliances.

The Shift of Production to Developing Countries

From the mid-1970s, many firms, especially multinational enterprises (MNEs) began to reduce their costs by utilizing cheaper developing-country labour in their production processes. This resulted in the transfer of some production to developing countries such as Mexico, Tunisia and Taiwan. This transfer intensified as developing countries, especially those in East Asia,[3] improved the quality of local infrastructure and the skills of their workforce. By the early 1980s, although foreign direct investment (FDI) between Triad countries (North America, Western Europe and Japan) remained paramount, MNEs were increasingly locating manufacturing facilities[4] in East Asia, with the initial footfall being in Singapore, Hong Kong, South Korea and Taiwan (Figure 9.1). It is worth mentioning that the transfer of production to East Asia was a highly complex process. For instance, although the establishment of manufacturing industries in Singapore was overwhelmingly due to the efforts of foreign MNEs, in other newly-industrializing economies (NIEs) local companies were often to the fore, albeit frequently as suppliers and subcontractors to major Triad companies. These local companies, which ultimately became East Asia's DCMs, were also heterogeneous. Thus in South Korea the principal vectors in the industrialization process were large industrial groups (the chaebol); in Taiwan, SMEs were the driving force; in Hong Kong the picture was very mixed, with foreign MNEs, large combines and SMEs all playing a role. Such complexity has persisted as industrialization has spread beyond these 'first order' NIEs to other parts of the region and helps explain the variegated nature of EA-DCMs, as will be seen later.

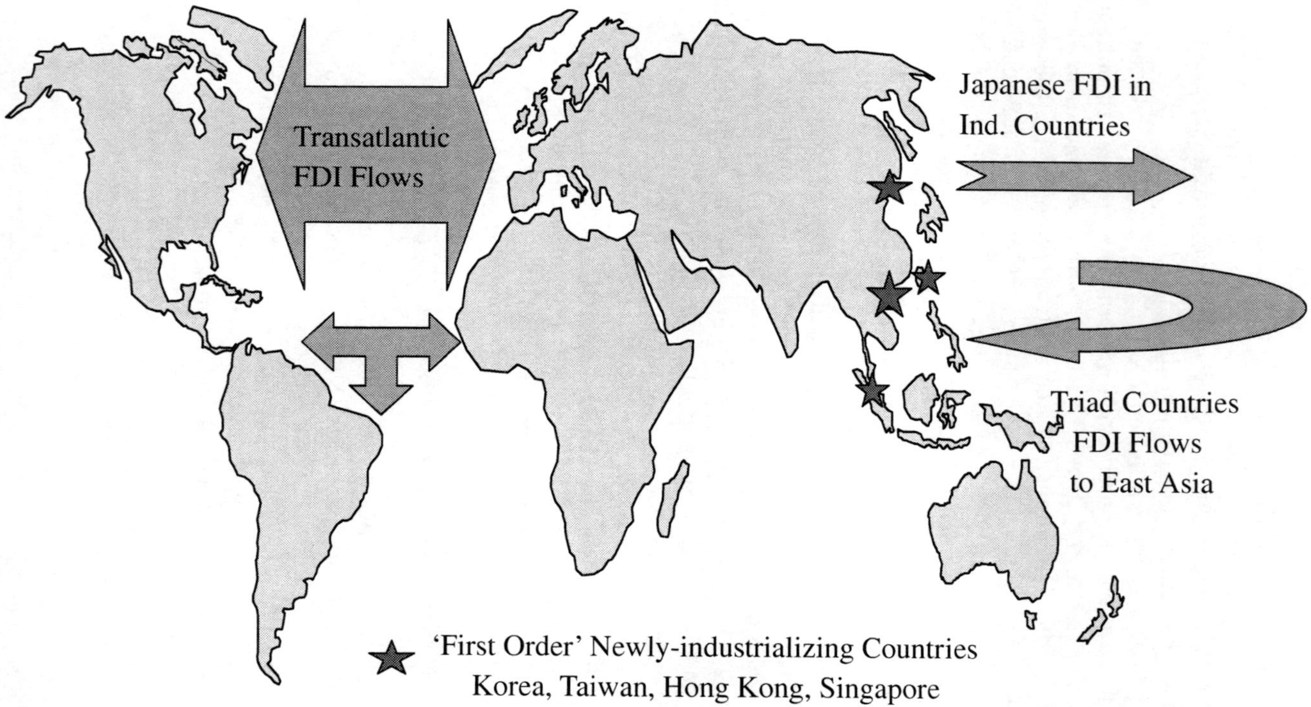

Figure 9.1 Incipient globalization circa 1980

With the internationalization of production, foreign and local firms were able to seize new opportunities. For instance, Figure 9.2 shows schematically how the East Asian production system of a 'typical' US MNE has evolved from the 1970s through the 1990s, from one which was merely re-exporting further processed goods to the home economy using non-skilled labour (that is, 'offshore production') to one which *also* exported *fully*-processed goods using increasingly skilled labour. This latter phase also went through a cycle. In the first instance, products were exported to third (non-USA) markets (2); then to local markets, created as host-economies developed and workers took home sizeable pay cheques (3); and finally to all international markets, including the USA (that is, 'global production',

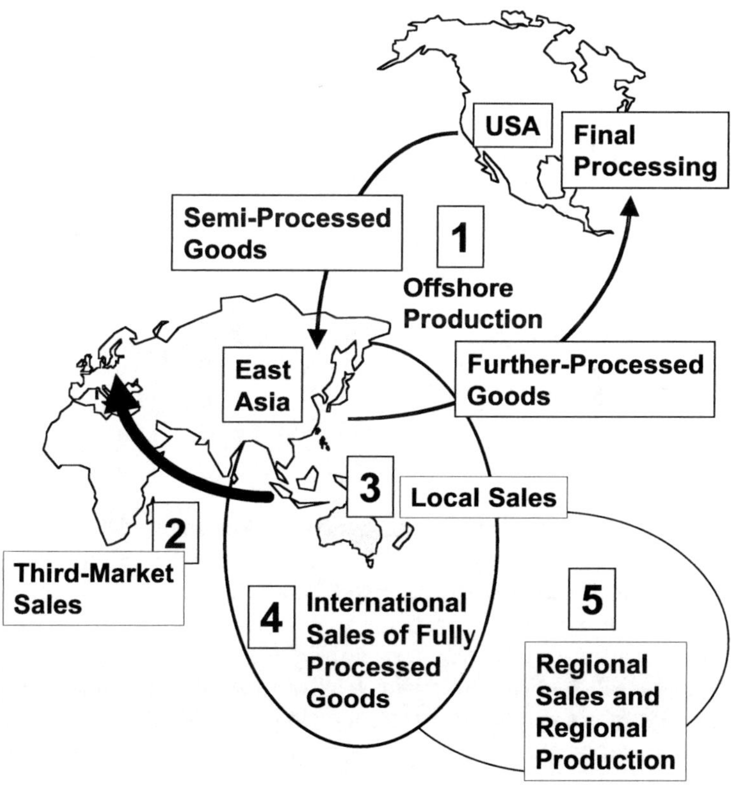

Figure 9.2 From offshore production to global production: a schematic depiction of the evolution of international production by USA MNEs

(4)). The latest phase in this dynamic process has been an increasing emphasis on sales to the *region* (5) and the utilization of a regional division of labour for international production (see Mirza *et al.*, 1997 for a discussion of this *vis-à-vis* ASEAN[5]). Figure 9.3 depicts the consequence of such processes at the macro-level. Triad MNEs and EA-DCMs have acted as vectors for East Asian regionalization by moving production into nearby countries. For example, Taiwanese, Hong Kong and Overseas Chinese[6] DCMs led the drive into China. ('May a million joint-ventures bloom!': for a number of years in the early 1990s China received up to a quarter of rapidly expanding annual international direct investment flows (UNCTAD, 1997).) Similarly, Singapore-based Triad MNEs have expanded throughout Southeast Asia, a move increasingly followed by EA-DCMs from Singapore, Malaysia, Thailand and other ASEAN countries.

The long-term result of these regional developments has been the arrival of new *industrialized* economies such as South Korea, Taiwan and Singapore – and developing-country multinationals[7] – onto the world scene; and the process of industrialization and development continues apace in increasingly larger countries, such as Vietnam and China. Despite tremendous social and economic costs, as well as the Asian financial crisis, East Asia has now emerged as a major economic region (Asian Development Bank, 1997; World Bank, 1993) and its dynamism is spreading to South Asia, Central Asia and further afield. It is important to recognize that most foreign capital currently being invested in East and South Asia comes from other countries in the region (EC/UNCTAD-DTCI, 1996; Dunning, 1998a), *not from the West*. In other words a significant number of East Asian MNEs have emerged.

The Search for New Markets and Strategic Alliances

A second international corporate survival strategy pursued from the 1970s onwards was the search for new markets which increasingly took MNEs to non-industrialized, non-Western countries. One interesting angle on this was the rapid proliferation of international bank loans and flows of portfolio capital. During the 1980s, miscalculations by the international banks, in the context of a depressed global economy, led to the international debt crisis which almost brought down the world financial system. It is not possible to go into the intricacies of this crisis here, but suffice it to say that one consequence was

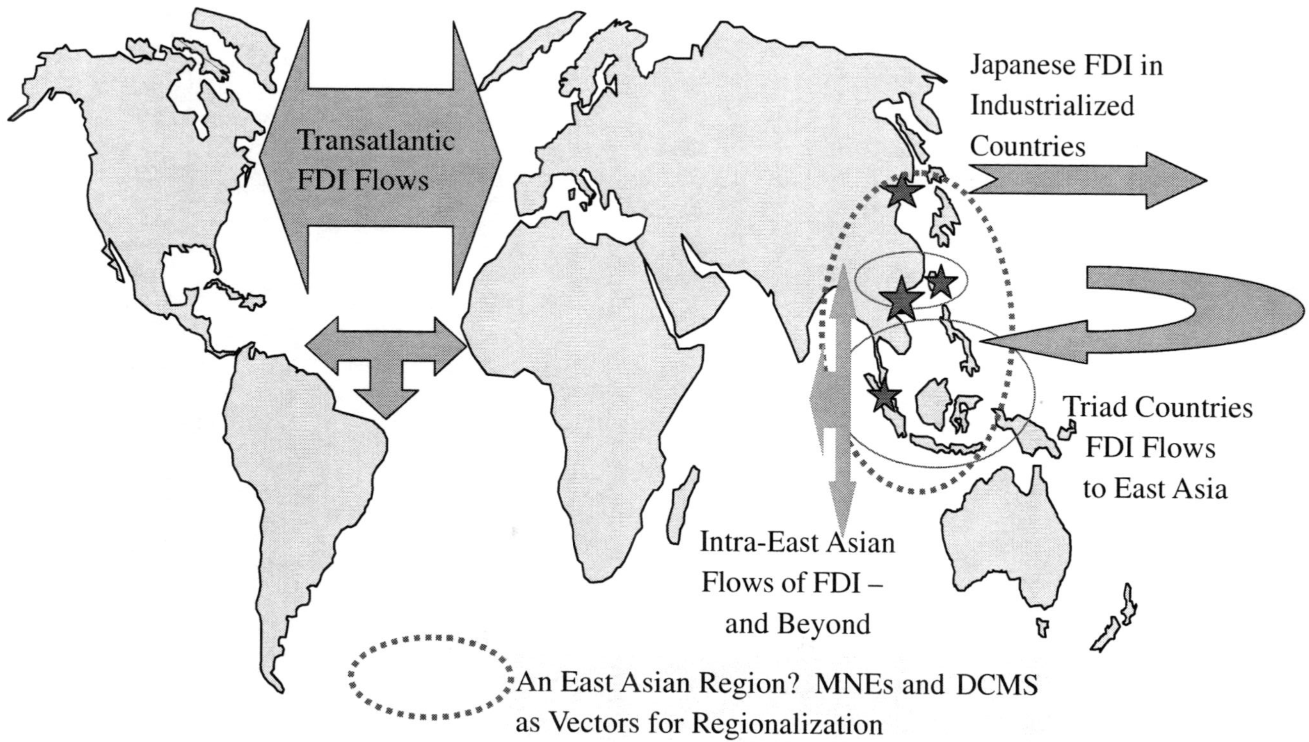

Figure 9.3 Globalization and East Asian 'regionalization' circa 2000

a thorough and ongoing overhaul of the international institutional framework, particularly through the establishment of the World Trade Organization (WTO) and a revamp of both the International Monetary Fund (IMF) and the World Bank.[8] As a consequence of the internationalization of the financial sector, huge amounts of capital became available for investment in 'emerging markets', thereby facilitating the globalization of production.

Another survival strategy utilized by firms was to reduce competition by establishing international strategic alliances, for example, through cooperation with other firms when, for instance, entering new markets or developing new technologies. There was an echo of this at the political level with the establishment or reinvigoration of regional groupings, such as the European Union (EU), the Association of Southeast Asian Nations (ASEAN), the North American Free Trade Agreement (NAFTA) and Mercosur (in South America).[9] If nothing else, these new groupings afford opportunities for economic expansion by many companies and countries. Government policies have clearly played a key role in the simultaneous globalization and regionalization of the world economy (Dunning, 1997).

Globalization and Developing-Country Multinationals

Although the globalization of production, induced by the actions of firms after the crisis of the 1970s, has been a chaotic process at times, it has resulted in fundamental changes in the structure of the global political economy. Growth zones exist the world over and new ones are coming into existence because of the activities of firms, governments and international institutions. These zones are sometimes linked to politically created regions (for example, Mercosur), sometimes not (for example, southern Africa). Most importantly, the ongoing industrialization of the developing and transitional world has developed its own momentum. A recent report by the World Bank indicates that by the year 2020, developing countries (including the successor states of the former Soviet Union) will account for a half of international trade; and, furthermore, just five of these countries (Brazil, China, India, Indonesia and Russia) will be responsible for 22 per cent of international trade.[10] Developing country multinationals will be responsible for much of this trade, as well as an increasing amount of FDI, especially at the regional level.

Regionalization, East Asia and Developing-Country Multinationals

As indicated above, FDI by East Asian DCMs needs to be analysed in terms of the impact of 'globalization' on East Asia as a region (and sub-regions) and the ensuing political–economic consequences. In this context it is worth examining more closely the complex interaction between MNEs, governments and regionalization *processes*. These processes can be conceptually divided into four types:

- First, economic development and proximal expansion across borders can lead to integration between countries, as in the case of France and Germany, and between regional growth zones, for example in the developments along the USA–Mexico border. This is essentially a 'spillover' model of regionalization, and the extent to which such tendencies are regional as opposed to global can be explained in terms of growth pole and location theories (Hansen, 1972), as well as other contingencies including government policies and MNE strategies. Many East Asian DCMs invest overseas because of the spillover process. Examples include Malaysian firms in investing in Sumatra (Indonesia), or Taiwanese firms operating in Fujian province (China). In both cases geographical and cultural-ethnic proximity/familiarity are important reasons for the spillover, as well as a welter of other causes such as cheaper labour.
- Secondly, a regional impulse might also be imparted or intensified by a variety of corporate strategies. Examples of this include, MNE expansion to growth zones (some of the large inflow of FDI to 'greater China' in recent years has been of a 'me too' character); initial foreign direct investment in countries such as Singapore and Hong Kong, often driven by government incentives, which created the conditions for later spillover into nearby countries; the North American, Japanese and Asian investment in Europe from the mid-1980s, which occurred because of fears of a 'Fortress Europe' after the EU's decision to establish a Single European Market (SEM)[11] and which helped to accelerate the industrial and economic integration of the European Union. The growth zones of East Asia clearly affect both East Asian MNEs and Triad MNE subsidiaries in Asia more immediately than companies further afield. This explains, at least in part, why regional companies are

the primary source of new FDI in this part of the world (UNCTAD, 1996).

- Thirdly, a regionalization momentum might be created or intensified by *specific regionalization strategies* pursued by MNEs. For example, economies of scale may lead to 'spillover' because the size of a national market is insufficient for efficient operations (though these do not need to be confined to the regional level). Similarly, many MNEs take advantage of regional divisions of labour. Thus in Southeast Asia, for example, electronic firms such as Matsushita are utilizing the variable factor endowments, competencies and markets of countries such as Malaysia, Singapore, the Philippines, Vietnam and Indonesia (Mirza *et al.*, 1997). Many Singaporean and Malaysian companies have a broader ASEAN or Asian strategy precisely because their home markets are so small; similarly, although larger South Korean firms are looking globally for their markets, their vision nevertheless includes a regional dimension (O' Neil, 1998).
- Finally, government policies, some deliberately designed to encourage regionalization, are also important. A number of examples can be cited. For instance, the establishment of customs unions, free trade areas, regional institutions and incentives can help create or formalize growth zones. Having said this, creation or intensification 'by decree' is not a foregone conclusion. On the one hand, for instance, the southern ASEAN growth triangle (parts of Malaysia, Singapore and Indonesia) has been successful because it further extends an existing growth region, namely, Singapore and Johore in Malaysia. On the other hand, however, the eastern ASEAN growth triangle (Brunei and parts of the Philippines, Malaysia and Indonesia) is less successful because it lacks an obvious industrial or corporate motor for growth. International organizations can also get into the act. For example, the gravity model (Garnaut and Drysdale, 1994) partly underlies the Asian Development Bank's policy of encouraging growth through the mega-dollar infrastructural development in the 'Greater Mekong Sub-region' (a territory comprising Cambodia, Laos, Myanmar, Thailand, Vietnam and Yunnan Province of China with a population of a quarter-billion people). The idea is that infrastructural development will play a catalytic role in encouraging corporate activity in the region by both local and foreign firms. Thai and Malaysian DCMs have been particularly involved in these Mekong developments.

Governments and companies also cooperate directly in regional activities, an instance being the close collaboration between these entities in both East Asia and the European Union in encouraging trade and investment links *between* the regions as part of the ASEM (Asia Europe Meeting) process. The ASEM initiative began at a meeting in Bangkok during March 1996 because of the relatively weak links between Europe and East Asia (as opposed to their respective links with North America). The process has continued through a variety of initiatives, including two reports (EC and UNCTAD, 1996; and UNCTAD, 1996), whose recommendations require MNEs and governments to work very closely in order to further future investment, trade and other technology, capital and labour flows in, and between, the two regions. Thus, for example, South Korean, Taiwanese and Singaporean FDI in Europe is encouraged, as well as EU FDI in Asia. ASEM 1998, held in London in March 1998, further underlined these objectives. A final point worth mentioning is that, as will be seen later in the chapter, government policies on outward FDI (for instance, in Singapore, Thailand and Malaysia) are frequently regional in orientation, thereby circumscribing the sort of international strategies that some DCMs can pursue.

THE SCALE AND SCOPE OF DEVELOPING-COUNTRY MULTINATIONALS

The globalization of production has meant that developing-country multinationals (DCMs) are playing an increasing role in international trade and investment compared to Triad MNEs. As Table 9.1 shows, for instance, foreign direct investment from developing countries has been rising in recent years. In 1980 the stock of DCM FDI stood at

Table 9.1 FDI outward stock by country, 1980–96 (per cent)

Country groups and economies	*1980*	*1990*	*1996*
World (US$ billions)	519	1615	2893
Developed countries	98	96	91
Developing countries	2	4	9
East Asian countries	1	2	7

Source: Derived from UNCTAD (1997), Table B.4.

only 2 per cent of the world total; in contrast, the DCM share of world FDI in 1996 was a more respectable 9 per cent of a much greater total stock (US$2893 billion). Moreover, as hinted at earlier, East Asian MNEs account for the lion's share of developing country FDI (7 per cent). Seven of the 10 largest developing FDI source countries (Hong Kong, Singapore, Taiwan, China, South Korea, Malaysia and Thailand) are located in East Asia, with three disparate countries, Brazil, Nigeria and Kuwait representing the rest of the developing world (Table 9.2). Of course these figures have to be treated with caution. For example, Hong Kong's outward FDI is undoubtedly inflated by 'round-tripping' by Chinese firms which use it as a base for investment back in China and elsewhere. In addition, Hong Kong is the regional headquarters for many North American, European and Asian firms and their outward investment (especially in China) will also appear in the statistics as outward Hong Kong FDI flows/stock, although clearly this does not constitute FDI by Hong Kong companies. The same issue applies for Singapore which is also a major location for regional Triad MNE headquarters. On the other hand, many investments go unreported (often for political reasons) including, for instance, a proportion of Taiwanese investments in China and Indonesia.

Table 9.3 underlines East Asia's preeminence as an economic power in the developing world, with 27 companies ranking among the world's 500 largest in 1997. As might be anticipated, Hong Kong,

Table 9.2 The ten largest sources of FDI in the developing world, 1996

Economy	*Investment stock (US$ billions)*
Hong Kong	112.2
Singapore	37.5
Taiwan	27.3
China	18.0
South Korea	13.7
Nigeria	11.9
Malaysia	10.8
Kuwait	8.5
Brazil	7.4
Thailand	4.1

Source: Derived from UNCTAD (1997), Table B.4.

Table 9.3 The location of the world's 500 largest firms (by market capitalization), 1997

Location	*Number of firms*	*Location*	*Number of firms*
North America	235	East Asia	27
Europe	145	Hong Kong	11
Japan	71	Taiwan	8
Latin America	8	Singapore	4
Africa	4	Malaysia	2
Other	9	South Korea	1
Middle East	1	Indonesia	1

Source: 'The Financial Times 500', *Financial Times*, 22 January 1998.

Taiwanese, Singaporean and Malaysian firms rank among the region's largest. Examples of these companies include, HSBC, Hutchison Whampoa, Singapore Airlines, Taiwan Semiconductor and Telekom Malaysia. The scale of EA-DCMs is actually understated for a number of reasons. First, East Asia's stockmarkets are depressed because of the Asian financial crisis and thus comparisons based on capitalization show EA-DCMs in a poor light compared to some other more buoyant markets. Secondly, South Korean firms figure quite low in the FT survey because the country's chaebol (industrial groups such as Samsung and Hyundai) list their individual constituent companies separately on the stock exchange. Thirdly, Chinese companies do not appear in the FT survey because the country's state-owned enterprises are not listed at all on the stock exchange. Overall, the above analysis shows that East Asia is now the source of a significant amount of FDI and home to a number of large DCMs. The next section will examine the specific characteristics of FDI from East Asia and will reveal, among other matters, that the region's small and medium-sized enterprises (SMEs) are also sizeable international investors.

RIPPLES AND REPERCUSSIONS: THE CHARACTERISTICS OF EAST ASIAN MNES AND THE PATTERN OF FDI

As discussed earlier, the irruption of a burgeoning globalization process into the East Asia arena in the 1970s in the form of new and varied MNE strategies was one critical factor in the rapid development of the region and the subsequent proliferation of DCMs. Equally important were two other factors. Firstly, there were a range of socio-economic endowments of long and short-term provenance, including the skills bases of Singapore and South Korea derived from the colonial period; the raw materials of Indonesia; and the advanced regional infrastructural capacity established with assistance from Japan's multi-billion dollar 'recycling plan'.[12] Secondly, there was the role of the developmental state in countries as diverse as Malaysia, Thailand and China.

Given the range of factors involved and the sheer diversity of East Asia, it is not surprising that the impact of globalization on the region was heterogeneous in the extreme. In the earliest stages, among first-order NIEs, South Korea relied primarily on large indigenous chaebols for its industrialization, whereas Singapore depended heavily on FDI, and Taiwan on SMEs subcontracting their operations to North American and Japanese MNEs; Hong Kong's industrialization was a cordial mix of all of these strategies. As the industrialization process spilled over into Malaysia, Thailand, Indonesia, China and beyond, the range of potential DCMs diversified even further to include, for example, Thai conglomerates, Singaporean state-owned enterprises (SOEs) and firms belonging to China's People's Liberation Army. It is therefore not easy to summarize the nature of East Asia's MNEs, but Table 9.4 provides an overall evaluation of some key attributes of DCMs from the six largest source countries of FDI in the region and indicates the characteristics of FDI from these countries. The summary table relies heavily on research by other scholars, but given that this is an under-researched area the analysis below should be treated as being preliminary and provisional.

An examination of Table 9.4 suggests that there may be four types of EA-DCM involved in foreign direct investment. The first type is represented by large industrial groups in comparatively advanced industries such as electronics, automobiles and speciality chemicals, emanating from countries such as South Korea, Singapore (including SOEs) and, to a progressively lesser extent, Hong Kong, Taiwan, Malaysia, Thailand, China and the Philippines. They are often regionally focused because of their relatively lower technological base compared to major Western and Japanese MNEs, but many have a global perspective, especially with regard to sales. This is often reflected in a large proportion of FDI in commerce-related activities in North America and Europe. This orientation towards industrialized country markets is likely to intensify, mostly in the short term, because of the impact of the Asian financial crisis on regional markets. In addition

Table 9.4 Analytical summary of EA-DCMs and FDI characteristics by source country

Characteristic	*South Korea*	*Taiwan*	*Hong Kong*	*Singapore*	*China*	*Malaysia*
Scale of FDI (circa 1996)	US$13.7bn	US$27.3bn (possibly under-reported)	US$112.2bn (perhaps 60–70% of this is by Hong Kong companies)	US$37.5bn (Singapore sources indicate S$46bn, 5159 ventures abroad in 1995 – implying that roughly 50% of FDI is by Singaporean companies)	US$18.0bn	US$12.3bn
Type of Firm	Large chaebols (industrial groups) such as Samsung and Daewoo. SMEs	Primarily SMEs, often OEMs subcontracted to foreign MNEs. A few large companies such as Acer and Tatung	SMEs, especially companies manufacturing in China and ASEAN. Larger conglomerates in the financial, services and infrastructural/ property areas	Principally large firms, many state-owned or state-influenced. Larger conglomerates in the financial, services and infrastructural/ property areas	Principally large state-owned (at the national, provincial and municipal levels); some controlled by the People's Liberation Army	Principally conglomerates – many have Government support – many are Chinese-owned with regional family links. Larger firms are resources-based
Sectors/ Industries	Manufacturing 56% Commerce 20% Mining 6% Others 18% (In manufacturing: textiles, metal products and footwear in Asia; electronics, automobiles, and petrochemicals in North America)	Manufacturing 60% Financial 25% Commerce 6% Other 9%		Financial 50% Manufacturing 25% Commerce 10% Real estate 7% Other 8%		Finance, Real estate, Business services 52% Manufacturing 19% Agroindusties 16% Mining 5% Trade and tourism 3% Other 5%

Table 9.4 *Continued*

Characteristic	*South Korea*	*Taiwan*	*Hong Kong*	*Singapore*	*China*	*Malaysia*
Location of FDI	China & ASEAN 44% N. America 31% Europe 15% S. America 4% Other 6%	China 35% ASEAN 20% N. America 16% Other Asia 6% Europe 3% Others 20%	China ASEAN North America Europe Oceania	ASEAN 47% Other Asia 16% Europe 20% N. America 2% Oceania 1% Other 14%	Hong Kong & Macau 61% N. America 4% Oceania 8% Other 6% Other 21%	ASEAN 33% China 9% Other Asia 2% Europe 8% N. America 9% Oceania 25% Africa 16%
Location of FDI in manufacturing	USA, UK, Indonesia, Vietnam, Malaysia, the Philippines	China, Malaysia, Thailand, Vietnam, Indonesia, the Philippines	China, Indonesia, Thailand, Singapore, Vietnam	Malaysia, Hong Kong, Indonesia, China, Thailand, Vietnam, India	Diverse locations incl. Malaysia, Brazil, Poland, China, Tanzania etc.	China, Indonesia, the Philippines, Cambodia
Characteristics of subsidiaries	Large, wholly-owned in industrialized countries; small, joint-ventures in developing countries	Majority joint ventures or wholly-owned	Joint ventures, often with local Chinese	67% of subsidiaries are wholly or majority controlled	Relatively small, mostly greenfield joint ventures, frequently with local Chinese	Joint venturing is common, esp. because of Malaysian firms' conglomerate nature and government influence
Motives	Markets in industrialized countries; Growing	Currency appreciation; Rising costs of	Rising costs of production; Growing	Rising costs of production in the home market;	Export promotion; Acquisition of	Soaring labour costs in Malaysia; Small

	opportunities in Asia-Pacific markets; Rising costs of production in the home market; Need for resources; Ethnic Koreans (in China, Kazakhstan and the USA)	production; Growing opportunities in Asia-Pacific markets	opportunities in Asia-Pacific markets; Conglomerate opportunism	Small local market; Growing opportunities in the Asia-Pacific; Need to access industrialized country markets; Government 'Regionalization' policy	technology and expertise; Export of manpower; Government measures; Political ties with foreign countries	local market; Opportunities in regional markets; Government encouragement, including 'south–south' deals with the Philippines, Vietnam, India and Tanzania; ASEAN schemes and incentives. Regional partners for non-ASEAN entrants to, say, Cambodia and the Mekong region
Other characteristics	Larger firms are responding to global competition with regional policies (among other measures); SMEs play a significant role, especially in terms of FDI in ASEAN	Little joint investment by Taiwanese SMEs and their MNE 'principals'; this contrasts for example with Japanese investments, esp. within keiretsu	Expatriate MNEs, many now headquartered overseas, generally behave similarly to Hong Kong 'Chinese' conglomerates	FDI in Europe (esp. UK) and N. America is chiefly in the financial sector, followed by commerce	The only truly developing country among EA- DCM investors in this table	FDI in Europe (esp. UK) and N. America is chiefly in the financial sector, followed by commerce. Some evidence of technology acquisition activities in manufacturing
Source material UNCTAD (1996)	Shin (1998), O'Neil (1998); Chaponnier (1998), Kim (1996), Kim (1997)	Chen (1996), McDermott (1998), Giroud and Mirza (1998), Mirza *et al.* (1998), Tu (1994)	Chen and Ng (1998), Yeung (1996)	Oh (1996), Goh (1997), SMF (1993), SDS (1995, 1996)	Tseng (1997), Zhan (1995), McDermott and Huang (1996)	Yeo (1996), Joi (1998)

these DCMs are also often involved in technology acquisition activities, again particularly through FDI in North America, Western Europe and, increasingly, Central and Eastern Europe.

A second type of EA-DCMs are multisector, diversified conglomerates from countries such as Hong Kong, Malaysia and Singapore. These include many 'overseas Chinese' conglomerates and 'expatriate MNEs' such as Jardines, which tend to invest overseas in areas such as finance, tourism, property and construction. This also tends to lead to a regional focus, but opportunistic purchases in industrialized and developing countries are not uncommon. For example, Malaysian enterprises such as Petronas and Telekom Malaysia recently acquired assets valued at US$1.5bn (JOI, 1998). Such strategies occur where the apex of the conglomerate is a holding company and the acquired products are sold locally, as for example in designer goods. In many respects their development has been sustained through industries *ancillary* to manufacturing which until recently have been highly profitable; they also often enjoy government support and links, especially in ventures related to construction and infrastructure. They frequently operate in alliance with other companies, hence the preponderance of joint ventures in their overseas operations.

Thirdly, many EA-DCMs are small and medium-sized enterprises which play a significant role in the economies of Taiwan, South Korea and Hong Kong. Under cost pressures some of these have relocated to China and ASEAN in order to take advantage of cheap labour. Many are subcontractors and retain their links to larger MNEs from both the region and Triad countries. It is not untypical for a Taiwanese SME to move its entire production base to China with only a small sales office in the home economy. Joint ventures, usually keeping a majority stake, are common in order to take advantage of relationships with local companies and officials. Finally, China's DCMs are usually large SOEs which are engaged primarily in state-determined activities, such as the acquisition of foreign currency and technology. Moreover, many overseas manufacturing ventures have been undertaken to cement political ties with friendly regimes. In the future these firms may evolve into one or other of the first two types above.

Apart from Chinese DCMs, however, all the others, it would appear, are analogous to similar types of MNEs from the West and Japan. The key differences are in their relative technological level, experience and expertise and – possibly – the nature of their firm-specific advantages. Having said this, there are always idiosyncrasies. Ethnic ties, for instance, play a role in determining the location of a proportion of the

FDI. Examples include: Taiwanese companies locating in certain parts of Fujian province; Overseas Chinese firms similarly locating in parts of Guangdong and neighbouring provinces; and Korean firms entering markets such as Kazakhstan, partly because of the local Korean diaspora. The FDI patterns of EA-DCMs are also, to some extent, determined by government policies. This reflects the continuing role of the 'development state' and good examples include Singapore, which has a fully-articulated regional FDI policy (SMF, 1993), and Malaysia. The Malaysian government is keen to encourage investment into Indo-China and Thailand has a similar policy. Malaysia has also been promoting FDI by its enterprises in the Philippines and Vietnam. ASEAN policies, such as the growth triangles and the ASEAN Investment Area (AIA) (Mirza *et al.*, 1997; Chia, 1996) are also government-induced incentives to internationalize regionally, although in this case the relevant benefits are available to all MNEs. This government influence will remain significant for a period, but arguably will subside in the future.

CONCLUDING REMARKS

This chapter has argued that, perhaps in contradistinction to the major DCMs of the past,[13] the internationalization of East Asian MNEs is primarily the consequence of a simultaneous process of globalization and regionalization. However, as with stones thrown into turbulent waters, the ripples are far from homogeneous and the patterns of industrialization and internationalization are diverse and disparate. Nevertheless, it has been suggested that there are four main types of East Asian DCMs, with distinctive characteristics. All of these, arguably, have analogues among Western and Japanese MNEs, albeit their relative position in the international division of labour circumscribes the types of strategies they can pursue. Of course there is a need to further examine this proposition and related ones, especially because of the growing role EA-DCMs are likely to play in the world economy.

For example, it is clear from the above discussion that East Asian MNEs pursue all four traditional types of FDI (resource-seeking, market-seeking, efficiency-seeking and strategic asset-seeking), but it would be useful to get a better sense of which types are more prominent, especially by source country and type of DCM. Furthermore, are the characteristics of locational variables for each type of FDI similar to or different from those displayed by Western and Japanese MNEs? (Dunning, 1998b). This might depend on the fashion in which existing EA-DCMs will evolve. For example, many East Asian conglomerates exist because they have hitherto been able to ride the interstices created by market imperfections – a not unusual situation in a region with developing industries and institutions and one in which the government has had to play a considerable role. However, in view of increasing competition after the Asian financial crisis – including further inroads by global players – the overriding emerging question is whether their internal markets are efficient or whether, in fact, inefficiencies have been disguised by monopoly power they have been able to yield because of their imperfections-generated dominance. If the latter is accurate, EA-DCMs will change dramatically over the next few years through a process of divestment, mergers and acquisition – in other words they will become even closer in form to Triad MNEs, albeit with a degree of distinctiveness.

On the other hand, if they have been able to generate internal-market efficiencies (and this might vary by type of conglomerate, that is, from chaebol to expatriate MNE) the situation will be very different. Their evolution will also be determined by the extent to which their activities compete with or are complementary to Triad MNEs now and in the future. With heroic oversimplification it could be argued that industrial groups (type 1 in the previous section) compete, conglomerates (type 2) cooperate and SMEs (type 3) are subcontractors: after appropriate modifications it would be useful to predict how this 'model' will apply in the future. Furthermore, depending on the answers to earlier questions, it may also be possible to judge whether the impact of DCMs on host countries is more or less beneficial when compared to other MNEs. For instance, if East Asian conglomerates are the primary vehicle for FDI, is the technology and expertise associated with them too ephemeral for sustainable development?

In summary, there are many possible avenues for future research regarding East Asian (and other) developing-country multinationals. This is an appropriate juncture to utilize and extend existing theories and use them to investigate this interesting phenomenon which is important from the perspective of both strategic and developmental considerations.

Notes

1. The term 'globalization' is more fully discussed elsewhere in this volume.
2. A number of developing-country multinationals pre-date the globalization process, but they will not be discussed directly here except insofar as they participated in the globalization/regionalization process analysed in this chapter.
3. Although the policies of East Asian economies were very important in encouraging investment by both foreign and local companies, it is worth mentioning that East Asia was fortunate in at least two respects compared to other developing economies. On the one hand, there was the proximity of Japan, the first non-Western industrialized country which was both a model and a source for much early investment. On the other hand, local political conditions made Eastern Europe, South America and the Mediterranean countries less attractive to foreign investors.
4. Although this discussion is posited in terms of manufacturing, a similar discussion could be constructed for services. Indeed, the internationalization of services is today more important than manufacturing, and East Asia has very much shared in this process.
5. The Association of Southeast Asian Nations which currently is composed of nine countries: Brunei, Indonesia, Laos, Malaysia, Myanmar, the Philippines, Singapore, Thailand and Vietnam.
6. In this chapter the term 'Overseas Chinese' refers to the Chinese migrant populations of Southeast Asia (and their enterprises). This is in analytical contradistinction to the Chinese in Hong Kong and Taiwan who are likely to exhibit different behaviour patterns – with (possibly) contrasting corporate strategies' consequences. Arguably, given the country's majority population, many Singaporean enterprises may behave similarly to those from Hong Kong and Taiwan.
7. For ease of exposition this chapter will continue to use the term 'developing-country multinational' for MNEs from South Korea, Singapore and Taiwan, even though the case can be made that these are industrialized economies.
8. However, in view of the continuing financial crises in Mexico, East Asia and Russia during the 1990s, the problems of financial volatility have clearly not been solved.
9. Mercosur currently consists of Argentina, Brazil, Paraguay and Uruguay, as well as a number of associate members.
10. Reported in the *Guardian*, 10 September 1997.
11. Similarly European MNEs have more recently turned their attentions towards East Asia because of their low levels of FDI in the region compared to USA and Japanese companies (UNCTAD, 1996).
12. Japan recycled some of its trade surpluses as aid for developing regions, especially East Asia during the 1980s and 1990s – one goal being the establishment of first-rate infrastructure for the expansion of Japanese MNEs into the region. Of course, this infrastructure has also benefited other firms.

13. Including, perhaps, non-East Asian DCMs from Brazil, Nigeria, Kuwait and elsewhere.

References

ANDERSON, O. and L.W. KEAM (1998), 'Resource-based Theory and International Growth Strategies: An Exploratory Study', *International Business Review*, vol. 7, no. 2, pp. 163–84.

ASIAN DEVELOPMENT BANK (1997), *Emerging Asia: Changes and Challenges* (Manila: ADB Publications).

BAIROCH, P. and R. KOZUL-WRIGHT (1996), *Globalization Myths: Some Historical Reflections on Integration, Industrialisation and Growth in the World Economy*, UNCTAD Discussion Papers, no 113 (Geneva: UNCTAD).

CERACI, V.J. and W. PREWO (1977), 'Bilateral Trade Flows and Transport Costs', *Review of Economics and Statistics*, vol. 59, no. 1, pp. 16–27.

CHAPONNIERRE, J.R. (1998), 'Korean Outward Investment: Too Large, Too Soon?', paper presented at the LVMH Conference, *Asian Foreign Investment in Asia*, INSEAD Euro–Asia Centre, Fontainbleau, 6–7 April.

CHEN, E.K.Y. and R.C.W. NG (1998), 'Foreign Direct Investment of Hong Kong in ASEAN', in H. Mirza and K.H. Wee (eds), *The Strategy of Transnational Corporations in the ASEAN Region* (London: Edward Elgar).

CHEN, T-J. (1996), 'Taiwan's Small Transnational Firms in Southeast Asia: Invest and Localise', paper presented at the ASEAN–UNDP Experts' Seminar on *Promotion of Foreign Direct Investment in the Context of the ASEAN Investment Area*, Felix Arnoma Swissôtel, Bangkok, 23–24 May.

CHIA, S.Y. and T.Y. LEE (1992), 'Subregional Economic Zones: A New Motive Force in Asia-Pacific Development', paper presented at the *20th Pacific Trade and Development Conference*, Washington, September.

CHIA, S.Y. (1996), 'Foreign Direct Investments into ASEAN and Intra-ASEAN Investments', paper presented at the *ASEAN Investment Workshop*, Manila, September.

DUNNING, J.H. (1998a), 'Globalization and the New Geography of Foreign Direct Investment', *Oxford Development Studies*, vol. 26, no. 1, pp. 47–9.

DUNNING, J.H. (1998b), 'Location and the Multinational Enterprise: A Neglected Factor?', *Journal of International Business Studies*, vol. 29, no. 1, pp. 45–66.

DUNNING, J.H. (1997), *Governments, Globalization and International Business* (Oxford and New York: Oxford University Press).

DRYSDALE, P. and R. GARNAUT (1994), 'Trade Intensities and the Analysis of Bilateral Trade Flows in a Many-Country World', in R. Garnaut and P. Drysdale, *Asia Pacific Regionalism: Readings in International Economic Relations* (Pymble: Harper International).

EUROPEAN COMMISSION AND UNCTAD–DTCI (1996), *Investing in Asia's Dynamism: European Direct Investment in Asia* (Luxembourg: Office for Official Publications of the European Communities).

GARNAUT, R. and P. DRYSDALE (1994), *Asia Pacific Regionalism: Readings in International Economic Relations* (Pymble: Harper International).

GIROUD, A. and H. MIRZA (1998), 'Taiwanese Firms Technology Transfer to South East Asian Countries', paper presented at the LVMH Conference, *Asian Foreign Investment in Asia*, INSEAD Euro–Asia Centre, Fontainbleau, 6–7 April.

GOH, E. (1997), 'Foreign Direct Investment: Experience of an SME from a Developing Country in Asia', paper presented at a conference on SMEs–FDI–Development organized by UNCTAD and MOFTEC, *Attracting SMEs and Promoting Development in Developing Asia*, Kunming, 29–31 October.

HANSEN, N.M. (ed.) (1972), *Growth Centres in Regional Economic Development* (New York: The Free Press).

HUNTINGTON, S.P. (1996), *The Clash of Civilizations and the Remaking of World Order* (New York: Simon & Schuster).

INTERNATIONAL MONETARY FUND (1997), *World Economic Outlook, May 1997: Globalization – Opportunities and Challenges* (Washington: IMF).

JAPAN INSTITUTE FOR OVERSEAS INVESTMENT (JOI) (1998), 'The Investment Climate of South Africa', *JOI Review*, March, pp. 1–34.

KIM, H-Y. (1997), 'Korean Outward Direct Investment', paper presented at a conference on SMEs–FDI–Development organized by UNCTAD and MOFTEC, *Attracting SMEs and Promoting Development in Developing Asia*, Kunming, 29–31 October.

KIM, W-P. (1996), 'Globalization and FDI of Korean Automakers', paper presented at the 13 Annual Euro–Asia Management Studies Association Conference, Chuo University, Tokyo, November.

LINNEMANN, H. (1966), *An Econometric Study of World Trade Flows* (Amsterdam: North-Holland).

McDERMOTT, M. (1998), 'Taiwanese Outward FDI: The Response to Regionalization', in H. Mirza (ed.), *Global Competitive Strategies in the World Economy* (London: Edward Elgar).

McDERMOTT, M. and HUANG, C.H. (1996), 'Industrial State-Owned Multinationals from China', *Asia-Pacific Business Review*, vol. 3, no. 1, pp. 16–27.

MIRZA, H. (ed.) (1998), *Global Competitive Strategies in the World Economy* (London: Edward Elgar).

MIRZA, H. (1997), 'The Emerging Cultures of Capitalism', paper presented at the 14th Sino-European Conference, co-organized by the Modern Asia Research Centre, University of Geneva and the Institute of International Relations, *Civilizations, National Powers and Economics: Convergence or Clash?*, Geneva, 23–24 September.

MIRZA, H., F. BARTELS and M. HILEY (1997), *The Promotion of Foreign Direct Investment into and within ASEAN: Towards the Establishment of an ASEAN Investment Area* (Jakarta: ASEAN Secretariat).

MIRZA, H. and K.H. WEE (eds) (1998), *The Strategy of Transnational Corporations in the ASEAN Region* (London: Edward Elgar).

MIRZA, H., A. GIROUD, K.H. WEE and F. BARTELS (1998), 'The Investment Strategies of Asian and Non-Asian Firms in ASEAN', paper presented at the LVMH Conference, *Asian Foreign Investment in Asia*, INSEAD Euro–Asia Centre, Fontainbleau, 6–7 April.

OH, J. (1996), *Singapore's Regionalization Strategy: The Internationalisation of State and Enterprise*, MBA management project, Bradford, University of Bradford Management Centre.

O' NEIL, K. (1998), 'Samsung's Views on Global and Regionalization Strategies', in H. MIRZA (ed.), *Global Competitive Strategies in the World Economy* (London: Edward Elgar).

PETRI, P.A. (1994), 'The Regional Clustering of Foreign Direct Investment and Trade', *Transnational Corporations*, vol. 3, No. 3, pp. 1–24.

RUGGIERO, R. (1996), 'The Road Ahead: International Trade Policy in the Era of the WTO', *The Fourth Annual Sylvia Ostry Lecture*, Ottawa, 28 May.

SAUVÉ, P. and D. SCHWANEN (1996), *Investment Rules for the Global Economy: Enhancing Access to Markets* (Toronto: C.D. Howe Institute).

SHIN, MANNSOO (1998), 'Korean Investment in ASEAN', in H. Mirza and K.H. Wee (eds), *The Strategy of Transnational Corporations in the ASEAN Region* (London: Edward Elgar).

SINGAPORE DEPARTMENT OF STATISTICS (SDS) (1996), *Singapore's Investment Abroad, 1994–1995* (Singapore: SDS).

SINGAPORE DEPARTMENT OF STATISTICS (SDS) (1995), *Singapore's Investment Abroad, 1994*, Occasional Paper series, Singapore.

SINGAPORE MINISTRY OF FINANCE (SMF) (1993), *Final Report of the Committee to Promote Enterprise Overseas* (Singapore, SNP Publishers).

TINBERGEN, J. (1962), *Shaping the World Economy – Suggestions for an International Economic Policy* (New York: Twentieth Century Fund).

TSENG, C.S. (1997), *Foreign Direct Investment by PRC First-Time Investors*, PhD thesis, Bradford, University of Bradford Management Centre.

TU, J-H. (1994), 'Intra-Regional Direct Foreign Investment and Technology Transfer: Implications of the Taiwanese Experience', in *Intra-Regional Investment and Technology Transfer in Asia: A Symposium Report*, Tokyo, Asian Productivity Organization.

UNCTAD (1997), *World Investment Report 1996: Transnational Corporations, Market Structure and Competition Policy* (New York and Geneva: United Nations).

UNCTAD (1996), *Sharing Asia's Dynamism: Asian Direct Investment in the European Union* (New York and Geneva: United Nations).

WOLF, C. Jr. and D. WEINSCHROTT (1973), 'International Transactions and Regionalism: Distinguishing "Insiders" from "Outsiders"', *American Economic Review*, vol. 63, no. 2, pp. 54–71.

WORLD BANK (1993), *The East Asian Miracle: Economic Growth and Public Policy* (Oxford: Oxford University Press).

WORLD TRADE ORGANIZATION (1995), *Regionalism and the World Trading System* (Geneva: World Trade Organization).

YEO, R. (1996), *Malaysian Foreign Direct Investment in Transition*, MBA Management Project, Bradford, University of Bradford Management Centre.

YEUNG, H.W.C. (1996), 'Sectoral Specialisation and Competitive Advantage: Hong Kong Investments in the ASEAN Region', *ASEAN Economic Bulletin*, vol. 13, no. 1, pp. 16–27.

ZHAN, J.X. (1995), 'Transnationalization and Outward Investment: The Case of Chinese Firms', *Transnational Corporations*, vol. 4, no. 3, pp. 61–93.

10 Small- and Medium-sized MNCs, Industrial Clusters and Globalization: The Japanese Experience

Terutomo Ozawa

INTRODUCTION

While Japan's big enterprises such as Toyota, Toshiba, Matsushita, and Sony are household names throughout the world, the Japanese economy is crowded with a large number of unknown small and medium-sized enterprises (SMEs). For instance, the latter category of enterprises (defined as those with less than 300 employees) accounted for 95.9 per cent of the total number of establishments in manufacturing, contributing to 51.3 per cent of the total value of shipments and 55.9 per cent of total value-added in 1994 (Small and Medium Business Agency, 1997). SMEs are often described as *Kagemusha* or 'shadow *samurai*' in Japan. Without them, Japan's large business sector would not have developed such formidable competitiveness in the global market. Many industries exhibit close symbiotic relationships between the two sectors.

The high weight of the SME sector in Japan is, however, actually not unique. All other developed countries exhibit more or less similarly high proportions of business activities by SMEs in total employment and output (Fujita, 1997). Is there, then, anything unique about Japan's small business sector? Perhaps Japan's SMEs have been exposed to much more drastic and faster-paced structural changes at home, and hence required to be much more adaptive and flexible than in other advanced countries. There are also much closer affiliational relations between SMEs and their large counterparts in Japan, particularly by way of well-coordinated subcontracting. The rapid structural transformation and the high levels of business collaboration have left distinctive marks on the changing patterns of the international business operations of Japanese SMEs. Their overseas investment activities in particular have by and large been *macro-structurally compelled* (because of drastic structural changes), rather than *micro-motivationally/autonomously induced* (though this latter attribute is becoming increasingly pronounced in present-day Japan).

Scattered throughout Japan, SMEs in manufacturing tend to congregate in certain local communities. For good reasons, they operate in industrial clusters rather than isolated from each other and from their customers. No discussion about Japan's small business sector can be made without reference to its localization features, although the localization phenomenon itself may not be so unique to Japan. Furthermore, Japanese SMEs seem to be driven to engage in international business, notably foreign direct investment (FDI), to a much greater extent than their counterparts in the other countries. In this regard, the Japanese experience provides a good laboratory to study the interactions between the economic phenomenon of industrial clusters and the internationalization process of SMEs, a new topic in the field of international business and economics.

THEORETICAL CONSIDERATIONS

Situated in an over-inhabited and geographically confined archipelago, Japan's policy-makers and captains of industry have been conscious of the critical importance of how productive activities are located, organized, and managed. Besides, industry itself tends to settle and cluster rather naturally in certain regions by necessity, since Japan is 85 per cent mountainous, leaving only limited flat space to be used for both agriculture and industry. Enterprises are compelled to localize in regions where flat space is available. This localization tendency is even more pronounced for SMEs than for large ones, since the former more consciously rely on the external economies of agglomeration at the time of business establishment. In the context of this study of locally-clustered SMEs, it is also important to keep in mind that the nature of industrial clustering has changed and exhibited various organizational structures *pari passu* with the rapid structural transformation of the Japanese economy as it has gone through the sequential stages of growth. Moreover, the nature of small producers in such evolving industrial regions has accordingly changed.

The Smithian 'Town' and the Principle of Surplus Resource Transmogrification

Conventional wisdom posits that the concept of industrial clustering in a particular region was first introduced by Alfred Marshall (1920). Marshall's industrial district has become a standard point of reference in the mainstream economics literature. Surprisingly, however, it is scarcely known among conventional economists that 144 years earlier, Adam Smith (1776) already introduced the concept of industrial agglomeration by conceptualizing the growth of a manufacturing 'town.' It could be argued that Smith's concept is actually *far more dynamic* than Marshall's and is even *far more relevant* as a framework in which to analyze the trade-driven type of industrial clusters that have been in existence in Japan (Ozawa and Ferrer, 1997).

Adam Smith emphasized *inter-sectoral* growth complementarity between 'country' (agriculture) and 'town' (manufacturing). Here, it should be noted that the Smithian 'town' is nothing but the phenomenon of industrial clustering where small manufacturers of 'artifices' come and settle initially in response to the needs of farmers and, later on, in response to the needs of each other:

> Without the assistance of some artificers, indeed, the cultivation of land cannot be carried on . . . Smiths, carpenters, wheel-wrights, and plou[gh]-wrights, masons, and bricklayers, tanners, shoemakers, and tailors, are people, whose service the former has frequent occasion for. Such artificers too stand, occasionally, in need of the assistance of one another, and as their residence is *not*, like that of the farmer, *necessarily tied down to a precise spot, they naturally settle in the neighbourhood of one another, and thus form a small town or village*. [They all] contribute *still further to augment the town.*
>
> (Smith, 1776, p. 403, emphasis added)

Thus, compared to Marshall's single-sector model, what Smith had in mind was a *two-sector* model in which the 'town' provides manufactured goods to the 'country' in exchange for farm goods as provisions and materials. This means that *the more productive the 'country' is, the larger (and richer) the 'town' becomes* – and vice versa in an interactive cumulative causation.

What is more fascinating is that Smith explicitly brings in the role of *international trade* in agglomeration and makes a fascinating observation: namely that the more fertile the 'country' is, but the more isolated from opportunities for trade 'on account of the expense of land carriage, and inconveniency of river navigation' (namely, isolated from ports), the more 'difficult to send this surplus abroad'. Then, the 'town' (manufacturing) serves as an intermediary to *virtually transmogrify a farm surplus into exportable manufactures circuitously via an expansion of an industrializing town*:

> . . . a great number of workmen [settled in the town] give a new value to the surplus part of the rude produce, by saving the expense of carrying it to the water side, or to some distant market; . . . as the fertility of the land had given birth to the manufacture, so that progress of the manufacture re-acts upon the land, and increases still further its fertility. *The manufacturers first supply the neighbourhood, and afterwards, as their work improves and refines, more distant markets . . . The corn, which could with difficulty have been carried abroad in its own shape, is in this manner virtually exported in that of the complete manufacture, and may easily be sent to the remotest corners of the world.*
>
> (Smith, 1776, pp. 430–1, emphasis added)

What may be identified here as the *surplus-resource-transmogrification* principle of trade is critical to our understanding of industrial clusters in an open economy. Smith then cites the manufacturing regions of Leeds, Halifax, Sheffield, Birmingham and Wolverhampton as the typical examples of this type of manufacturing town based on rich agricultural areas and trade.

The trade-driven growth of Smithian industrial clusters rests on Smith's other famous dictum: 'the division of labour is limited by the extent of the market'. The most desirable effect of trade is an *expansion* of market size, which enables manufacturers to cultivate increasing returns to scale, both internal and external; division of labour and specialization; skill formation and technological improvement; and enhanced agglomeration economies in industrial clusters. These are all the dynamic effects created by an expansion of the market through trade. In modern parlance, they culminate in productivity growth or 'total factor productivity'. As a result, the nature and quality of manufactures – that is, 'their extension and improvement' – occurs, changing from 'necessaries' and 'conveniences' to 'elegancies' under 'a natural progress to opulence', according to Smith's terminology. These are the dynamic gains from trade that promote economic development and constitute 'the nature and causes of the wealth of nations'.

Put differently, trade transforms endowed assets (location-specific advantages) into created assets (ownership-specific advantages).

In Smith's model, indeed, industrial agglomeration occurs in *triple* ways: inter-sectorally and intra-sectorally, as well as across borders (namely, inter-nationally). This process is dynamic, structural and functionally specified in terms of sectoral interactions, and evolutionary in technological and structural upgrading, and explicitly focused on international trade as an *augmenter* of market size. This is in sharp contrast to Marshall's conceptualization, in which agglomeration takes place only intra-sectorally, and the role of trade, domestic and foreign alike, is left unconsidered. Marshall's model depicts only an intra-country (closed economy), *intra-industry* phenomenon.

In short, the Smithian open-economy multi-sectoral approach provides a much more appropriate analytical framework for evaluating the experiences of Japan's small industry which has been employing external commercial links (trade, foreign direct investment and technology flows) as strategic instruments for evolutionary corporate growth.

STRUCTURAL TRANSFORMATION, GLOBALIZATION AND SMEs IN JAPAN

The Evolutionary Structural Changes

The Japanese economy has gone through rapid structural changes since the end of the Second World War, accompanied by rapid globalization. The relationships between Japan's structural upgrading and the roles of SMEs as wealth creators and business globalizers are summarized in Table 10.1. Japan's structural upgrading can be chronologically divided into four phases: (1) Phase I: the development of Heckscher–Ohlin industries; (2) Phase II: undifferentiated Smithian industries; (3) Phase III: differentiated Smithian industries; and (4) Phase IV: Schumpeterian industries (Ozawa, 1994). These are now considered in turn.

Heckscher–Ohlin Industrialization and SMEs as the Vanguards of Transnationalization

Phase I (1950 to the mid-1960s) was characterized by the expansion of labour-intensive low-wage goods in light industries such as textiles,

Table 10.1 Structural upgrading, industrial clusters and SME globalization

Stages of growth	*Factor-driven ('Heckscher–Ohlin')*	*Scale-driven ('Undifferentiated Smithian')*	*Assembly-driven ('Differentiated Smithian')*	*Information-driven ('Schumpeterian')*
I *Economy at large*				
Representative industries	Textiles, toys, sundries	Steel, chemicals, heavy machinery, shipbuilding	Automobiles, electronics	Biotechnology, optoelectronics, new materials, super-micro-chips
Types of industrial cluster	'Transmogrifier' clusters	'Konbinato'	'Just-in-time' delivery zone	'Virtual industrial district; non-place' 'techno-konbinato'
II *SME sector*				
Involvement	Light industry	Sectional subcontractors	Suppliers of parts, components & accessories	'Niche' exporters
Advantages	Economies of factor-based clustering	Subcontracted specialization	Economies of affiliation	Economies of networking (strategic alliances)
		Scale economies, internal/interlinked/ external	Scale & scope economies	External economies in information
Globalization	Cross-border surplus-resource-transmogrifiers Vanguards of Japan's overseas FDI	Mainly licensing & technical assistance	'Follow-the-client' FDI as parts suppliers	Strategic alliances in R&D, production, and marketing and so on

toys and sundries, the Heckscher–Ohlin industries whose competitiveness derives from the abundant endowment of resources, including 'raw' (unskilled) labour. This was the period during which SMEs were the most active employers of low-cost labour, producing standardized light industry goods and exporting them. Indeed, they were the major earners of foreign exchange which was particularly precious at that time. Their competitive strength stemmed from low-cost labour and the highly developed *social (inter-firm and inter-functional) division of labour* among the small producers themselves who specialized in divided-up tasks of processing and fabrication, and between these producers and the distributors and traders who were able to serve as *business-makers* (both at home and cross borders).

Many of these SMEs are clustered in so-called *jiba-sangyo* (locality-embedded industries), which are found throughout Japan. These clusters currently number no less than 300, more than one-third of which are engaged in exporting (Yamazaki, 1980), although their export orientation used to be much more pronounced in the 1950s and 1960s. Although the trade competitiveness of the *jiba-sangyo* has weakened in labour-intensive manufacturing, they are still surviving as 'flexible' sub-regions through diversification into new industries and upgrading of their products.

Overpopulated Japan used to result in the poor emigrating to Latin America and North America, but this alone could not solve the problem of surplus labour. The real solution was found in the Smithian principle of surplus resource transmogrification, accompanied by the expansion of the *jiba-sangyo*. But such Smithian clusters soon hit limits to growth. In fact, *the faster and the more successful the growth of the Smithian district, the greater the need for adaptability*. The very success leads to two self-constraining factors, namely, labour shortages (hence, higher wages) and home currency appreciation (especially if the initial rate is undervalued to promote exports).

In response to a 'deteriorating' industrial milieu, the firms had to alter their business activities and choose new courses of adaptive action. There were basically four possible avenues to take for survival. They could raise labour productivity (for example, via automation and training); upgrade their products to higher value-added types so that they could pay higher wages; diversify into a new line of business; or transplant production to a low-wage country (via subcontracting, licensing, or foreign direct investment). Large and small enterprises alike were confronted with the need to adapt by means of these possible measures. To succeed in these endeavours, however, requires a great deal of entrepreneurship and risk-taking.

All these options, except the last one, take time to bear fruit. As a short-run response, therefore, many SMEs – especially those which were only marginally competitive at home – had to choose the last avenue and went to nearby countries where low-cost labour was then still in abundant supply. In fact, they were the pioneers of Japan's incipient multinationals in the late 1960s, so far as manufacturing is concerned.[1] Moreover, additional competitive pressures were exerted on the SME sector by the appreciation of the Japanese yen which began in the early 1970s.

Those SMEs that quickly turned to overseas investment may be called 'cross-border surplus-labour transmogrifiers'. While securing low-cost labour overseas, however, many of them simultaneously strove to raise competitiveness with the measures mentioned above. Some became higher value-added in their operations while maintaining the production segment of their value-added chain abroad (as is illustrated in the case study of Swany Co. in Box 10.1).

Box 10.1
Swany and Comparative Advantage Recycling[1]

(Surplus-resource transmogrifier)
Home office: Shiratori, Shikoku
Employment (home office): 50
Main product: gloves

- Swany was originally established in 1937 as a family-owned shop to manufacture gloves, and incorporated under the present company name in 1950. It was one of several hundred small glove-makers who clustered together in a small rural town, Hiratori, on the island of Shikoku. In the town's heyday (1955–65) when exports brought prosperity, as many as 90 per cent of the townsfolk (totalling about 4000) were either directly or indirectly engaged in manufacturing of all kinds of gloves, from dress gloves to sporting and gardening gloves.
- The labour shortages and wage hikes that began to occur in the 1960s put a profit squeeze on this local industry. The appreciation of the yen in the early 1970s (after the dollar's devaluation in 1970) added difficulties, and the town's exports declined precipitously year after year. To overcome rising labour costs at home and the appreciating yen, Swany chose the Masan Export Processing Zone in Korea as the location of its first wholly-owned manufacturing sub-

sidiary abroad. It started out by employing as many as 450 workers. The unique feature of the factory was an assembly-conveyor system contrived by Swany to mass-produce gloves cost-effectively. This venture's earnings moved into the black after two years.

- Swany's export sales expanded rapidly thanks to the company's direct marketing strategy with big American merchandisers such as Sears Roebuck. In this case the approach to market was not intermediated by trading companies unlike so many products manufactured by SMEs. So much so that in 1976 it opened another wholly-owned subsidiary in Korea employing 300 workers. This expansion was followed by the opening of a third plant with a workforce of 250 in Korea. At the same time, however, Swany closed its three factories in Japan and ended up only with the home-office activities of product development, procurement, and quality and production controls. It began to operate with a staff of only 50 people in Japan.
- Each factory was assigned only one type of product to manufacture. The first subsidiary specialized in synthetic-fabric winter gloves, the second in ski gloves, and the third in leather winter gloves. Along with the conveyor-work-flow system, this inter-subsidiary product specialization proved to be cost-effective, as it enabled local workers to learn and develop specialized skills in a short period of time. Swany thus came to manage 1000 Korean workers with such a small staff at home. With an eye to further expanding export sales in North America, Swany opened an office in New York with a showroom and a small sales staff of 10. It also established a sales office in Canada in 1983. Process technologies are basically simple and labour-intensive, but the company's strength lies in its effective product development, including for example the introduction of 'idea products' such as children's mittens that can make a picture appear with a drop in temperature.
- Sooner than expected, however, the rapid rise in wages and labour shortages in Korea forced Swany to find a new production site in China where low-cost labour was still plentiful. In 1984, it established a 52 per cent-owned joint venture, Swany China, with local interests (48 per cent), and simultaneously closed one of its three Korean operations in 1985. Swany was among the first groups of Japanese manufacturers which moved to China in the early years of opening for inward FDI. Initially, Swany had a problem with low labour efficiency in China, but soon was able to motivate workers (stitchers and knitters) to a higher level of productivity under a piece-work incentive programme. Its operation turned profitable after one year.
- Swany then decided to open up more factories in China, concentrating on sporting gloves. Three new factories were established in 1988 and 1989, and the fifth one was added in 1993. And, simultaneously, the remaining two Korean factories were closed, thereby completely the shift of production from Korea to China.

Continued

- Swany's experience illustrates a case of *comparative advantage recycling* involving labour-intensive products, first from Japan to South Korea (one of the NIEs), and then from the NIEs to China, while the company retains its export markets, mostly in the United States.

[1] Information about Swany is from Small and Medium Business Agency (1986) and Imai, Satoshi *et al.* (1997).

Undifferentiated Smithian Industries, 'Konbinato' and Subcontracting

By the end of the 1960s, however, Japan had already entered the phase of heavy and chemical industrialization. Back in 1955, for example, labour-intensive light industries accounted for 74.7 per cent of the total value of manufacturing, while capital-intensive industries (industrial machinery, chemicals, transportation equipment) 25.3 per cent. But by 1970 these ratios had changed to 46.4 per cent and 53.4 per cent, respectively; while in 1980 they stood at 38.9 and 61.2 per cent, demonstrating a rapid structural upgrading (Ozawa, 1995). Reflective of such structural change was also a reduction in the export contribution of small manufacturers.

The heavy and chemical industries, such as machinery and shipbuilding, are popularly described as *Ju-dai-cho-ko* (*heavy-big-long-thick*) because of the characteristics of the goods they produce. Japan had already succeeded in developing basic (traditional) heavy and chemical industries before the Second World War, but at the war's end they stood damaged and obsolete in both technology and physical facilities. Besides, Japan found itself way behind the West in its modern industries such as speciality steel, alloys, petrochemicals and plastics. A wave of reconstruction and modernization thus emerged in the late 1950s. But these modern industries were not only capital-intensive but also technology-based and, most importantly, resource-intensive. How could resource-deficient Japan develop competitiveness in such resource-based industries?

It decided to set up industrial sites on the coastal areas by building new port facilities, so that low-cost sea transportation could be taken advantage of in both the importing and unloading of bulky raw materials and loading and shipping-out processed products. For example, in petrochemicals an oil refinery, a set of adjunct petrochemical plants and a power-generating plant were all placed in close proximity with each other in a coastal industrial site. This arrangement made it possible to achieve efficient (least costly) flows of input and output from, and to, the outside world. Since these key facilities were arranged in an optimal possible combination, these industrial clusters (complexes) came to be called '*kobinato*' in Japan.

This form of spatial organization was likewise capitalized on by Japan's fully-integrated steel complexes which are heavily dependent on imported coking coal and iron ore, and which are above all dependent on imported state-of-the-art technologies. Moreover, all these facilities were designed to exploit internal scale economies at the plant level. Large volumes of output were achieved through Japan's devoted efforts to export; that is, trade made it possible to capitalize on scale economies by expanding 'the extent of the market'. *The Smithian dynamic effect of cumulative causation was thus incorporated into the 'konbinato' efficiency*. Because of the attained efficiency, paradoxically, resource-exiguous Japan ended up becoming one of the most resource-based economies by the end of the 1960s.

This phase of industrialization was clearly the age of big business and large-scale plants. The Japanese economy and its competitiveness were basically scale-driven in steel and petrochemicals, whose materials processing activities were integrated at industrial site level. However, in other segments of heavy and chemical industries, such as general machinery, shipbuilding and precision machinery, where vertical division of labour was possible, SMEs still had substantial opportunities to grow. They served as vital subcontractors.

Japan's industrial organization in these industries was built on a pyramidal formation. The machine tool industry, for example, had 106 major manufacturers who were supported by as many as 5616 primary subcontractors in such areas as forging, machine processing, subassembly, preparing of metal sheets and plates (MITI, 1989 p. 36). These primary subcontractors in turn depended on even larger numbers of the lower-tier firms. Shipbuilding is another example. The industry was dependent on subcontracting for 38 per cent of shipbuilding, and 53 per cent for ship repairing and maintenance (as of March, 1981) (Mizota, 1983, p. 120). Two types of subcontracting were involved: firstly, inside-plant subcontracting in which independent subcontractors engaged in such specialized works as welding, riveting, painting, scaffolding, equipment fitting and cleaning on the premises; and, secondly, outside-plant subcontracting (mostly suppliers of specialized machinery and equipment such as engines, motors, boilers, air-conditioners, navigational equipment and pantry equipment).

These heavy industries created their own unique industrial systems in which SMEs came to be actively used as subcontractors. This development provided ample and precious opportunities for SMEs to upgrade and further specialize in niche technologies and production, since strong export orientation required higher technical standards and because their large firms' customers were able to provide any necessary technical and managerial assistance. These specialized firms were eventually to emerge as technologically advanced firms later on. Being in the machinery sector, many small subcontractors were able to shift to the next wave of assembly-based growth industries (that is, automobiles and electronics) as specialized producers of parts, components and accessories. Others also succeeded in becoming highly specialized in product development, capturing the niche markets. They have thus become the supporting industries of Tier-II assembly-based industries and the vanguards of Tier-I Schumpeterian industries.

Heavy and chemical industries (such as steel mills and petrochemical plants) as a whole are not so footloose. Yet, they rapidly accumulated a large stock of technologies, and began to engage in technology exports more actively through licensing agreements than via outward FDI. For example, by the early 1970s the steel industry in Japan became a net exporter of technological licences. Some heavy machinery producers (for example, Komatsu, a construction equipment maker) did invest overseas but these investments were by and large limited to distribution, repairs, maintenance services and final assembly operations (involving imported knock-down kits). There were not many cases in which SMEs subcontractors followed their major clients.

Differentiated Smithian Industries and 'Just-in-Time' Delivery Districts

The growth of highly assembly-based, components-intensive industries, notably automobiles and electronics, represented Japan's third phase of industrialization and export expansion. This group of assembly-based industries are oriented to the product characteristics of *kei-haku-tan-sho* (*light-thin-short-small*). This is in sharp contrast to heavy and chemical industries whose traits are *ju-ko-cho-dai* (*heavy-thick-long-big*). Because of the introduction of so-called 'lean production' at Toyota Motor Corporation (Womack, Jones and Roos, 1990) and its rapid spread throughout the assembly-based industries, vertical stages of production became more tightly integrated among firms along the pyramidal structure with a final assembler at the pinnacle and layers (primary, secondary, and so on) of parts, components and accessories (PCA) suppliers. Because of this vertically-integrated nature of operations, these industries cannot be simply identified as 'oligopolistic', because only several major firms (such as Toyota, Nissan, Honda, Mitsubishi and Mazda in automobiles, and Matsushita, Sony and Toshiba in electronics) control the market. In fact, it is an *amalgamation* of different market structures: oligopoly at the top, monopolistic competition in the middle, and near perfect competition at the bottom.

In the course of organizing such a production system (in part encouraged by the Japanese government), SMEs began to be recruited as subcontractors for particular final assemblers. They gradually developed affiliational relationships as parts and components suppliers. This formation of closely-knit industrial groups facilitated such organizational/managerial innovations as 'design-in' subcontracting and 'just-in-time' delivery, which gave an unbeatable source of competitiveness to the final assemblers in both autos and electronics.

The growth of Japan's automobile industry illustrates another unique form of organizing production in terms of space (geography), time and interfirm relations. In the postwar period, the production of automobiles was conventionally regarded as mass production, the method of assembly perfected under Fordism and Taylorism. The automobile industry is deep in vertical integration and requires a large number of parts, components and accessories (PCAs) – 7000 to 10000 units, depending on how these inputs are classified. Consequently, what Thorstein Veblen (1927) called 'interstitial coordination' is a critical managerial function in determining production efficiency (Ozawa, 1994). Fordism and Taylorism emphasized centralization and internalization, that is, in-house production of parts, components and accessories. Ford even runs its own steel mills.

In contrast, Japanese automakers took a different approach. Instead of producing PCAs in-house, they outsourced a substantial portion of inputs to their primary subcontractors, who in turn farmed out to a variety of secondary subcontractors. The latter further use a host of smaller firms as their own subcontractors. Hence the formation of pyramidal *keiretsu* production structures, each led by major final assemblers.

The most prominent auto-related industrial cluster is so-called 'Toyota Castle Town'. Toyota took advantage of locational factors by clustering its suppliers within a radius of approximately one hour's driving time for 'just-in-time' delivery of PCAs (Ikari, 1981). The whole area, encompassing two large cities (Toyoda and Kariya), became a self-contained 'virtual factory', in which about one hundred primary and secondary supplies were all located in close proximity to Toyota's eight major plants. Because of the rapid growth of Toyota Motor it had to build two new plants outside the original cluster, thus expanding the JIT district, and also create an entirely new complex in a distant location in Kyushu, involving a locational replication.

Compared to the subcontracting arrangement seen in heavy industries, the relationships between the final assemblers and their PCA suppliers in the assembly-based industries became much closer in joint product designing/engineering and manufacturing processes. The automobile industry came to develop a 'design-in' or 'black box parts' system, in which the major assemblers work closely with their parts suppliers from the very beginning of a new model change for both approved and consigned drawings and engineering (Fujimoto, 1995). This collaborative product development practice has led to Japanese automakers' formidable strengths in time-based and quality-based competition.

In the course of developing this unique type of 'just-in-time' delivery district, SMEs were recruited by major auto assemblers into the latter's closely knit outsourcing network of PCA suppliers. Inter-process and inter-parts division of labour was pursued, and a substantial part of PCA production was outsourced and externalized. As a result, Japan's automobile industry evolved into a highly SME-dependent system of production, with as much as 87.7 per cent of its firms in the category of SMEs in 1981 (Kiyonari, 1985, p. 94).

The efficiency and export competitiveness of this Japanese industry, however, soon caused trade friction in both North America and Europe. It was against this background that Japanese automobile makers began to set up assembly operations abroad, accompanied by their own PCA suppliers as direct investors or as technology suppliers (licensers) to local suppliers. Unlike the previous phase of heavy and chemical industrialization, small suppliers in assembly-based industries were compelled to establish overseas ventures mostly at the request of their major customers. They may thereafter be called 'assembler-pulled affiliational investors' in PCA supplies.

Hence, it is no surprise that statistics on Japan's outward FDI indicate a close correlation between large firms and SMEs in advancing into overseas markets simultaneously (though often with some lags). Unfortunately, there is no detailed data on the comparative FDI behaviour of SMEs *vis-à-vis* large enterprises in different host countries and across different industries. Nonetheless, the aggregate numbers of overseas ventures set up by SMEs and large enterprises over the 1984–96 period (Figure 10.1) reflect to some extent the characteristics of FDI in the differentiated Smithian industries.

The crest of Japan's outward FDI in the latter half of the 1980s (1985–91) constituted the *third* wave of outward FDI in the postwar period. The first wave occurred during 1969–73, and the second during 1978–85, whose trough (1985) alone is glimpsed in Figure 10.1. In terms of number of ventures, SMEs have been almost as equally active as large enterprises in outward FDI. SMEs' overseas ventures accounted for anywhere between 31 per cent and 60 per cent of the total. The overseas investments made by both SMEs and large enterprises exhibited a similar pattern of fluctuations, moving together in ups and downs, a strong indication of their equal susceptibility to some similar set of factors.

The third wave of outward FDI was actually brought about by Japan's assembly-based industries, notably cars and electronics, in which SMEs serve as PCA suppliers. Although many other factors no

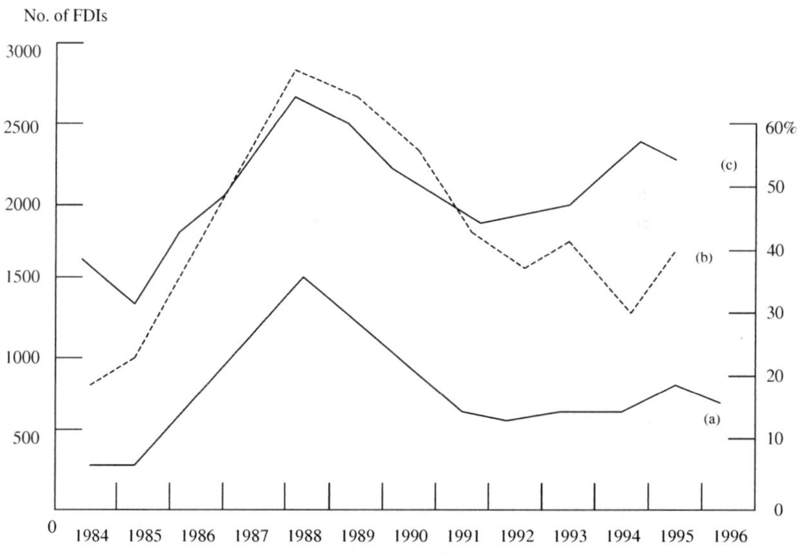

Source: Small and Medium Business Agency (1997).

Figure 10.1 SMEs' overseas FDI and its proportion to total FDI, 1984–96

doubt caused the simultaneous rising and ebbing of the waves of FDI by SMEs and large enterprises over the 1985–91 period, the assembler-pulled type of FDI also contributed to this phenomenon.

Schumpeterian 'Information-driven' Industries and SME Mavericks

Japan has recently reached the phase of what may be called the era of Schumpeterian industries in which innovations play the dominant role in competitiveness. As stressed by Joseph Schumpeter (1934), innovations cover a wide range of new activities, including technological, organizational and marketing innovations. They are based more directly on scientific and technological breakthroughs (such as bio-engineering, opto-electronics, computer science, metallurgy and material science). They are at the forefront of new growth industries which are more customer-oriented. Their production is more tailor-made rather than mass-produced or lean-produced. They contribute to both 'inter-structural upgrading' (establishing a new higher value-added industry) and 'intra-structural upgrading' (qualitative improvement in existing industries).[2]

The firms active in this incipient sector are both existing ones and start-ups. The established firms in lower-tier industries have been striving to diversify into new growth businesses by stepping up their R&D activities. In this process, small new independent units have been spun off from large firms; these spin-offs are usually high-tech ventures. At the same time, small-scale start-ups are also mushrooming, and are also on the cutting edge of technology in highly specialized niche markets. They may be called 'niche market trail-blazers', the new breed of small ventures that may also be called 'satellite enterprises', since they specialize in the 'brain' functions of R&D and product planning and development, contracting out the 'brawn' function of manufacturing to others.

In fact, some of these SMEs have started to use larger and better-known corporations as their subcontractors, thereby turning the tables on the big manufacturers. These upstarts are the never-heard-of-before firms. For example, Kankyo (with less than 100 employees) is Japan's number-one supplier of household air-cleaners and air-dehumidifiers (see Box 10.2). It uses such giant companies as Matsushita as its original equipment manufacturing (OEM) subcontractor. Other examples are Akia, a personal computer company which is now 'outselling Toshiba, NEC and even IBM in Japan's discount electronics stores'; Atlus, a photo-print machine company that sells its

Box 10.2
Kankyo[1] and OEM Operations

Yokohama-city, Tokyo
Established in 1984
Capital: Y495.3 million ($3.96 million)
Employment: 80 people
Sales (1995): Y5 billion ($40 million)

- The Japanese name of this company, *Kankyo*, means the 'environment'. Its major product lines are household air-cleaners and air-dehumidifiers, electronics devices to clean the air in the room from dust particles and to remove humidity. In 1995, the Japanese demand for this product reached the level of 950 000 units, and this small company emerged as a number-one supplier, acquiring a more than 20 per cent market share.
- Yasuyuki Fijimura, the man who started this company used to work as a researcher at Komatsu Corporation, Japan's top construction machinery manufacturer. In 1984 he quit the company and established his own business. A bubble economy was then about to start in Japan and banks were interested in high-tech ventures. Fijimura had no difficulty securing venture capital from major banks such as the Fuji Bank and the Sumitomo Trust Bank as equity investors. The company invested about Y500 million ($4 million) every year and succeeded in securing a number of patents on air-cleaning and air-dehumidifying principles and electronics air-filters. Its current best-seller is an air-cleaner called 'Clear Veil', capable of absorbing invisible dust particles as small as 0.001 micron, a device very popular with those suffering from allergy and asthma.
- Actual R&D is often consigned to outside private research institutions and universities. Hence, there are currently only a dozen pure researchers at the company. About half the company's total of 80 employees have engineering backgrounds, and the majority of them are engaged in technical assistance and quality controls on outsourcing. In fact, the company has no manufacturing facilities. Its products are produced under the OEM (original equipment manufacturing) arrangement with well-known large manufacturers at home, such as Matsushita Electric Industries, Kobe Steel and Minebea, as well as overseas (in the United States, Canada, Israel and Korea). This is indeed a new pattern of subcontracting in which small firms 'hire' large manufacturers as their subcontractors. Traditionally, small firms do the manufacturing work for large firms.
- The reason the company does not manufacture in-house is that Fujimura believes that the product life-cycle is only eight years. They strive to introduce at least one new product a year and develop one

Continued

of them into a major line in four years, thereby maintaining two major products all the time. As the product nears the end of its life-cycle, it is quickly dropped. The absence of manufacturing makes it much easier to remove such a product.

[1] Information about this company is based on Nikkei Business (1995).

Print Club photo machines to teenagers; and Sangi, a toothpaste supplier 'that has given Japan's big consumer-goods producers a fright'.[3]

Many other mavericks are forming R&D associations with business partners inside their *jiba-sangyo*. For example, the Sumida Ward of Tokyo is noted for its dense cluster of small machine shops. Forty-eight small firms organized a joint organization called 'Rush Sumida', for R&D, product development, technological exchange and manufacturing in order to innovate high-tech products. They are mobilizing the varied craftsman skills possessed by diverse small companies into a complementary whole. The group recently succeeded in commercializing a brand-new product, a visual sensor with 360 degrees of vision that can be used as a vital component for robots, watches, cameras and medical instruments. The sensor was designed by a university professor in engineering and developed by the team of craftsmen. The production required extremely high-precision lathe work and intricate mirror manufacturing (involving, for instance, one metal lathe craftsman shaping brass bars into bowl-shaped mirrors, which are then plated by another craftsman). The organization, which now accounts for as much as 80 per cent of the Ward's business, includes metal-parts manufacturers, plating specialists, plastic and rubber processors and trading companies.[4]

Since this new phase of growth has just begun, innovation-oriented firms are still largely focusing on the domestic market. But when some of them go abroad as direct investors, intra-*jiba-sangyo* collaboration is often extended to overseas production in the form of joint investments.

In short, Japan's small manufacturing sector ensconced in *jiba-sangyos* has come a long way from those days when it was considered the backwater of Japanese industry. Indeed, *jiba-sangyo* was once synonymous with low value-added, low-tech cottage-type manufacturing that survived on the cost advantages of low wages and family members' toils. This was perhaps the most accurate description of the

SME sector in the early postwar period (as well as in the prewar period) when Japan began to reconstruct industry, namely, in the Phase I labour-driven industrialization. Yet out of the adverse environment characterized by an extremely high rate of turnover (free entries and exits) under the principle of the 'survival of the fittest', high-tech niche firms have eventually emerged with nimbleness and adaptability. No doubt the high degree of utilization of SMEs as subcontractors during Phase II heavy and chemical industrialization, and as PCA suppliers during Phase III assembly-driven industrialization under the rigorous supervision of modern large corporations, unwittingly contributed to the rapid modernization of the SME sector in technology and skills. They were exposed to the process of natural selection, since only those that were able to learn and meet the ever-rising technological and quality standards of manufacturing demanded by Japan's large world-class corporations survived. This spillover effect of technological and structural upgrading in the large business sector is the unique feature of Japan's industrial organization. Many SME mavericks are in the making. It remains to be seen, however, if some of these mavericks transform themselves into Casios and Hondas. Indeed, it may be that this way of thinking is already obsolete, since these mavericks are organizing businesses in an entirely new fashion, fabless- or satellite-style, as is the case with Kankyo in Box 10.2.

Will Japan's SME Industry be Hollowed Out?

Despite the vitality exhibited by Japan's small business sector, it is often feared that the sector is eroding and may be gradually hollowed out due to two major developments, namely, globalization and the lack of successors as craftsmen and entrepreneurs.

The rapid globalization (the transfer of production overseas and increasing competition from imports) is, indeed, contributing to the continuous shrinkage of the SME sector. Japan's outward FDI is accompanied by four basic effects: the 'intermediate-goods-export' effect; the 'capital-goods-export' effect; the 'export-substitution' effect; and the 'reverse-import' effect. The first two are positive, while the last two are negative for the SME sector. The net outcome of the four effects combined used to be positive in the 1970s and the early 1980s, but it turned negative in the mid-1980s and its negative balance has been growing steadily; it reached a negative ratio of 0.64 in 1994 (Small and Medium Business Agency, 1997). This trend is closely related to the overseas transplantation of components-intensive, assembly-based industries (namely, the third wave of outward FDI) and the inevitable rise in the overseas production of both intermediate and capital goods, some of which are also increasingly imported back to Japan.

The rate of startup in manufacturing has not only declined in absolute terms, from about 4 per cent in 1988–90 to 2 per cent in 1993–95, but also became much lower than the rate of closure. The latter has been about 2.5 per cent to 4 per cent over the same period for SMEs with employment of 20–299 workers (Small and Medium Business Agency, 1997). In contrast, both rates are about the same (at 1 per cent annually) for Japan's large business sector. This trend is perhaps inevitable with the continuous tertiarization of the Japanese economy in which the small business sector is moving into services faster than the large business sector.

The decline of Japan's supporting industry is also unavoidable to a certain extent as assembly-based industries have seen their best days. For example, automobile production in Japan already reached its pinnacle in 1990 (Toyota, 1998). The third phase of industrial growth driven by differentiated Smithian industries is now being replaced by the fourth phase based on Schumpeterian industries.

The lack of successors as craftsmen and entrepreneurs is a more serious problem, since successful small businesses cannot continue beyond the first generation. The SMEs in manufacturing are often engaged in so-called three-K (or-D) jobs – *Kiken* (dangerous), *Kitanai* (dirty), *Kitsui* (demanding). Young Japanese are not attracted to such unglamorous jobs. Craftsmanship is the product of many years' apprenticeship and on-the-job experiences at rather drab small factories. In fact, many craftsmen have a limited formal schooling with only junior- or senior-high-school education. All in all, talented college graduates seek jobs in large firms rather than joining the SME sector. The government's measures introduced in 1995 allow a 'limited stock option system' to attract such people to venture business (Whittaker, 1997). There is an encouraging sign, however, that a new generation of better educated, risk-taking entrepreneurs is on the rise, especially in the urban *jiba-sangyo*, as exemplified by companies such as Kankyo, Akira, Atlus and Sangi. Restructuring and modernization of the SME sector is slowly but steadily in the making, mainly from traditional subcontracting activity to venture businesses in the niche markets.

OVERALL ASSESSMENT

The topic of industrial clusters and international business activities (trade and direct overseas business operations) has not yet been fully explored, and the interactive nature and links between these economic phenomena remain largely unconceptualized. The importance of SMEs and their high concentration in industrial clusters (hence, a vigorously competitive market structure) has been described by several authors but without reference to the phenomenon of SMEs' internationalization (*inter alia*, Piore and Sabel, 1984; Porter, 1990; Best, 1990; and Enright, 1991). Also, the transnationalization process of their business activities has been explored but outside the context of industrial clusters (Buckley *et al.*, 1997).

Japan's SME manufacturers – particularly those export-oriented ones – ensconced in *jiba-sangyos* have gone through a rapid process of structural transformation and transnationalization simultaneously. To explain this phenomenon, the Smithian model of international-business-driven agglomeration and structural change in an industrial cluster has been conceptualized as the basic prototype for the *jiba-sangyo*, and expanded in such a way as to take into account their organizational and structural changes. The Japanese experiences illustrate how international business has impacted on SMEs through its effects on local industrial clusters, and reveal the development-phase-specific dynamic/evolutionary process of spatial organization, involving SMEs as active participants in global business.

In fact, SMEs, once they turn into multinationals, are committed to overseas production to a much greater extent than large firms. All in all, small transnationals are more 'transnationalized' than large ones. The case in which overseas production is more than 90 per cent of total sales accounts for 25.0 per cent for small transnationals, 4.8 per cent for medium transnationals, but practically none for large ones. Indeed, the 'more-than-60 per cent' case accounts for merely 1.3 per cent (Small and Medium Business Agency, 1996).

SMEs' motivations for outward FDI vary with each destination. Three sources of motivation are predominant: attraction of local markets; low wages and abundant labour; and following parent firms and/or customers. According to the result of an official survey (Small and Medium Enterprise Agency, 1997, p. 204), the 'attraction of local markets' reason is the most important (45 per cent) for North

America-bound FDI, followed by the 'following parent firms and/or customers' reason. In contrast, for developing country FDI the 'low wages and abundant labour' reason is expectedly the most dominant (25 per cent), while the 'attraction of local markets' is the close second (21 per cent) with 'following parent firms and/or customers third'. This difference indicates that those SMEs headed for China include mostly the 'surplus labour transmogrifiers' and the 'assembler-pulled PCA suppliers' (that is, strongly 'macro-structurally induced'), and that those in North America are strongly represented by the mavericks whose competitiveness comes from their own created assets (that is, 'micro-autonomously induced'). Small trading companies are also engaged in the 'invest and import' type of procurement. No data on Europe are available, but the same observations made about North America equally apply to Europe.

Although, in general, Japanese firms often moved out in search of low-cost locations and away from home because of its 'deteriorating' business milieu (high-cost conditions due to rising wages and the sharp appreciation of the yen before mid-1995), they have often found the new locations after all not as attractive as initially expected. This development is particularly pronounced among SMEs. This has resulted in a high rate of withdrawal in the recent past. One key factor for withdrawals was a sharp rise in local wages and the difficulty of securing workers in rapidly-growing host countries, especially NIEs, which made their low value-added, labour-intensive type of ventures unprofitable. Many small transnationals of the 'transmogrifier' type therefore have been shifting production from the NIEs to ASEAN, China, Vietnam and Myanmar (as exemplified by Swany in Box 10.1). Some of these which set up operations in the advanced West, the USA and Europe, also experienced difficulties.

But these experiences belong mostly to SMEs of the early postwar generation. The mavericks in the present era of Schumpeterian industries are at the moment strongly domestic-market oriented, simply because they are recent start-ups and in their early stages of growth. As they accumulate new advantages, they will expand their horizons beyond the domestic markets. Their globalization decisions will be largely micro-motivationally determined in contrast to their older postwar generation. They are also likely to adopt more flexible ways (such as strategic alliances in R&D, production and marketing) of running international businesses than conventional equity-based FDIs.

Notes

1. Until 1970, for example, as many as 87.6 per cent of their ventures were located in the neighbouring Asian countries or territories: those set up in Taiwan alone accounted for 43.9 per cent of the total. Korea, Hong Kong and Okinawa were other major host economies, together receiving 23.1 per cent (Japanese investments in Okinawa prior to its return to Japan in May 1972 were officially treated as overseas investment (Ozawa, 1985)). It should also be noted that resource-scarce Japan began to invest in resource-related ventures abroad in order to secure vital supplies for its heavy and chemical industries.
2. The concept of 'intra-structural upgrading' was introduced by Pearce and Papanastassiou (1996) in connection with their discussion of the author's stage-based model by way of distinguishing it from the concept of 'inter-structural upgrading' used in the model.
3. The three examples are given in 'Small Firms in Japan: Fabulous and Fabless', *The Economist*, 29 March 1997, p. 69.
4. As reported in 'Small Businesses Flourish in Virtual Village', *Nikkey Weekly*, 26 January 1998.

References

BEST, M.H. (1990), *The New Competition: Institutions of Industrial Restructuring* (Cambridge, Mass.: Harvard University Press).

BUCKLEY, P.J., J. CAMPOS, H. MIRZA and E. WHITE (1997), *International Technology Transfer by Small and Medium-Sized Enterprises: Case Studies* (London: Macmillan; and New York: St Martin's Press).

ENRIGHT, M.J. (1991), *Geographic Concentration and Industrial Organization*, PhD dissertation, Harvard University, printed by U.M.I. Dissertation Services, Ann Arbor, Michigan, 1995.

FUJIMOTO, T. (1995), 'A Note on the Origin of the "Black Box Parts" Practice in the Japanese Motor Vehicle Industry', in H. Shiomi and K. Wada (eds), *Fordism Transformed: The Development of Production Methods in the Automobile Industry* (Oxford: Oxford University Press), pp. 184–218.

FUJITA, M (1997), 'Small and Medium-sized Enterprises in Foreign Direct Investment', in P Buckley *et al.* (eds). *International Technology Transfer by Small and Medium-Sized Enterprises: Country Studies* (London: Macmillan) pp. 9–70.

IMAI, S. *et al.* (eds) (1997), *Nihon no Chusho Kigyo wa Ima* [What Japan's SMEs are up to] (Tokyo: JETRO).

IKARI, Y. (1981), *Nohon no Jidosha Kogyo* [Japan's Automobile Industry] (Tokyo: Nihon Noritsu Kyokai).

KIYONARI, T. (1985), *Chusho Kigyo* [Small and Medium Enterprises] (Tokyo: Nihon Keizai Shimbunsha).

KRUGMAN, P. (1991), *Geography and Trade* (Cambridge, Mass: MIT Press).

LOCKWOOD, W.W. (1954), *The Economic Development of Japan: Growth and Structural Change 1868–1938* (Princeton: Princeton University Press).

MARSHALL, A. (1920), *Principles of Economics* (London: Macmillan).

MITI (Ministry of International Trade and Industry) (1989), *Niju-I'seiki no Sangyo Kikai Vision* [A Vision for the Industrial Machinery Industry in the 21st century] (Tokyo: Tsusho Sangyo Chosakai).

MIZOTA, S. (1983), *Zosen Gyokai* [The Shipbuilding Industry] (Tokyo: Kyoikusha).

MYINT, H. (1958), 'The "Classical Theory" of International Trade and the Underdeveloped Countries', *Economic Journal*, vol. LXVIII, no. 270 (June), pp. 317–37.

NIKKEI BUSINESS ed. (1995), *Chi'isana Tsuyoi Kaisha* [Small Strong Companies] (Tokyo: Nikkei BP).

OHLIN, B. (1933), *Interregional and International Trade* (Cambridge, Mass.: Harvard University Press).

OZAWA, T. (1994), 'Japan's External Asymmetries and Assembly Industries: Lean Production as a Source of Competitive Advantage', *Transnational Corporations*, vol. 3, no. 3, pp. 25–51.

OZAWA, T. (1985), *International Transfer of Technology by Japan's Small and Medium Enterprises in Developing Countries* (Geneva: UNCTAD).

OZAWA, T. (1979), *Multinationalism, Japanese Style* (Princeton: Princeton University Press).

OZAWA, T. and C. FERRER (1997), 'Strategic Organization and Structural Dynamism: Spatial Underpinnings of Japan's Phase-Based Industrial Competitiveness', *CEMS Business Review*, vol. 2 (Supplement), pp. S19–35.

PEARCE, R. and M. PAPANASTASSIOU (1996), *Technological Competitiveness of Japanese Multinationals: The European Dimension* (Ann Arbor: University of Michigan Press).

PIORE, M. and C.F. SABEL (1984), *The Second Industrial Divide: Possibilities for Prosperity* (New York: Basic Books).

PORTER, M. (1990), *The Competitive Advantage of Nations* (New York: Free Press).

SMALL AND MEDIUM BUSINESS AGENCY (1997), *Chusho Kigyo Hakusho* [White Paper on Small and Medium Business] (Tokyo: Finance Ministry Printing Office).

SMALL AND MEDIUM BUSINESS AGENCY (1996), *Chusho Kigyo Hakusho* [White Paper on Small and Medium Business] (Tokyo: Finance Ministry Printing Office).

SMALL AND MEDIUM BUSINESS AGENCY (1986), *Chusho Kigyo Kaigai Shinshutsu Jireishu* [SMEs' Overseas Advances: Case Studies] (Tokyo: Small and Medium Business Agency, Research Department).

SMITH, A. (1776/1908), *An Inquiry into the Nature and Causes of the Wealth of Nations* (London: Routledge; and New York: E.P. Dutton).

TOYOTA MOTOR CORPORATION (1998), *The Automobile Industry* (Toyota City: Toyota Motor Corporation).

UCHINO, T. (1983), *Japan's Postwar Economy: An Insider's View of Its History and Its Future* (Tokyo and New York: Kodansha).

WHITTAKER, D.H. (1997), *Small Firms in the Japanese Economy* (Cambridge, UK: Cambridge University Press).

WOMACK, J., D. JONES and D. ROOS (1990), *The Machine that Changed the World* (New York: Macmillan).

YAMAZAKI, M. (1980), *Japan's Community-based Industries: A Case Study of Small Industry* (Tokyo: Asian Productivity Organization).

Part IV
The Policy Perspective

11 The World Trade Organization: Global Rule-maker?[1]

Thomas L. Brewer and Stephen Young

INTRODUCTION

Globalization at the corporate level has been strongly influenced and facilitated by, *inter alia*, a worldwide trend, especially during the 1990s, towards the liberalization of governments' FDI policies; the latter have been linked to wider programmes of deregulation, privatization and market reform. There is still a long way to go in investment liberalization, particularly in some major developing nations and transition economies, and the process is far from irreversible. Since MNEs' investment may generate economic benefits for nation-states and the world economy, as international trade has, locking-in the liberalization that has been achieved, providing a coherent global policy framework for FDI[2] and extending policy into new areas are critical if the momentum of corporate globalization is to be sustained. This requires a system of investment rules to complement the multilateral trade regime negotiated and implemented through the General Agreement on Tariffs and Trade (GATT) and the World Trade Organization (WTO).

Interest in a multilateral framework for investment has ebbed and flowed over a period of 50 years; but a significant step forward was taken with the inclusion of a number of investment-related issues in the GATT Uruguay Round, negotiated over the period 1986–94. The Uruguay Round agreements establishing the WTO on 1 January 1995, are sometimes referred to as a 'constitution for world business'. Though the phrase is hyperbolism, it is suggestive of the scope and significance of the agreements, for the WTO implements rules in a broad range of areas of importance to international business beyond trade in goods. In particular, WTO rules cover some foreign direct investment (FDI) policies directly, as in the General Agreement on Trade in Services (GATS)[3] and Trade-Related Investment Measures

(TRIMs), and other investment-related issues in the agreement on Subsidies and Countervailing Measures (SCMs) and agreement on Trade-Related Intellectual Property Rights (TRIPs). Further, the basic telecommunications agreement signed in the spring of 1997 and the financial services agreement signed in the fall of 1997 – both as annexes to the GATS – extend multilateral rules on investment to two service sectors of considerable economic significance. Thus, by early 1998 there had already been a substantial expansion of multilateral investment rules in the services sector through the GATS framework.

At the same time, it is widely recognized that there are many investment issues that are *not* covered by current WTO rules. Indeed, the WTO ignores most investment issues. For instance, there are no multilateral rules concerning international mergers and acquisitions or other competition policy issues, despite the extraordinary increases of recent years in international strategic alliances among putative competitors. Nor are there multilateral rules to control the increasingly common beggar-thy-neighbour investment incentives that governments use to attract inward FDI. Further, the agreement on Trade-Related Investment Measures (TRIMs) is frequently interpreted to represent a failure of the Uruguay Round to make significant progress on investment issues; that agreement does not prohibit governments' investment-related performance requirements affecting trade that were not already prohibited by GATT. In sum, therefore, the totality of the present array of WTO rules is mixed as far as their coverage of investment issues is concerned – with significant coverage in some services sectors, but minimal coverage in manufacturing, and no direct, explicit coverage in agriculture, textiles or mining.

As for the future, there are institutionalized arrangements in place to focus attention on investment issues at the WTO during the next several years. In particular, there is a provision in Article 9 of the TRIMs for a 'review' by the end of 1999 to consider whether that agreement 'should be complemented with provisions on investment policy and competition policy' (GATT, 1994, p. 156). A Working Group on the Relationship between Trade and Investment was consequently created in 1997 in order to explore issues for the potential future agenda of the WTO. Similarly, a Working Group on Competition Policy and Trade has been created, and its agenda has inherent investment policy implications. Further, at the time of writing, there was an extensive series of studies, expert meetings, and regional symposia on a possible multilateral framework on investment

(MFI) in progress at the UN in Geneva (UNCTAD, 1999). Some of those activities are being conducted jointly with the WTO (WTO and UNCTAD, 1998). The agenda of investment issues at the WTO, therefore, is not only marked by much complexity and uncertainty, but also by much activity.

A clarification of the status of – and prospects for – multilateral investment rules is thus timely in the context of this volume on globalization. The chapter accordingly addresses the following questions: To what extent and in what ways has the WTO become a rule-maker on investment issues? What aspects of investment issues have been included or excluded in the Uruguay Round agreements and in their implementation? What investment issues have emerged in the dispute settlement process? How does the WTO experience thus far compare with the history of the GATT? What implications can be drawn for the globalization of MNE activity and economic development?

Dispute cases provide one set of data that is relevant to answering these questions. The paper therefore includes an analysis of the 115 WTO dispute cases that entered the dispute settlement process during 1995–7, and compares the WTO record of those three years with 325 GATT cases during the 1948–94 period. Before turning to the analysis of the cases, however, the chapter briefly discusses the 'architecture' of investment rules at the WTO and in the international investment regime more broadly.

THE ARCHITECTURE OF RULES ON INVESTMENT[4]

The current multilateral system of rules on international investment is often referred to as 'patchwork' marked by gaps, overlaps and inconsistencies – across sectors, across types of business transactions, across domains of government policy, and across countries. Furthermore, these features not only characterize the relationships among WTO agreements; they also describe the relationship of WTO rules to other arrangements at the multilateral, regional and bilateral levels. The most conspicuous gaps include the following: no investment rules in the agricultural, mineral and textile sectors; limited rules concerning only performance requirements and subsidies in the manufacturing sectors; complex and highly variable rules across services industries, and across types of business transactions and government policies within them. This patchwork, at a minimum, substantially increases transaction costs for firms in their global business activities;

and may significantly distort decision-making and reduce cross-border integration.

The complexities and confusion that emerge from the patchwork of agreements are illustrated by Korea's liberalization programme in the financial services sector, and its agreements as a member of the WTO, the OECD and the IMF. In particular, Korea's agreement in December 1997 with the IMF provides for increased foreign ownership of banks and foreign ownership of stock brokerage firms, as well as other commitments that were not included in its agreement with the OECD during its accession agreements. Further, its commitments in the WTO financial services agreement do not bind either its IMF or its OECD agreements. Korea's international agreements in financial services thus vary depending on whether it is viewed as a member of the WTO, the OECD or the IMF.

The Uruguay Round agreements with relevance to FDI-related issues are summarized in Box 11.1. The patchwork problem is confirmed and there is a good deal of ambiguity in a number of the

Box 11.1
Summary Features of Uruguay Round Agreements Relevant to FDI-Related Issues

Highlights	**Limitations**
GATS	
• Establishes framework agreement for liberalization of all service industries • Includes separately negotiated agreements for telecommunications, transportation (air and maritime), and financial services • Covers all modes of supply – investment, as well as cross-border trade, movement of consumers, and movement of persons as service suppliers • Limits restrictions on joint ventures and percentages of foreign ownership • Opens previously protected domestic services sectors to foreign competition through trade and FDI	• Some services are not covered • Provides many industry- and country-specific exceptions to MFN and national treatment principles • Use of positive lists of industries in the schedules of national commitments is less transparent than negative lists would be

TRIMs	
• Prohibits domestic content, import–export balancing, and foreign exchange balancing requirements that could otherwise be imposed on FDI facilities • Provides for phase-in periods of 2 years (for developed countries), 5 years (for developing countries), and 7 years (for least developed countries) • Explicitly establishes linkages between trade policy and investment policy	• Applies only to investment in manufacturing and trade in goods • The list of prohibited measures is not exhaustive and does not include export performance requirements in particular • The transition period allows countries to phase-out measures that were (at least arguably) already prohibited by GATT rules on trade
TRIPs	
• Establishes uniform standards for national laws for the protection of intellectual property rights (IPRs) • Includes copyrights, trademarks, industrial designs, patents, and designs of integrated circuits • Mandates transparent and equitable domestic judicial procedures for the enforcement of IPRs • Provides for interception at borders of counterfeit trademark or pirated copyright goods in international trade • Establishes phase-in periods of 1 year (developed countries), 5 years (developing countries), and 10 years (least developed countries)	• Difficulties of establishing IPR regimes in countries that had none or only rudimentary ones • Difficulties of enforcement
SCMs	
• Prohibits various export subsidies in manufacturing that are contingent on the use of domestic over imported goods or export performance. Includes currency retention schemes	• There is complexity and ambiguity in terms of the specific types of subsidies that are or are not allowable • No recognition of FDI

Continued

with bonuses for exports; favourable transportation rates for exports; tax remissions, export credits and guarantees • Permissible subsidies include those for pre-competitive R&D, assistance for disadvantaged regions, and adaptation of facilities to new environmental regulations	incentives in the form of subsidies that are not available to domestic investors and that are used to compete for inward FDI

Source: Adapted from Brewer and Young (1998).

provisions. Yet there is also the potential to significantly influence MNEs' strategies and operations through, for example, liberalization of service industries; the prohibition of various performance requirements and export subsidies in potential host countries; and the prospect of better protection for companies' intellectual property and hence encouragement for licensing and FDI.

All of these agreements – GATS, TRIMs, TRIPs, SCMs – were at issue in various disputes during the first three years of the WTO, and an analysis of those cases in the context of the dispute settlement process more generally is undertaken in the following.

DISPUTE SETTLEMENT PROCESS AND CASES

Process

A significant achievement of the Uruguay Round was agreement on much stronger dispute settlement processes than those previously operating under the GATT. The key elements of the Dispute Settlement Understanding (DSU) are as follows:

- Dispute cases can include government–government disputes concerning investment, trade, technology transfer and other policies affecting FDI projects and MNEs' other international business activities.
- Specially formed, case-specific dispute panels conduct investigations and file reports, which can be appealed by a (losing) government.

- The complete dispute settlement process involves four main phases – consultation, panel deliberation/report, appellant deliberation/report, and implementation – each with a specific maximum period of time.
- Any given case can be settled directly by the parties throughout the process.
- Unanimous agreement of members is needed to override dispute case reports.
- If a losing party fails to comply, compensation or even retaliation is a possibility.
- The dispute settlement procedures are subject to a review, scheduled to begin by the end of 1998.

As noted above, the WTO's current procedures for settlement of investment disputes *pertain only to government–government disputes*; they do not pertain to investor–government disputes, as do many of the existing international investment agreements at the bilateral, regional, plurilateral and multilateral levels. There is an issue, therefore, about whether the WTO dispute procedures should eventually include investor–government disputes, as suggested for instance by Julius (1994). The question of whether or not such an expansion of the coverage of the WTO's dispute procedures should occur can only be understood in relationship to the distinction between international rules concerning government policy *liberalization*, on the one hand, and international rules concerning investment *protection*, on the other. Although the correlation is far from complete, there is a tendency for government–government disputes to be about government policy liberalization, while investor–government disputes tend to be about investment protection. Exceptions include, for instance, investor–government disputes that could arise from the liberalization of government right of entry measures, or government–government disputes when a home government becomes an agent for an investor in a dispute with the host government where the investment has been made.

This important and complex topic about the future of investment issues and dispute settlement in the WTO will become a central issue in the integration of investment issues into the WTO process. A more extensive analysis of the issue, however, is beyond the scope of the present chapter. Instead, focus is placed on the record of dispute cases in the GATT and in the WTO through early 1998.

Cases

The new WTO dispute settlement process was used extensively during its first three years, particularly in comparison with the 48 years of the GATT. During the period of the GATT, the average number of cases was seven per year, whereas during the first three years of the WTO it was 38 per year (see Table 11.1). Interestingly, although the membership of the GATT increased from 23 countries in 1948 to 128 in 1994, this did not seem to influence the incidence of dispute cases.

There has been an important shift in the distribution of cases, according to country groupings, from the GATT to the WTO. Whereas fully two-thirds of the cases under GATT involved developed countries as both complainant and respondent, the comparable proportion for the WTO was only slightly more than one-third during its first three years. Developing countries thus became more involved as both complainant and respondent in disputes under the WTO (see Table 11.2). But developing countries' involvement as complainant increased much less (rising from 23 per cent of all complaints under GATT to 33 per cent under WTO) than their involvement as respondent (rising from 9 per cent to 39 per cent of the total). The US and EU, in any event, remain the most common parties as either complainant or defendant (Table 11.3), as they were in the GATT.[5]

In WTO terminology, there had been four distinct dispute 'matters' explicitly involving investment brought to the WTO by the end of 1997 (see Table 11.4). A 'matter' can include several 'cases' when they involve similar complaints by different countries about one country's practices. In short-hand terminology, these matters/cases were: the EC bananas matter (one case), the US Helms–Burton matter (one case), the Indonesian auto matter (four cases), and the Brazilian auto matter (four cases).

The EC bananas case involved complaints by Ecuador, Guatemala, Honduras, Mexico and the United States. They contended that the EC regime for the importation, sale and distribution of bananas was inconsistent with several agreements: GATT94, GATS, Import Licensing, Agriculture and TRIMs. Its significance in relation to investment issues in the context of the present paper is that the panel report found that EC regulations that discriminated against imports distributed by foreign-owned firms in favour of domestically-owned firms violated provisions in TRIMs and GATT94. However, it also concluded that the TRIMs was in a sense redundant because all the measures that violated the TRIMs also violated the GATT. The pro-

Table 11.1 Number of GATT and WTO dispute cases by time periods

Years	*Number of cases during period* *Disputes*	*Consultations*	*Total*	*Mean number per year*
GATT years				
1948–59	53	9	62	5.2
1960–69	6	16	22	2.2
1970–79	29	12	41	4.1
1980–89	93[a]	42	135	13.5
1990–94	46[a]	19	65	6.5
GATT total (1948–94)	227	98	325	6.9
WTO years (1995–97)	115	[b]	115	38.3

Notes:
[a] Including cases concerning Tokyo Round Codes.
[b] Not tabulated separately in this table for WTO.
Source: Computed from GATT (1994, pp. 577–82, 718–34); WTO web site, http://www.wto.org, 14 January 1998.

visions concerning quantitative measures in the TRIMs therefore did not prohibit any measures not prohibited by the GATT. The panel report was upheld by the Appellate Body and adopted by the Dispute Settlement Body. This confirmed, then, the long-standing interpretation of the GATT held by some countries, including the United States, that trade-related investment measures that involved quantitative import measures were covered by GATT rules on trade and that additional rules on trade-related investment measures pertaining specifically to discriminatory quantitative import restrictions were not needed. In sum, this early WTO dispute case suggested that the TRIMs had no incremental value as an investment agreement in at least this respect.

The Indonesian and Brazilian TRIMs matters were similar in several respects. Each matter involved four separate cases which were considered together by a dispute panel since they all referred to the same practices. Further, in each matter the complainants were the same: the EC, Japan and the USA (in the Indonesian matter, Japan filed two complaints, the first involving TRIMs and GATT, and the second involving the SCM agreement. In the Brazilian matter, the US

Table 11.2 Country groups in GATT and WTO dispute settlement cases[a]

	GATT cases: 1948–94 *Respondents*		
Complainants	*Developing countries*[b]	*Developed countries*	*Subtotals*
Developing countries	3[b] (1%)	71 (22%)	74 (23%)
Developed countries	27 (8%)	224 (69%)	251 (77%)
Subtotals	30 (9%)	295 (91%)	325 (100%)
	WTO cases: 1995–97 *Respondents*		
Complainants	*Developing countries*[c]	*Developed countries*	*Subtotals*
Developing countries	9 (8%)	29 (25%)	38 (33%)
Developed countries	36 (31%)	41 [44][d] (36%)	77 [80][d] (67%)
Subtotals	45 (39%)	70 [73][d] (61%)	115 (100%)

Notes:

[a] Includes cases under 1958 Consultation Procedures (*n* = 75), 1989 Consultation Improvements (*n* = 23), and Tokyo Round Codes (*n* = 24), as well as disputes under original GATT agreement (*n* = 203).

[b] Two cases involved India and Pakistan (1949 and 1952); one case involved India and Poland (1993).

[c] Hungary and Poland were listed among 'developed' countries in the sources, but are classified as 'developing' in this table.

[d] There were three cases involving developed countries as both complainant and respondent – cases which also included developing countries.

Source: GATT cases: computed by the authors from GATT (1994, pp. 577–82, 718–34) and Petersmann (1997, pp. 247–84). WTO cases: computed by the authors from http://www.wto.org, 14 January 1998.

filed two complaints, the second involving Brazilian measures that were adopted after the US had already asked for consultation in the first case). In all of these cases, the precipitating policies were the TRIMs in the motor vehicle industry in the two countries (Brazil and Indonesia). TRIMs have long been widely used in that particular industry in many developing countries, and given the sizes of the

Table 11.3 WTO members as respondents or complainants in dispute cases (1995–97)[a]

Members	*Respondent*	*Complainant*	*Total*
EC	23	25	48
Japan	11	5	16
US	22	37	59
Canada	[a]	9	9
Mexico	[a]	5	5
Brazil	7	5	12
India	8	[a]	8
Korea	8	[a]	8
Others	36	44	80
Total	115[b]	130[b]	245[b]

Notes:
[a] Entries in the cells are limited to those instances where the number of cases is 5 or more in order to highlight the members that are relatively frequent respondents and/or complainants.
[b] Although each case has only one respondent, the number of complaints per case varies from 1 to 6. There were 4 cases with more than 1 complainant.
Source: Computed by the authors from http://www.wto.org, 14 January 1998.

markets in Brazil and Indonesia and their particularly salient use of TRIMs, it was not surprising that they would be targets of early dispute cases in the new WTO regime. In both matters, the panel reports found that the countries' measures were inconsistent with the TRIMs, SCM and GATT. Further, as in the EC bananas case, the TRIMs was found to be redundant because it did not prohibit practices that were already prohibited by GATT.

The case concerning the US Helms–Burton Act was still pending at the time of writing, technically still in the consultation phase and the subject of continuing negotiations between the USA and the EC. The investment-related issues in the Helms–Burton case were fundamentally different from the cases above; they were not about TRIMs, but rather concerned the US use of economic sanctions that included the denial of entry into the US by employees of non-US firms that had bought property in Cuba that had been owned by US firms and indi-

Table 11.4 WTO disputes, directly involving investment issues (1995–97)[a]

DS No.	*Case*	*TRIMs*	*GATS*	*TRIPs*	*SCMs*	*GATT*	*Other*
27	EC Bananas (US + 4)	Yes	Yes			I, II, III, X, XI, XIII	Agriculture
38	US Cuban Liberty (EC)		I, III, VI, X VI, XVII			I, III, V, XI, XIII	
54	Indonesia auto (EC)	2			3	I, III	
55	Indonesia auto (Japan)	2, 5, 4				I:1, III:2, III:4, X:3(a)	
59	Indonesia auto (US)	2		3, 20, 65	3, 6, 28	I, III	
64	Indonesia auto (Japan)				3, 6, 28		
51	Brazil auto (Japan)	2			3, 27.2, 27.4	I:1, III:4, XI:1, XXIII:1(b) (non.vio.)	
52	Brazil auto (US)	2			3, 27.4	I:1, III:4, XI:1, XXIII:1(b) (non.vio.)	
65	Brazil auto (US)	2			3, 27.4	I:1, III:4, XI:1, XXIII:1(b) (non.vio.)	
81	Brazil auto (EC)	2			3, 5, 27.4 (also non.vio.)	I:1, III:4 (also non.vio.)	

Note: a. Figures in table refer to articles within particular Agreements.
Source: WTO Website, 'Dispute Settlement', 6 September 1997.

viduals before being expropriated by the Cuban government. The specific complaint by the EC was that those US measures (as embodied in legislation commonly referred to as the Helms–Burton Act) violated the US commitments in the GATS. More broadly, however, the case concerned the US assertion of a national security exception and the extra-territorial application of US law to the investments of non-US firms on non-US territory. The case thus had serious implications for the WTO far beyond the narrow, technical issue of whether the US measures violated investment related rules in the GATS. The Dispute Panel's authority lapsed on 22 April 1998 without any resolution, and the problem could re-emerge in future.

In sum, it would appear on the surface that these four matters had not had much significance as far as the development of the WTO as a global rule-maker on investment issues was concerned as of early 1998. They only confirmed that the specific provisions of the TRIMs agreement concerning quantitative import restrictions were covered by GATT provisions concerning trade in goods, and in that sense the TRIMs agreement provided no incremental coverage of investment issues. The prospective resolution of the Helms–Burton case, though, had much potential significance.

However, the rulings in motor vehicles provide a warning shot to emerging nations which may wish to support the development of an indigenous industry, as the case of Indonesia reveals. Here the 1996 national car programme granted sales tax and import-duty exemption to cars which met given local content requirements. But, the only car authorized under the scheme was the Timor saloon, controlled by (the then) President Suharto's youngest son in cooperation with Kia Motors of Korea. In the early stages of the programme, Kia Motors exported 45 000 fully-assembled cars to Indonesia with the same tax and duty exemptions. The WTO panel found that the programme violated rules prohibiting investment measures linked to local content, as well as WTO commitments not to discriminate between trading partners or like products. Indonesia was also in breach of the subsidies agreement because the tax concessions enabled the Timor unfairly to undercut its foreign rivals in the domestic market (*Financial Times*, 23 April 1998).

The focus on the motor vehicle sector is also highly significant given its visibility and its importance in international investment and trade. There were reports (*Financial Times*, 11 June 1998) that Japan was preparing a WTO challenge against Canada over its 'preferential' treatment for US vehicle manufacturers: Ford, Chrysler and General

Motors can import vehicles duty free from anywhere in the world under the terms of the USA–Canada automotive pact, whereas Toyota and Honda (with large manufacturing facilities in Canada) are subject to a 6.7 per cent tariff on imported vehicles.[6] This illustrates both the wider applicability of WTO rules and the interrelatedness of investment and trade (see the following).

After three years of dispute-settlement experience, investment issues had explicitly entered into a small fraction of the cases – in fact, only 10 of 115 cases in total (see the Appendix for the entire list of cases with a summary of selected features). It would be incorrect, however, to underestimate the importance of WTO rules. Because of their significance in international trade and technology transfer as well as FDI, MNEs are clearly strongly affected by the substantial upsurge in dispute settlement cases under the WTO. Many cases had investment-related implications even though they were not technically and narrowly about WTO members' investment measures. Among the most conspicuous illustrations were the Kodak–Fuji case and the Indian intellectual property rights (TRIPs) case, for instance. Overall there were seven cases where issues concerning patent and copyright protection arose. In addition, there were 11 disputes relating to anti-dumping and countervailing duties. This latter topic has aroused controversy for many years because of a belief that such cases commonly derive from lobbying by weak domestic producers, and that they have encouraged FDI as a means of circumventing actual or potential duties; the opposing view is that they are necessary to counter mercantilist national strategies and government-supported over-production in, for example, Asia. There is also a need to understand more fully the ways in which trade rules influence MNEs' international operations. For instance, one case involved a complaint to the WTO concerning EU countries' (UK and Ireland) reclassification of computer networking equipment to higher tariff categories: the complaint involved \$2.5 bn of US exports of local area networks (LANs) adapter equipment, clearly involving major MNEs. The case above relating to Japanese car exports to Canada is also relevant.

THE NEGOTIATING AGENDA

As for the near future, negotiations are scheduled for services, agriculture, intellectual property, government procurement and other issues as a result of the built-in agenda provided in various Uruguay Round agreements. The WTO Director General has indicated that the linkages and trade-offs across those negotiations suggest that they will amount, as an ensemble, to another general round of negotiations (*Inside US Trade*, vol. 15, no. 52, 26 December 1997, pp. 1, 21). In any case, whether or not a general round of negotiations materializes, there are already ongoing activities that are tantamount to negotiations – or at least negotiations about negotiating – and they definitely include investment issues.

There are several ways that investment issues are manifest in the ongoing and emerging negotiating agenda at the WTO. Key issues can be briefly highlighted as follows:

- The inclusion of investor–government disputes as well as government–government disputes has been raised as a possible item on the agenda by some observers.
- More commonly, investment issues are addressed in relationship to the two Working Groups that are already in progress in the context of the review of the TRIMs agreement – that is, the groups focusing on (a) the relationship between investment and trade, and (b) the relationship between competition policy and trade. Both are marked by difficult analytic and diplomatic hurdles, particularly the latter. The inclusion of competition issues on the built-in post-Uruguay Round agenda reflected a frequently expressed desire by many developing countries that there be an agreement on the restrictive business practices of MNEs – a desire which was generally opposed by the developed countries. The EU Commission, however, has recently been pushing for WTO action on competition-policy issues; the USA, in contrast, remains essentially opposed to movement on such issues in the WTO, although during 1998 agreement was reached between the USA and the EU to strengthen transatlantic cooperation in the enforcement of competition rules.
- A broad range of other types of investment issues are receiving increasing interest, and there are joint UNCTAD–WTO activities in progress on them – such as jointly-sponsored workshops for Geneva delegates to those organizations (WHO and UNCTAD, 1998). In addition, UNCTAD has in progress a series of technical papers on issues for a possible multilateral framework for investment (MFI); they are intended to assist policy-makers and others to understand the concepts, principles, issues and options that arise

in diverse negotiating fora when international investment agreements are under consideration (UNCTAD, 1999). The review of the TRIMs agreement provides an institutionalized focus for some of those issues, though the substantive issues extend far beyond the scope of TRIMs.

- Investment incentives – which have been largely ignored in both investment and trade negotiations (Brewer and Young, 1997) – could enter the WTO agenda more expansively in the context of the agreement on Subsidies and Countervailing Measures (SCMs). Beggar-thy-neighbour policies among would-be host countries in the competition for inward FDI continue to become more intense, and poorer countries are at a disadvantage in that competition and would thus like restraints imposed.
- The review of the GATS provides numerous opportunities for further liberalization of particular sectors within individual countries, as they reconsider their schedules of national commitments. Though they are in some respects the most esoteric and technically complex, these items also entail some of the most economically important investment issues. The potential importance of investment issues in further GATS negotiations lies in the combination of several facts: first, the services sectors are the fastest growing sectors in most economies; second, they have been subjected to relatively stringent protectionist measures as well as discriminatory regulatory policies in the past; and, third, FDI as a mode of servicing foreign markets is especially important in service industries because service transactions tend to involve a disproportionately high number of face-to-face encounters as compared with goods.

For all of these reasons, therefore, it seems likely that investment issues will become increasingly important in WTO negotiations for the indefinite future. What is not so clear is the tangible forms any agreements will take and therefore what specific types of investment issues will be included and excluded from WTO rules.

Further, as of mid-1998 it was not clear to what extent any future WTO rules concerning investment would apply to China and Russia and several other countries since they had not yet completed accession negotiations. What is apparent, however, is that the vast majority of the world's FDI outflows and inflows are already represented by the 132 WTO member countries – more than 95 per cent of the outflows and more than 85 per cent of the inflows. If all of the countries in line for admission actually gain admission – for a total membership of 163 – the FDI outflows and inflows of WTO members would constitute more than 99 per cent of the world totals. In that sense, the WTO clearly has the potential to become a truly global rule-maker on FDI issues. Whether its members have the political will and negotiating skill to create a substantially more effective set of WTO rules concerning FDI obviously remains to be seen.

CONCLUSIONS

This chapter has provided evidence, through dispute cases, of the progress which has been made in the WTO forum to formulate a set of multilateral investment rules. The assumption is that the undoubted worldwide economic benefits generated by trade liberalization would be replicated by investment liberalization. At the macro-level, more favourable and stable economic environments would stimulate worldwide investment flows. At the micro-level, there would be greater opportunities for MNEs to exploit the international division of labour and pursue global strategies; liberalization would reduce transaction costs in decision-making as well as distortion in choices among modes of market supply. An effective international competition policy would, of course, be a necessary concomitant to liberalization to prevent abuse of market power.

The information presented in the chapter shows that only a very small step has been taken towards multilateral investment liberalization (but perhaps it would be wrong to expect too much, given that trade liberalization in the GATT has taken place over a 50-year period). Many investment issues have already been explicitly or implicitly included in the WTO – in specific provisions of agreements from the Uruguay Round and in dispute cases that have been brought to it. But those issues have not been addressed in a systematic or comprehensive way. Instead, in some agreements and sectors, as in the TRIMs for goods, only a very limited range of government measures is covered; in other agreements, as in the GATS on services, there are many exceptions across industries and countries in commitments to core principles such as national treatment; in yet other agreements, as in SCMs, an important dimension (incentive competition) is ignored; and, finally, on some topics there is no WTO agreement at all, for instance the implications of international mergers and acquisitions for competition.

However, there are several existing agreements and institutionalized procedures for dispute settlement and for further negotiations to expand or refine agreements. Investment issues are therefore likely to become more salient (as well as contentious items) on the WTO agenda for many years.

In terms of the impact of what has been achieved, it is possible to see signs from the investment dispute cases of the removal of some investment-related barriers; the cases themselves are simply the tip of the iceberg – what is more important are the signals they send to the world as a whole. The early involvement of the motor vehicle industry is also very significant given its international visibility. And although not reflected in the cases, the stimulus of the Uruguay Round to liberalization in services and to the protection of intellectual property rights is of major significance.

The principal problem for the future lies in the inability of the citizenry of individual countries to recognize the potential gains from multilateral investment liberalization, and hence a reluctance to surrender national sovereignty. In the first years of the WTO, the public and media emphasis has been on the losers in dispute cases. For example, the Vice-President of the European Commission, Sir Leon Brittan, found it necessary to argue in the *Financial Times* (10 September 1997) that the EU should not lose faith with the WTO because two cases (including the outlawing of the EU's banana import regime) had gone against it. He pointed out that the EU was using WTO action to remove obstacles hindering production by European car firms in Brazil and Indonesia, and it was seeking to influence America's car tax regime; and he added that: 'Individual disputes aside, the EU has increasingly used the WTO as a multilateral forum to negotiate open markets worldwide in high tech sectors where European industry has a competitive edge'.

The need to take a rounded view is also evident in the USA, where there was anger in Congress when the WTO disputes panel rejected a US complaint that Japan had rigged its photofilm market against imports (the so-called Kodak–Fuji case). In developing countries, too, there is a strong requirement to publicize the economic benefits from MNE investment, policy-liberalization and international rule-making. Exacerbated by the Asian financial crisis, there is still substantial scepticism, even antagonism, in major developing countries such as Egypt concerning global liberalization and the WTO regime. Yet the Bangalore software case (Chapter 6) provides an excellent example of the opportunities for linkage into the global economy.

Overcoming the attitude that multilateral rules are desirable providing they suit individual countries' own interests represents a formidable challenge. Equally problematic is the piecemeal and highly legislative approach being pursued in the WTO forum which means that it is easy to lose sight of long-term objectives and encourages cynicism. To take the case of the telecommunications agreement, it is agreed that the WTO will have its hands full enforcing its regulatory principles for this agreement, while most member countries lack proper machinery for implementing the rules (*Financial Times*, 2 March 1998).

The conclusion from all of this is that the WTO is a long way from becoming a global rule-maker on investment issues. To achieve further progress it will be necessary both to prove and to publicize the benefits to countries from a multilateral framework of rules. It is easy to point to greater security for investors from a more stable, predictable, transparent and liberal investment regime; but the output in terms of an increase in the quantity, quality and pattern of FDI flows, linking MNE globalization to economic development, has also to be proved.

APPENDIX: WTO DISPUTE SETTLEMENT CASES, 1 JANUARY 1995 – 31 DECEMBER 1997

DS no.[a]	*Respondent*	*Complainant*	*Product*	*Issue*	*Agreement*[b]	*Status*[c]
1	Malaysia	Singapore	polyethylene & polypropylene	imports prohibition	GATT	S
2 (4)	US	Venezuela	gasoline	environmental regulations	GATT, TBT	C
3 (41)	Korea	US	agriculture	testing & inspection	GATT, SPS, TBT, Agri	P
4 (2)	US	Brazil	gasoline	environmental regulations	GATT, TBT	C
5	Korea	US	various	shelf-life regulation	GATT, TBT, SPS, Agri	S
6	US	Japan	autos	import duties	GATT	S
7 (12, 14)	EC(France)	Canada	scallops	trade description	GATT, TBT	S
8 (10, 11)	Japan	EC	liquor	tax	GATT	C
9 (13, 17, 25)	EC	Canada	cereals	duties	Agri	S
10 (8, 11)	Japan	Canada	liquor	tax	GATT	C
11 (8, 10)	Japan	US	liquor	tax	GATT	C
12 (7, 14)	EC(France)	Peru	scallops	trade description	GATT, TBT	S
13 (9, 17, 25)	EC	US	cereals	duties	Agri	S
14 (7, 12)	EC(France)	Chile	scallops	trade description	GATT, TBT	S
15	Japan	EC	telecommunications	purchase agreement	GATT	S
16 (27, 105)	EC	Guatemala, Honduras, Mexico, US	bananas	importation, sale, distribution	GATT, ILA, Agri, TRIMs, GATS	C
17 (9, 13, 25)	EC	Thailand	cereals	duties	Agri, GATT	S
18 (21)	Australia	Canada	salmon	quarantine regulation	GATT, SPS	P
19	Poland	India	automobiles	tariff scheme	GATT	S
20	Korea	Canada	bottled water	regulations	GATT, SPS, TBT	S
21 (18)	Australia	US	salmon	quarantine regulation	GATT, SPS	P
22 (30)	Brazil	Philippines	desiccated coconut	countervailing duty	GATT	C
23	Venezuela	Mexico	oil country tubular goods	anti-dumping investigation	AD	S

24	US	Costa Rica	underwear	import restriction	ATC	C
25 (9, 13, 17)	EC	Uruguay	cereals	duties	Agri	S
26 (48)	EC	US	meat & meat products	import restriction	GATT, SPS, TBT, Agri	A
27 (16, 105)	EC	Ecuador, Guatamala, Honduras, Mexico, US	bananas	importation, sale, distribution	GATT, ILA, Agri, TRIMs, GATS	C
28 (42)	Japan	US	sound recordings	copyright regime	TRIPs	S
29 (34, 47)	Turkey	Hong Kong	textiles	import restrictions	GATT	P
30 (22)	Brazil	Sri Lanka	desiccated coconut	countervailing duties	GATT, Agri	P
31	Canada	US	periodicals	import prohibitions, tax & postage rates	GATT	C
32	US	India	wool coats	safeguard measure	ATC	S
33	US	India	wool shirts & blouses	safeguard measure	ATC	C
34 (29, 47)	Turkey	India	textiles	import restrictions	GATT, ATC	P
35	Hungary	Argentina, Australia, Canada, New Zealand, Thailand, US	agriculture	export subsidies	Agri	S
36	Pakistan	US	pharmaceutical & agricultural chemicals	patent protection	TRIPs	S
37	Portugal	US	industrial property	patent protection	TRIPs	S
38	US	EC	LIBERTAD Act	Cuban trade sanctions	WTO, GATT, GATS	A
39	US	EC	general	tariff increases	GATT, DSU	S
40	Korea	EC	telecommunications	procurement	GATT	S
41 (3)	Korea	US	agriculture	testing & inspection	GATT, SPS, TBT, Agri	P
42 (28)	Japan	EC	sound recordings	copyright regime	TRIPs	S

APPENDIX: *Continued*

DS no.[a]	*Respondent*	*Complainant*	*Product*	*Issue*	*Agreement*[b]	*Status*[c]
43	Turkey	US	foreign films	taxation of revenues	GATT	S
44	Japan	US	photographic film & paper	distribution & sale regulations	GATT	A
45	Japan	US	distribution services	dept. store & supermarket regulations	GATS	P
46	Brazil	Canada	aircraft	export subsidies	SCM	P
47 (29, 34)	Turkey	Thailand	textiles	import restrictions	GATT, Textiles	P
48 (26)	EC	Canada	livestock & meat	import restrictions	GATT, SPS, TBT, Agri	A
49	US	Mexico	tomatoes	anti-dumping investigation	GATT, AD	S
50 (79)	India	US	pharmaceutical & agricultural chemicals	patent protection	TRIPs	C
51 (52, 65, 81)	Brazil	Japan	automotives	investment measures	TRIMs, GATT, SCM	P
52 (51, 65, 81)	Brazil	US	automotives	investment measures	TRIMs, GATT, SCM	P
53	Mexico	EC	various	customs valuation	GATT	P
54 (55, 59, 64)	Indonesia	EC	automobiles	duties & luxury tax	GATT, TRIMs, SCM	A
55 (54, 59, 64)	Indonesia	Japan	automobiles	duties & luxury tax	GATT, TRIMs	A
56	Argentina	US	footwear, textiles & apparel	duties	GATT, TBT, ATC	A
57 (106)	Australia	US	leather	subsidies	SCM	S
58 (61)	US	India, Malaysia, Pakistan, Thailand	shrimp	import prohibition	GATT	A
59 (54, 55, 64)	Indonesia	US	automobiles	duties & luxury tax	GATT, TRIMs, SCM, TRIPS	A

60	Guatemala	Mexico	portland cement	anti-dumping investigation	AD	A
61 (58)	US	Philippines	shrimp	import prohibition	GATT, TBT	P
62 (67, 68)	EC	US	computer equipment	customs classification	GATT	A
63	US	EC	solid urea	anti-dumping measures	AD	P
64 (54, 55, 59)	Indonesia	Japan	automobiles	duties & luxury tax	SCM	A
65 (51, 52, 81)	Brazil	US	automotives	investment measures	GATT, TRIMs, SCM	P
66	Japan	EC	pork	import restrictions	GATT	P
67 (62, 68)	UK	US	computer equipment	customs classification	GATT	A
68 (62, 67)	Ireland	US	computer equipment	customs classification	GATT	A
69	UC	Brazil	poultry	import quota	GATT, AILP	A
70 (71)	Canada	Brazil	civilian aircraft	subsidies	SCM	P
71 (70)	Canada	Brazil	civilian aircraft	subsidies	SCM	P
72	EC	New Zealand	butter	import classification	GATT, TBT, AILP	A
73	Japan	EC	navigation satellite	procurement	GPA	S
74 (102)	Philippines	US	pork, poultry	tariff-rate quotas	GATT, Agri, AILP, TRIMs	P
75 (84)	Korea	EC	liquor	tax	GATT	A
76	Japan	US	agriculture	quarantine measures	SPS, GATT, Agri	A
77	Argentina	EC	textiles, clothing, footwear	duties & tariffs	GATT, ATC, TBT	A
78	US	Colombia	brooms	safeguard measure	Safeguards, GATT	P
79 (50)	India	EC	pharmaceutical & agricultural chemicals	patent protection	TRIPs	A
80	Belgium	US	telephone directory services	licensing & regulation	GATS	P
81 (51, 52, 65)	Brazil	EC	automotives	investment measures	GATT, SCM, TRIMs	P
82 (115)	Ireland	US	intellectual property	copyright & neighbouring laws	TRIPs	P

APPENDIX: *Continued*

DS no.[a]	*Respondent*	*Complainant*	*Product*	*Issue*	*Agreement*[b]	*Status*[c]
83	Denmark	US	intellectual property	provisional measures	TRIPs	P
84 (75)	Korea	US	liquor	tax	GATT	A
85	US	EC	textiles	rules of origin	ATC, Rules of Origin, GATT, TBT	P
86	Sweden	US	intellectual property	provisional measures	TRIPs	P
87 (109, 110)	Chile	EC	liquor	tax	GATT	A
88 (95)	US	EC	government procurement	contract regulation	GPA	P
89	US	Korea	television receivers	anti-dumping duties	GATT, AD	P
90 (91, 92, 93, 94, 96)	India	US	agriculture, textile, industrial	quantitative restrictions	GATT, Agri, AILP	A
91 (90, 92, 93, 94, 96)	India	Australia	agriculture, textile, industrial	quantitative restrictions	GATT, Agri, AILP	P
92 (90, 91, 93, 94, 96)	India	Canada	agriculture, textile, industrial	quantitative restrictions	GATT, Agri, AILP	P
93 (90, 91, 92, 94, 96)	India	New Zealand	agriculture, textile, industrial	quantitative restrictions	GATT, Agri, AILP	P
94 (90, 91, 91, 93, 96)	India	Switzerland	agriculture, textile, industrial	quantitative restrictions	GATT, Agri, AILP	P
95 (88)	US	EC	government procurement	contract regulation	GPA	P
96 (90, 91, 92, 93, 94)	India	EC	agriculture, textile, industrial	quantitative restrictions	GATT, Agri, AILP	P
97	US	Chile	salmon	anti-dumping investigation	AD	P
98	Korea	EC	dairy	safeguard measure	Safeguards, GATT	P
99	US	Korea	semiconductors	anti-dumping duty	AD	P
100	US	EC	poultry	ban on imports	GATT, SPS, TBT	P

101	Mexico	US	high-fructose corn syrup	anti-dumping investigation	AD	P
102 (74)	Philippines	US	pork, poultry	tariff-rate quotas	GATT, Agri, AILP, TRIMs	P
103	Canada	US	milk, dairy	export subsidies	GATT, Agri, SCM, ILA	P
104	EU	US	processed cheese	export subsidies	GATT, Agri, SCM	P
105 (16, 27)	EU	Panama	bananas	importation, sale, distribution	GATT, ILA, Agri, TRIMs, GATS	P
106 (57)	Australia	US	automotive leather	subsidies	SCM	P
107	Pakistan	EU	hides and skins	export measures		P
108	US	EU	foreign sales corporations	tax treatment	GATT, SCM	P
109 (87, 110)	Chile	US	alcoholic beverages	tax	GATT	P
110 (87, 109)	Chile	EU	alcoholic beverages	tax	GATT	P
111	US	Argentina	groundnuts	tariff rate quota	GATT, Agri, Rules of Origin, ILA	P
112	Peru	Brazil	buses	countervailing duty investigation	SCM	P
113	Canada	New Zealand	dairy	subsidies	Agri	P
114	Canada	EC	pharmaceuticals	patent protection	TRIPs	P
115 (82)	EU	US	intellectual property	copyright & neighbouring laws	TRIPs	P

Source: WTO Website, 'Dispute Settlement', 14 January 1998; http://www.wto.org.

Note:

[a] DS no. in parentheses refers to related case on same matter.

[b] Agri = Agreement on Agriculture; AD = Anti-Dumping; AILP = Agreement on Import Licensing Procedures; ATC = Agreement on Textiles and Clothing; GPA = Government Procurement; ILA = Import Licensing Agreement; SCM = Subsidies; SPS = Sanitary and Phytosanitary Measures; TBT = Technical Barriers to Trade.

[c] As of 31 December 1997; A = Panel active; C = Panel process completed; P = Consultations pending; S = Settlement notified or apparent.

Notes

1. Portions of this chapter have been adapted from Brewer, T.L. and S. Young (1998), 'Investment Issues at the World Trade Organization', *Journal of International Economic Law*, vol. 1, no. 2, pp. 1–14.
2. The FDI flow data are *not* meant to suggest that these FDI flows were 'covered' by GATT rules or even necessarily by WTO rules; rather, they only suggest the magnitudes of their members' FDI flows relative to world totals.
3. The significance of the GATS to FDI is due in part to the fact that FDI in the services sector has been growing more rapidly in recent years than FDI in other sectors (UNCTAD and the World Bank, 1994, Tables 1.8 and 1.9, pp. 16–17).
4. This section of the paper draws extensively on Brewer and Young (1998, pp. 124–30).
5. For previous statistical analyses of dispute cases in the GATT, see Hudec (1993) and especially the summary and extension in Jackson (1997, p. 120). There is some variability and discretion in the range of cases to be counted from the GATT era. However, the 325 included here is within the range represented by Hudec's lower count of 207 as of 1992–93, and Jackson's higher count of 418 as of mid-1994, the latter of which includes conflicts that did not formally become cases in the GATT system.
6. The US–Canada Automotive Pact of 1965 requires MNEs to produce one vehicle in Canada for every one sold there, and to have at least 60 per cent of the vehicle's value added in Canada. The Japanese manufacturers have argued that they meet these requirements and thus should qualify for duty-free importation of imported vehicles.

References

BREWER, T.L. (1995a), 'International Investment Dispute Settlement Procedures: The Evolving Regime for Foreign Direct Investment', *Law and Policy in International Business*, vol. 26, pp. 633–73.

BREWER, T.L. (1995b), 'Investment Issues in the WTO and Implications for APEC's Agenda, in C.J. Green and T.L. Brewer (eds), *Investment Issues in Asia and the Pacific Rim* (New York: Oceana), pp. 113–33.

BREWER, T.L. and S. YOUNG (1998), *The Multilateral Investment System and Multinational Enterprises* (Oxford: Oxford University Press).

BREWER, T.L. and S. YOUNG (1997), 'Investment Incentives and the International Agenda', *World Economy*, vol. 20, pp. 175–98.

CAMERON, J. and K. CAMPBELL (1997), *Dispute Resolution in the World Trade Organisation* (London: Cameron May).

FINANCIAL TIMES, various items as cited.

GEORGETOWN UNIVERSITY LAW CENTER and SECTION OF INTERNATIONAL LAW AND PRACTICE OF THE AMERICAN BAR ASSOCIATION (1998), *A Symposium on the First Three Years of the WTO Dispute Settlement System*, Washington, DC.

GATT (1994), *Law and Practice of the GATT* (Geneva: GATT).

HUDEC, R.E. (1993), *Enforcing International Trade Law* (Salem, N.H.: Butterworth).

INSIDE US TRADE, various items as cited.

INTERNATIONAL LAWYER (1998), *The First Three Years of the WTO Dispute Settlement System*, vol. 32, no. 4.

JACKSON, J.H. (1997), *The World Trading System*, 2nd edn (Cambridge, Mass.: MIT Press).

JULIUS, DE ANNE (1994), 'International Direct Investment: Strengthening the Policy Regime', in P.B. Kenen (ed.), *Managing the World Economy* (Washington, DC: Institute for International Economics) pp. 269–86.

PETERSMANN, E-U. (1997), *The GATT/WTO Dispute Settlement System* (Boston: Kluwer Law International).

STEWART, T.P. and M.M. BURR (1998), 'The WTO Panel Process: An Evaluation of the First Three Years', Symposium on the First Three Years of the WTO Dispute Settlement System (Washington DC: Stewart & Stewart).

UNCTAD (1999), Technical Paper Series on Issues for a Possible Multilateral Framework on Investment (Geneva: UNCTAD).

UNCTAD (1997), *World Investment Report* (Geneva: UNCTAD).

WTO and UNCTAD (1998), A Seminar for Delegates in Geneva on Investment, Trade and Economic Development, Glion, Switzerland (Geneva: WTO and UNCTAD).

12 Locational Tournaments for FDI: Inward Investment into Europe in a Global World

Lynn K. Mytelka[1]

INTRODUCTION

Globalization has many dimensions, and two of these are dealt with in this chapter. The first has to do with the substantial rise in flows of foreign direct investment (FDI) to and from industrialized countries over the past two decades, the emergence of a global market for investment sites and the locational tournaments[2] that now take place across them. The second concerns the globalization of an innovation-based mode of competition. As production has become more knowledge-intensive, a shift has taken place within most industries from competition that is primarily based on price, to competition that is both price and innovation-based. The process of liberalization has helped to diffuse this new mode of competition, putting a premium on the ability of firms to learn and to innovate.[3]

It is within this new context that innovation and inter-firm linkages of various sorts have become particularly important (Mytelka, 1991). Many now stress that a major stimulus to learning and innovation within the firm comes from interactivity and this, they argue, occurs most readily within national and regional systems of innovation (Nelson and Rosenberg, 1993; Lundvall, 1988, 1992, 1995; Storper, 1998). Such interactivity is thought to be of particular importance for sustained innovation in small and medium-sized enterprises (SMEs) (Kuhlmann and Kuntze, 1991; Maskell and Malmberg, 1996).

This chapter explores the effects of high levels of inward and outward FDI, or what is here termed 'turbulence', on the learning environment for firms in the European Union. It does so in two ways. Section one examines the relationship between inward and outward foreign direct investment flows and their impact on innovative activity and local linkages through country-level aggregates. These, however, are, at best, suggestive of a link between the turbulence created by heightened capital mobility and innovation. Section two, therefore, moves to the regional level and explores the impact of bidding wars for FDI within the automobile and electronics industries on the potential for local linkages and learning. Section three draws some preliminary conclusions with respect to the competitive environment for foreign investment in the medium-term. It also considers the impact of accelerated capital mobility on innovation networking by small and medium-sized enterprises (SMEs) over the longer term.

TURBULENT LEARNING ENVIRONMENTS

As markets and competition globalized and direct foreign investment flows rose dramatically over the 1980s and 1990s, municipal, regional and national authorities within Europe sought every opportunity to enhance their attractiveness as sites for international capital. Remaining capital controls were lifted, nominal exchange rates were stabilized and subsidies and other inducements were offered to influence locational decisions. This was accompanied by reductions in tariff and some non-tariff barriers to trade, and a wide repertoire of policies customized to attract FDI and provide 'after-care' services to foreign firms were developed (Phelps, Lovering and Morgan, 1998, p. 121). Within the European Union, the result was a rapid acceleration in capital mobility and an intensification in cross-investments.[4] Inflows of FDI from non-European sources and outflows of FDI from Europe also rose significantly in this period.[5]

From a dynamic innovation perspective, it might be hypothesized that this accelerated capital mobility, involving both the ingress and exit of firms, carries with it both new opportunities for learning but also the threat of increased turbulence. The latter affects trust-based networking relationships and thus makes innovation stimulated by longer-term interaction more difficult. Measuring both learning and turbulence would require detailed, regionally-specific studies of the inflow and outflow of capital by both nationally-owned and foreign firms and an evaluation of the consequences for networking and innovation by locally-based firms. But a first approximation might be had by looking at some aggregate figures on foreign investment flows and relating these to a few rough measures of learning. We can start, for example, by looking at changes in average annual flows of FDI by country. Between 1980–85 and 1989–94, there was a sharp rise in average annual flows of inward FDI, which more than doubled in all advanced EU countries.[6] In a period of rising capital mobility, the share of a country like France in total inward FDI thus rose from 4.7 per cent in the period 1980–85 to 8.4 per cent in 1989–94. Similarly, outward FDI also rose dramatically for a number of these countries.

Another indicator of turbulence is the extent to which a country has passed (or come close to) the bar of 10 per cent of gross fixed capital formation (GFCF) being accounted for by FDI inflows over the past 15 years or so, since this places them well above the annual average for all developed countries which over this period never rose above 5 per cent. With the progressive creation of a single market in the 1980s and 1990s, the EU tended to attract higher levels of foreign investment, but, even then, the ratio of average annual inflows of FDI to GFCF never exceeded 6 per cent. Countries which are above the 10 per cent mark and where the pace of change has been rapid are thus significantly different. So, too, are the few countries where ratios have stayed very low, Germany and Japan, for example. These data are presented in Table 12.1.

But turbulence is not only generated by capital inflows. Of equal interest for this purpose is the sharp rise in the share of GFCF accounted for by FDI outflows. Combining these ratios and comparing them across the three time periods, 1981–85, 1986–90, 1991–95 provides a very rough measure of the growing turbulence in a large number of European Union countries as the ratios rose, sometimes quite precipitously (Table 12.1). By 1986/90 the share of inflows and outflows in GFCF had risen to over 20 per cent in the Netherlands, the UK, Benelux and Sweden. In the latter two, the rate of change has been exceptionally high and continued to substantially increase during the third period. In three other countries, Spain, France and Portugal, the ratio was over 10 per cent by 1990 and continued to rise in France. In Denmark and Ireland, where inward and outward FDI flows as a share of GFCF has risen to only 7.2 and 8.2 respectively in 1986–90, the ratio rose rapidly to over 20 per cent in each of these countries in the 1991–95 period.

What might be the significance of this accelerated capital mobility for the kind of learning economy or 'national system of innovation' that researchers such as Lundvall, Storper, Maskell and Malmberg, Freeman, Nelson and others have described? Clearly one would wish to examine the impact of the turbulence created by a high level of inward and outward capital flows on the potential for local *linkages*

Table 12.1 The share of inward and outward foreign direct investment in gross fixed capital formation in the EU, North America and Japan

	(A) FDI inflows/GFCF			*(B) FDI outflows/GFCF*			*(A) + (B)*		
	1981/1985	*1986/1990*	*1991/1995*	*1981/1985*	*1986/1990*	*1991/1995*	*1981/1985*	*1986/1990*	*1991/1995*
Benelux	7.6	16.1	23.9	1.3	14.7	16.7	8.9	30.8	40.6
Canada	1.0	5.8	6.0	4.9	4.9	5.5	5.2	10.7	11.5
Denmark	0.4	2.5	11.7	0.9	4.7	11.1	1.3	7.2	22.8
France	2.0	4.1	7.7	2.5	8.5	9.3	4.5	12.6	17.0
Germany	1.2	2.0	0.8	3.4	6.8	4.9	4.6	8.8	5.7
Greece	6.0	7.9	5.2	N/A	N/A	N/A	N/A	N/A	N/A
Ireland	4.0	1.1	16.8	2.3	7.1	4.5	6.3	8.2	21.3
Italy	1.1	2.2	1.5	1.8	2.3	3.0	2.9	4.5	4.5
Japan	0.1	0.1	0.3	1.5	4.1	1.7	1.6	4.2	2.0
Netherlands	6.1	13.3	12.6	15.5	21.1	21.9	21.6	34.4	34.5
Portugal	3.0	10.0	8.0	0.2	0.5	2.3	3.2	10.5	10.3
Spain	5.3	9.4	8.8	0.9	1.7	3.0	6.2	11.1	11.8
Sweden	1.6	4.0	23.5	7.7	23.0	15.8	9.3	27.0	39.3
UK	5.7	14.6	10.0	12.0	18.7	16.6	17.7	33.3	26.6
USA	2.9	6.9	4.2	2.1	4.7	6.4	5.0	11.6	10.6
Developed Countries	2.2	4.6	3.6	2.7	5.6	5.4	4.9	10.2	9.0
EU	2.6	5.9	5.7	4.3	8.8	7.7	6.9	14.7	13.4

N/A = Not available.
Source: UNCTAD (1995), Annex Tables 5 and 6; UNCTAD (1997), Annex Tables B5.

and the stimulus this provides for *innovation*. Recent OECD science and technology indicators provide some rather crude proxies for these two potential impacts since they are aggregated at the national level.[7] Innovation, for example, might be measured by resident patent applications, and linkages by gross domestic expenditure on R&D in higher education financed by business.[8]

Data for all EU countries and for both variables over the 10-year period 1985–95 were not always available. To make the comparisons more meaningful, the less favoured regions of the EU have been excluded from this analysis. With respect to the indicator of innovation, it was possible to find data on resident patent applications for seven of the advanced industrial countries of the EU and these data are graphed in Figure 12.1.[9] The indicator for linkages is more problematic since several of the countries did not collect these data on an annual basis and the data are not available for the most recent period. But broad trends can nonetheless be perceived. Data for linkages as reflected in Gross Domestic Expenditure on R&D in Higher Education Financed by Business are presented in Table 12.2.

A number of interesting patterns emerge from an analysis of the data on innovation as reflected in resident patent applications. The 1980s, it will be remembered, were a period of intense competitive pressure giving rise to higher R&D expenditures and higher levels of national patenting in all seven EU countries in each of the years from 1985 to 1992.[10] It would be expected, therefore, that resident patent-

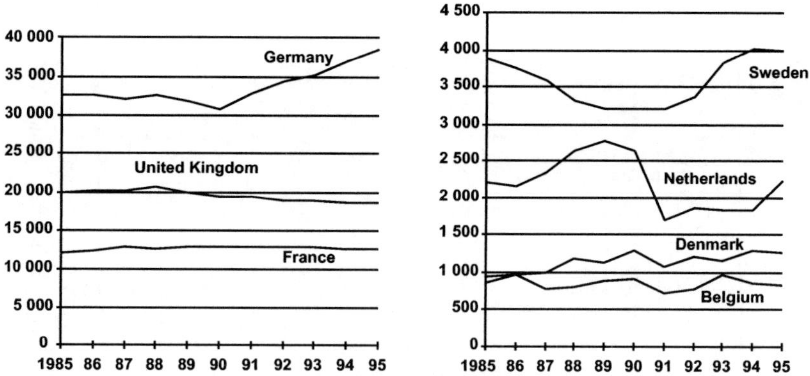

Source: OECD (1995) Table 20; (1997) Table 72.

Figure 12.1 Innovation: number of resident patent applications, 1985–95

Table 12.2 Linkages: gross domestic expenditure on R&D in higher education financed by business (1990 constant US$ millions)

Capital mobility (FDI inflows + outflows/GFCF)	*1987*	*1988*	*1989*	*1990*	*1991*	*1992*
High: >25%						
Belgium	40.6	44.1	86.8	N/A	11.4	N/A
Netherlands	11.1	12.0	11.3	12.5	17.1	18.0
Sweden	69.5	N/A.	102.1	N/A	58.8	N/A
UK	166.6	217.7	229.7	235.8	244.7	246.6
Medium: 10–15%						
France	107.4	125.0	154.6	168.2	150.7	135.7
Portugal	N/A	0.9	N/A	1.3	N/A	1.2
Spain	12.8	46.9	62.3	70.8	91.2	91.6
Low: <10%						
Denmark	3.5	4.2	4.7	5.1	5.4	6.0
Germany	69.7	298.6	319.4	367.3	389.9	397.4
Greece	N/A	3.1	7.7	N/A	7.4	N/A
Ireland	4.3	4.7	6.3	8.2	7.9	7.6
Italy	20.2	36.9	57.3	59.0	98.8	117.8

N/A = Not available.
Source: OECD (1995) Table 1.

ing activity would follow suit. Instead, quite noticeable differences in resident patenting activity are found. When these differences are examined in the context of variations in the intensity of capital mobility in each country, irrespective of the size of the economy, an association between the level of domestic capital mobility and resident patent applications appears. Thus, countries with high levels of domestic capital mobility over the 1980s such as UK, Sweden and the Netherlands, tended to exhibit a downward trend in resident patent applications by the late 1980s/early 1990s, whereas countries with lower levels of domestic capital mobility, such as Germany and Denmark, have rising levels of resident patent applications. France, which has moderately high levels of capital mobility, had a rather flat curve throughout this period, suggesting that resident patenting activity was not keeping pace with non-resident patent applications. Clearly further research along these lines is needed.

For several of the countries in which the composite index for turbulence is over 20, such as Benelux, Ireland and Sweden, the share of FDI inflows in GFCF rose far higher over the period than did the share of FDI outflows in GFCF. In Denmark and the Netherlands, the reverse was true. It might be expected that this would lead to a difference in innovation as measured by resident patent applications. Interviews with head offices in 150 firms led Warrant, for example, to conclude that local subsidiaries in Europe have considerable autonomy in research and development, resource allocation and alliance formation (Warrant, 1991). Madeuf *et al.*, on the other hand, argued that subsidiaries in France performed research that was unrelated to their local environments (Madeuf, Lefevre and Savory, 1992). The data in Figure 12.1 provide a limited test of this hypothesis, and reveal a decline in the number of resident patent applications over the ten-year period 1985–95 in Sweden, Netherlands, Denmark and Belgium. This would suggest that turbulence created by both capital inflows and outflows may be a factor contributing to a breakdown in the kind of trust-based relations and in the interactivity required for innovation.

The relationship of capital mobility to linkage formation as illustrated by gross domestic expenditure on R&D in higher education financed by business (Table 12.2) is more difficult to interpret. This is in part because of the correspondence between low levels of capital mobility and strong traditions of university–industry R&D in countries such as Germany and Italy where the trend in business-financed university R&D steadily rose over the 1980s. Of the advanced industrial countries, only Denmark falls into the category of countries with low levels of capital mobility and there, too, the trend in business-financed university R&D is rising, albeit from a very low level. At the other extreme, no clear pattern emerges in the four countries with very high levels of capital mobility. A declining trend might have been expected, but only Sweden exhibits this pattern clearly. Once again, the difficulty of interpretation lies with other factors that explain these trends. For example, the significant increases in business-financed university R&D in Belgium and the UK might reflect the high level of participation by research institutions from these countries in European R&D programmes alongside local firms (Mytelka, 1991). But it might also be an indication of the attractiveness of the latter as a site for R&D activities by multinational corporations as a number of studies suggest (Pearce and Singh, 1992; Papanastassiou and Pearce, 1994).

Clearly there is a need to get behind these aggregate data and look more closely at local linkages, embeddedness and innovation, not only in large but also in small and medium-sized firms. One way of doing so is to examine some of the effects of locational tournaments at the regional level as they interface with the changing competitive conditions in specific industrial sectors. Although much of this discussion will deal with greenfield investment, it is important to recognize that a large percentage of the 'new' investment in Europe consists of mergers and acquisitions, joint ventures, and/or extensions to existing plants. In recognition of this characteristic of inward FDI, agencies such as the Invest in Britain Bureau, for example, assign a high priority to inducing transnational firms to choose the UK when undertaking expansions.[11] Locational tournaments thus take place both when the issue is the extension of an existing investment, and when it is a question of attracting a first-time investor. The subsequent section explores these issues in two specific industries.

LOCATIONAL TOURNAMENTS IN THE AUTOMOBILE AND ELECTRONICS INDUSTRIES

Although competition among nation-states is not new[12] and incentives, in themselves, do not create the flow of foreign capital nor are they wholly determinant of its location,[13] two features of contemporary locational tournaments suggest that the nature of that competition has significantly changed and that these changes might have a bearing on localized learning and innovation potential. The first is the widening range of incentives offered to non-local investors by an increasing number of *industrialized* countries based on static considerations of employment and exports. A recent UNCTAD survey of incentives in 103 countries, for example, showed that 22 of the 26 developed countries offered a reduction in the standard income tax rate for foreign investors; 15 offered an accelerated rate of depreciation; while 11 gave tax holidays and other sorts of fiscal incentives such as deductions from social security contributions and exemptions from import duties (UNCTAD, 1995, pp. 292–3).[14] The second feature is the extension of competition to all levels of government.[15] For example, in the competition for a Mercedes-Benz plant in 1993, some 170 cities and regions across two continents were initially in the running (*Wall Street Journal*, 25 November 1993).[16] To illustrate these trends, a few examples of locational tournaments in two of the most globalized industries, namely the automobile and electronics industries,[17] will clarify the magnitude of the changes currently under way and some of the contradictions they are beginning to generate.

Automobiles

In the immediate post-World War II period both European and Japanese producers sought to replicate the American model of mass production of standardized products and vertical integration. Within a few years, however, financial difficulties and market instability led Japanese automobile producers to dismiss a large numbers of workers and to begin nearly three decades of experimentation with new supplier–client relationships (van Tulder, Trefers and Ruigrok, 1996, p. 5; Womack, Jones and Roos, 1990). Some of these were transferred through outward investment by Japanese automobile companies to the United States during the 1980s (Helper and Sako, 1995; Kenney and Florida, 1991; Martin, Mitchell and Swaminathan, 1995).

Strategies of vertical disintegration and the use of strategic partnerships to build new forms of supplier–client relationships represented a significant break with existing organizational technology in United States and European automobile firms. Gradually, however, this new organizational model spread to other automobile manufacturers. By 1996, for example, only Ford and Volvo manufactured more than 60 of their parts in-house. Vertically-integrated firms still supplied some 43 of Volkswagen's parts, but only 38 of those for Mercedes-Benz, 37 for GM, 33 for BMW, Renault and Peugeot, 30 for Fiat and 25 for Honda, Nissan and Toyota (Kurylko, 1996, p. 14). Automobile companies now expend considerable resources to develop new technologies to manage international supply chains and global logistical systems.

Closer links between parts suppliers and assemblers have enhanced both the direct and indirect contribution of the automobile industry to employment. This has made it particularly attractive to less favoured regions in the industrialized countries and the object of major bidding wars. Thus, for example, Japanese automotive companies in the early to mid-1980s secured record subsidies in exchange for new plants in Ohio, Tennessee and Kentucky. State subsidies per employed person rose from $2500 in the case of Honda's Marysville, Ohio plant in 1982, to $6470 to Nissan (TN) in 1983, $14263 to Mazda (MI) in 1987, $42771 to Toyota (KY) in 1988 and $98059 to Subaru-Isuzu (IN) in 1989 (Kenney and Florida, 1991, p. 30). Politicians at the time vowed to bring the bidding wars under control, but nothing came of it, and over the 1980s the level of incentives offered to foreign firms escalated further.[18]

One of the issues raised by the rise of bidding wars was the question of value for money with the latter most often defined in terms of employment gains. The decision to locate a BMW plant in Spartanburg, South Carolina in 1992 is illustrative. Of an initial investment of $400 million through 1995, $240 million, or some 60 per cent of investment costs was borne by state and local sources. The incentive package included[19] a freeze on the level of taxation for 20 years – worth $71 million, a tax credit equal to $1500 per employee for five years – with a projected level of 1200 employees this was worth $9 million; and the right to finance construction costs using domestic, low interest industrial reserve bonds. As these bonds carry an AAA rating, they resulted in considerably lower financing charges than a traditional loan. Borrowing locally, moreover, reduces the firm's exposure to exchange rate fluctuations and by marshalling local savings avoids the need to bring in fresh capital for investment. This particular package also included subsidized training of workers to BMW specification at state technical colleges with a value of about $90 million; a $1.00 per year lease on a 900 acre tract of land purchased for BMW by the city; $25 million for site preparation, mainly for electricity, gas, water and sewage; $45 million to build the required highway and airport facilities; as well as an extension of the airport's free trade zone to cover the BMW site thus enabling BMW to avoid the payment of customs duties on parts imported from Germany or elsewhere. Since BMW intended to import its engines and axles by air from Europe, this represented considerable savings. However, given the substantial incentives which BMW received, value for money in employment terms would depend heavily on the growth of indirect employment as suppliers moved to the area.

Further changes in the nature of competition in the automobile industry during the late 1980s have created contradictory tendencies with regard to the employment gains generated by bidding wars. Of critical importance in this respect is the emergence of preferred first-tier suppliers with whom new forms of partnership were developed for the design of principal components and subsystems. The interactive nature of this relationship implied that preferred first-tier suppliers were most often based in the home markets of the major automobile manufacturers. While in the past most automobile assemblers had tended to create parallel supplier networks in each of the foreign locations in which they established major production facilities (Humphrey, 1998), long-term contracts and special pricing arrangements with preferred first-tier suppliers is inducing the latter to organize the supply of parts and subsystems in other locations (Le Gall, 1998; Young, 1996).[20] This, in turn, has led to an increase in mergers and acquisitions within the auto-parts industry and has accelerated the internationalization of auto-parts manufacturers either through the establishment of subsidiaries or through the creation of joint ventures with existing companies.

Under these new competitive conditions, bidding wars for automobile assemblers bring with them a host of secondary changes, which have the potential to disrupt existing ties between local auto-parts suppliers and automobile assemblers. In so doing, they diminish the incentive to strengthen local R&D and design capacity to serve new investors. At the same time, however, the new relationship between assemblers and preferred first-tier suppliers offers the possibility of raising the indirect employment gains from both expansion and new investment. It thus contributes to the intensification of bidding wars in this industry and to the contradictions they generate for local learning and innovation. Recent experiences in the UK and France are illustrative of these two effects.

In the mid-1980s, following a first set of bidding wars, two major Japanese automobile manufacturers built greenfield plants in the United Kingdom. Nissan established a European manufacturing base at Sunderland in Northern England, one of the UK regions hardest hit by the decline in its traditional industrial base; while Toyota located an assembly plant in Burnaston, Derbyshire, and an engine plant at Deeside in Northern Wales, another disadvantaged region. Over the next ten years the Nissan subsidiary grew into a company producing 270000 vehicles per year and employing 4350 people. Much of its output was exported and it was rated the most efficient automobile plant in Europe. Moreover, 26 of Nissan 'synchronous first-tier suppliers' located in the region, but only a few of these were not among Nissan's traditional suppliers. The US firm TRW is one example. Fewer still were, like the British auto-parts firm Lucas Varity, suppliers to the world from a Northern England base. These suppliers and their sub-contractors, however, collectively account for a further 20000 employees in the region (Bridge, 1998, p. 2). The employment stakes are thus very high in this industry, but so, too, are the difficulties which local SMEs are facing as a result of the changing nature of supplier–client relationships in this industry.

In early 1997 Nissan announced its decision to produce a third model at its Sunderland facility raising capacity to 350000 vehicles per year and adding a further 800 jobs. This announcement came on the heels of a decision by Ford to cut 1300 jobs at its Halewood plant and end the production of its Escort model at Merseyside, another disfavoured region. All Escort production would be consolidated at Ford's plants in Saarlouis, Germany, and Valencia, Spain, where an eventual replacement model would be built. The Nissan expansion would compensate only partially for these losses, but an announcement that Toyota would also introduce a new model was expected to lead to a positive overall balance. In competition with Burnaston, however, were sites in France, Germany, Spain, Austria and Poland.

While penetration of continental markets was a key Toyota objective and Valenciennes, the chosen location in the Nord–Pas-de-Calais region, was on major transportation routes making supply and sales easier than for some of its rivals, incentives were clearly a major factor in Toyota's decision to locate a further operation in France.[21] Located in a disadvantaged region, the Valenciennes plant was eligible for a wide variety of regional and national incentives. These reportedly included exemptions from some of the normal employers' social charges, reduced energy and land prices as well as grants from the French government amounting to nearly 20 per cent of the factory's building costs – a rate of subsidization double that which the United Kingdom's Department of Trade and Industry could offer.

The Toyota plant will involve an investment of $655.6 million and create some 2000 jobs by the year 2005, and the company has already invited its preferred first-tier suppliers to locate in the region. Unlike the North of England or Wales, Nord–Pas-de-Calais, however, was already a centre for the production of automobiles and auto-parts. Renault is the second largest employer in the region and the region is home to major auto-parts subsidiaries of Renault and Peugeot such as ECIA; joint ventures of Renault/Peugeot (STA manufacturing gear boxes, Française de Mécanique motors); and many large and smaller French auto-parts producers, such as Valeo, Plastic Omnium, Sotexo, a subsidiary of Bertrand Faure. In 1996 and 1997 a number of American auto-parts firms, Valmex (Textron), Japanese companies, Ogura, Akebono (Toyota Group) and US/Japanese joint ventures (Delphi/Calsonic of the Nissan Group) located in the region or announced plans to do so.

While these new investments will create jobs, they may not increase overall employment in the Nord–Pas-de-Calais region. Nor are they likely to strengthen the regional system of innovation. Most of the newcomers, such as those cited above, will fall within the group of 'preferred' suppliers and their local joint venture partners. Their contributions to deepening learning and innovation within the region are likely to be small despite an earlier move in this direction by locally-based firms.[22] The effect of having attracted a new Toyota plant to the region will also be felt indirectly by local suppliers as a result of the significant overcapacity in the European automobile industry; the age of existing Renault and Peugeot plants in the region; and the difficulties which the latter face in securing fiscal and financial advantages similar to those which Toyota has obtained. This set of factors is likely to increase the vulnerability of local assemblers and their suppliers, reducing the ability of the former to maintain existing levels of production and sustain local linkages.

Electronics

Similar examples concerning the high cost of locational tournaments and the contradictory forces generated by the deepening process of globalization can be cited in the electronics industry. Two of these are reviewed in this section.

In the case of IBM's recent decision to locate a 64 Mb Dram production at Corbeil-Essone in France, the investment was about $1 billion but the number of jobs it would directly generate was only 600. This must be understood in the context of an earlier downsizing at this location, where one semiconductor line was closed in 1994 with a loss of 400 jobs and closures of production lines for bipolar and Cmos integrated circuits planned for 1996 and 1997, resulted in a further loss of 1100 jobs.[23] The creation of 600 new jobs at this site thus left a considerable shortfall. Nevertheless, the local (Corbeil), regional (Ile-de- France) and national authorities in France competed actively to attract this investment away from rival sites in Germany (Dresden), Singapore and Taiwan. In total, financial incentives including reductions and exemptions from professional taxes and investment subsidies amounted to 300 million francs or 6 per cent of investment costs.[24] In addition, however, the national and regional governments agreed to fund training activities and subsidize the purchase of equipment by area research laboratories. According to one source, regional and national authorities have also extended the promise of contracts for the purchase of IBM PCs produced in France.

Within the electronics industry hard-disk drives form one of the most globalized sectors. The major competitors include IBM, Seagate, Maxtor, Quantum and Western Digital. Until the early 1980s almost all production was located in the United States. In 1982, Seagate, only three years after its founding, moved a large part of its disk-drive assembly operations to Singapore and a year later established a second affiliate in Thailand. Since then all major competitors have moved most of their final assembly to Asia. In addition to its high level of concentration and globalization, the hard-disk-drive industry '... is characterised by continuous price wars, very short product cycles and highly volatile market positions' (Ernst, 1997, p. 2). The price–performance curve in the disk-drive industry is even steeper than that described by Moore's Law for the semiconductor industry, according to which processing power of chips double every 18 months (Markoff, 1998, p. 10).

The investment promotion authorities in Ireland have long been aware of the volatile nature of the international electronics industry. Yet much of the rapid growth in inward FDI has been a result of investment by electronics firms, many of which are in the most volatile segments of this industry. In the mid-1990s, the Industrial Development Authority (IDA) successfully attracted Seagate, the world's leading independent disk-drive manufacturer to locate in Ireland.[25] Incentives totalling $16 million were offered, and of these 88 per cent consisted of capital grants. An assembly operation employing 1400 people was opened at Clonmel in 1996. Barely a year later, Seagate announced its decision to close this plant and consolidate disk-drive assembly in Penang, Malaysia. The Asian financial crisis was certainly a factor in the decision to relocate these highly price-sensitive assembly operations to Malaysia, where costs had so dramatically fallen. But the market glut for hard-disk drives caused by a rapid expansion of disk-drive assembly plants built by Japanese and South Korean groups such as Fujitsu, Samsung and Hyundai had led to a collapse in prices before the current financial crisis. Moreover, the capital mobility was encouraged by the limited local supply linkages which this assembly operation had established. The rationale for remaining in Ireland was further eroded by the difficult financial situation faced by Apple, one of its two major Irish-based clients. In the wake of Seagate's withdrawal, the Irish authorities have recognized the high volatility of capital in the electronics industry as 'a cause for concern' and likely to affect a further 15 of Ireland's 150 foreign-owned electronics firms.[26]

While locational tournaments and the subsidies they provide are justified mainly in terms of employment creation, the reality is that these jobs are being generated at high cost and, with the exception of less-favoured regions where much of the investment is greenfield investment, in net terms the increment is often quite small. Approximately 60 per cent of all inward foreign direct investment in Europe is ownership-changing investment and much of it results in downsizing. IBM, in the course of its restructuring in Europe, sold off several of its plants and in each case there was a substantial reduction in employment. Nonetheless, even this investment is often subsidized with the subsidies justified as required to save jobs, as illustrated above. If from a short-term, allocative perspective one might seriously put locational tournaments into question, what can be said about the extent to which these newcomers generate 'growing territorial cores of learning-based industries . . . involv[ing] dense, local input-output linkages . . . [or] specialised knowledge and organisational talents . . . due to knowledge spillovers and complementarities . . .' (Storper, 1995, p. 13).

In so far as the less-favoured regions of Europe are concerned, there is increasing evidence that locational tournaments do not attract the kind of investment that generates learning and innovation. A comparative study of 'flagship' plants attracted to four less-favoured regions – Scotland, Ireland, Portugal and Brandenburg for the European Union, for example – found few 'multilocal performance-oriented firms' likely to move into new functional or product areas, innovate locally or secure world product mandates for their output (Amin, 1994; Young, Hood and Peters, 1994). Local supplier–client linkages were also weak, confirming the points raised by Morgan and Sayer (1988) in their study of Japanese transplants in the electronics industry in South Wales. Evidence that foreign firms have become 'embedded within regional clusters' in the UK is very slim (Phelps *et al.*, 1998).

Although Kenney and Florida (1993) have provided data on the extensive network of suppliers created by Japanese transplants in the automobile and steel industries in the American rust belt, more recent studies suggest that many of these are recreations of earlier links with Japanese suppliers with whom '. . . long-term relationships facilitate inter-organisational learning and lead to inter-organisational interdependence' (Martin, Mitchell and Swaminathan, 1995, p. 605). The Nissan plant at Sunderland, which began production in 1986, largely replicates this pattern. In the early years of its development it 'relied on imported components . . . but did establish immediately one or two key suppliers in critical component areas: car seats (Ikeda Busan), panel formings (Nissan Yamato) and large injection mouldings (Magna Kansei)' (Bridge, 1998, p. 2).

In regions known for the density of their R&D infrastructure (such as Ile de France or Rhône-Alpes in France), the innovativeness of established firms and the existing fabric of potential suppliers, innovative firms are being attracted from elsewhere. In the electronics sector these companies join large French firms such as Thomson-CSF, SGS-Thomson, SNECMA and Renault in creating R&D linkages with local research organizations and dynamic, innovative supplier–client networks with local firms.[27] But no systematic studies have been made of the extensiveness of the local linkages which newcomers have established.[28] There is increasing evidence that globalization of competition is pushing local firms to follow their clients overseas[29] and global restructuring is leading to the rupture of networks that had been developed over the course of a decade or more.[30] This is particularly true in the auto-parts industry where cross-investments and M&As have risen sharply between European and American auto-parts firms as the industry accelerated its internationalization and assemblers divested part of their component operations in the 1990s. In self-defence, a number of regional governments have taken the lead in supporting local SMEs. In North Rhine-Westphalia, for example, the Automotive Initiative involves R&D collaboration between suppliers and clients and has a high level of participation by SMEs. It was launched in 1993 by the Länder government in collaboration with automobile assemblers, their suppliers, unions, banks, business associations and technical institutions at precisely the time that German automobile assemblers began to internationalize production, and there was every sign that some of their major suppliers would follow suit (von Bandemer, Kalff, Tellechea and Watson, 1996, p. 43).

CONCLUSIONS

This review of the relationship between turbulence generated by accelerated capital mobility and local learning and innovation has demonstrated that attracting large firms to a locality will not necessarily contribute to greater innovative activity in the region. Nor from a learning perspective, and with particular regard to the automotive and electronics industries, are there guarantees that locational tournaments will contribute to the involvement of local SMEs in either production or R&D networks. Such linkages are increasingly difficult to bring about where, as in Britain, turbulence has increased because '. . . successive rounds of investment fail to replace closures and rationalisations among existing firms from earlier rounds' (Phelps *et al.*, 1998, p. 121). In addition, as John Bridge of the Northern Development Company acknowledges with respect to Nissan and its suppliers, globalization and the changing nature of supplier–client relationships make it difficult for smaller more specialized local companies '. . . to sustain captive, local markets . . . SMEs that are going to succeed will [have to] develop competencies across markets and sectors' (Bridge, 1998, p. 3). Policies to stimulate and support the kind of learning that firms need in order to move in this new direction will be required, yet locational tournaments and the incentive policies they involve seem to be moving in quite the opposite direction, as the Valenciennes case suggests.

Most governments, however, remain convinced that FDI is critical for growth, and within Europe countries and regions continue to gird themselves for battle. After noting the fall in investment by foreign firms between 1995 and 1996 in France, *L'Usine Nouvelle* (1997, p. 10) pointed out that Britain has successfully 'played the card of massive incentives' in attracting 40 per cent of the Asian and American foreign investment in Europe. The message was clear and as the Valenciennes case illustrates, two can play this game. Yet the costs have risen dramatically and some of the very regional authorities that figured among its most active players are beginning to question whether bidding wars have not gone too far. Ron Davies, Welsh Secretary, recently made this point when he emphasised that, 'The future of the Welsh economy depends on small and medium-sized enterprises. That's not to dismiss the importance of inward investment, but they must be our number one priority'.[31]

Locational tournaments are also pitting region against region within Europe's two main host countries – the UK and France. Worse still, efforts to maintain their frontrunner status in attracting foreign investment are not likely to slacken as new competitors enter the lists in the wake of the financial meltdown in Asia. Although within the EU incentives are capped, this appears to have led to the search for innovative ways to get around them. Countries have thus taken each other before the EU on the grounds that they have exceeded their caps. Measures are clearly needed to convert this wide variety of incentives into comparable and quantifiable indicators,[32] which can be related more easily to the longer-term costs, and benefits of locational tournaments. This alone would enable regional authorities to undertake a more substantial evaluation of the alternative uses to which such incentives might be put.

Lastly, it should be pointed out that no current international treaty limits the continuance of bidding wars as a means to attract inward foreign direct investment. The OECD-based Multilateral Agreement on Investment (MAI) is under pressure from many sources, and even if it were to be signed at some point over the next year or two the current text contains few provisions to limit incentives or develop stronger rules governing competition. Indeed, the call for global competition rules by Karel Van Miert, the European Union's competition commissioner at the World Economic Forum in Davos this year, went largely unheeded.[33] Uruguay-Round liberalization measures do include a phase-out for performance requirements, but this is unlikely to have much of an impact on locational tournaments given the kinds of incentives being offered within the European Union. These tend to be directed towards less-favoured regions and the need for reconversion and/or training and R&D activities that are not limited by WTO disciplines. Under WTO rules, however, there may be a problem for states that seek to introduce contractual clawback provisions into agreements with firms attracted through locational tournaments. Such provisions would require repayment of grants when a project fails to achieve the objectives for which such grants were made. WTO rules make the formulation of such objectives more difficult. Nonetheless, Seagate, in the case discussed above, was asked to repay the Irish government for its grants and they have done so. Despite mounting criticism, bidding wars are thus likely to continue.

Notes

1. Director, Division on Investment, Technology and Enterprise Development, UNCTAD, Geneva, on leave from Carleton University (Ottawa) and Forum-Cerem, Université Paris-X. An earlier version of this paper was presented at the EMOT Workshop on 'Learning and Embeddedness: Evolving Transnational Firm Strategies in Europe', Collingwood College, University of Durham, 27–29 June 1996. The views expressed here do not reflect UNCTAD positions nor do they in any way engage that organization. The author wishes to thank Carol Cosgrove-Sacks, Ed Safarian and Karl Sauvant for their helpful comments and gratefully acknowledges the support of the Social Sciences and Humanities Council of Canada in the research leading to this paper.

2. The term is borrowed from Paul David (1984) and signifies bidding wars to attract inward FDI.
3. A variety of indicators ranging from evidence of shortened product life-cycles, to estimates of the growth of 'intangible investments' in design, R&D and training within the firm and changes in the level and mix of skills within the economy are used to illustrate this point. See Cantwell and Randaccio (1992), Chesnais (1991), Dosi and Soete (1991), Freeman and Perez (1988), Mytelka (1983 and 1987), OECD (1992), Porter (1990).
4. Cantwell and Randaccio (1992) argue that within the EU, oligopolistic rivalry under conditions of falling NTBs and for firms which do not invest strictly to serve the domestic market, that is, import substituting M&As or greenfield investments, has led to considerable cross-investment and particularly cross-investment that is partially motivated by MNC interests in establishing EU-wide networks of technological activity (p. 104).
5. Average annual inflows of FDI into Europe rose 62 per cent between 1985–90 and 1991–95, and outflows increased 83 per cent over this period. Calculated from Annex B1, p. 303 and Annex B-2, p. 308 of UNCTAD, *World Investment Report 1997.*
6. The situation is somewhat different in the less-favoured regions of Europe. All data are calculated from the UN's *World Investment Reports* (UNCTC, 1988, and UNCTAD, 1995 and 1997).
7. Ideally we would wish to measure linkages and innovation at the local level since many studies show that the most dense interactions are most often with firms and R&D institutions that fall within a radius of 50 miles/60 kilometres of the company. Local-level networking and indications of the kinds of changes taking place within firms can only be tapped through extensive interview data. Comparative studies of this sort are not yet available.
8. Inter-firm linkages would be another indicator but little of this information is available at the regional level. In more aggregate terms, the most recent data on inter-firm technology partnerships involving firms from the developed countries do show that the number of such partnerships continues to grow (UNCTAD, *World Investment Report 1998*) and like resident patent data they are affected by overall economic conditions. During the recessionary years 1990/91 there was a drop in the number of in inter-firm technology partnerships similar to that in resident patent applications. The data on technology partnerships, however, are mainly collected from public sources such as newspapers and professional journals that tend to favour partnerships involving TNCs and exclude the vast majority of inter-firm agreements involving SMEs.
9. No data on resident patent applications were available for Italy in the period prior to 1992.
10. The sole exceptions were 1987 in the case of Denmark, and 1991 for all countries except Germany and Denmark.
11. 'Inward Investment into the UK', *Financial Times*, 18 July 1996. Agencies such as the Datar in France are similarly attentive to the need to

compete to retain investors already committed to France. As a recent OECD study pointed out, in France, some 500 people are now involved in investment promotition activities (OECD, 1996, p. 29).

12. Interwar beggar-thy-neighbour policies were one of the factors leading to the postwar GATT liberalization process. Despite this process, competitive devaluations, the use of subsidies and the mercantalistically motivated imposition of countervailing duties have become commonplace (UNCTAD, 1994).
13. As John Dunning points out, however, 'incentives offered by regional authorities within the European Union (EU) and of states within the United States have been shown to be a decisive factor in influencing the intra-regional location of inbound MNE activity' (Dunning, 1998, p. 52).
14. This contrasts with the 1960s and 1970s, for example, when most such incentives were offered by developing countries.
15. This is leading to a number of aberrant results. St Louis and Kansas City both in the State of Missouri, for example, were competing along with New York City to become the new headquarters for Trans World Airlines then in bankruptcy. The two Missouri cities offered competing sets of incentives, and St Louis eventually won. As Kenneth Thomas points out (Thomas, 1995, pp. 2–3) 'From the point of view of Missouri unemployment, the same number of jobs would have come to the state' whether St Louis or Kansas City had won. But each lost relative to a situation in which they had not offered additional incentives to those provided by the State of Missouri, because the cost of attracting these jobs rose. Moreover, 'from the standpoint of the United States as a whole, it is even more irrational. Not only would the same number of jobs have been generated in New York City, Kansas City or St Louis, there are offsetting job losses at the company's former headquarters at Mt. Kisco, New York. Thus, sub-national governments prepared three sets of investment incentives to reward TWA for creating *no* new jobs in the U.S.'
16. Although the runner-up to Alabama in the Mercedes case was another American State, North Carolina, the competition among municipalities and regions is increasingly international. Livingston, Scotland, for example, won out over Roseville, California, in its bid to attract NEC Corporation's latest computer chip fabrication facility (*International Herald Tribune*, 22 September 1994).
17. UNCTAD's *World Investment Report 1997* (pp. 29–30) provides a list of the top 100 TNCs ranked by foreign assets. All of the world's largest automobile companies – Ford, GM, VW, Toyota, Nissan, Daimler-Benz, Renault, BMW, Honda and Volvo – and ten of the world's largest electronics firms – General Electric Corporation, Hitachi, IBM, Matsushita, Siemens, Sony, Fujitsu, Philips, Hewlett Packard and Motorola – figure in this list. For each of these firms a composite 'transnationality index' is calculated as the average of three ratios: the foreign share of total assets, total sales and total employment. The average transnationality index is 43.8 for the ten automobile companies in this list, and 44.7 for the ten electronics firms. LG Electronics and Samsung have smaller

total assets but the former has a transnationality index of 40 and the latter, 14.2.

18. Governor Evan Bayh of Indiana, for example, won election in 1988 after accusing his predecessors of overpaying to attract Mitsubishi's Diamond Star plant in 1985, but by 1991 he was being attacked by neighbouring governors for offering United Airlines $291 million in incentives to build a new maintenance facility in Indianapolis (*Wall Street Journal*, 25 November 1993). High levels of subsidization were also a feature of Hyundai's investment in Bromont, Québec (Rourke, 1989).
19. These data were compiled from articles published in the *Financial Times Survey* (UK) of 20 October 1992, *La Tribune* (France) of 26 June 1992 and the *Independent on Sunday* (UK) of 9 May 1993.
20. In the VW truck plant at Resende in Brazil suppliers have been brought within the plant and actually carry out production using their own components and workers.
21. These data were drawn from articles published in the on-line *Daily Telegraph* of 18 March 1997, 8 May 1997, 21 October 1997, 9 December 1997 and 10 December 1997, *The Financial Times* of 10 December 1997 and the *International Herald Tribune* of 10–11 January 1998.
22. In 1996 Cofimeta, the automobile division of Arbel, was planning to establish a centre for machine design for the automobile industry in the Nord-Pas-de-Calais employing an expected 200 engineers and technicians. *L'Usine Nouvelle* 'La France de l'Industrie', edition 1996, p. 144.
23. These data were drawn from articles published in *L'Usine Nouvelle* of 9 and 23 November 1995, *Le Figaro-Eco* of 4–5 November 1995, and *La Tribune* of 3 November 1995 and 5 February 1996.
24. Less-favoured regions must often bid higher to attract such investment. Thus Ireland offered Intel a subsidy equivalent to 18.5 per cent of investment costs for a plant that opened in Kildare in 1994, and a subsidy amounting to 11.8 per cent of investment for a second wafer-fabrication plant in Kildare in 1995. This represents a subsidization rate per job created of close to $US80 000 (*Financial Times*, 19 November 1995, and *Wall Street Journal* 23 November 1995).
25. This case study is based on information contained in Markoff (1998), and *Financial Times* 13 December 1997, 15 December 1997 and 9 January 1998.
26. The estimate is that of Kieran McGowan, chief executive of Ireland's Industrial Development Agency as cited in 'Asian turmoil hits Irish Plant', *Financial Times*, 13 December 1997.
27. Sun Micro Systems and SCI were attracted to Grenoble (Rhône-Alpes) by the pull of local research into open systems (interconnectability of rival computer systems) and ties to clients (*Financial Times*, 18 April 1996).
28. See for example the most recent study of the Zirst-Meylan outside of Grenoble, one of France's most successful Technopoles (Bernardy de Sigoyer and Boisgontier, 1996).
29. Six American parts suppliers, for example, purchased companies divested by Fiat and several others, component companies shed by

Daimler-Benz. Reverse flows also exist. French auto-parts suppliers, large firms such as Valeo and medium-sized companies such as Electricfil have invested recently in the United States, following American and European clients (*L'Usine Nouvelle*, 22 February 1996, *Les Echoes* 8 March 1995).

30. The case of Montpellier in the wake of IBM's drastic reduction in operations is another example (*L'Usine Nouvelle*, 31 August 1995).
31. Reported in 'Welsh Businesses Reassured over Support', *Financial Times*, 16/17 May 1998.
32. I am grateful to Ed Safarian for this point. He drew the analogy here to the way in which non-tariff barriers were turned into 'tariff equivalents' under GATT. It would, of course, require greater transparency than currently exists in the competitive race to attract foreign investors.
33. Reported in 'Van Miert Seeks Global Competition Rules Accord', *Financial Times*, 1 February 1998.

References

AMIN, A. (1994), 'The Regional Development Potential of Inward Investment in the Less Favoured Regions of the European Community', paper presented at the Conference on Industrial Policies for Small, Less Favoured Countries in the EC, Athens, 1–2 February.

BANDEMER, S. VON, P. KALFF, J. TELLECHEA and J. WATSON (1996), *Study on the Typology of Partnerships in the European Research and Innovation System*, Brussels, DG13, March, mimeo.

BERNARDY DE SIGOYER, M. and P. BOISGONTIER (1996), *La Technopole* (Paris: L'Harmattan).

BEST, M. (1990), *The New Competition: Institutions of Industrial Restructuring* (Cambridge: Polity Press).

BRIDGE, J. (1998) 'Supply-Chain Dynamics – A Case Study of the Automotive Sector', paper presented at the International Workshop on Global Production and Local Jobs: New Perspectives on Enterprise Networks, Employment and Local Development Policy, Geneva, ILO, 9–10 March.

CANTWELL, J. and F. SANNA RANDACCIO (1992), 'Intra-Industry Direct Investment in the European Community: Oligopolistic Rivalry and Technological Competition', in J. Cantwell (ed.), *Multinational Investment in Modern Europe* (Cheltenham: Edward Elgar), pp. 71–106.

CHESNAIS, F. (1991), 'Technological Competitiveness Considered as a Form of Structural Competitiveness', in J. Niosi (ed.), *Technology and National Competitiveness* (Montreal: McGill-Queen's University Press), pp. 142–76.

DAVID, P. (1984), *High Technology Centers and the Economics of Locational Tournaments* (Stanford: Stanford University), mimeo.

DOSI, G. and L. SOETE (1991), 'Technological Innovation and International Competitivenes', in J. Niosi (ed.), *Technology and National Competitiveness* (Montreal: McGill-Queen's University Press), pp. 91–118.

DUNNING, J. (1998), 'Location and the Multinational Enterprise: A Neglected Factor?', *Journal of International Business Studies*, vol. 29, no. 1 (first quarter), pp. 45–66.

ERNST, D. (1997) 'High-Tech Competition Puzzles, How Globalization Affects Firm Behaviour and Market Structure in the Electronics Industry', paper presented at the DRUID Seminar, Aalborg, Denmark, 1–3 June.

FREEMAN, C. and C. PEREZ (1988) 'Structural Crises of Adjustment: Business Cycles and Investment Behaviour', in G. Dosi, C. Freeman, R. Nelson, G. Silverberg and L. Soete (eds), *Technical Change and Economic Theory* (London: Pinter), pp. 38–66.

HELPER, S. and M. SAKO (1995), 'Suppliers Relations in Japan and the United States: Are They Converging?', *Sloan Management Review*, vol. 36, no. 3 (Spring), pp. 77–84.

HOFFMAN, K. and P. KAPLINSKY (1988), *Driving Force* (Boulder, Col.: Westview Press).

HUMPHREY, J. (1998), 'Globalisation and Supply Chain Networks in the Auto Industry: Brazil and India', paper presented to the International Workshop on Global Production and Local Jobs: New Perspectives on Enterprises, Networks, Employment and Local Development Policy, ILY, Geneva, 9–10 March.

KENNEY, M. and R. FLORIDA (1991), 'Rebuilding the Rust Belt', in *Technology Review*, Feb./March, pp. 25–33.

KUHLMANN, S. and U. KUNTZE (1991), 'R and D Cooperation by Small and Medium-Sized Companies', Proceedings of PICMET 1991, Portland National Conference on Management of Engineering and Technology, 27–31 October, pp. 709–12.

KURYLKO, D. (1996), 'Makers Aim for Vertical Disintegration', *Automotive News Europe*, 24 June, p. 14.

LE GALL (1998), 'L'Industrie Automobile: La Décomposition de L'Oligopole Traditionnel', in Forum/Cerem (eds), *L'Emergence d'Oligopoles en Réseau Fondés sur la Connaissance* (Paris: Commissariat Général du Plan), March.

LUNDVALL, B.A. (1995), 'The Social Dimension of the Learning Economy', Denmark, Aalborg University, Danish Research Unit for Industrial Dynamics Working Paper no. 96-1.

LUNDVALL, B.A. (1992), *National Systems of Innovation* (London: Pinter).

LUNDVALL, B.A. (1988), 'Innovation as an Interactive Process: From User–Producer Interaction to the National System of Innovation', in G. Dosi, C. Freeman, R. Nelson, G. Silverberg and L. Soete (eds), *Technical Change and Economic Theory* (London: Pinter), pp. 349–69.

MADEUF, B., G. LEFEVRE and A. SAVORY (1992), 'Les Activités de Recherche en France Des Sociétés Etrangères', Rapport de fin d'Etude pour la Direction Générale de la Recherche et de la Technologie, Ministère de la Recherche et de l'Espace, Paris, December.

MARKOFF, J. (1998), 'Disk-Drive Madness: How Far Can it Go?', *International Herald Tribune*, 26 February, p. 10.

MARTIN, X., W. MITCHELL and A. SWAMINATHAN (1995), 'Recreating and Extending Japanese Automobile Buyer–Supplier Links in North America', *Strategic Management Journal*, vol. 16, pp. 589–619.

MASKELL, P. and A. MALMBERG (1996), 'Localised Learning and Industrial Competitiveness', paper presented at the Regional Studies Association European Conference on 'Regional Futures', Gothenburg, 6–9 May.

MORGAN, K. and A. SAYER (1988), *Microcircuits of Capital: 'Sunrise' Industry and Uneven Development* (Boulder, Col.: Westview Press).
MYTELKA, L.K. (1991), 'States, Strategic Alliances and International Oligopolies: The European ESPRIT Programme', in L.K. Mytelka (ed.), *Strategic Partnerships and the World Economy*, (London: Pinter), pp. 182–210.
MYTELKA, L.K. (1987), 'The Evolution of Knowledge Production Strategies within Multinational firms', in J. Caporaso (ed.), *A Changing International Division of Labour* (Boulder, Col.: Lynne Reiner), pp. 43–70.
MYTELKA, L.K. (1983), 'Le Capitalisme Fondé sur la Connaissance et le Changement dans les Stratégies des Entreprises Industrielles', *Etudes Internationales,* vol. XIV, no. 3 (September), pp. 433–52.
NELSON, R.R. and N. ROSENBERG (1993), 'Technical Innovation and National Systems', in R. Nelson (ed.), *National Innovation Systems: A Comparative* Analysis (Oxford: Oxford University Press), pp. 3–22.
OECD (1998), *Technology, Productivity and Job Creation. Best Policy Practices* (Paris: OECD), DSTI/IND/STP/ICCP (98) 2/Part 1, 27 February 1998.
OECD (1997), *Main Science and Technology Indicators* (Paris: OECD).
OECD (1996), *Examens de l'OCDE sur l'Investissement Direct Etranger* (Paris: OECD).
OECD (1995), *Basic Science and Technology Statistics* (Paris: OECD).
OECD (1992), *Technology and the Economy the Key Relationship* (Paris: OECD).
PAPANASTASSIOU, M. and R. PEARCE (1994), 'La Mondialisation de L'innovation et L'organisation de la R and D dans les Multinationales', in F. Sachwald (ed.), *Les Défis de la Mondialisation Innovation et Concurrence* (Paris: Masson), pp. 69–106.
PEARCE, R.D. and S. SINGH (1992), *Globalising Research and Development* (London: Macmillan).
PHELPS, N.A., J. LOVERING and K. MORGAN (1998), 'Tying the Firm to the Region or Typing the Region to the Firm? Early Observations on the Case of LG in South Wales', *European Urban and Regional Studies,* vol. 5, no. 2, pp. 119–37.
PORTER, M.E. (1990), *The Competitive Advantage of Nations* (New York: The Free Press).
ROURKE, P. (1989), 'Hyundai and the Canadian Automotive Industry: The Influence of Canadian State Policies', MA research essay, Ottawa, Carleton University, Norman Paterson School of International Affairs.
STORPER, M. (1998), 'Industrial Policy for Latecomers: Products, Conventions, and Learning', in M. Storper, T. Thomadakis and L. Tsipouri (eds), *Latecomers in the Global Economy* (London: Routledge), pp. 13–39.
STORPER, M. (1995), 'Regional Economies as Relational Assets', paper prepared for presentation to the Association des Sciences Régionales de Langue Française, Toulouse, 30 August–1 September.
THOMAS, K.P. (1994), 'European Union Regulation of competition for Investment: Lessons for North America', Paper presented at the International Conference on Economic Integration and Public Policy, NAFTA, the EU and Beyond, Toronto, 27–29 May.
UNCTAD (1997) *World Investment Report Transnational Corporations, Market Structure and Competition Policy* (New York and Geneva: UN).

UNCTAD (1995), *World Investment Report Transnational Corporations and Competitiveness* (New York and Geneva: UN).
UNCTC (1988), *Transnational Corporations in World Development Trends and Prospects* (New York: UN).
UNCTC (UNCTAD) (1993), *World Investment Report 1993: Transnational Corporations and Integrated International Production* (New York: UN).
L'USINE NOUVELLE (1997), La France de l'Industrie, édition 1997, 'Le Poids des Étrangers Augmente', pp. 10–12.
VAN TULDER, R.A. TREFERS and W. RUIGROK (1996), 'Cars and Institutions, or Cars as Institutions', paper presented to the EMOT Workshop on Learning and Embeddedness: Evolving Transnational Firm Strategies in Europe, Durham, 27–29 June.
WARRANT, F. (1991), 'Déploiement Mondial de la R&D Industrielle', FAST Research Paper, Commission of the European Communities, Brussels, April.
WOMAC, J., D. JONES and D. ROOS (1990), *The Machine that Changed the World* (New York: Harper).
YOUNG, L. (1996), 'Auto Companies Bring More Suppliers in Early', *Electronic Business Today*, June, pp. 61–4.
YOUNG, S., N. HOOD and E. PETERS (1994), 'Multinational Enterprises and Regional Economic Development', *Regional Studies*, vol. 28, no. 7, pp. 657–77.

13 The Globalization of Competition and the Localization of Competitive Advantage: Policies towards Regional Clustering

Michael J. Enright[1]

INTRODUCTION

Two seemingly competing tendencies, the globalization of economic activity and the localization of industries, have captured the interest of scholars, economic development professionals, and policy-makers in recent years. While trends towards globalization of industries and companies appear to reduce the importance and distinctiveness of (subnational) regions, a tendency towards localization of certain industries and economic activities appears to do exactly the opposite. The simultaneous globalization and localization tendencies have created policy challenges for national and local governments. One response to these challenges has been a dramatic proliferation of regional development policies based on regional clusters of firms and industries.

This chapter argues that the globalization of competition is completely consistent with the localization of competitive advantage in some industries and activities. It goes on to describe the similarities and differences among the cluster-based strategies that have emerged in nations and regions around the world to deal with the globalization–localization nexus. It suggests that many such programmes lack a sufficiently rigorous process of cluster identification, characterization and selection. As a result, there is a danger that instead of providing a basis for distinctive programmes tailored to the specific nature of the local economy and society, the focus on regional clustering will result in the same policies chasing the same industries in different places. On the other hand, when properly formulated and implemented, such strategies hold promise precisely because they can address the challenges presented by a globalizing–localizing world.

The Globalization of Competition

One of the most important trends in the world economy in recent years has been the globalization of economic and business activity. International economic activity of all kinds has been on the increase. World trade has grown significantly faster than world output over the last few decades and foreign direct investment flows have grown faster than world trade. In 1996, the worldwide stock of foreign direct investment reached US$3.2 trillion and sales by foreign affiliates, roughly US$7 trillion a year, were some 30 per cent greater than world exports (UNCTAD, 1997). Foreign portfolio investment has increased in importance as well. Private holdings of long-term foreign securities by United States residents and entities alone reached an estimated US$1.1 trillion at the start of 1997 (International Monetary Fund, 1997). And finally, international currency transactions, at US$1.5 trillion to US$1.8 trillion a day, dwarf all other forms of international economic activity.

Some of the major features of the globalization phenomenon have been the development of global finance and financial markets, the spread of knowledge facilitated by improved communication, the widespread availability and use of technology, the active expansion of multinational firms, the decoupling and decentralization of economic activities within and between firms, the blurring of nationality of multinationals, the development of global oligopolies, reductions in barriers to trade and investment, the increased importance and power of supranational organizations such as the European Union, and the emergence of regions and regional identities that transcend borders (See Amin and Thrift, 1994; Dicken, 1992, 1994; Dunning, 1998; Hagström, 1990; and Reich, 1991, for example). Added to this list today would be the rise of electronic communities over the Internet and the fact that nations comprising nearly one-half of the world's population (including China, India, South Africa, the former Eastern bloc, and the formerly import substitution driven economies of Latin America) have either entered the world economy or have dramatically changed their relationship to it in the last two decades (Enright, 1997).

The result has been an unprecedented globalization of business competition and competition for attracting economic activity. To some (Cooke and Imrie, 1989; Amin and Robins, 1990; Amin, 1994 and Ettlinger 1994), globalization has broken down formerly strong local and regional economic identities. It is only a slight exaggeration to state that the process of globalization is one that is often portrayed as pitting large, powerful multinational firms and supranational organizations against virtually powerless and increasingly identityless regions and regional governments. In such a world, one role of government is to ensure that such regions are not bypassed by the globalization of economic activity.

The Localization of Competitive Advantage

As globalization has accelerated, interest in localized groups of firms in the same or related industries, or 'regional clusters', has accelerated as well. Porter (1990), Enright (1991, 1996, 1998), and Storper (1992) point out that in many industries the leading firms are located in the same nation, region, or even city. Regional clustering is found in virtually every advanced economy and increasingly in developing nations as well (Humphrey and Schmitz, 1996). It can be seen in the industrial districts of Northern Italy, the high-technology agglomerations of Silicon Valley or Route 128, the company towns of Ludwigshafen or Toyota City, and the metropolitan business service centres of New York or London. It can even be seen in the emergence of 'anti-cluster clusters', clusters of firms in non-location-sensitive activities which would not normally be thought of as subject to clustering at all. Omaha in telemarketing, South Dakota in credit-card processing, Ireland in back-office processing for financial services, Sydney in information processing, Bangalore in software services, and Manila in data entry are only a few examples of mobile activities that one generally thinks of as being decentralized *from* places being decentralized *to* places. The fact that even such 'placeless' activities have shown tendencies to cluster indicates the strength of the phenomenon.

Storper (1992) concludes that the clustering phenomenon places a fundamental limit on the process of globalization. In addition, even large multinationals have their local characteristics. Despite the emergence of so-called 'transnational corporations' (Bartlett and Ghoshal, 1989), most multinational companies are 'home-based multinationals', with a distinct centre of gravity for their management and critical activities (Dicken, 1994; Sölvell and Zander, 1995). ABB, a firm that is often characterized as virtually stateless, has its business units headquartered in specific locations with specific identities. The motion picture industry is dominated by multinational firms, all headquartered in the Los Angeles area. The pharmaceutical industry has been consolidating on a worldwide basis, but more than half of the leading firms have headquarters and/or have major research facilities between New York City and Philadelphia. The financial services industry is globalizing, but New York and London have maintained or increased their dominance.

Even the fact that some regional clusters decline in the face of competition from multinational firms does not diminish the importance of location. Some (though certainly not all) regional clusters have been displaced, not by randomly located multinationals, but by other regional clusters of either small firms or multinationals. Birmingham's craft-based gun cluster was displaced by mass production and interchangeable parts, but the new firms were concentrated in the Connecticut Valley, still the leading production area for firearms in the United States today. The cutlery industry of Sheffield (UK) was displaced by a similar cluster in Solingen (Germany), which in turn has battled with another cluster in Seki (Japan). Producers of low and medium-priced watches in the Swiss Jura came under great pressure first from Japanese companies and then from a cluster of Hong Kong companies. North American and European motorcycle companies were displaced largely by four Japanese firms, including three from the small city of Hammamatsu, which was also home to the top three Japanese multinational musical instrument companies that displaced craft-oriented firms in North America and Europe. This is not to say that the regional clustering phenomenon is present in all industries or even most industries (in fact the geographic profile of different industries varies widely – Enright, 1993a), but that it is an important part of the economic landscape.

Globalization and Localization: Resolving the Paradox

The numerous examples of regional clustering provide evidence that even as competition and economic activity globalize, that competitive advantage can be localized. This is the economic equivalent of what ten years ago the present author started to call 'the Brussels paradox'. That is, if current trends towards increasing the power of European Union institutions and growing (subnational) regionalism within the EU continue, Brussels will be capital of one Europe, but two Belgiums.

Of course, the apparent economic paradox is really no paradox at all. Globalization can result in a geographic spread of economic activities over space, but it also can allow firms and locations with specific sources of competitive advantage to exploit their advantages over ever wider geographic areas, often, though not always, at the expense of other areas. Enright (1993b) claims that as long as globalizing forces move at a faster pace than forces that influence the geographic sources of competitive advantage (such as localized human capital, presence of key suppliers, tastes of local consumers, demand patterns of industrial customers, the nature and levels of local competition and cooperation, and local institutions), economies will become in some ways more distinct, rather than less distinct. Thus, geographic sources of competitive advantage will become more, not less, important.

These tendencies can be reinforced by the location choices of multinational firms, which are slicing their activities more and more finely, and are more carefully arbitraging differences in locational sources of advantage, even having locations compete for product mandates in some cases (Birkinshaw, 1998). In some industries, design, research and development, finance, and even business unit headquarters activities have been concentrating on a global basis. Nissan performs a substantial portion of its new design work in Southern California, a noted centre for automotive design. Samsung designs new semiconductors in Silicon Valley. Several European pharmaceutical and chemical companies do the bulk of their biotechnology research in biotechnology clusters in the United States. In a study of the geography of innovation in Europe, Tödtling (1994) found that globalization and moves to more flexible production systems tend to strengthen existing innovation centres. Financial and managerial centres, such as New York, London and Tokyo, appear to be consolidating their power (OECD, 1995); most major Western financial institutions have their Asia-Pacific regional headquarters in Hong Kong or Singapore (Enright *et al.*, 1997); German banks buy British merchant banks, but then move their merchant banking headquarters to London; while the world's first major pharmaceutical company, Hoechst, recently moved the headquarters of its pharmaceutical operations to the United States. In each case, the decisions of multinationals have reinforced pre-existing clusters.

Although the globalization of competition should raise, and arguably has raised, the average level of economic well-being around the world, there are winners and losers in this process as well as shifts in the relative power of economic actors. Dicken (1994), Amin (1992) and Schoenberger (1991) point out that not every local economy can hope to participate in the localization process brought about by the globalizing activities of multinational firms. In particular, excluded regions are likely to become more excluded and the degree of differentiation across locations will increase with the globalization of economic activity, perhaps resulting in destructive competition among regions for a place in the productive networks of multinational companies.

Where one stands in terms of whether the globalization–localization nexus provides opportunity or threat seems to depend on where one sits. Those who study innovative high-technology clusters, industrial districts that have succeeded in international competition and dynamic metropolitan clusters tend to focus on the advantages of localization and the opportunities of globalization. Those who study regions that have declined, have lost branch plants and have had difficulties in regenerating their economies focus on the loss of local industries, the difficulties in obtaining a position in the global economic hierarchy and the loss of local economic power and autonomy. In either case, globalizing and localizing tendencies make 'place', in particular the attributes that determine whether a given place will benefit or suffer from the globalizing and localizing tendencies, more important, rather than less important, to a region's economic well-being (Enright, 1993b; and Scott, 1998).

CLUSTER-BASED DEVELOPMENT POLICIES IN THE GLOBAL–LOCAL NEXUS

The globalization–localization nexus described above has had an important impact on national and regional economic development policies. One response has been a growing interest in local development policies geared towards support for regional clusters, defined as localized agglomerations of firms in the same or related industries. In the last decade, dozens of regions, states, provinces, cities and local communities have instituted development plans based on regional clusters. In addition, multilateral organizations such as the World Bank, UNIDO, the OECD, the European Commission and others have taken up cluster strategies as tools for regional and local development. The reasons have included the globalizing and localizing forces mentioned above, perceived difficulties with development through large firms, trends towards outsourcing and downsizing among larger firms, case studies on successful clusters, and the tendency to push economic policy-making from the national to the regional or local level in several nations. Perhaps the most important reason, however, is that other strategies have not worked to the satisfaction of policy-makers and their constituents (see Doeringer and Terkla, 1996; Scott, 1992, 1998; OECD, 1995; Gittell *et al.*, 1996; and Enright, 1996).

Governments with widely different ideologies and philosophies have instituted cluster-promotion policies. In the United States, conservative states, liberal states, and states in between have adopted cluster-based strategies. In Canada, the most interventionist (the Atlantic Provinces and Quebec) and least interventionist (Alberta and British Columbia) provinces have done the same. Cluster-based strategies are being employed in Europe by governments across the spectrum from left to right and right to left. In the Asia-Pacific, national or local governments in such diverse places as Australia, New Zealand, Malaysia and Singapore have adopted cluster-development strategies. With such different governments all adopting cluster-based strategies, it is easy to conjecture that we have either stumbled across universal truths, mass delusions, or the same words used to describe very different programmes. In reality, it is probably a mixture of all three.

An exhaustive enumeration of cluster-based strategies is beyond the scope of this chapter. However, it is useful to identify some of the similarities and differences found in such strategies.

Common Elements of Cluster Strategies

Cluster-development strategies tend to have a number of elements in common. Though not necessarily linked specifically to clusters, efforts to *improve the generalized business environment*, by reviewing tax policy, examining regulations, reducing costs of services, streamlining administration and maintaining a favourable business climate, often become parts of cluster-development policies. So too do efforts to *provide information and data* on business and economic trends as well as information and data specific to individual clusters, such as market data, information on customers and competitors, information on technological trends, and so on. In many instances, governments have commissioned detailed consulting reports that identify and profile clusters, and make suggestions to cluster participants. Such activities are justified on the basis that it is often too difficult or expensive for firms to carry out such activities on their own.

Most jurisdictions, at least in advanced economies, provide basic *infrastructure, education and training*. In cluster-based programmes, these investments tend to become far more focused on the specific infrastructure, skills and capabilities required by specific clusters. This can include effluent treatment facilities for specific industries (Catalan leather), dedicated water (Malaysian electronics) or electricity lines (Venezuelan metals), and specialized port (Singapore shipping) or air-freight (Dutch flowers) facilities. It can mean specific education and training programmes in software (Bangalore), motion pictures (Los Angeles), materials science (Sassuolo), winemaking (Napa Valley) and electronics (Taiwan), among others. The purpose is to provide specific infrastructure, skills and capabilities that can be a source of localized competitive advantage.

Cluster-development programmes have used a variety of means to foster *business networking and inter-firm collaboration*. Some programmes have relied on informal networking through introductions, referral lists, industry associations and other mechanisms. More formal programmes, such as those in parts of Canada, parts of Australia, New Zealand, the United Kingdom and Finland have added a cluster dimension to the networking programmes pioneered in Denmark and Norway, in which small and medium-sized enterprises can receive government support to create networks and develop collaborative activities. These policies, some of which have run their course and have expired, have received mixed reviews, with some observers pointing to the number of networks that were formed under the programmes and with others pointing out the large number of networks that survived only as long as government funding was available (Korhonen, 1996).

In several regions, governments have made investments to *provide business services* ranging from basic research, to market research, to materials testing, to business process consulting, to accounting and record keeping, to advice on business management. The idea is to provide scale and experience-sensitive services that small and medium-sized firms cannot perform or afford for themselves individually. The best-known examples are Northern Italy's locally-run 'real service centres', the many offices of Germany's Steinbeis Foundation scattered around the country, and the manufacturing and business extension services attached to several public universities in the United

States. Such centres provide services such as contract research and development, transferring technology from universities to firms, applied technology research, materials testing, managerial training, and other services. While such institutes are often initiated with public investments, several have become partially or fully self-funding.

Finally, many groups interested in promoting cluster development engage in activities that can be best termed *community building*. As Scott (1998), Putnam (1993), Rosenfeld (1995) and Cooke and Morgan (1994) have observed, it is difficult or impossible to separate a region's economic development from its social and community development. These authors indicate that communities that can develop a shared sense of purpose, work toward the common good, and engender information-sharing and inter-firm trust perform better economically than other communities. This knowledge has informed cluster-development programmes in North America (in places like Arizona, Austin, Chihuahua, Florida, North Carolina, Silicon Valley and Quebec) and Europe (Germany, Italy and Spain, for example), where attempts have been made to develop institutions to foster community development. Such efforts are subject to the caveat that successful institutions in a specific location can be very difficult to reproduce elsewhere (Amin and Thrift, 1994).

Differences in Cluster Development Strategies

Although there are elements common to many cluster-development programmes, there are important differences among programmes that are rarely highlighted. Such programmes, for example, differ in the origin of the industrial base and in the degree of government intervention, with different approaches that depend on different views of (or positions in) the globalization–localization nexus.

Origin of Industrial Base

Cluster-development programmes can focus on the expansion and deepening of the indigenous economic base, on attracting activities of foreign firms, or on a combination of the two. *Organic cluster strategies* seek to broaden and deepen a region's existing economic base by identifying the region's clusters and then trying to promote development by improving information flows, increasing the interaction among local firms, removing infrastructure bottlenecks, developing human resources and fostering inter-firm collaboration. Although some efforts might be made to attract firms from outside the region, the primary focus is on development based on firms already present in the region. Most of the programmes in the United States, Spain, Italy, Austria and New Zealand, among others, are in this category.

Transplant cluster strategies attempt to build clusters by attracting the facilities of outside companies and developing or attracting suppliers and related firms. Such strategies resemble the traditional transplant strategy that fell into disrepute in some places in the 1970s and 1980s, albeit with refinements. One refinement is the use of clustering to focus on particular targets or sets of targets that might fit particularly well with the local economic environment. Another is a realization that regional headquarters, research and development, and certain other high value-added activities are more desirable targets than manufacturing alone. Another is the use of the policies associated with cluster development to foster better linkages within the local economy. Ireland, Scotland, Wales, Northern England, Malaysia and Singapore, among others, have used this type of strategy.

Hybrid strategies result when organic cluster-development programmes start actively to recruit outside investment, or when transplant strategies become successful enough to create a critical mass of locally embedded facilities and firms that can be engaged in more organic programmes. In the United States, Massachusetts, Arizona and others have added promotion of foreign investment into their programmes. Singapore and Ireland, on the other hand, have developed a sufficient mass of foreign-owned firms to treat them as a base for cluster development.

Each strategy has its pluses and minuses. Organic strategies, since they build on unique features of the local environment, can foster distinct advantages that are difficult to copy. Organic strategies, however, are predicated on the presence of a solid economic base to build upon, which is not the case in many regions. Transplant strategies can help develop a regional economy rather quickly, but are limited to the investments available for attraction, are subject to imitation and destructive competition, and face the risk that poorly-embedded facilities will eventually close. Hybrid strategies, while perhaps intrinsically attractive, can result in confusion and competition between policies directed at indigenous and foreign firms.

For the purposes of this chapter, the point is that different strategies indicate different approaches to the globalization–localization nexus. Organic policies view economic development primarily coming through local firms and their ability to inject themselves into international markets, in other words to become vital multinational companies or to extend their international presence. Globalization and localization primarily provide opportunities and the role of government is to accelerate the development of latent or potential clusters already in the environment. Transplant strategies attempt development by attracting the globalizing activities of multinational firms and using these activities to provide a nucleus around which other activities will develop or can be attracted. The globalization of competition and the activities of multinational firms provide opportunities to attract some activities to locations that have either lost out in global competition in other industries or to locations that have not been developed previously. Implicitly, transplant strategies indicate a realization that indigenous development is unlikely to achieve the desired results or the belief that globalization might bypass the location in question, the downside to the globalization–localization nexus.

Extent of Government Intervention

Cluster-development strategies also differ in their level of government intervention, another fact rarely highlighted in the literature. *Catalytic strategies* limit government to an indirect, supporting role. In these strategies, governments attempt to facilitate the development of clusters by encouraging private-sector efforts. In Arizona, for example, an important part of the state's activities involved identifying the head firms in related industries and introducing them to each other. The firms were then largely left to their own devices (Waits *et al.*, 1992). Today, government provides some support in the form of defraying the expense of an organizer for industry associations that are part of the cluster programme, but direction is clearly given by the private sector. In New Zealand, a government entity, TRADENZ, tries to educate individuals in specific industries to the potential benefits of clusters and provides a limited amount of support for networking, but again it is up to the private sector to form relationships and gain from the process (Ffowcs-Williams, 1997).

Interventionist strategies, on the other hand, involve more active attempts to support cluster development. Several regions in Europe have active transplant cluster strategies that seek out potential investors and then offer tax breaks, direct subsidies, training grants and other forms of direct aid to firms (Mytelka, 1998). Malaysia is embarking on a similar strategy, targeting several high-technology industries, and providing infrastructure, facilities, training, tax breaks, grants and other subsidies (Malaysia, 1996). Singapore has evolved its activist industrial attraction policies into policies intended to develop and expand the clusters that have been attracted in the past. Quebec, on the other hand, has taken a somewhat different approach, with significant government investments in research, education, training, infrastructure and networking programmes, but more limited direct support to specific firms (Ferland *et al.*, 1996).

Again, the differences in levels of government intervention imply different views of the globalization–localization nexus. Catalytic strategies assume that providing the means for clusters to accelerate their own development will allow localized clusters to take advantage of the globalization of competition in the marketplace. Interventionist strategies assume that market forces will not be sufficient to foster the development of vibrant clusters in the region without more substantial government support and resources. The latter can reflect beliefs that global competition is too tough, other clusters are too well supported, or local firms are too weak to go it alone.

It appears that cluster-based strategies or at least strategies that claim to be based on a cluster logic can be adopted by, or sold to, governments of virtually any persuasion. Interventionist governments find that cluster-based strategies provide them with finer tools with which to pick and promote industries of choice. At the same time, even the most non-interventionist policy-makers and economists realise that some market failures can be addressed through government action. Cluster-based strategies give them a means and a rationale for doing so. Despite the apparent similarities in cluster-based development programmes, it seems that part of the reason that cluster-based strategies can be adopted by different types of governments is that a fairly wide range of strategies, with varying tools and tactics, actually are being subsumed under the same rubric.

Cluster Selection

Another area in which cluster-development programmes show both similarities and differences is in the process of cluster identification and selection. Some programmes use an involved process of identifying and selecting clusters for support (see Rosenfeld, 1995; Massachusetts Technology Collaborative, 1997; Gouvernment du Quebec, 1997; Regional Planning Association, 1996; and Conejos *et al.*, 1997 for examples). The Greater Tucson Strategic Economic Development Plan, for example, identifies 24 specific target industries (at the 4-digit

SIC level), all within the categories of optics, environmental technologies, aerospace, bioindustries, teleservices and software and information services. These clusters were identified using a detailed set of criteria, including industry growth rate, multiplier effect, job-creation and income potential, match with local resources, environmental considerations, relationships with local suppliers, contribution to quality of life, and synergy with local institutions and businesses (Greater Tucson Economic Council, 1996).

Other programmes are not so focused. According to one government:

> Priority sectors are characterised by a reliance on significant R&D investment, value-added production, a skilled workforce, intellectual property assets, and global exports. They enjoy high margins and high growth, but only if they identify and service new markets, develop and apply new technology, attract and develop human resources, and operate at a world class level of quality.
> (British Columbia Ministry of Employment and Investment, 1997)

The literature from this government makes no mention of suitability to the local environment or economy, which presumably would have an important influence on the success of the programmes.

Some jurisdictions target so many industries and clusters that one wonders how many are really targeted at all. Malaysia's list of targeted industries is actually several pages long. Both Alberta and its largest city, Calgary, have identified long lists of industries for support. The Calgary Economic Development Authority helpfully adds that, 'If your company is not in one of these sectors that does not mean that we are not interested in providing assistance to you' (Calgary Economic Development Authority, 1997). Some 'clusters' such as 'tradable business services', 'engineering' and 'technology' (Northern Ireland Growth Challenge, 1997), while useful perhaps in a broad-brush description of an economy, are too broad to be of much use for cluster-development programmes. Other selections, such as 'tourism/heritage/lifestyle', 'agriculture/aquaculture/forestry', 'knowledge-based cluster', and 'government services cluster' (Cape Breton, 1995), are hardly clusters at all.

Despite some of the differences cited above, perhaps the most striking feature of the lists of clusters identified for development programmes is their similarity. A random selection of such programmes shows that 'business services' has been selected in Alberta, British

Columbia, Chihuahua, Connecticut, Malaysia, Massachusetts, New York, New Jersey, Northern Ireland, Singapore and Tennessee; 'Electronics' in Alberta, Chihuahua, Ireland, Malaysia, Massachusetts, Scotland, Singapore, Tennessee and Wales; 'Information technology' in Alberta, Arizona, British Columbia, Cairns, Connecticut, Hunter, Ireland, Malaysia, Massachusetts, North Tyneside, Northern Ireland, Scotland and Quebec; 'Telecommunications' in Alberta, Arizona, Connecticut, Finland, Hunter, Massachusetts, Scotland, Singapore and Wales; 'Medical and biomedical industries' in Alberta, British Columbia, Cairns, Connecticut, Massachusetts, New York, New Jersey, Northern Ireland, Scotland, Tennessee and Wales; as distinct from 'Pharmaceuticals and biotechnology', selected in Arizona, British Columbia, Connecticut, Hunter, Ireland, Malaysia, Massachusetts and Quebec.

Despite the different processes that have been employed to identify clusters for support programmes, there is a surprising similarity in those identified. Either economies around the world are far more similar than they initially appear, or some other force is influencing the selection process. Such conclusions, and the overly diffuse 'clusters' identified in some locations, lead one to wonder how many programmes are based on a real knowledge of what clusters are and how they can promote economic development.

SHARPENING CLUSTER ANALYSIS AND CLUSTER-DEVELOPMENT STRATEGIES

Several issues arise from the above discussion of cluster-development strategies. These include characterizing the variety of clusters, understanding the state of development of clusters, the importance of cluster identification and selection processes, the links between market failures and cluster-based strategies, and whether cluster-based strategies are appropriate in a particular context. The discussion indicates that we must sharpen our analysis of regional clusters and cluster development policies if clustering is to be used successfully as a basis for economic development.

Dimensions of Clusters

First for consideration is what a cluster is in the first place. One of the more confusing features of the recent literature and policy-making based on regional clusters is the fact that a variety of phenomena are grouped under the term. 'Regional clustering' has been used to describe industrial districts of small craft firms, high-technology centres, agglomerations of financial and business service firms in cities, company towns, and large branch plants and their supply chains. 'Cluster' terminology seems so embedded that one despairs of redefining or sharply defining the term. However, clusters at least must be characterized along relevant dimensions if appropriate policies are to be devised. It is suggested that thinking along the following dimensions is particularly useful (see Table 13.1):

- The *geographic scope* of a cluster refers to the territorial extent of the firms, customers, suppliers, support services and institutions that are embedded in the ongoing relationships and interdependent activities that characterize the cluster. *Localized clusters* are tight groupings found in a small geographic area, often a single town, whereas *dispersed clusters* are spread across wider geographies.
- The *density* of a cluster refers to the number and economic weight (in terms of market shares of relevant industries) of the firms in the cluster. *Dense clusters* can be populated by hundreds, thousands or even tens of thousands of firms with total sales reaching hundreds of millions or billions of dollars, whereas *sparse clusters* do not have the same economic weight, either because they have fewer firms or fewer substantial firms.
- The *breadth* of clusters refers to the range of horizontally-related industries (industries related by common technologies, end-users, distribution channels and other non-vertical relationships) within the cluster. *Narrow clusters* consist of one of a few industries and their supply chains. *Broad clusters* provide a variety of products in closely-related industries.
- Cluster *depth* refers to the range of vertically-related industries within the cluster. *Deep clusters* are those in which a region does not just contain an industry or set of related industries, but complete or nearly complete supply chains, whereas *shallow clusters* are those that rely principally on inputs, components, equipment, technology and support services from outside the region.
- The *activity base* of a cluster involves the number and nature of the activities in the value-added chain performed with the region. In *activity-rich clusters,* most or at least many of the critical activities in the value-added chains of the relevant industries are

Table 13.1 The dimensions of regional clusters

Dimension	*Types*	*Examples*
Geographic scope[a]	Localized	Sassuolo ceramic tiles
	Dispersed	Japan synthetic fabrics
Density	Dense	New York financial services
	Sparse	New Hampshire instrumentation[b]
Breadth	Broad	Osaka electronics
	Narrow	Dalton tufted carpets
Depth	Deep	Danish agroindustry
	Shallow	Ireland pharmaceuticals
Activity base	Activity-rich	Silicon Valley
	Activity-poor	Chihuahua maquilas
Growth potential/	Sunrise/competitive	Los Angeles multimedia
industry growth/competitive position	Sunrise/uncompetitive	
	Noonday/competitive	Quebec transport equipment
	Noonday/uncompetitive	

	Sunset/competitive	Boston minicomputers
	Sunset/uncompetitive	
Innovative capacity	High-innovation	Boston biotechnology, Milan fashion, Singapore electronics
	Low-innovation	
Industrial organization[c]	Core–Ring with coordinating firm	Veneto garments
	Core–Ring with lead firm	Toulouse aircraft
	All ring, no core	Carpi knitwear
	All core, no ring	
Coordinating mechanisms[d]	Spot markets	Prato textiles
	Short-term coalitions	Hollywood motion pictures
	Long-term relationships	Turin factory automation equipment
	Hierarchies	Detroit autos

Sources:
[a] Enright (1993b).
[b] Kaufman *et al.* (1994).
[c] Storper and Harrison (1991).
[d] Enright (1995).

performed locally. Firms in such clusters tend to carry out their core strategy-setting, product or service development, marketing strategy and corporate coordination activities within the region in question. *Activity-poor* clusters, on the other hand, involve one or only a few activities in a given industry or set of related industries.

- The *growth potential* of an individual cluster depends not only on the growth in demand for the products and services supplied by the cluster, but also the competitive position of the cluster relative to outside competitors and the availability (or ability to create or attract) resources necessary to support growth. Thus one can specify *sunrise*, *noonday*, and *sunset* clusters, but it is far more useful to include the relative competitiveness of the firms in the cluster versus outside competition (*sunrise/competitive*, *sunrise/non-competitive*, and so on) and an assessment of the region's circumstances with respect to the resources required for growth.
- The *innovative capacity* of the cluster refers to the ability of the cluster to generate the key innovations in products, processes, designs, marketing, logistics and management that are relevant to competitive advantage in the industries in question. The distinction between *high-innovation* and *low-innovation* clusters is far more useful than that between 'high-technology' and 'low-technology' clusters. Some 'high-technology' clusters are not at all innovative, and some 'low-technology' clusters are. A cluster's ability to sustain itself is related more to its innovative capacity than to the level of technology produced or used in the process.
- A cluster's *industrial organization* refers to the governance structures and relationships among firms in the cluster, including the nature of relationships and distribution of power among firms.
- *Coordination mechanisms* involve the ways that inter-firm relations are organized, through hierarchies, markets or other forms.

Characterizing clusters along these dimensions allows one to understand their potentials and problems in ways that can inform policy. Localized clusters, dense clusters, deep clusters, and activity-rich clusters have a greater chance of fostering close inter-firm communication and interaction that can be a source of competitive advantage. These clusters are, other things being equal, more likely to be high-innovation clusters that benefit from the globalization of economic activity. Policy towards clusters with these attributes can be organic, focusing on enhancing the information, relationships and skills necessary to project further into the international market place.

Dispersed, sparse, shallow and activity-poor clusters are less embedded into the local economic and social systems and are less likely to be sources of self-sustaining growth. These clusters are, other things being equal, less likely to be high-innovation clusters. In addition, while they might benefit in the short run from the globalization of economic activity, they might be more subject to competition over time since the core competitive advantages of constituent companies are created somewhere else. This description fits many of the clusters created through transplant strategies. No matter their origin, development in clusters with the attributes listed above is likely to be far more difficult. Concentration on fostering the conditions under which suppliers or related firms can be attracted, developed or spun off is likely to be a high priority.

Knowledge of industrial organization, governance structures and coordination mechanisms can guide policy towards the most efficient use of scarce resources. Policies directed at SMEs, for example, will be ineffective if the cluster has lead firms or core firms that are not interested in the programmes. On the other hand, atomistic, decentralized, 'all-ring' structures with activities coordinated by spot markets might be very difficult structures in which to foster inter-firm collaboration due to coordination difficulties.

In general, local policy should be designed to help localize, deepen, broaden, activity-enrich, and/or improve the innovation capacity of clusters. In reality, it can be difficult or fruitless to move in all directions at once. Policy should benefit from characterizations and analyses that identify the key constraints and leverage points of relevant clusters along these dimensions. In addition, different clusters, even in the same location, might have very different characteristics and therefore a very different appropriate policy mix. 'One size' does not fit all, even for clusters in the same location. This is another fact that has been largely overlooked in cluster development programmes and the literature on regional clusters.

State of Development of Clusters

The state of development of a cluster will also have an important influence on its future and the appropriate policy mix to support the cluster. The state of development refers not to the age of the cluster, but rather whether the cluster is benefiting from the co-location of firms, is self-aware, and is self-reinforcing:

- *Working clusters* are those in which a critical mass of local knowledge, expertise, personnel and resources create agglomeration economies that are used by firms to their advantage in competing with those outside the cluster. Working clusters tend to have dense patterns of interactions among local firms that differ quantitatively and qualitatively from the interactions that the firms have with those not located in the cluster. Working clusters often have complex patterns of competition and cooperation and often are able to attract mobile resources and key personnel from other locations. Even if participants do not call themselves a 'cluster' there tends to be knowledge of the interdependence of local competitors, suppliers, customers and institutions. Italy's industrial districts, Silicon Valley, and Hollywood would be prime examples.
- *Latent clusters* have a critical mass of firms in related industries sufficient to reap the benefits of clustering, but have not developed the level of interaction and information flows necessary to truly benefit from co-location. This can be due to a lack of knowledge of other local firms, a lack of interaction among firms and individuals, a lack of a common enough vision of their future, or a lack of the requisite level of trust for firms to explore and exploit common interests. In any case, such groups of firms do not think of themselves as clusters and, as a result, do not think of exploring the potential benefits of closer relationships with other local organizations. Arizona's optics cluster, for example, consisted of a group of firms that operated without knowledge of each other until a cluster development initiative brought them together. Today, there is an active industry association, joint selling of bundled products, and numerous other industry activities. New Zealand's wine industry also went from a latent cluster, with limited interaction, to an industry that has been able to develop and jointly market New Zealand wines as high quality wines in major markets.
- *Potential clusters* are those that have some of the elements necessary for the development of successful clusters, but where these elements must be deepened and broadened in order to benefit from the impact of agglomeration. Often there are important gaps in the inputs, services, or information flows that support cluster development. Like latent clusters, they lack the interaction and

self-awareness of working clusters. New York is showing signs of the emergence of a multimedia cluster, but is not as far along as the multimedia clusters in Los Angeles and San Francisco.

- *Wishful-thinking clusters* are those chosen by governments for support, but which lack a critical mass of firms or favourable conditions for organic development. Many of the electronics and biotechnology 'clusters' found in government programmes fall into this category. Other 'wishful thinking' clusters are those such as 'manufacturing' or 'high-technology' that are far too broad to act meaningfully as clusters. Sometimes such entities are called 'policy-driven clusters' because they rely on government rather than market forces for development.

Knowledge of the state of development of clusters is extremely useful in determining where to focus the details of cluster-promotion policies. For working clusters, policy emphasis should be placed on helping them to further their penetration into export markets. For latent clusters, emphasis should be on helping them reach a level of self-realization that will allow for development of inter-firm linkages, institution building and information generation. For potential clusters, emphasis should be on helping develop or attract a sufficient critical mass of economic activity to become a working cluster. For wishful-thinking clusters, emphasis should be on either more creative approaches or exclusion from resource-constrained programmes.

Selection Processes

The process of selecting clusters for inclusion in development programmes can be quite important. A critical question is the role that economic analysis and political forces play in the decisions. Rosenfeld (1995) describes a detailed process combining statistical analysis of a region's economy with other information to identify the key linkages and leverage points, but as shown by some of the 'clusters' identified above, the cluster selection process is not always so informed or scientific. In fact, such processes can be highly political, with 'wishful-thinking clusters' suddenly discovered in places where no one had ever supposed they existed or could exist. While it is beneficial to include some 'potential clusters' in a cluster development programme, and it makes sense for a region to 'stretch', the trouble with politically-motivated selections is that they often receive a disproportionate share of attention and resources and wind up undermining the entire effort.

Care should be taken that selection processes do not retard the self-realization of clusters that happen not to be chosen for the programmes. When the very definition of 'cluster' is based on some programme, there are unintended consequences. The president of a firm in what by all appearances should have been a dynamic cluster once told me, 'We thought we were a cluster. We wanted to be a cluster, but we were not approved', as if a cluster only exists if it is identified by some authority.

Market Failures and Cluster Strategies

Other issues are intrinsic to the cluster-development strategies themselves. In theory, government action is justified by market failures, but in practice relatively few cluster programmes explicitly identify the market failures that they are designed to correct. The most obvious market failures that can be addressed by cluster strategies are impacted information, managerial myopia, underprovision of public goods, and coordination failures. Impacted information occurs when information that would be useful to the firms is not available to them or is only available at a cost that would be prohibitive. Managerial myopia occurs when information that is available is not used to optimum benefit due to lack of understanding, or to a failure to link knowledge with action. Public goods, such as education, training, infrastructure and others tend to be undersupplied by markets. Coordination failures occur when information is available and is understood, but is not acted upon because disparate actors cannot organize themselves to act in concert.

Public entities can clearly play a vital role in providing information, education and public goods, and in helping to provide coordination mechanisms for local firms. However, these activities often are applied as recipes rather than as attempts to overcome specific, identified market failures. Nor is the nature of the 'public goods' that are being provided fully scrutinized. The legitimacy of cluster-promotion policies towards SMEs, for example, is rarely questioned. If, however, international experience indicates that only 10 per cent of the SMEs in a given jurisdiction will use government support programmes (as found in the EU by Thomas, 1995), then unless this 10 per cent will have a decisive impact on a regional economy, programmes involving even small levels of direct government support (as in many network programmes) are providing private rather than public goods.

Finally, of course, market failures should be real, not imagined ('This specific set of firms is unable to coordinate to carry out this specific valuable activity by themselves' as opposed to, 'We aren't the biotechnology capital of the world so there must be a market failure').

Failure to explicitly identify the market failures that cluster-development programmes are designed to address leaves the programmes open to rent-seeking and political lock-in. If in Adam Smith's time competitors spoke of raising prices whenever they conversed, in our time they are just as likely to ask for government support and handouts. Cluster programmes are new potential sources of such support. Even in New Zealand, a nation that has largely withdrawn from state support of industry, one participant in a cluster-development programme told me that firms participated, 'because that is the only way we can get money from government'. A related danger is that the same cooperation that allows a cluster to have a voice in shaping local economic policy, to partner with local governments to identify infrastructure needs, and to set up cluster-specific education and training programmes, can also be used to lobby for protection or support that goes well beyond the provision of public goods (Grabher, 1993).

The Appropriateness and Sufficiency of Cluster Strategies

There is also a danger that cluster-based strategies will be used in situations in which they are not appropriate. In some countries, particularly developing nations, there is a danger that industry or cluster-based strategies will be viewed as substitutes for developing the preconditions for development. Only when these preconditions, such as the existence of real markets, coherent macroeconomic policies, a certain level of proficiency among government agencies, and so on, are in place will an industry-based or cluster-based strategy be helpful or appropriate. Otherwise, 'cluster programmes' result in hopelessly piecemeal solutions to systemic problems, or, even worse, become tools to subsidize politically-connected companies or industries.

Venezuela is an interesting case in point. From 1994 to 1998, instead of following the basic prescriptions necessary to turn the economy around (see Enright *et al.*, 1994, 1996), the Venezuelan government spent much of its time, efforts and resources on wasteful programmes focused at the industry and cluster level. The result was economic calamity evidenced by a rapid fall in the standard of living and a bolivar that fell from 110 per US $ on 31 December 1993 to 525 per

US $ on 1 April 1998. Cluster-based strategies have their place but, in some cases, industry or cluster-based strategies can be worse than useless.

In addition to appropriateness, there is the issue of sufficiency. Cluster-based policies are unlikely to be sufficient to generate sustained economic development in the absence of a generally business-friendly environment, a certain level of skills and capabilities in the region and the institutions and attitudes that will support economic growth. This suggests that governments must look beyond cluster-based policies alone in their efforts to foster development. Locations must be developed, not just clusters. Cluster development is a means, not an end. The economic rebounds of Massachusetts and New Zealand in the early 1990s, for example, were due far more to deregulation, reductions in intervention, lower taxes and the restoration of a business-friendly environment than to the existence of any cluster-development policies. One reason that cluster-development policies have the potential to be extremely useful is that, when properly assessed, planned and implemented, they are directly targeted on the globalization-localization nexus described above and they point towards other policy areas that require attention.

CONCLUSIONS

Although distance might be less important for certain industries or activities today, geography in the sense of 'place' is not. In fact, the globalization–localization nexus described above makes the specific attributes of particular places more important to their economic development and prosperity rather than less important. This is true whether one is located in a dynamic region which is home to firms that can take advantage of globalization trends and the tendency of firms in some industries to be localized, or in a less dynamic region which might suffer. It also is true for multinational firms that choose the best locations for their activities, local firms that might lose out to global competitors, and firms that use the benefits they find within their clusters to succeed in world markets.

The opportunities and threats associated with the nexus have helped foster an interest in cluster-based development strategies, especially on the part of local and regional governments. For some, the goal is to enhance the development of existing clusters and their penetration into world markets. For others, the goal is to make sure that their regions are not left behind by the process of globalization. Although many of the elements of cluster-development strategies have similarities with more traditional development policies, the strong emphasis on groups of firms in related industries (rather than individual industries or firms), the focus on inter-firm linkages, the potential for organic development programmes, and the orientation towards business and community organizations and institutions are each distinctive aspects of cluster-based strategies. In addition, cluster-development policies, intentionally or not, tend to be aimed precisely at the globalization–localization nexus that has created such challenges for policy-makers around the world.

Many cluster-development programmes are remarkably similar, both in their main features and in the specific clusters that they tend to focus upon. Some observers have even concluded that there is enough convergence in policies or programmes to conclude that there is little doubt as to what to do, but only as to how to do it (OECD, 1995). Such similarities often mask the differences of the origins of the target industrial base, the level of government intervention in cluster development, and even in the understanding of what a cluster is in the first place. The general failure to acknowledge such differences leads one to wonder if in becoming all things to all people, cluster-development strategies will ultimately mean little to anyone. After all, it would be ironic if a concept that holds out the promise of development tailored to the specifics of local economies were to become the rationale for 'one size fits all' policies where all regions follow the same policies in pursuit of the same industries. It would be particularly ironic if a process predicated on the embeddedness of economic activity into local society results in the same set of disembodied policies regardless of the local context. This would nearly ensure that the 'nightmare' scenario of faceless, identityless regions fighting each other for a place in the production networks of multinational firms would ensue.

The best way to avoid this result is to ensure that cluster-development programmes are tailored to the local economic and social reality. This implies careful identification and characterization of local clusters in all their dimensions, explicit recognition of their needs, and programmes that clearly target specific market failures. It implies an understanding of the motivations and needs of multinational corporations that are in tough competitive environments as well. It implies a growing differentiation of regions and a further geographic division of labour. When viewed in this way, cluster-development programmes can be useful tools for policy-makers as they seek to maximize the potential of their own economies to effectively deal with a globalizing–localizing world.

Note

1. The author wishes to thank Ash Amin, Neil Hood, Stephen Young, Kevin Morgan and the participants in the Workshop on the Globalization of Multinational Activity and Economic Development held at the University of Strathclyde, Glasgow, Scotland, on 15 and 16 May 1998 for helpful suggestions.

References

ALBERTA ECONOMIC DEVELOPMENT (1997), *Alberta Business Opportunities* (Calgary, Alberta Economic Development).

AMIN, A. (1994), 'Holding Down the Global', in A. Amin and N. Thrift (eds), *Globalization, Institutions, and Regional Development in Europe* (Oxford: Oxford University Press), pp. 257–61.

AMIN, A. (1992), 'Big Firms versus the Regions in the Single European Market', in M. DUNFORD and G. KAFKALAS (eds), *Cities and Regions in the New Europe: The Global–Local Interplay and Spatial Development Strategies* (London: Belhaven Press), pp. 127–49.

AMIN, A. and K. ROBINS (1990), 'The Re-Emergence of Regional Economies? The Mythical Geography of Flexible Accumulation', *Environment and Planning D: Society and Space*, vol. 8, pp. 7–34.

AMIN, A. and N. THRIFT (eds) (1994), *Globalization, Institutions, and Regional Development in Europe* (Oxford: Oxford University Press).

BARTLETT, C.A. and S. GHOSHAL (1989), *Managing Across Borders* (Boston: Harvard Business School Press).

BIRKINSHAW, J. (1998), 'Multinational Corporate Strategy and Organisation', paper delivered at the Workshop on the Globalization of Multinational Enterprise Activity and Economic Development, University of Strathclyde, Glasgow, Scotland, 15–16 May 1998.

BRITISH COLUMBIA MINISTRY OF EMPLOYMENT AND INVESTMENT (1997), *Invest in BC!* (Victoria, BC: Government of British Columbia).

CALGARY ECONOMIC DEVELOPMENT AUTHORITY (1997), *A Great Place to do Business* (Calgary: Calgary Economic Development Authority).

CAPE BRETON COUNTRY ECONOMIC DEVELOPMENT AUTHORITY (1995), *Economic Times*, vol. 1, pp. 1–7.

CHANDLER, Jr, A.D., Ö. SÖLVELL and P. HAGSTRÖM (eds) (1998), *The Dynamic Firm: The Role of Technology, Strategy, Organization and Regions* (Oxford: Oxford University Press).

CHIHUAHUA NOW (1997), *Locating Your Business in Chihuahua* (Chihuahua, Mexico: Chihuahua Now).

CONNECTICUT DEPARTMENT OF ECONOMIC AND COMMUNITY DEVELOPMENT (1997), *Connecticut Business Agenda: Building the State of the Future* (Hartford, Conn.: State of Connecticut).

CONEJOS, J., E. DUCH, J. FONTRODONA, J.M. HERNÁNDEZ, A. LUZÁRRAGA, and E. TERRÉ (1997), *Cambio Estratégio y Clusters en Cataluña* (Barcelona: Gestion 2000).

COOKE P. and R. IMRIE (1989), 'Little Victories: Local Economic Development in European Regions', *Entrepreneurship and Regional Development*, vol. 1, pp. 313–27.

COOKE, P. and K. MORGAN (1994), 'Regional Growth Under Duress: Renewal Strategies in Baden Württemberg and Emilia-Romagna', in A. Amin and N. Thrift (eds), *Globalization, Institutions, and Regional Development in Europe* (Oxford: Oxford University Press), pp. 91–117.

DICKEN, P. (1994), 'Global–Local Tensions: Firms and States in the Global Space-Economy', *Economic Geography*, vol. 70, pp. 101–28.

DICKEN, P. (1992), *Global Shift*, 2nd edn (London: Paul Chapman).

DOERINGER, P.B. and D.G. TERKLA (1996), 'Why Do Industries Cluster?', in U.H. Staber, N.V. Schaefer and B. Sharma (eds), *Business Networks: Prospects for Regional Development* (Berlin and New York: de Gruyter), pp. 175–85.

DUNNING, J.H. (1998), 'Globalization and the Theory of MNE Activity', paper delivered at the Workshop on the Globalization of Multinational Enterprise Activity and Economic Development, University of Strathclyde, Glasgow, Scotland, 15–16 May 1998.

ENRIGHT, M.J. (1998), 'Regional Clusters and Firm Strategy', in A.D. Chandler, Jr, Ö. Sölvell and P. Hagström (eds), *The Dynamic Firm: The Role of Technology, Strategy, Organization and Regions* (Oxford: Oxford University Press), pp. 315–42.

ENRIGHT, M.J. (1997), 'Hong Kong: The Interconnected Economy', University of Hong Kong working paper.

ENRIGHT, M.J. (1996), 'Regional Clusters and Economic Development: A Research Agenda', in U.H. Staber, N.V. Schaefer and B. Sharma (eds), *Business Networks: Prospects for Regional Development* (Berlin and New York: de Gruyter), pp. 190–213.

ENRIGHT, M.J. (1995), 'Organization and Coordination in Geographically Concentrated Industries', in D. Raff and N. Lamoreux (eds), *Coordination and Information: Historical Perspectives on the Organization of Enterprise* (Chicago: University of Chicago Press), pp. 103–42.

ENRIGHT, M.J. (1993a), *The Determinants of Geographic Concentration in Industry*, Harvard Business School Working Paper.

ENRIGHT, M.J. (1993b), 'The Geographic Scope of Competitive Advantage', in E. Dirven, J. Groenewegen and S. van Hoof (eds), *Stuck in the Region?: Changing Scales of Regional Identity* Utrecht, Netherlands Geographical Studies, vol. 155, pp. 87–102.

ENRIGHT, M.J. (1992), 'Why Local Clusters are the Way to Win the Game', *World Link*, vol. 5 (July/August), pp. 24–5.

ENRIGHT, M.J. (1991), 'Geographic Concentration and Industrial Organization', PhD dissertation, Harvard University, available through University Microfilms.

ENRIGHT, M.J. and P. TENTI (1990), 'La Competitività della Ceramica Italiana', *Harvard Espansione*, September, pp. 28–41.

ENRIGHT, M.J., A FRANCES and E. SCOTT-SAAVEDRA (1994, 1996), *Venezuela: El reto de la competitividad* (Caracas: Fondo Fintec/Ediciones IESA) (in Spanish); *The Challenge of Competitiveness* (New York: St Martin's Press) (in English).

ENRIGHT, M.J., E.E. SCOTT and D. DODWELL (1997), *The Hong Kong Advantage* (Hong Kong: Oxford University Press).

ETTLINGER, N. (1994), 'The Localization of Development in a Comparative Perspective', *Economic Geography*, vol. 70, pp. 144–66.

FERLAND, M., B. MONTREUIL and D. POULIN (1996), 'Quebec's Strategy to Foster Value-Adding Interfirm Cooperation', in U.H. Staber, N.V. Schaefer and B. Sharma (eds), *Business Networks: Prospects for Regional Development* (Berlin and New York: de Gruyter), pp. 82–96.

FFOWCS-WILLIAMS, I. (1997), 'Stimulating Local Clusters', paper delivered at the World Bank Workshop for Practitioners of Cluster Formation, Chihuahua, Mexico.

GITTELL, R., A. KAUFFMAN and M. MERENDA (1996), 'Rationalizing State Economic Development', in U.H. Staber, N.V. Schaefer and B. Sharma (eds), *Business Networks: Prospects for Regional Development* (Berlin and New York: de Gruyter), pp. 82–96.

GOUVERNMENT DU QUEBEC (1997), *Business Directory* (Quebec: Gouvernment du Quebec).

GRABHER, G. (1993), 'The Weakness of Strong Ties: The Lock-In of Regional Development in the Ruhr Area', in G. Grabher (ed.), *The Embedded Firm: On the Socioeconomics of Industrial Networks* (London: Routledge), pp. 255–77.

GREATER TUCSON ECONOMIC COUNCIL (1996), *Greater Tucson Strategic Economic Development Plan* (Tucson: Greater Tucson Economic Council).

HAGSTRÖM, P. (1990), 'Unshackling Corporate Geography', *Geografiska Annaler, Series B, Human Geography*, vol. 72B, pp. 3–12.

HUMPHREY, J. and H. SCHMITZ (1996), 'The Triple C Approach to Local Industrial Policy', *World Development*, vol. 24, pp. 1859–77.

INTERNATIONAL MONETARY FUND (1997), 'United States Introduces New Measures of its Portfolio Assets Abroad and U.S. Currency Flows', *Balance of Payments Statistics Newsletter*, vol. v (December), pp. 14–18.

KAUFMAN, A., R. GITTELL, M. MERENDA W.N. NAUMES and C.W. WOOD (1994), 'Porter's Model for Geographic Competitive Advantage: The Case of New Hampshire', *Economic Development Quarterly*, vol. 8, pp. 43–66.

KORHONEN, K.J. (1996), 'Finland: A History of Networking', in OECD, *Networks of Enterprises and Local Development* (Paris: OECD), pp. 169–73.

MALAYSIA (1996), *Second Industrial Development Programme* (Kuala Lumpur: Government of Malaysia).

MASSACHUSETTS TECHNOLOGY COLLABORATIVE (1997), *Index of the Massachusetts Innovation Economy* (Boston: Massachusetts Technology Collaborative).

MYTELKA, L.K. (1998), 'Locational Tournaments for FDI: Inward Investment into Europe in a Global World', paper delivered at the Workshop on the Globalization of Multinational Enterprise Activity and Economic Development, University of Strathclyde, Glasgow, Scotland, 15–16 May 1998.

NORTHERN IRELAND GROWTH CHALLENGE (1997), 'Cluster for Success' (Belfast: Northern Ireland Growth Challenge).

OECD (1995), *Local Economies and Globalization* (Paris: OECD).
PORTER, M.E. (1990), *The Competitive Advantage of Nations* (New York: Free Press).
PUTNAM, R. (1993), *Making Democracy Work* (Princeton, N.J.: Princeton University Press).
REGIONAL PLANNING ASSOCIATION (1996), *Improving the Regional Economy: The Competitive Region Initiative* (New York: Regional Planning Association).
REICH, R. (1991), *The Work of Nations* (New York: A.A. Knopf).
ROSENFELD, S.A. (1995), *Industrial Strength Strategies: Regional Clusters and Public Policy* (Washington DC: The Aspen Institute).
SCHOENBERGER, E. (1991), 'Globalization and Regionalization: New Problems of Time, Distance, and Control in the Multinational Firm', paper presented at the Annual Meeting of the Association of American Geographers.
SCOTT, A.J. (1998), 'The Geographic Foundations of Industrial Performance' in A.D. Chandler Jnr, Ö. Sölvell and P. Hagström (eds), *The Dynamic Firm: The Role of Technology, Strategy, Organization, and Regions* (Oxford: Oxford University Press), pp. 384–401.
SCOTT, A.J. (1992), 'The Collective Order of Flexible Production Agglomerations: Lessons for Local Economic Development Policy and Strategic Choice', *Economic Geography*, vol. 68, pp. 219–33.
SÖLVELL, Ö. and I. ZANDER (1995), 'Organization of the Dynamic Multinational Enterprise: The Home-Based and Heterarchical MNS', *International Studies of Management and Organization*, vol. 25, pp. 17–38.
STABER, U.H., N.V. SCHAEFER and B. SHARMA (eds) (1996), *Business Networks: Prospects for Regional Development* (Berlin and New York: de Gruyter).
STORPER, M. (1992), 'The Limits to Globalization: Technology Districts and International Trade', *Economic Geography*, vol. 68, pp. 60–96.
STORPER, M. and B. HARRISON (1991), 'Flexibility, Hierarchy and Regional Development: The Changing Structure of Industrial Production Systems and Their Forms of Governance in the 1990s', *Research Policy*, vol. 20, pp. 407–22.
TENNESSEE BOARD FOR ECONOMIC GROWTH (1996), *Opportunity 21: An Economic Vision for Growth and Prosperity in the 21st Century* (Knoxville, Tenn.: Tennessee Board for Economic Growth).
THOMAS, M. (1995), 'Business Support Services in Europe', *Welsh Economic Review*, vol. 8, no. 1, pp. 6–7.
TÖDTLING, F. (1994), 'The Uneven Landscape of Innovation Poles: Local Embeddedness and Global Networks', in A. Amin and N. Thrift (eds), *Globalization, Institutions, and Regional Development in Europe* (Oxford: Oxford University Press), pp. 68–90.
UNCTAD (1997), *World Investment Report* (New York: UNCTAD).
WAITS, M.J., K. KAHALLEY and R. HEFFERNON (1992), 'Organizing for Economic Development: New Realities Call for New Rules', *Public Administration Review*, vol. 52, pp. 612–16.

14 Plant Subsidiary Upgrading: Some Evidence from the Electronics Industry

Ewen Peters

INTRODUCTION

Context

To date the success of Scotland's Silicon Glen has largely been based on world-class manufacturing activity. For example, according to Scottish Enterprise (SE), the leading local development body, over 75 000 people are currently employed both directly and indirectly in over 450 manufacturing establishments in Scotland's electronics industry. Furthermore, Scotland has developed particular manufacturing strengths in high-volume product areas such as information systems, telecommunications equipment and semiconductors.[1] Most of this capacity is overseas-owned. In 1993, research concluded that the long-term viability of Silicon Glen was threatened because of, *inter alia*, over-dependence on manufacturing, an underdeveloped local supply base and, importantly, insufficient local innovation (Monitor, 1993). The Scottish Electronics Forum, which represents the views of leading manufacturers locally, has since expressed its concerns regarding Scotland's apparent inability to develop higher value-adding activity around existing manufacturing, especially functions such as product-related design and development.

In response to these concerns, SE commissioned research to benchmark Scotland's experience. This work included a study of plant upgrading in the overseas manufacturing subsidiaries of eight leading electronics corporations. Drawing on this research and relevant aspects of the academic literature, this chapter seeks to examine four important aspects of plant upgrading in a global context:

- the nature and extent of plant upgrading based on the co-location of product-development activity with manufacturing;
- the extent to which the investment supporting upgrading was contestable;
- the role of the public sector in stimulating and supporting the plant-upgrading process; and
- the main impact of upgrading on the subsidiary and the local host economy.

Finally, some preliminary observations on the implications for public policy in host countries are offered.

What is the Nature and Extent of Plant Upgrading?

Several important studies and reviews conducted over the last 15 years have established and confirmed the emergence of various types of manufacturing subsidiary which are relatively innovative and high value-adding. These include, for example:

- 'Strategic Independents' and 'Product Specialists' (White and Poynter, 1984);
- 'Strategic Leaders' and 'Contributors' (Bartlett and Ghoshal, 1989);
- 'Autonomous' and 'Active' Subsidiaries (Jarillo and Martinez, 1990);
- 'World Mandate' (Birkinshaw and Morrison, 1995);
- 'Partner' and 'Militant' Subsidiaries (Taggart, 1997);
- 'Enhanced Mandate' (Delany, 1998).

The relevance and reliability of these and other related findings (D'Cruz, 1986; Rugman and Douglas, 1986; Morrison and Roth, 1993; Chang and Rosenzweig, 1998) continue to be the focus of academic discussion and debate (for example, Taggart, 1997). This chapter presents some additional industry-specific evidence on the nature and extent of the functional upgrading of manufacturing subsidiaries with specific reference to product development activity in electronics. This particular aspect is explored because of the potential importance of the link with localized innovation processes which are held to underpin successful industry clusters (Porter, 1990; Young *et al.*, 1994; Malmberg *et al.*, 1996).

How Contestable is Plant Upgrading?

For over a decade, economic development professionals and government policy-makers, mainly in the advanced economies, have been alert to the growing relative importance of expansion activity as a key driver of overseas direct investment in strategic production industries such as electronics. While much expansion-related investment is incremental and non-contestable, host-country experience also demonstrates that such investments can to some degree be contestable. Recent theorizing on the process of subsidiary development has sought to incorporate this dynamic (Birkinshaw and Hood, 1997). To date, however, there has been relatively little empirical research into the nature, extent and influence of rivalry on the plant-upgrading process. Such evidence again helps, for example, to test the general applicability of cluster theory (Porter, 1990) where the emphasis is on the primacy of inter-firm, rather than intra-firm, rivalry in upgrading. This chapter seeks to present some new evidence on this matter.

What is the Role of the Public Sector in the Upgrading Process?

Research has also established that there are local pre-conditions[2] which can improve the chances of subsidiary success in securing contestable projects. This has encouraged the public sector to develop more specific policies of support for local plant subsidiaries: this is seen, for example, in the first-time adoption of formal 'aftercare strategies' by local economic development bodies (Young and Hood, 1995). Moreover, a higher premium is now being placed on the attraction of quality reinvestment as a key component of strategic aftercare. This reflects the growing need for the more peripheral areas of the advanced economies to ensure that their competitive advantage rests on their ability to add value and provide suitable advanced factor conditions (see Figure 14.1) in order to attract and retain the productivity-maximizing investment that increasingly typifies world-class corporations in the electronics industry (see Figure 14.2).

This premium is perhaps best reflected in the number and quality of interventions by the public sector and various attempts to better integrate relevant aspects of fiscal, industrial, technology and training policy to achieve new economies of flexibility and scope. Again, there is little current research that attempts to detail and assess the value of such interventions in the upgrading context. This chapter presents a preliminary view on some of these issues.

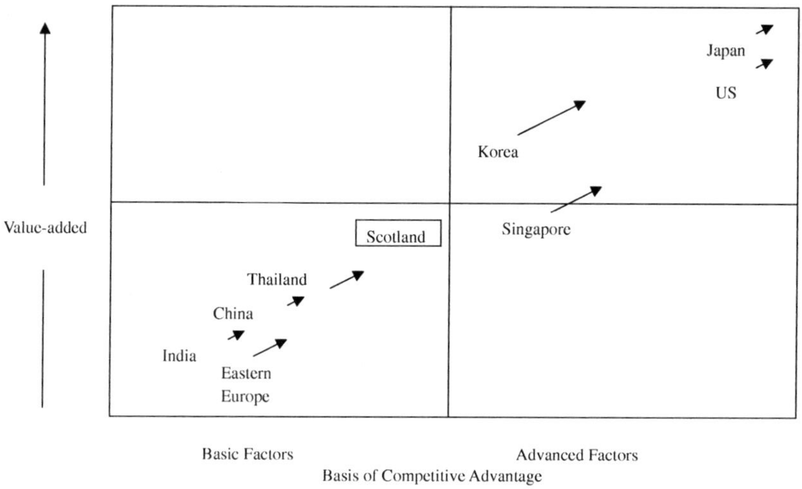

Note: Arrow length represents relative speed of upgrading.
Source: Consultant's Report (1993).

Figure 14.1 The basis of competitive advantage – country positioning

What is the Nature and Significance of Post-Upgrading Impacts?

Studies of best practice in manufacturing and technology management (for example, Pittiglio *et al.*, 1990; Booz, Allen and Hamilton, 1993; Kluge *et al.*, 1996) continue to demonstrate the primacy of rapid innovation in the electronics industry, though the specific form of innovation necessary for competitive success clearly varies by product type and maturity. Thus, from the parent company perspective, the development of more innovative capacities at subsidiary level may, under certain circumstances, allow it to more vigorously pursue sustainable competitive advantage. For example, decentralization of development activity can facilitate fuller integration of the actors central to the product innovation process in key local markets and reduce cycle times for product development. It can also enable the more rapid adoption of flexible systems of production and thereby reduce time-to-market for new product introductions. From the subsidiary perspective, developmental upgrading can help to raise general skill levels in the plant, broaden and update the plant's product portfolio, and add more value to existing operations.

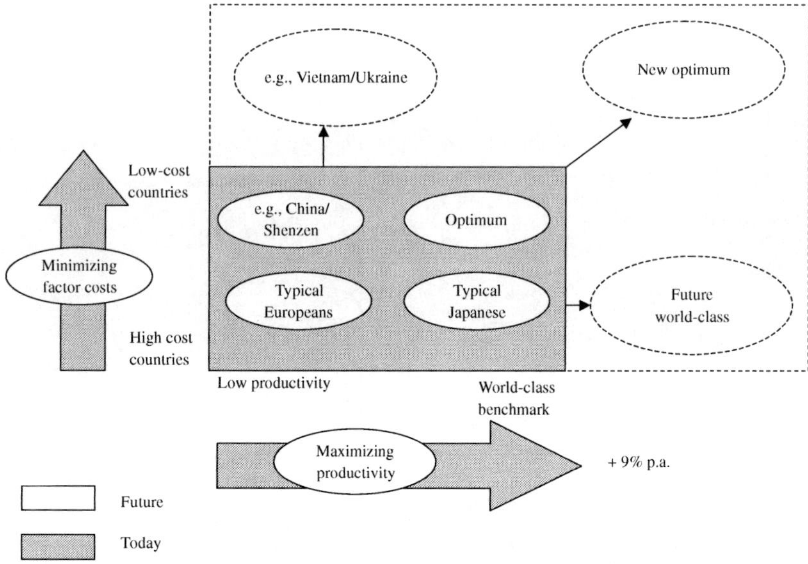

Source: Kluge *et al.* (1996).

Figure 14.2 Consumer electronics example

From the economic development perspective, it is the local linkage between product development and manufacturing associated with fuller integration which host countries are perhaps most keen to explore and exploit. A virtuous circle of cause and effect is envisaged: successful product innovation is seen to lead to greater expansion and upgrade opportunities for existing manufacturing operations than might otherwise be expected; stronger linkages may be forged with existing suppliers and local centres of R&D expertise; and, in turn, the proximity benefits associated with a strengthened process of local innovation attracts new entrants. Thus, the prospects of developing a larger and more firmly anchored cluster of activity are enhanced, one which better proximates the form[3] and function[4] of Porter's 'home-base' model of development (1990).

While Porter allows, in theory at least, for the uprooting and relocation of a firm's entire home-base as a necessary part of a global strategy, the possibility of an evolutionary progression from single-function subsidiary to home-base for a product group/division is not considered. However, some initial thinking on the type of development path this implies has been attempted elsewhere (Young, Hood and Peters, 1994). The model envisaged is perhaps most relevant to peripheral and less-favoured regions in the advanced economies characterized by a relatively high historical dependence on overseas manufacturing investment in key industries. This chapter attempts to further test this refinement of Porter by presenting some new evidence on the number, type and strength of post-upgrading impacts and their relevance to clustering.

THE STUDY AND FINDINGS

Method

In 1995 a leading firm of international consultants was jointly commissioned by SE and the Scottish Electronics Forum to undertake a study which benchmarked Scotland's experience of subsidiary plant upgrading in the electronics industry with that of near international competitors. The consultant was selected on the strength of its client base amongst the world's top 500 electronics corporations.

The main selection criteria for subsidiary plant upgrading included: the match with Scotland's sectoral strengths in electronics; rather than basic research or product maintenance activity, the plant upgrade had to involve the co-location of advanced development (that is the development of underlying technologies and key components for incorporation into new products) and/or new product development (that is the design of new products and product families and transfer to manufacturing) with existing manufacturing activity; plant upgrades had to be strategically important both to the parent and the host country/region; and plant upgrades had to have commenced product development activity within the previous three to five years.

Given the complex nature of the enquiry and the small population of 20 manufacturing subsidiaries which met the selection criteria, a case-study approach was adopted based on in-depth interviews with senior managers with direct responsibility for plant upgrading at both parent and subsidiary levels. Eight corporations agreed to participate fully in the work. In the interest of confidentiality, their names have been disguised and sensitive information omitted. The results of this work are summarized by company and by main industry segment in Appendix 14.1. The study was conducted over an 18-month period in 1995 and 1996.

The Nature, Size and Extent of Plant Upgrading

When analysed by the strategic orientation of the parent, four types of upgrade emerged (Table 14.1):

- *Rationalizers ('SemCo' and 'TestCo')*: belonged to parents with overlapping development capabilities in similar product areas at different locations, largely as the result of acquisition. As sites develop products for more than one main geography, they are not protected from each other by product regionalization. Parents have the option of either rationing development budgets and activity between sites, or concentrating development at one site on the basis of reducing costs, improving resource utilization and exploiting local research strengths.
- *First-time decentralizers ('LapCo' and 'DeskCo')*: belonged to large, but relatively young parents which are upgrading subsidiary locations for the first time and where the entrepreneurship of the local plant or local development agency was key in initiating and securing the upgrade. Decentralization was undertaken for a variety of reasons including the need to be closer to key customers in order to improve the flow of new product ideas, the need to improve the efficiency of new product transfer to manufacturing, and the desire to exploit favourable local incentives.
- *Strategic planners ('TelCo' and 'TevCo')*: belonged to parents that develop initiatives and make decisions strategically at the centre with little or no opportunity for entrepreneurship by local actors. The site-selection process for development activity is similar to that for manufacturing investment – a combination of strategic analysis and formalized analysis of candidate locations – and provides a similar opportunity for development agency involvement. The main reasons for decentralization included the need to overcome non-tariff barriers to entry (technical standards), the need to reduce time-to-market for new product introductions and to improve resource utilization in development.
- *Established matrices ('ConCo' and 'AudioCo')*: belonged to parents with an established business/geographic matrix operation. Each corporation had separate well-defined business groups operating globally with development activities well-established at several different locations. In certain instances the development activity of one business group coincided with the location of development activity of another business group. The suitability of these

Table 14.1 Nature and size of subsidiary plant upgrading

Type	*Rationale*	*Description*	*Size* (emp)*
Rationalizers			
SemCo	Better resource utilization; reduced time-to-market; plus exploit local research expertise	Corporate responsibility for the development of specialized product for global markets	20+
TestCo	Low-cost product development	Group-wide responsibility for the development of specialized products which meet North American and European technical standards	30
First-time decentralizers			
LapCo	Improved flow of ideas for new products serving key local markets; exploit local financial incentives	Corporate-wide responsibility for the development of a young product family for global markets	80+
DeskCo	Proximity to key customers; more efficient transfer of new product to manufacturing	Principal regional site for the development of advanced technology for all Pacific-rim products	60+

Table 14.1 *Continueed*

Type	*Rationale*	*Description*	*Size** *(emp)*
Strategic planners			
TelCo	Overcome technical barriers to market entry; reduce time-to-market on new product introductions	Group responsibility for the development of GSM-related technologies	16
TevCo	Release resources at the centre for work on new emerging technologies	Corporate responsibility for the maintenance and development of core technology for mature product family	35
Established matrix			
ConCo	Proximity to key customers and suppliers; reduce time-to-market on new product introductions	Global centre of excellence for the development of core technology for a mature product family	400+
AudioCo	Exploit cost advantages; secure efficiency gains from fuller integration with manufacturing	Regional centre of excellence for developing core technology for mature family of products	200+

* Size refers to the employment (full-time equivalent) engaged in on-site development activity.
Source: Author, based on consultant's report.

> locations for development activity in specific product areas had been proven in the parent's eyes through many years of continuous operation. For example, in one instance the parent had been performing development activity at the overseas manufacturing site for over 20 years. Most product development was of an incremental, ongoing nature and undertaken to further exploit existing proximity benefits with key customers and suppliers, to take advantage of lower development costs, to secure efficiency gains from fuller integration with manufacturing and reduce time-to-market for new product introductions.

The scale of the above activities varied. Subsidiaries of *first-time decentralizers*, *rationalizers* and *strategic planners* operated development teams of less than 100 people, indeed most teams numbered 20 to 30 people. The subsidiaries of *established matrix* organizations were significantly larger and operated with development staffs of 200–400.

The absence of reliable longitudinal data on population size and characteristics precludes any precise assessment. However, it is instructive to note that the extensive screening and selection undertaken by the leading industry consulting practice could only identify twenty potentially relevant examples of plant upgrading in the most recent five-year period. Given recent trends towards greater decentralization, the rise of the multi-centred transnational corporation, the perceived growing importance of value-added networks and self-organizing systems, and the well-developed global presence and perspective of the electronics industry, these numbers, albeit intuitively, seem relatively small.

Plant Upgrading, Rivalry and Public-sector Support

The degree of rivalry present in the plant upgrading process varied within and between subsidiary types (Table 14.2). Five plant upgrades involved some degree of rivalry. Three of these involved 'internal rivalry' from other subsidiaries (this included both *rationalizers* and an *established matrix* company). The two other upgrades involved an element of 'external rivalry' from other locations rather than from other sites within the corporation. This included, for example, a *first-time decentralizer* whose parent ran a 'shadow pricing' exercise to test the merits of a local plant initiative by examining the advantages of alternative greenfield sites in three other countries.

Interestingly, three upgrades were largely uncontested. The reasons for this included: unique site advantage (for example, in one instance

Table 14.2 Contestability and public sector support for plant upgrading

Type	*Contestability*	*Public sector support*	*Size* (emp)*
Rationalizers			
SemCo	Four sites considered worldwide: two existing manufacturing locations and two high-technology greenfield sites	Reactive support, largely in the form of general financial incentives (grants for job creation and investment)	20+
TestCo	Four sites undertake some D&D activity which overlaps. These sites compete directly for relevant development investment from the parent, largely on cost	Proactive support to establish development 'partnerships'. Provision of specific financial incentives (tax credits for company-based RD&D activity)	30
First-time decentralizers			
LapCo	Three other greenfield sites considered in the region.	Proactive support: local development agency formulated the initial investment proposal and partnered the subsidiary in negotiations with the parent. Provision of general and specific financial support (tax holiday for general manufacturing operations; grant support on project costs and training)	80+
DeskCo	No other locations considered	As above	60+

Strategic planners			
TelCo	Limited. Only one country considered within wider region due to policy of distributing investments between main national markets; four greenfield sites for co-location of manufacturing and development considered within the country of preference.	Reactive development agency support. Provision of general financial support (grants for job creation plus interest-free loan)	16
TevCo	Site self-selected because of the need to co-locate with existing manufacturing activity	Reactive development agency support. Provision of specific financial support (grants for project costs)	35
Established matrix			
ConCo	Four other sites within the corporation were considered globally for incremental investment.	Reactive development agency support on negotiation of incentives with other arms of government. Provision of specific financial support (grants for project costs)	400+
AudioCo	No other sites considered as investment was follow-on and incremental	Provision of specific financial incentives (grants for project costs)	200+

* Size refers to the employment (full-time equivalent) engaged in on-site development activity.
Source: Author, based on consultant's report.

the site was the only one where overseas manufacturing operations were conducted in the market area and co-location with manufacturing was a key site-selection criterion for the parent); the nature of the investment supporting plant upgrading (that is where investment was follow-on and incremental in nature); and the nature of the upgrade process (where the local plant initiative conferred first-mover advantage) in combination with some location-specific advantage.

Generally speaking, competition encouraged rival subsidiaries and locations to put forward their best case for meeting the parent's investment requirements: incentives along with value-adding factors such as local research competence and expertise, proximity to world-class manufacturing and key customers, and the availability of engineering skills featured as key ranking criteria (see Figure 14.3). However, data limitations prevented detailed analysis of the potential distorting effects of subsidies. As such the relationship between rivalry and the size, type and quality of upgrading were difficult to establish. Generally, however, where discretionary incentives were involved, parents sought to lever maximum advantage from rivalry in their negotiations with public bodies in host countries/regions.

At least four types of intervention are evident from the case studies: this could be proactive or reactive and could involve both financial or non-financial support. Where plant upgrading was non-contestable or rivalry limited, strategic aftercare was absent and public sector support was largely reactive, responding to parent demands for information on location advantages (including incentives), administering grant applications, and negotiating the type and level of grant award. In the interests of 'customer-led' strategies (a euphemism in this context for securing the maximum grant available under discretionary rules), and in the absence of rivalry from elsewhere, there was some evidence of local development bodies 'project championing' the parent's case with other grant awarding public bodies in order to lever advantage. This behaviour was more characteristic of the larger, older manufacturing sites with relatively mature product portfolios.

Where plant upgrades are more fully contested, different public sector behaviour was apparent. Strategic aftercare was a pronounced feature. In its most developed form, such policies were thoroughly proactive. This was seen in the ability of local development agencies to 'initiate' as well as 'pump prime' the upgrade process. Specifically, development agencies: formulated initial investment proposals; secured buy-in from senior managers at subsidiary level; then supported the plant management in their efforts to sell proposals to the parent. Such initiatives often represent a new and unsolicited demand on scarce capital resources. As such, parents carefully assessed the risks and returns against their investment policy line, existing capital commitments and the needs of long-term corporate strategy. On this basis, proposals were rejected or accepted. If accepted, proposals were usually modified and took a less ambitious form. For example, projects were downsized and focused on proven, rather than leading-edge technology. Where powerful financial incentives were available, local development agencies played these directly into the strategic conversation with the parent in a planned and tactical manner.

The above represents something of a step change in past behaviours. In this context the primary task of the development agency can no longer be conceived as one of area 'selling' on the basis of USPs (unique selling points). The traditional sales role is expanded, evolving into something more strategic. Credible investment proposals (CIPs) are now developed with project partners from within the existing stock of overseas-owned plant subsidiaries. This implies a broadening and deepening of the skills set and expertise of leading development agencies either directly or by finding new ways of accessing necessary know-how, while maintaining the appearance of a 'seamless transaction' with the customer.

Post-Upgrading Impacts

The most commonly reported effect of upgrading on the local subsidiary was role enhancement (see Table 14.1). The achievement of 'centre of excellence' status, for example, raised the subsidiary in the eyes of the parent and sister plants elsewhere in the product group/division. Senior managers at both parent and subsidiary level were agreed that this improved the prospects of the subsidiary securing future manufacturing and development investment.

Traditional Economies of Agglomeration

From the local economic development perspective, a variety of post-upgrading effects which strengthen traditional economies of agglomeration (Marshall, 1890) in host countries/regions were apparent. These included:

- The creation of new, highly-skilled engineering jobs in the local economy. This served to strengthen 'skills specialization' as a driver of agglomeration. This effect was cited both by relatively

young subsidiaries in locations where economies of agglomeration were relatively weak, and by older subsidiaries that were part of larger, well-established industrial complexes.
- 'Technological spillovers' which were most pronounced in locations where skills shortages were acute, key skills remained relatively immobile, and high staff turnover was being experienced.
- The co-location of key suppliers from overseas which added further breadth and depth to the range of 'specialized support industries' available locally.

Cluster Effects

In his cluster theory, Porter identifies a number of additional factors which underpin the long-term sustainability of local industrial agglomerations in a fast globalizing, competitive world (Porter, 1990). These include, *inter alia*, local demand which is sizeable and sophisticated and which anticipates need in the international market place; local infrastructure and factor conditions which are advanced and highly customized; customers, suppliers, related industries, institutions and government bodies that are world-class and well-linked and aligned; well-developed and fully-integrated strategic functions that serve as the 'home-base' for internationally successful corporations; dynamic rivalry and entrepreneurship which encourages rapid innovation and upgrade amongst all the key cluster partners and stakeholders; and a degree of localization which enhances and elevates the operation of the cluster as a system of competitive advantage (see Table 14.3).

A number of effects which strengthen these factors were identifiable from the research:

- First and foremost, the co-location of development activity with manufacturing was associated with positive anchoring effects and boosted the rate of subsidiary upgrade. This was rooted in the successful concurrent engineering of new products and associated manufacturing processes at the same location which led to significant economic spin offs:

  (a) manufacturing skills were upgraded;
  (b) as new product is higher in value than more mature, commodity-like products – plant profitability increased; this led to a higher ROI which in turn improved plant prospects of securing further reinvestment;

Table 14.3 Key features of Porter's industrial clusters

Features	*Comment*
Industrial specialization	Evident in some degree of product homogeneity
Internationally successful	Evident in significant world market share and the internationalization of production by leading firms and predicated upon a well developed and fully functioning 'diamond of competitiveness' including: • advanced and sophisticated local demand • strong domestic rivalry • world-class specialist suppliers and related industries • advanced factor conditions
Key actors	Dominant firms, leading institutions, government bodies and individuals linked in vertical *and* horizontal relationships to form a local network of high value-adding activity. Social capital – shared values, beliefs and objectives in a unique social and historic context – are also important
Key functions	At the level of the firm these include: the development of corporate strategy and network leadership; the research, development and design of new products; strategic marketing; advanced manufacturing; and global procurement. Together these comprise Porter's 'home-base' model of development
Key processes	Sustainable competitive advantage is dependent on the strength and dynamism of two fundamental processes – innovation and rivalry; these processes are supported by dynamic entrepreneurship/intrapreneurship, strategic partnerships and networking
Localization	A key feature which facilitates more rapid upgrading by amplifying and elevating the operation of the diamond of competitiveness as a system

Source: Author based on Porter (1990).

(c) fuller functional integration, the relative immobility of key engineering skills, and the generation of higher value also helped offset any loss of cost competitiveness.

- Taken together the above factors countered to some extent the competitive threat from least-cost locations and helped to focus the parent's mind on the risks and uncertainties of relocation.
- Given that the pursuit of global sourcing policies was widespread, local linkages with suppliers remained generally poorly developed. However, some opportunities to forge new links locally with key suppliers (for example, Microsoft and Intel) were found and exploited. In one instance, the manufacturing model was changing to one based on outsourcing. Accordingly, local linkages were strengthened with those sub-contractors enjoying key-supplier status.
- Post-upgrading, however, it was linkages with the parent's core R&D function and with local research institutes that benefited most in terms of the number and quality of interactions. This significantly boosted the subsidiary's innovative capacity and the rate of technology transfer. In turn, this enhanced the process of local innovation and upgrade which is held to be fundamental to clustering and the neo-Schumpetarian view of competition adopted by Porter.
- In certain instances functional upgrading resulted in the subsidiary achieving 'centre of excellence' status and becoming an important specialized node on the corporate web of innovation.
- In two instances where development was more broad-based and had been underway for longer, the subsidiary had evolved into a 'strategic business unit' which better proxied Porter's home-base model or D'Cruz and Rugman's flagship model (1993) in scope and function.

Finally, as noted elsewhere (Enright, 1998), the policy ideal would be to encourage the formation of industrial clusters which demonstrate 'all' the characteristics associated with sustainable competitive advantage. However, to expect to be able to move forward on all possible development fronts simultaneously is untenable. This is especially true for many peripheral and less-favoured regions for whom the cluster ideal can seem no more than a rather distant, long-term aspiration. Thus, characterizations which help to identify key development opportunities and constraints in relevant emerging clusters can be especially useful, particularly where these help to identify specific issues and actions to which costs and benefits may be attached. Accordingly, Table 14.4 sets out an analytical framework, suggested by the research, which attempts to identify and capture the main types of cluster effect specifically associated with the developmental plant upgrading of a manufacturing subsidiary. This may be of particular interest to policy-makers in the peripheral regions of the more advanced economies.

CONCLUSIONS

Implications for Theory

Allowing for the indicative nature of the findings, the research provides new evidence of interest to international business theorists that single-function overseas subsidiaries may, under certain circumstances, evolve into higher-value multiple function units through functional upgrading. Specifically, the evidence of this study demonstrates that plant upgrading in the electronics industry can enable manufacturing subsidiaries to become 'centres of manufacturing and development excellence'. Furthermore, the research shows that where upgrading has been broad-based and continuous over an extended period of time (usually 10 years plus), manufacturing sites may also evolve into more full-blown 'strategic business units' within the corporation.

The study identified a number of effects that enhanced the rate of specialized skills formation, added to the number of specialized suppliers, boosted the rate of technological spillover and generally strengthened local agglomeration economies as traditional theory would predict. Furthermore, in terms of cluster theory, the study identified a number of effects which add positively to the size, structure and functionality of emerging local industry clusters and which enhanced their operation as adaptive value-adding networks. In particular, the innovative attributes associated with developmental plant upgrading helped to create new local linkages with other key functions (for example, high-volume world-class manufacturing and components supply) and processes (for example, local innovation) which helped to root the emerging cluster more firmly in the local economic and technological milieux. While this pattern of development may in certain respects better proxy Porter's home-base model of development, the continued absence (or relative weakness) of key functions,

Table 14.4 Examples of main cluster effects associated with subsidiary plant development

	Direct effects	*Indirect effects*	*Induced effects*
Structure (economic resources and & activity)	Establishment of sales and manufacturing activities in a new product area	Local suppliers expand upstream from manufacturing	Overseas suppliers and related industries establish and expand within the cluster
	Cluster enlargement occurs through expansion of existing activities	Other local industries develop 'related industry characteristics'	New rivals establish via indigenous start-up or inward investment
	Local factor conditions improve through higher rates of factor formation, especially advanced and specialized factors	Local demand is strengthened	
		Public and private sector bodies align factor creation activity with cluster needs	
Linkages (vertical and horizontal)	Strategically important links are established/extended with other co-located functions or key functions elsewhere in the MNE	Strategically important links are established/ extended with existing key customers, suppliers, rivals, related industries and non-business partners	Strategically important links are established by new arrivals

Key processes (ability to innovate and upgrade continuously)	Higher level functions and capabilities are acquired: • strategic marketing; • design and development responsibilities for new products and processes; • capacity to generate/absorb and integrate technology into new products and processes	Existing innovative capacities of key buyers and suppliers (including sub-contractors and service providers) and efficient technology transfer are enhanced	New investment is made by suppliers, firms in related industries and rivals to establish/enhance innovative capacities and capabilities
	Tech transfer links are forged/strengthened with parent and other parts of MNE	Institutional arrangements are developed in partnership with government and others to enhance the rate of advanced factor formation and upgrade	New investment in commercialization mechanisms is made by cluster partners and stakeholders Inward investment in standalone RD&D activity is attracted

Source: Author, based on Porter (1990).

linkages and processes at the firm and institutional level constrains the development of self-sustaining clusters. For example, the study indicates that even where 'centres of development excellence' emerge, more often than not local linkages remain underdeveloped and that key functions such as strategic marketing and fundamental research into next-generation product technology are absent.

Policy Implications

The small number of fully contestable strategic plant upgrades identified in the study perhaps give local development bodies cause to pause and consider the balance and focus of their aftercare programmes. For the electronics industry, the findings suggest that this type of upgrading appears to offer limited, but important, niche opportunities. To engage effectively with these, the study indicates that a new approach to 'partnership' may be emerging. Rather than the traditional role of 'selling' the location-specific advantages of their region, some development bodies are now assuming a fundamentally different role, one which is much more proactive. This involves the development of CIPs in order to initiate strategic conversations with senior local plant managers and their parents concerning new plant upgrade opportunities. This role is clearly more sophisticated and astute, both technically and commercially, than the more traditional sales/marketing role and requires the acquisition of new knowledge and skills, especially deep industry understanding. As the millennium fast beckons, this approach may represent another expression of the type of local collaboration and partnership implied by the emergence of alliance capitalism (Dunning, 1997).

The absence of any evidence for 'rivalry' leading to functional upgradings which were significantly larger or of better quality than would otherwise be expected, is potentially significant. Indeed, where the plant upgrading was initiated locally, there was evidence that the parent's influence resulted in the acceptance of proposals that were 'downsized', based on 'proven' rather than 'leading-edge technology', and phased over longer time periods than originally proposed by the subsidiary. The study also showed that parents used 'rivalry' to lever maximum advantage from host countries/regions in their negotiation of discretionary incentives. Though the level of direct subsidies used by governments in the advanced economies is known to be on a downward trend (for example, Fourth Study of State Aids in Manufacturing, EC, 1996), the evidence to hand suggests that incentives still feature strongly in the investment decision. Thus, concerns over the possible distorting effects of incentives on location decisions and competitiveness remain (Porter, 1990). Moreover, given the parent behaviour identified, the policy concern must also be with the potential 'dead weight' associated with the level of incentive attracted by contestable investment projects of this kind. As such, this issue remains a concern for the global community and continues to merit fuller study and investigation in the interests of economic fairness and efficiency.

As noted elsewhere (Enright, 1998), policy-makers cannot proceed on all fronts simultaneously in pursuing cluster-based strategies for local economic development. Key issues and actions relative to emerging clusters offering the greatest development potential must be identified at the earliest stage possible. Much care and attention has therefore to be given by policy-makers to developing and applying relevant 'cluster characterizations' which achieve such a focus. This is especially important for policy-makers in less-favoured, peripheral regions. In the case of this research, for example, a significant number of post-upgrading impacts were evident which strengthened both the traditional drivers of agglomeration and general cluster formation. These effects are potentially many and varied. Accordingly, Table 14.4 represents a framework which seeks to capture and systematize, and offers policy-makers a starting point in their assessment of the nature and extent of clustering effects, perhaps as a prelude to more detailed cost–benefit analysis of policy choices.

As note above, 'cluster characterization' which is relevant and appropriate to the local setting is a fundamental, but challenging, *sine qua non* for the policy-maker. However, many development agencies, especially in the less favoured and peripheral regions of the advanced economies, are now actively pursuing the 'cluster approach' to local economic development with only partial appreciation of the relevance of the cluster approach and partial understanding of where cluster baselines might lie, and what growth potentials may exist. In particular, deep industry knowledge, necessary to accurate and effective cluster mapping, may often be lacking, along with the consultancy skills and credibility with private sector partners needed to generate it.

Finally, for industries where overseas-ownership is a pronounced and perhaps dominant feature, it is recognized that Porter's original framework needs further development and careful application (for example, Dunning, 1993). This study suggests that overseas-owned plant subsidiaries, under certain conditions, can strengthen local innovation – a process fundamental to successful clustering – through development upgrade. However, the best examples of this in the study are largely based on proven and mature technology which parents see benefit in developing remote from the centre. Accordingly, policy-makers may wish to bear in mind that the processes considered here are not helping redefine where 'the leading edge' of technology lies. More often than not, this remains where it always has, at home, in the backyard of the corporate parent.

APPENDIX: COMPANY CASES

Computers and Components ('Lapco', 'Deskco' and 'Semco')

Box 14.1
'LapCo'

LapCo is the Singaporean subsidiary of a leading computer manufacturer headquartered in the United States. The plant was established in 1986 as the first major production facility overseas with manufacturing responsibility for printed circuit boards. Manufacturing responsibilities have been progressively expanded with respect to product scope (production of central processing units and desk-top computers commenced in 1990 and lap-top computers in 1994). Market scope has also been enlarged and LapCo now has the worldwide mandate for lap-top manufacture. The plant employs over 2000 people and has an annual turnover in excess of £600m. In 1995, for the first time in the corporation's history, the parent devolved some development responsibility: LapCo was given development responsibility for the support of existing products manufactured. Subsequently, full product development responsibilities were devolved for lap-tops, a relatively young and strategically important product within the parent's portfolio. This created employment opportunities for over 80 developers and engineers.

The parent considered decentralization following an approach by the local development agency which first proposed the creation of a new product development facility on the basis of the tax and grant incentives specifically available for product development activity. This coincided with the parent's growing concern that its generation of new product ideas for the global market may be limited by having only one development location in the United States. This argument was further reinforced by the growing relative importance of Asian markets in terms of their size and growth potential, and the challenge presented by their distinctive tastes, culture and language.

The interest stirred in the parent led to a formal assessment of Singapore's suitability against three other Pacific-rim locations. The criteria used, in rank order of importance, included: proximity to main markets; level of financial incentives available; proximity to world-class manufacturing; the excellence of local research institutes in supporting the corporation's development activities; the level of training assistance available; the ability to attract skilled labour; and the general ease of doing business. Against these criteria, Singapore emerged as the only serious candidate. In particular, the proven success of the manufacturing operation allied to a powerful incentives package (namely, the promise of a five-year extension to LapCo's tax exempt status, significant direct subsidization of start-up costs and the costs of sending key personnel to the United States for training etc.) could not be matched.

Securing a global development remit for a strategically important product category has raised LapCo's corporate profile. Under present plans, this is expected to lead to even greater autonomy as the parent intends to run the plant as an independent strategic business unit to exploit emerging market opportunities. In particular, the large and fast growing Chinese market is expected to boost manufacturing volumes. The development investment has: created new job opportunities for over 80 experienced engineers (most of these posts will be recruited locally) and helped to safeguard around 2000 manufacturing jobs (most new products and related manufacturing processes will be engineered and implemented concurrently by LapCo); encouraged a key supplier to relocate a product support unit to work alongside LapCo on new product introductions (NB while regional sourcing from Malaysia, Thailand and India accounts for up to 70 per cent of raw material and component purchases, local sourcing from suppliers in Singapore is very low); strengthened technology links with the parent's core R&D function; and is expected to lead to the establishment of more local linkages with research institutes and supply companies.

Thus, with the increased competition faced from lower cost locations for manufacturing investment, developing 'own-product' expertise has helped to anchor existing manufacturing activity by increasing the interdependence of manufacturing and development, and by raising the risks associated with relocation as development competence resides primarily in staff, most of whom would not move.

Box 14.2
'DeskCo'

Established in Singapore in 1981, DeskCo is the manufacturing subsidiary of a leading US computer company. It employs around 1000 people and has an annual turnover of £275m. Originally chartered to

Continued

produce printed circuit boards, DeskCo's manufacturing remit has since been expanded to include personal computers which are made primarily for the Asian market. In 1992, DeskCo entered into a joint venture with a local institute to undertake research into language recognition systems. A year later, the parent decided to co-locate a multi-million pound design centre with manufacturing. Employing 60 staff, this centre was established to develop printed circuit boards and software diagnostic technologies.

The decision to establish a development centre was based on three main factors: first, proximity to a large market of key customers offered a better opportunity to develop products which well met regional needs; secondly, the parent's experience of the most important national market in the region demonstrated that careful product customization significantly increases market penetration; and, finally, it was recognized that co-locating development with manufacturing would enhance the speed and efficiency of the product realisation process. The initial impetus for this investment came, however, from the public sector of the host country (specifically, the public bodies responsible for economic development and science and technology who approached both the parent and the local subsidiary directly).

The level of financial incentive offered (namely around 50 per cent of the investment start-up costs were directly subsidized and the exchange costs of training local engineers in the USA was fully subsidized) combined with the strength of the case for co-location and the confidence which the parent had in the development competence of the location (based on the experience of the joint venture) meant that no other locations were considered by the parent.

DeskCo is now the principal site for developing and manufacturing products for all main Pacific-rim markets. A number of economic impacts flow from this: 60 new highly-paid jobs have been created, largely for local engineers and developers (the local economy is also benefiting from the technological spillovers associated with increased skill shortages as turnover rates amongst qualified staff have trebled in as many years); because of the benefits arising from increased cooperation between manufacturing and development, most new products developed locally will also be manufactured locally – this will safeguard production jobs in DeskCo; new products also add greater value than more mature ones; linkages with local suppliers are likely to be strengthened (that is, the parent is especially interested to promote closer ties with the local subsidiaries of key suppliers such as Microsoft); and technology links with both with the parent and local centres of excellence are likely to be enhanced.

Box 14.3
'SemCo'

First established in 1983, SemCo is an Irish-based plant subsidiary which manufactures power semiconductors for European and World markets. The plant was acquired in the early 1990s by a large US electronics corporate with similar manufacturing facilities in Asia and North America. The acquisition completed the globalization of manufacturing for this product division. Since its acquisition, plant employment and sales turnover have doubled over three years and stand at 500 and £32m respectively. Product development responsibilities have also been expanded and upgraded from two engineers performing minor product modifications to over 20 developers and support staff with sole responsibility for developing new products and associated manufacturing processes for introduction on a worldwide basis.

The parent's decision to close its existing standalone development facilities in the United States and move these elsewhere was prompted by three main concerns: first, the existing facilities were remote and serious problems were being experienced in the introduction of new products to manufacturing sites around the world; second, because of existing linkages with a local research institute, the Irish plant acquisition created an overlap with development activities elsewhere; third, due to the rationalization of other departments, development activities in the United States had been left in premises too big for their needs.

The parent sought to rationalize this position by creating a single centre of development excellence for the product division. The initial candidate sites included two existing manufacturing sites in Europe and Asia and two high-technology locations in the United States and Southern Germany. In rank order of importance, the four main site-selection criteria applied by the parent were: the ability of the region to undertake product development based on factors such as the competence (both technical and commercial) of local centres of research excellence; and the quality of local skills and the plant subsidiary; the level of financial incentive offered by the public sector; the ability to introduce new products to manufacturing more rapidly and efficiently; and low labour and infrastructure costs.

The absence of local manufacturing sites mitigated against the United States and Southern Germany. When financial incentives and labour and infrastructure costs were factored into the cost–benefit analysis, Ireland emerged ahead of the competing Pacific-rim site. Finally, the proven success of the established relationship with the local research institute confirmed Ireland as the preferred location.

Post-upgrading, SemCo's standing and status has risen within the corporation: SemCo now controls the global development resource for an entire product division and is the first choice manufacturing location for all new products developed there; and the cycle-time for new product introductions worldwide has been halved. A number of benefits

Continued

flow from this for the local host economy: new products have high margins (typically 80 per cent compared with 30 per cent for more mature products) and this increases the security of manufacturing operations and provides a basis for further expansion – the workforce of SemCo is expected to double again over the next three years and the jobs created are expected to be of higher calibre than that needed for the manufacture of 'commodity' items; technology transfer links with the local research institute have been strengthened and this has provided more local job opportunities for engineering skills that tend naturally to migrate; however, linkages with local semiconductor suppliers remain weak because specialist materials and equipment are needed and these tend to be sourced globally. In particular, the creation of a larger pool of enhanced engineering skills is regarded as a potentially important driver of agglomeration.

Communications Equipment ('Testco' and 'Telco')

Box 14.4
'TestCo'

This is an Australian subsidiary of a US parent which is one of the world's top-10 electronics corporations. First established in 1986, it was primarily responsible for the local-for-local development and manufacture of telecommunications test equipment. However, manufacturing is now mostly sub-contracted out to local firms. Since the start of the decade, the parent's investment in TestCo's product development activities have grown by 40 per cent per annum, plant turnover has more than tripled to around £50m, and total employment has grown to over 120. TestCo now has group-wide responsibilities for the maintenance and development of new specialized test equipment to meet the different technical standards that prevail in the United States and Europe. TestCo competes with four other sites which also host design and manufacturing activity. Though site competencies vary according to the different protocol levels which segment this product area, there is also some overlap in development activities. The European site is especially broad-based and dominant: TestCo has largely expanded its development activities at the expense of this site.

The parent pursues an aggressive least-cost strategy for the allocation of development investment based on: proven competence and expertise in specific test equipment technologies; the cost of performing development; and the return on previous investment. All sites are highly-regarded in relation to their technical competence and do not differ significantly on other ranking criteria such as infrastructure and skill levels. As such the cost of performing development work is the main factor which allows the parent to differentiate and rank site performance. Development costs are in turn principally influenced by the cost of labour and the level of financial incentive available from the public sector. Cost comparisons prepared by the parent illustrate TestCo's advantage in attracting contestable development investment based on Australian tax rules which allow the write-off of product development expenses against tax liabilities in the same year as incurred at 150 per cent.

The increase in development investment has broadened the geographic scope of TestCo's development capabilities and further enhanced its competitive position and corporate reputation as a natural location for future development investment. In particular, this is seen as fundamental to the creation, safeguard and upgrading of jobs in development and local sub-contract manufacturing, as it is widely recognized in this industry that development investment drives sales growth and that sales growth is the *sine qua non* of employment, given the productivity levels needed if the plant is to remain internationally competitive.

Box 14.5
'TelCo'

TelCo is one of three European manufacturing subsidiaries of a leading Japanese electronics corporation. Established in France in 1990, the plant manufactures digital mobile phones for the European market. It employs 300 people and has an annual turnover of around £40m. The parent formally devised plans to co-locate product development activities with manufacturing in 1989. These were realized in 1992, two years ahead of schedule, when a development group of 16 engineers and support staff was established to focus on GSM technologies for the European mobile phone market: especially chip-set design, microcontrollers, batteries and chargers, and interfaces and displays.

With deregulation pending and moves to create the Single European Market underway, the parent first conceived the idea of a European mobile phone operation in 1987. Near-to-market product development activities were required to generate the technologies needed to enter the European digital GSM market for mobile phones. Furthermore, product and process development were regarded as interdependent, hence the need for co-location. In order to achieve geographic balance in the parent's business portfolio in Europe, France self-selected as the preferred country location. However, site selection was contested by four French regions on the basis of their technical competence, infrastructure and skills, access/proximity to main markets, and development agency support – especially the level of financial incentives available. The final investment location was a recognized 'centre of excellence' in telecommunications and was able to offer job-creation grants, interest-free loans and a low-cost factory lease-back scheme which together

Continued

constituted 25 per cent of the capital costs of the investment. (Tax incentives for incremental product development investment were assessed to be unattractive and were not taken up by the parent.)

TelCo is now established as a global centre of manufacturing and development excellence in GSM technology within the corporation. New GSM products are rapidly replacing analogue products. This helps safeguard 300 jobs on site and is expected to create another 700 jobs by the year 2000. The numbers of people engaged in development are expected to grow threefold over this period. With the drive by GATT to reduce tariffs and controls, the parent has been able to pursue least-cost purchasing strategies: thus at 25 per cent, European content remains modest. According to the parent, this would be zero if product development was only performed in Japan. Market forces are also driving down the value added in manufacturing and the parent is now pursuing more vigorous outsourcing strategies. The effect of the TelCo's development activity is to maintain a stream of new products which are generally estimated to have 10 per cent higher added value than mature products, and this helps to offset the decline in value added locally due to increased outsourcing.

Consumer Electronics ('Tevco', 'Conco' and 'Audioco')

Box 14.6
'TevCo'

Established in 1978, TevCo is the Singaporean subsidiary of a large Japanese electronics company. It has worldwide responsibility for the production of TVs, CRTs and monitors, employs over 2000 people and has an annual turnover of £400m. Design responsibility for TV and CRT products were devolved by the parent in 1994. This created employment opportunities for 35 engineers.

The parent planned the devolution of development responsibilities in order to free scarce development resources in Japan for new and emerging technologies and to improve the efficiency of technology transfer between development and manufacturing. Accordingly, because manufacturing already existed in Singapore, no other location was considered. To ensure viability, however, the parent undertook a detailed assessment of local skills (TevCo's demonstrated ability to undertake minor product adaptations increased parent confidence in this regard); labour costs (though lower than Japan's these were found to be rapidly rising); and development agency support (grants available were worth 15 per cent to 20 per cent of the capital cost of the project).

Within the corporation, TevCo is now recognized as having global responsibility for the development and manufacture of TV and CRT products. In turn, this has further enhanced the strong reputation of

Singapore's consumer electronics cluster: the co-location of these activities has created an additional 35 engineering jobs and has helped to safeguard 2000 jobs in manufacturing. With the parent transferring all development responsibilities for TVs, CRTs and PC monitors, the major expected benefit to Singapore is the technological spillover to other companies developing similar products as engineering turnover rates continue to rise due to skill shortages. The pattern of local sourcing is likely to remain unaffected by the investment with basic components coming from least-cost locations such as China and advanced components still being purchased in Singapore. However, the maturity of the product area limits the long-term prospects for creating new jobs in manufacturing.

Box 14.7
'ConCo'

ConCo is a large European electronics corporation which first established a manufacturing presence in Singapore in 1967. Several of the parent's business groups are now represented there – this includes the corporate headquarters for the consumer electronics group, the first HQ to relocate outside of Europe. The combined sales turnover and employment of Singaporean activities is £1bn and 6500 respectively. Product development activities were first established in the early 1980s and have grown incrementally to support 400 people. However, significant new development investment was undertaken in 1994 when two centres of excellence were established (that is, a product-related development centre exploring RF (radio frequency) technology and a process-related centre developing manufacturing technology). Most products are made for worldwide markets.

The primary reason for the parent co-locating product development with manufacturing has been to reduce time-to-market for new product introductions: this has cut been cut by 40 per cent over recent years. It was also recognized that there were significant competitive advantages to be gained from developing products close to a major customer and supplier base. The RF centre is perhaps the most strategically important of recent investment projects. Four locations around the globe were assessed against three main criteria: the relevance and competence of subsidiary activities; the level of financial assistance available; and the competence of the region in the product area. In this instance, the reputation of Singapore in consumer electronics and the financial assistance which the local development agency was able to secure from government proved decisive (grants worth over 20 per cent of the capital costs were negotiated).

Singapore is now a recognized centre of manufacturing and development excellence within the corporation, especially in TV and

Continued

manufacturing technologies: the parent invests around £30m annually in product development, most of which is uncontested and is not subsidized. In particular, the RF centre confirms the subsidiary's 'centre of excellence' status. Furthermore, it is expected that the activity of this centre will help safeguard and upgrade the skills of around 2500 manufacturing jobs in ConCo. The recent co-location of development activities with manufacturing has improved competitiveness by halving time-to-market in product development. Moreover, the upgrading process is regarded as especially important to the long-term plant and place competitiveness of Singapore: the parent has already begun to relocate parts of its manufacturing operation to other lower-cost countries such as Indonesia. Higher rates of technology transfer from the parent are seen as key to the more rapid upgrading of workforce skills. However, present skill shortages are a growing concern causing salary levels and turnover rates amongst engineers to rise markedly. As lost skills tend to be quickly re-deployed, the main effect on the local economy is to enhance the rate of technological spillover.

Box 14.8
'AudioCo'

AudioCo is the Singaporean subsidiary of a large US corporation which manufactures consumer audio electronics products. While all fundamental research is undertaken in the United States, product development is carried out at two Pacific-rim locations including Singapore. Manufacturing operations commenced in 1971 and development activity started 10 years later. The principal focus for this work is RF and communication technologies for advanced telephone products and CD component applications. AudioCo employs 2600 people, including around 200 engineers, and has a turnover of £300m. The parent invests around £12m per annum on product development in Singapore.

The parent has pursued a strategy of product migration, manufacturing in the cheapest location capable of achieving acceptable quality. Product development activity has always been regarded as interdependent with manufacturing. Accordingly, development investment followed manufacturing investment as Singapore offered low costs and political stability. On this basis, AudioCo has benefited from 15 years of product development investment. Related activities now support 170 engineering jobs and 200 support staff and help to safeguard and upgrade 2600 manufacturing jobs. New products developed and manufactured locally also add more value than more mature lines. Well-developed internal communications facilitate the exchange of information and ideas between staff on different development sites globally.

The emergence of a robust cluster of consumer electronics activity has confirmed Singapore's position in the parent's eyes as a prime location for development investment: staff exchanges between Singapore and the United States have enhanced the rate of technology transfer to Singapore. That said, growing skills shortages (reflected in rapidly rising salary levels and turnover rates of over 20 per cent) are beginning to undermine the benefits of clustering and cheaper near competing locations such as China and Malaysia (where the parent also has manufacturing operations) are becoming increasingly attractive as potential locations for product development. However, the risk of losing accumulated know-how and the uncertainty of labour quality elsewhere prevents the parent from relocating major manufacturing operations at present. The parent is also applying pressure on the government to offset the growing cost differential by increasing financial incentives. Linkages with Singaporean based suppliers are not especially strong: local content remains low as the parent aggressively pursues a least-cost global procurement strategy.

Notes

1. According to Scottish Enterprise, Scotland's share of European production capacity for workstations, ATMs, notebooks, branded PCs and semiconductors is 78 per cent, 60 per cent, 51 per cent, 40 per cent and 13 per cent respectively.
2. For example, in their study of the Scottish experience of plant upgrading in electronics, Anderson Lyall (1991) established that the chances of success were enhanced where the local subsidiary was world-class in fulfilling its manufacturing mission; demonstrably successful in developing innovative solutions to problems of process development and product adaptation; and had a strategically able general manager who was an effective ambassador and advocate for the local plant with the parent.
3. Flagship firms can play a central role in cluster formation and development through their investment, innovation and functional activity, especially the strategic leadership which can be provided to the wider cluster.
4. The key functions at the level of the firm that matter most in clustering are corporate leadership, core R&D, advanced manufacturing, strategic marketing and global procurement.

References

ANDERSON LYALL (1991), *R&D Activity in Scottish Electronics*, Confidential Report for the Scottish Development Agency.

BARTLETT, C.A. and S. GHOSHAL (1989), *Managing Across Borders: The Transnational Solution* (Boston Mass.: Harvard Business School Press).

BIRKINSHAW, J.M. and A.J. MORRISON (1995), 'Configurations of Strategy and Structure in Subsidiaries of Multinational Corporations', *Journal of International Business Studies*, vol. 26, no. 4, pp. 729–54.

BIRKINSHAW, J.M. and N. HOOD (1997), 'An Empirical Study of Development Processes in Foreign-owned Subsidiaries in Canada and Scotland', *Management International Review*, vol. 37, no. 4, pp. 339–63.

BOOZ, ALLEN, and HAMILTON (BAH) (1993), 'Mastering Technology Management for Competitive Advantage', monograph, BAH.

CHANG, S.J. and P.M. ROSENZWEIG (1998), 'Functional and Line of Business Evolution Processes in MNC Subsidiaries: Sony in the USA, 1972–1995', in J. Birkinshaw and N. Hood (eds), *Multinational Corporate Evolution and Subsidiary Development* (London: Macmillan).

D'CRUZ, J.R. (1986), 'Strategic Management of Subsidiaries', in H. Etemad and L.S. Dulude (eds), *Managing the Multinational Subsidiary: Response to Environmental Changes and to Host Nation R&D Policies* (London: Croom Helm), pp. 75–89.

D'CRUZ, J.R. and A.M. RUGMAN (1993), 'Developing International Competitiveness: The Five Partners Model', *Business Quarterly*, vol. 58, no. 2 (Canada), pp. 101–7.

DELANY, E. (1998), 'Strategic Development of Multinational Subsidiaries in Ireland' in J. Birkinshaw and N. Hood (eds), *Multinational Corporate Evolution and Subsidiary Development* (London: Macmillan), pp. 239–67.

DUNNING, J.H. (1997), *Alliance Capitalism and Global Business* (London: Routledge).

DUNNING, J.H. (1993), *The Globalization of Business* (London: Routledge).

ENRIGHT, M.J. (1998), 'The Globalization of Competition and the Localization of Competitive Advantage: Policies Toward Regional Clustering', paper presented at the Workshop on The Globalization of Multinational Enterprise Activity and Economic Development, University of Strathclyde, Scotland, 15–16 May.

HEDLUND, G. and D. ROLANDER (1990), 'Action in Heterarchies: New Approaches to Managing the MNC', in C.A. Bartlett, Y. Doz and G. Hedlund (eds), *Managing the Global Firm* (London: Routledge).

JARILLO, J.C. and J.I. MARTINEZ (1990), 'Different Roles for Multinational Subsidiaries: The Case of Multinational Corporations in Spain', *Strategic Management Journal*, vol. 11, pp. 501–12.

KLUGE, J. *et al.* (1996), *Shrink to Grow* (London: Macmillan).

MALMBERG, A., O. SOLVELL and I. ZANDER (1996), 'Spatial Clustering, Local Accumulation of Knowledge and Firm Competitiveness', *Geografiska Annaler*, vol. 78B, pp. 85–97.

MARSHALL, A. (1890), *Principles of Economics* (London: Macmillan).

MONITOR Co (1993), 'The Competitive Advantage of Scotland', confidential report for Scottish Enterprise.

MORRISON, A.J. and K. ROTH (1993), 'Developing Global Subsidiary Mandates', *Business Quarterly*, Summer, pp. 104–10.

PITTIGLIO, RABIN, TODD and MCGRATH (PRTM) (1990), 'International Manufacturing Strategies for Electronics Industry Companies: The Emergence of the Globally Integrated Corporation', Consultants Report, Copyright PRTM.

PORTER, M.E. (1990), *The Competitive Advantage of Nations* (New York: The Free Press).

RUGMAN, A.M. and S. DOUGLAS (1986), 'The Strategic Management of Multinationals and World Product Mandates', in H. Etemad and L.S. Dulude (eds), *Managing the Multinational Subsidiary: Response to Environmental Changes and to Host Nation R&D Policies* (London: Croom Helm), pp. 75–89.

SCOTT, A.J. (1992), 'The Role of Large Producers in Industrial Districts: A Case of High Technology Systems Houses in Southern California', *Regional Studies*, vol. 26, pp. 265–75.

TAGGART, J.H. (1998), 'Strategy Shifts in MNC Subsidiaries', *Strategic Management Journal*, vol. 19, pp. 663–81.

TAGGART, J.H. (1997), 'Autonomy and Procedural Justice: A Framework for Evaluating Subsidiary Strategy', *Journal of International Business Studies*, vol. 28, no, 1, pp. 52–76.

WHITE, R.E. and T.A. POYNTER (1984), 'Strategies for Foreign Owned Subsidiaries in Canada', *Business Quarterly*, Summer, pp. 59–69.

YOUNG, S. and N. HOOD (1995), 'Attracting, Managing and Developing Inward Investment in the Single Market', in A. Amin and J. Tomaney (eds), *Behind the Myth of European Union* (London: Routledge), pp. 282–306.

YOUNG, S., N. HOOD and E. PETERS (1994), 'Multinational Enterprises and Regional Economic Development', *Regional Studies*, vol. 28, no. 7, pp. 657–77.

15 Regions, Governance and FDI: The Case of Wales

Nick Phelps, Kevin Morgan and Crispian Fuller

INTRODUCTION

Recently there has been somewhat of a consensus among economists, political scientists, planners and geographers regarding the enhanced potential of sub-national territories and their institutions to influence the activities of multinational companies. To varying degrees, political scientists have stressed the growing powers and resources assumed by sub-national institutions and organizations as these have been redistributed among multiple levels of governance (for example, Jessop, 1997; Marks *et al.*, 1996; Ohmae, 1993). Geographers have recently re-emphasised the relevance of sub-national territories not merely as containers of economic activity but intrinsic to the very organization and accumulation of economic activity (Cox and Mair, 1991; Amin and Thrift, 1995; Storper, 1995).

Planners, too, have noted the contribution of distinct sub-national systems of governance to 'drawing down benefits from companies into the social and economic life of a place in environmentally sensitive ways' (Healey, 1997, p. 202). The creation of 'customised space' appears to be the primary way in which the planning system impinges on the attraction and development of inward investment (Peck, 1996; Phelps and Tewdwr-Jones, 1998). Finally, economists have noted the paradox that increased globalization of the activities of multinational companies has yet made some of the larger of these companies more sensitive to their numerous host economies and institutions. Here it would seem that globalization 'upgrades the capability of micro-regional spatial units to provide the complementary or support services necessary for . . . mobile assets to be properly assimilated and exploited' (Dunning, 1997, p. 115). For an alternative perspective, Chapter 6 in this volume should be consulted.

In this last respect there is clear evidence that the sub-national institutional capabilities involved with the attraction and development of multinational affiliates vary across EU and indeed UK regions. In the UK, for example, 'there is considerable evidence that "regional" institutions in Scotland and Wales are better able to understand, articulate, engage with and act upon regional problems and opportunities than their counterparts in England' (Evans and Harding, 1997, p. 24). As such, the increasing fine-tuning of institutional capacity has become somewhat of a policy orthodoxy among agencies concerned with inward investment attraction and development. Notable among recent institutional innovations has been the increased effort devoted to aftercare for existing investors in comparison to the attraction of new investors. Here then:

> in better recognising the contribution of the affiliates of foreign firms to cluster development, sub-national governments may need not only to upgrade the locational attractiveness of the micro-regions for which they are responsible, but do so in a way which maximises its spillover benefits. This may require some reprioritisation of the spatial distribution of social capital of national governments, and also of the taxation and expenditure plans of sub-national governments.
>
> (Dunning, 1997, p. 127)

Seen in this light the creation of a Parliament for Scotland and an Assembly for Wales may yet exacerbate regional differences in institutional capacities involved with the attraction and support of inward investors in the UK.

In this chapter the role of institutional support for inward investors in Wales is examined.[1] It begins by situating the role of sub-national institutions involved with inward investment attraction and development within a broader understanding of the increasing capacity of sub-national territories and their institutions. Consideration is then given to the evolution of the unique institutional capacity which has made Wales one of the most important destinations for manufacturing foreign direct investment (FDI) in the EU. Attention is then drawn to some important question marks over the contribution of a Welsh Assembly to the future attraction and development of FDI in Wales.

REGIONS, GOVERNANCE AND FDI

It has been argued that the current wave of regionalism is in fact the most recent of a number of crises of territorial representation in which centre–periphery relations within nation-states are being redrawn (Keating, 1997). In two previous crises, central states had accommodated territorial distinctiveness through administrative settlements in order to facilitate nation-building. The current regionalism 'is taking place in a new context, marked by global economic integration and European unification and thus escapes the confines of national politics' (Keating, 1997, p. 384). Many sub-national territories have evolved from territorial settlements or 'administrative regions' to use Cooke *et al.*'s (1997) terminology. Keating argues that the current regionalism can only be understood through an appreciation of the conjunction of different logics within given territories. Specifically, he identifies three forces – functional restructuring, institutional restructuring and political mobilisation – which to a greater or lesser extent have driven regionalism in different contexts. Regions may have several functional roles – economic, cultural, planning – but functional restructuring is seen to be most significant with respect to the role of regions as economic units. Here Keating stresses the celebrated paradox of the tendency for the globalization of economic flows to go hand in hand with the localization of activities. For the present purposes, concentration is on the changing functional role of Wales as a 'region', more specifically the economic functionality of Wales and, more specifically still, the contribution of FDI to the Welsh economy. Yet in doing so the authors also wish to highlight the centrality of institutional restructuring and political mobilization to FDI-led economic development in Wales.

Keating suggests that regions in this new context must be seen as 'systems of action' and that whilst regionalism can be situated descriptively within multiple levels of governance it is governmental *capacity* at the territorial level which is of analytical importance (Keating, 1997, p. 395). A similar emphasis on regional systems of action is to be found in a number of overlapping bodies of literature. For example, recent interpretations of the post-Fordist mode of accumulation which stress the uniqueness of local solutions to global economic restructuring (Painter and Goodwin, 1996; Tickell and Peck, 1995). As these more recent elaborations of regulation theory have stressed, 'regulation theory is not just about producing a "rigorous periodization of capital according to its own logic", it is also about analysing the institutional infrastructure around and through which capitalist development proceeds' (Tickell and Peck, 1995, p. 363). In this way modes of regulation are constituted geographically from diverse 'sites of regulation' (Painter and Goodwin, 1995).

In focusing on the distinctiveness of different sites of regulation visible at the local or regional level, Painter and Goodwin place considerable emphasis on the *process* of regulation and its geographical and temporal variability. 'The process of regulation is the product of material and discursive practices that generate and are in turn conditioned by social and political institutions' (Painter and Goodwin, 1995, p. 342). Having said all this commentators remain pessimistic about the coherence, durability and efficacy of many of these distinctive local or regional sites of regulation in the face of global economic restructuring, suggesting that 'Workable post-Fordist "solutions" at the national or local scales . . . will not stabilise until a new institutional fix is found at the global scale' (Tickell and Peck, 1995, p. 359).

Nevertheless, considerable weight has been placed on the contribution of distinctive local and regional sites of regulation or systems of governance to local economic development in general, and the attraction and development of foreign direct investment in particular within academic and policy circles. The term local governance implies that it is not simply the formal institutions of local government which have a bearing on local economic development, but also a wide range of other organizations and institutions including quasi-governmental organizations, the voluntary sector and important private sector concerns (Painter and Goodwin, 1996). Here the literature on 'institutional thickness' (Amin and Thrift, 1995) and 'regional innovation systems' (Cooke and Morgan, 1998) provide further detail on the capacities of, and capacity-building processes in, such local systems of governance.

MacLeod (1997), for instance, distinguishes four elements of institutional thickness: institutional presence – the number and powers of individual agents of governance; the density of interactions between the various agents of governance; structures of domination and coalition-building – essentially the quality of those interactions among agents of governance; and the cognitive mapping of place – where a locality or region possess a coherent identity and legitimacy as a single place. His examination of 'studied distrust' in the attraction of inward investment to the Central Lowlands of Scotland highlights the prevalence of the third of these elements and leads him to argue against a mechanical and quantitative reading of the idea of institutional thickness.

Most but not all of the agents of regional governance have some economic attachment to territory. For the likes of local authorities and regional arms of central state, economic prosperity at the sub-national level is important as a determinant of these organizations' own resources through tax revenues. Similarly, private sector firms have a degree of local dependence (Cox and Mair, 1991) which in turn can mean that they have an interest in the territorial politics of economic development. However, to date private sector involvement in the politics of economic development in the UK has been rather limited (Harding, 1990). This broad view of institutional capacity associated with the attraction and development of FDI in host economies is also warranted given changes in the dominant modes of entry of foreign firms in host economies.

In particular, the growing scarcity of new greenfield investments and the increasing significance of repeat investments within manufacturing FDI flows necessitate improved provision of after-care services on the part of inward investment agencies and an increasingly wide group of service-providing organizations and institutions. After-care services have become a major element in the building of institutional capacities among sub-national territories – requiring both an extension of, and qualitative change in, inter-agency relations. A distinction can be drawn between strategic, operational and informational forms of after-care services with a number of different models of after-care provision evident among sub-national territories and their institutions (Young and Hood, 1995).

Some strong claims have been made for the causal connection between institutional capacity and economic performance at a sub-national level, not least in relation to the Welsh economy (for example, Cooke *et al.*, 1995). However, the precise contribution of institutional capacity to sub-national performance in attracting and retaining FDI remains unclear (Amin *et al.*, 1994). The globalization of economic activity which Keating sees as fundamentally reshaping the functionality of a region like Wales is something over which local institutions have only an imperfect hold since contemporary corporate dynamics present important constraints on the possibilities for sub-national institutions to effect affiliate upgrading and embeddedness since 'internal decision-making processes of enterprises are an important part of any governance structure' (Teague, 1994, p. 280). Nevertheless, renewed optimism regarding the contribution of inward investment to economic development in older industrial regions has centred on changes in the structures and strategies of parent companies and the emergence of 'performance plants' or 'flagship' investments (Amin *et al.*, 1994; Rugman and D'Cruz, 1997) and the upgrading of the stock of inward investors.

There is some evidence of the gradual upgrading of an important part of the multinational sector in Scotland (Hood and Young, 1987) and indeed Wales (see Morgan, 1991; Cooke *et al.*, 1995), but the connection between such processes and local institutional support remain unclear. Furthermore, there is some evidence that upgrading and the acquisition of the likes of product mandates also entails a closer integration with parent company organizations (Birkinshaw, 1997; Roth and Morrison, 1992) possibly to the detriment of local economies and efforts of local institutions. In addition to this, the attitudes of multinational companies and their affiliates can vary from, at one extreme, an 'accommodation' with host-economy institutions through to 'avoidance'. In a few cases, the relationship between multinationals and host institutions can become sufficiently strained to prompt 'exit' (see Safarian, 1993). Seen in this light the likes of after-care policies are intended not only to maximize the benefits but also to minimize the threats inherent in the dynamism and global reach of multinational companies (MNCs).

Taking forward these general ideas regarding the political and cultural identity and the mobilization of institutional *presence* into a distinctive institutional *capacity*, and the latter's bearing on the attraction and development of multinational affiliates, the next section outlines the governance of FDI in Wales.

GOVERNANCE AND FDI IN WALES

In both economic and constitutional terms Wales is more closely integrated with England than are other national units within the UK, such as Scotland. Furthermore, the cultural and political identity of Wales has, to a significant degree, been defined in opposition to that in England. As such, the institutional capacity of Wales has developed only slowly, over a long time and essentially in opposition to nation-building by the English. A first phase in the development of distinctive institutional arrangements in Wales took place during the late nineteenth century and early twentieth century in the spheres of education, health, agriculture and religion. A second phase can be identified in the immediate postwar period when nationalization of industry embodied an element of obligation to particular regions. A third phase began in 1964 with the establishment of the Welsh Office and a Secretary of State for Wales. Initially the powers of the Welsh Office were rather limited but have gradually been extended under both Labour and Conservative governments to the point where the Welsh Office has been, 'for most purposes, the expression and means of government in Wales' (Jones, 1997, p. 390). The authors might add that a fourth, most recent, phase in the development of Welsh institutional capacity has begun with the establishment of an elected National Assembly for Wales after a closely fought referendum in September 1997. It is to the latter two of these phases of institutional development in Wales that concentration is directed when discussing the role of institutional capacity upon FDI.

Institutional presence has developed over time in Wales but in large measure has existed since the 1960s. It is only comparatively recently that this institutional *presence* has been galvanized – in opposition to English-dominated British politics and economic policy in the 1980s and 1990s – into providing a distinct and effective territorial *capacity* in terms of economic development in general and inward investment in particular.

Most of the Welsh quangos (quasi-autonomous non-governmental organizations) were established in the 1960s and 1970s. If the number of institutions has not proliferated markedly in Wales in recent times it is nevertheless the case that the orientation and capacities of individual institutions and organizations concerned with inward investment have changed over time. For example, although the Welsh planning system is identical in legal terms to that in England, it is nevertheless subtly different in terms of policy approach. In this regard 'the lack of an effective all-Wales tier of planning policy precipitated strong territorial political mobilization to counteract the perceived intrusive extension of metropolitan . . . non Welsh . . . institutions and policies' (Tewdwr-Jones, 1997, p. 58).

Economic development has been among the core policy areas around which this territorial opposition has emerged. Similarly, some quangos with all-Wales responsibilities such as the Land Authority for Wales (LAW) have worked closely with the Welsh Development Agency (WDA) for a number of years due to the imperatives of the inward-investment attraction process. As the Government's devolution proposals noted 'Increasingly it has operated alongside the WDA in the provision and marketing of strategic development sites [and] in assembling sites for inward investors' (HM Government, 1997, p. 12). Even quangos, such as the Countryside Council for Wales, with responsibilities somewhat at variance with economic development objectives have nevertheless adopted more sympathetic and cooperative stances (see Phelps and Tewdwr-Jones, 1998). Despite their limitations, then, these quangos have contributed considerably to the creation of a distinctive Welsh political and administrative identity (Jones, 1997).

The WDA was established by the Labour Government in 1975 and survived successive Conservative governments in the 1980s and 1990s to increase its capacity as the principal body concerned with inward investment attraction and development in Wales. Despite the breadth of its remit, until the early 1980s it had developed only a limited range of policies in pursuit of economic regeneration in Wales. The immediate emphasis at a time when traditional industries were haemorrhaging jobs and leaving derelict sites was upon providing the basic conditions to permit expansion of newer industries – on providing the 'hard infrastructure' for renewal through land reclamation, advance factory provision and investment (Cooke, 1980). Since this time, a number of important developments centred on the WDA have helped establish Wales as a major destination for overseas manufacturing investment in the UK and Europe.

The establishment and expansion of international activities through overseas offices greatly enhanced the Agency's ability to prospect for and attract foreign direct investment into Wales. Along with the Northern region of England, Wales had much less of a tradition than Scotland of attracting overseas investment but was the leading regional destination by 1987 (see Figure 15.1). At this time, Wales' position as the leading destination for FDI within the UK was reinforced by qualitative developments in the relationships between agents of governance in Wales. Even as the Committee on Welsh Affairs was taking evidence on the lack of coordination among the principal agents involved with attracting inward investment, relatively forward-thinking regional networking and partnership arrangements were being put in place between the WDA, local authorities and other bodies relevant to the immediate resolution of investor requirements (for example, LAW) (Bradbury and Mawson, 1997).

These partnerships were essentially a demand-driven, case by case, response to the requirements of inward investors involving the expedition of planning control procedures, fast-tracking of planning applications and allocation of additional housing sites where these had not

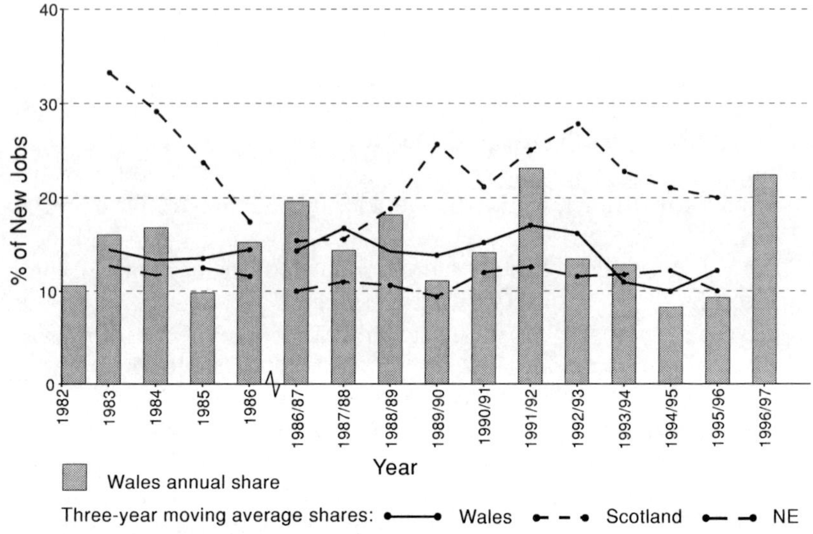

Source: 1982–86 Hill and Munday (1994) (percentage of GB total); Invest in Britain Bureau, unpublished tables (percentage of UK total).

Figure 15.1 Percentage share of new jobs associated with inward investment

been identified in relevant plan documents. These arrangements have evolved further both in their nature and the range of agents of governance included. For example, under the *Team Wales* approach, as it is now termed, organizations such as training and enterprise councils (TECs) are involved in one-stop-shop negotiations with prospective inward investors. The accumulated experience and improvements in the working relationships between institutions and organizations has meant that, along with Scotland, Wales continues to retain an advantage over English regions in the attraction and development of inward investment.[2] However care should be taken not to overstate the efficacy of the accumulated institutional capacity in Wales prior to the present institutional reforms.

Whilst Wales continues to attract a disproportionate share of inward investment in relation to the size of its economy, its inward investment performance has nevertheless tailed off markedly in the mid-1990s (see Figure 15.1).[3] Figure 15.1 shows both Wales' annual share of all new jobs from inward investment as well as three-year moving average annual shares of new jobs for Wales, Scotland and the

North East of England. This shows that whilst in certain years Wales has done well in securing inward investment, the trend has been one of decline since a relatively successful period in the late 1980s and early 1990s. Further, if one deducts the 6100 jobs associated with the proposed (and postponed) LG project which appear in the figures for 1996/97, the three-year average share of Wales at present would be less than half that at its peak in 1991/92.

The changing extent and nature of inter-agency interactions involved with the attraction of FDI to Wales is, in part, a product of the WDA's increasing efforts at providing after-care services. There have been several significant initiatives taken by the WDA in the realm of after-care services some of which have come to be regarded nationally and internationally as models of best practice. At the strategic level, a more focused sectoral approach to attracting inward investment projects has emerged. The situation has evolved from one in which there was little or no effective targeting in the 1970s and early 1980s, to one of tacit targeting in the late 1980s and eventually explicit targeting (under a *Sectoral Initiatives Programme*) by 1990 (Huggins, 1997). However, with up to 12 sectors being variously prioritized under four headings, there is scope for a yet more focused approach.[4]

At the operational level several important initiatives have underpinned the emerging sectoral focus. These include: the *Source Wales* programme for supply chain development; *collaborative training consortia* – an attempt to offer specialized training for a critical mass of inward investors perceived to exist in the automotive and electronics sectors; and the *Eurolink* and *Global Links* programmes concerned with assisting the globalization of indigenous firms through partnerships with similar firms internationally. At this point it is not intended to rehearse material which will be familiar to readers (see Cooke and Morgan, 1998; Cooke, 1992; Cooke, 1998; Morgan, 1997a, b). Instead, a number of key characteristics of the institutional arrangements for attracting and developing inward investors are outlined below.

Organization of the Inward Investment Attraction and Development Effort

As the organizational structure of the WDA has evolved, so too has the process of attracting foreign investments and the connection between attraction and the delivery of after-care services. Throughout the 1970s, 1980s and early 1990s the WDA operated a 'functional' divisional structure based on its various activities. The differing economic development needs of different parts of Wales were recognized in the late 1980s with the Agency identifying 'four zones into which it will channel investment advice and other services tailored specifically to the needs of local development' (WDA, 1987, p. 7). This represented a very weak form of regionalization of the WDA's activities (see Figure 15.2a). Under this divisional structure, and not long after introducing the main planks of its after-care services, the WDA introduced an accounts system for dealing with inward investors. At the time the WDA described how 'We have strongly reinforced our after-care programme in which we visit every inward investing company at least once a year to keep abreast of developments and to help with further expansion' (WDA, 1993, p. 23). However, *the* main organizational change, and one embodying a much stronger regionalization of the Agency's activities (see Figure 15.2b), has come in the mid-1990s with the creation of three regional divisions to deliver services within Wales (see Morgan, 1997a).

The responsibility for attracting inward investment remains centralized within the International division. Whilst resources directed to potential inward investors are not prioritized strictly in keeping with the regional divisions of the WDA, they are nevertheless prioritized so as to favour West Wales and even particular parts of West Wales. Furthermore, presently, there are both centralized and decentralized aspects to the provision of after-care services under the WDA's new 'regional' structure. After-care services had been spread across several functional divisions but are now provided as a full range of services through each of the regional divisions. 'Ordinary' accounts with inward investors are handled through the new regional structure with investors being dealt with according to local authority areas.

Recently this has been overlain with the formation of 'strategic' accounts with a top-20 or so inward investors handled centrally within the international division. The strategic accounts idea arose at the suggestion of one major inward investor. Although there are no fixed criteria on which strategic account investors have been defined they include some of the largest, usually multi-site, companies of strategic importance to the Welsh economy and those most likely to generate repeat or secondary investment. Whilst the generation of both new inward investment and repeat investment is crucially dependent on the exchange of knowledge generated separately in international and regional divisions, such exchanges are at best *ad hoc*. This in turn appears to be a product of the different nature of interactions of the divisions with potential and existing inward investors; international

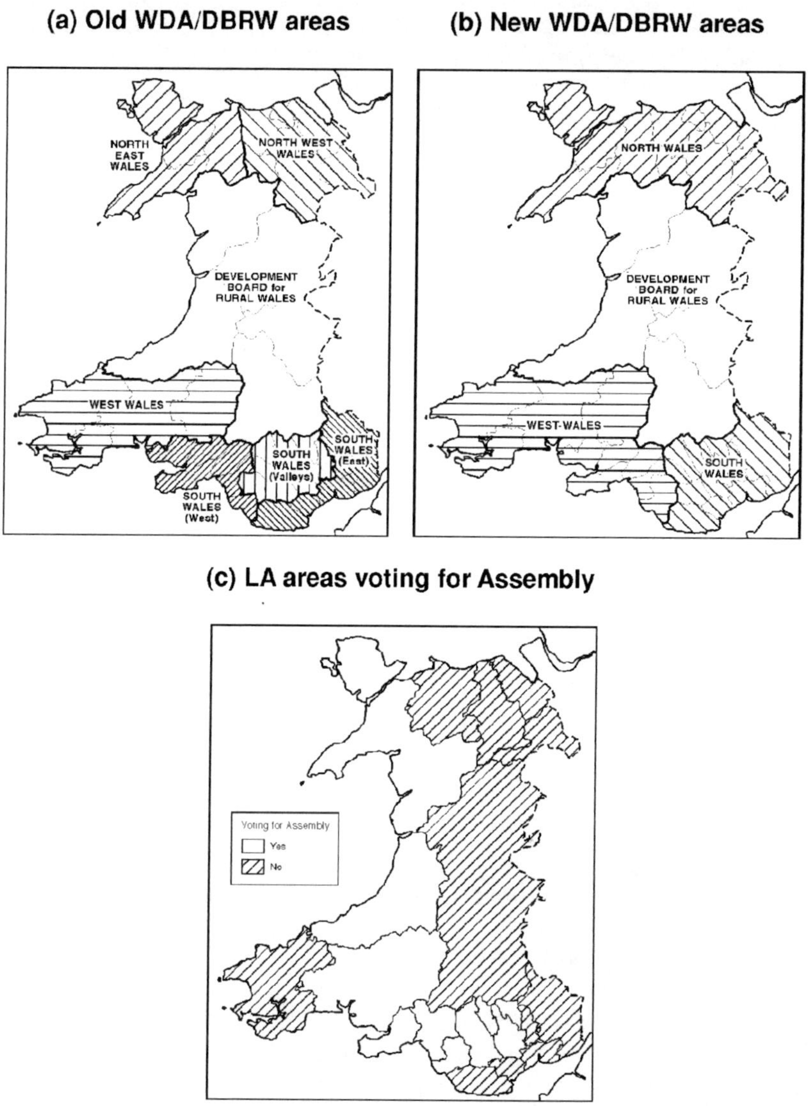

Figure 15.2 Old and new WDA/DBRW areas and LA areas voting for Assembly

offices being judged against *quantitative* targets, regional offices concerned with developing the *quality* of contacts.

Hierarchy and Exclusivity in Inter-agency Relations

Arguably, the distinctive institutional capacity involved with FDI has evolved in a societal context more favourable than that in English regions since 'Wales is a corporatist society, a culture which sets a high premium on collaboration between management and labour in the economy and between the public and private sectors in general' (Morgan and Henderson, 1997, p. 89). The unique institutional capacity that has built up around the attraction and development of FDI constitutes part of a broad consensus regarding the role of FDI in modernizing the Welsh economy. In the evolution of the system of governance connected with inward investment in Wales, then, Cooke (1998) has detected:

> more systematic co-ordination, driven by the hierarchical relationship between globally successful inward investors and local supplier companies . . . *animated* in a relatively non-hierarchic networked manner by a variety of intermediary agencies, notably, but not only, the WDA.
>
> (Cooke, 1998, p. 250; original emphasis)

This depiction of institutional capacity involved with inward investors speaks more to the *development* of inward investors in Wales than their initial *attraction*. Even so hierarchical coordination is visible in the fact that such networking is driven by major inward investors from whom the WDA is barely distinguishable as a partner in projects involving the mobilization of after-care services. The major repeat investment by Ford at its Bridgend engine plant was secured through a 'hand-in-hand' approach with the WDA (Roberts, 1995) – an approach which has been extended to other repeat investment projects among the strategic account investors.

Under the leadership of the Welsh Office, partnership arrangements in general have in the past been organized vertically and have been limited in scope (see Morgan and Henderson, 1997). This is especially true of the *attraction* of inward investment into Wales. Indeed, hierarchy and selectivity are vital to the attraction of FDI. The Committee on Welsh Affairs took evidence on the conflictual nature of inter-agency relations surrounding inward investment attraction in the

North East from the Northern Development Company (NDC) who nevertheless noted that 'to have an effective and efficient response mechanism you really need to go out to as few people as you possibly can' (Committee on Welsh Affairs, 1987, p. xxxiv). If the LG case is anything to judge by, the partnership arrangements created under *Team Wales* are similarly hierarchical and selective (Phelps and Tewdwr-Jones, 1998).

In the following section consideration is given as to how the creation and workings of the Welsh Assembly might affect the established institutional capacity devoted to the attraction and development of FDI in Wales.

GOVERNANCE, STRATEGY AND FDI IN WALES: PROBLEMATIZING THE ROLE OF THE ASSEMBLY

In July 1997 the new Labour government published its proposals for devolution, and at the time of writing it was taking evidence on the appropriate role and working arrangements for the National Assembly for Wales. The proposals made the case for an Assembly in terms addressing the democratic deficit which had developed from the proliferation of unelected quangos in Wales. However, the emphasis of the proposals is firmly on the Assembly enhancing economic development in Wales. The centrepiece of the proposals is the creation of 'a simpler institutional framework' within Wales given that the existing economic development effort is hampered by 'a multiplicity of national and local agencies, with overlapping responsibilities that are the source of confusion, inefficiency and unnecessary administrative costs' (HM Government, 1997, p. 12). There are two elements to this rationalization of institutional arrangements. The first is the creation of an 'economic powerhouse' or 'super WDA' from a merger of the existing WDA, the Development Board for Rural Wales (DBRW) and LAW (and possibly other bodies). The second is the desire to create geographical consistency, coterminosity even, in the jurisdiction of agents of governance (for example the WDA, the TECs, the Regional Committees of the Assembly and existing economic fora).

Economic development issues have been a centrepiece of arguments for devolution within the UK despite the equivocal connection between economic prosperity and institutional capacity (see Evans and Harding, 1997). The connection between institutional capacity-building, through democratic representation, and the attraction and development of FDI seems particularly unclear. In the remainder of this section we consider some important question-marks over the impact of the Assembly on inward investment attraction and development in Wales.

Objectives and Priorities of the Assembly and FDI

There is broad consensus that the primary advantages of the Assembly are, and its key objectives should be, economic development-related. The CBI, for instance, sees the remit of the Assembly in terms of increasing the competitiveness of Wales with an emphasis on 'concentrating funding to achieve this' (CBI Wales, in Committee on Welsh Affairs, 1998, p. 105). Similar concerns have been raised more specifically with an eye on the inward investment performance of Wales by the Wales TUC:

> The weakness for Wales for inward investment is funding . . . there is not enough money for us to attract the jobs if we could. Indeed jobs will go begging as a result of us not having sufficient funding in the budget to deal with the question. It may well be that there will be benefit for the English regions as a result of that.
>
> (Wright, quoted in Committee on Welsh Affairs, 1998, p. 132)

These sentiments represent part of one possible agenda behind the creation of a Welsh Assembly, namely the reprioritizing of expenditure plans in favour of economic development in a way which may confer a competitive advantage to Wales (and presumably Scotland) over English regions in attempts to secure inward investment. Reprioritizing expenditures towards economic development also has the advantage of 'having one's cake and eating it' in terms of inward investment attraction and development. If greater attention is to be paid to attracting investment to areas other than South East and North East Wales and to the needs of indigenous enterprise (see below), this might nevertheless be possible without having overly to sacrifice inward investment opportunities overall.

Beyond this, views divide as to exactly how democratic the Assembly should be in promoting economic development in Wales. As the Welsh CBI has argued 'There is no economic imperative for establishing a Welsh Assembly' (CBI in Committee on Welsh Affairs, 1998, p. 107). The CBI's argument here centres on the concern that the democratic process of the Welsh Assembly will increase the transaction costs facing business through increased regulation and delays in decision-making. In raising these concerns, the CBI has stressed the effectiveness of the hierarchical and selective inter-agency relations which have developed under *Team Wales*:

> The initial talk about an Economic Powerhouse we had some concerns over, because it could have turned into a monolithic body which did not deliver, which was just too wide ranging and not focused enough, whereas I think what we have now is at least in the economic development quangos, a very focused approach.
>
> (Haywood, quoted in Committee on Welsh Affairs, 1998, p. 110)

Thinking regarding the simplification of the institutional framework under the Assembly has centred on how to preserve the integrity of organizations which have been highly effective in the effort to attract and develop inward investors (Parkin, 1997).

Typical among architects of the Assembly is the view that:

> Regional economic development can be defined in a number of ways but in broad terms it should include education, skills, infrastructure, planning, environment, European programmes as well as local partnerships and the media.
>
> (Cardiff University Devolution Group, in Committee on Welsh Affairs, 1998, p. 67)

Such a breathtakingly expansive definition makes it clear that a whole range of normally legitimate and discrete policy areas will be subsumed under the Assembly's overall objective to promote economic development in Wales. Yet the Government of Wales Bill which is expected to receive Royal assent in June 1998 will impose a duty on the Assembly to promote sustainable development which may conflict with economic development objectives. Under existing less democratic institutional arrangements, the attraction and development of inward investment took place in a context in which economic development objectives took precedence over other policy concerns with little in the way of popular or organized political opposition. However, the democratic process seems likely, in due course, to bring forth alternative policy-agendas which challenge the economic development focus. For instance, the legitimate claims of different regions of Wales and of indigenous enterprise which have barely begun to be heard in policy circles in Wales are likely to come to the fore under an Assembly, indeed are acknowledged as vital emphases in the immediate work of the Assembly.

The Locus of Strategic Policy-making

Existing institutional arrangements in Wales have tended to be criticized from a perspective which assumes that greater accountability will promote economic development. But as we have seen, in their hierarchical and selective nature, the existing arrangements have been effective in promoting economic development especially through the attraction of FDI. The inter-agency partnership arrangements within the *Team Wales* approach may become more complex and unwieldy under an Assembly since 'in terms of inclusiveness, the Welsh Assembly will have a full range of political viewpoints within it, whereas the Welsh Office is generally only controlled by one political party at a time . . .' (Wales TUC, quoted in Committee on Welsh Affairs, 1998, p. 127).

Therein lies the rub, for political inclusiveness may have unforeseen economic consequences. To an extent this problem may be avoided by the definition of effective reporting structures and appropriate devolved executive functions within the Assembly and to existing and re-shaped institutions. The WDA, although recognizing the role of the Assembly in providing strategic direction, has argued that it will need to 'maintain and indeed enhance its capability to develop soundly based strategies' (WDA, in Committee on Welsh Affairs, 1998, p. 22). The Chief Executive of the WDA elaborated on this point, suggesting that 'the Assembly will need to reach its view on the strategic priorities and it will set these down after the Powerhouse, but the Powerhouse clearly needs the capability of putting together coherent economic strategies and proposing these to the Assembly for the Assembly to consider and dispose' (Willott, quoted in Committee on Welsh Affairs, 1998, p. 31). Despite the drift towards subsuming virtually all areas of policy within the Assembly's overriding objective of economic development, there is clearly some concern over the loss of the strategic capabilities of the WDA.

Subregional Identity and FDI in Wales

The creation of the Assembly seems certain to institutionalize and enhance sub-regional identities in Wales with important implications for the attraction and development of FDI. Political mobilization in Wales has been very uneven; its physical characteristics as a territory and the spatially skewed transportation and communication infrastructure, on the one hand, and institutional capacity, on the other, have not made for a single identity. Figure 15.2 above provides one illustration of some of the different 'regions' which may exist within Wales. Figure 15.2a shows the old regional structure of the WDA and DBRW, which represent relatively coherent sub-regions in economic terms. Figure 15.2b shows that the 'new' regions adopted by the WDA, and which form the basis of the new economic powerhouse and the Assembly, are a little less precise than those previously identified on the basis of economic needs. Finally, Figure 15.2c shows that, whilst the 'yes' vote overturned a 'no' vote of four to one in the 1979 referendum, the population of Wales is divided in its support for an Assembly (although see O'Leary, 1998, for a fuller discussion). Furthermore, neither of the sub-regional divisions defined broadly in economic terms coincide very closely with political support for the Assembly. The point here is that there is broad agreement among commentators that a strong common identity is imperative to the development of territorial institutional capacity (Amin and Thrift, 1995; Keating, 1997; Teague, 1994) but that no such common identity exists in Wales.

Within this context, concerns over the uneven distribution of economic activity and inward investment in particular have been growing:

> We would see the distribution of industry that has been attracted in as a product of the lack of a democratically accountable mechanism within Wales . . . because if you do not have a strategy but you have a market of foreign direct investors seeking a location and you have essentially a bureaucracy or technocracy managing the process of movement for them in a ferociously competitive global environment – you tend perhaps to take the technocratic decision and the most efficient location may be the one that is closest to the market and the easy option is to offer North East Wales and South East Wales.
>
> (Cooke, quoted in Welsh Affairs Committee, 1987, p. 91)

The case for, and deliberations over the structure of, the Assembly are closely identified with this need for accountability across some very different regions within Wales:

> One Welsh Assembly was not the answer. You need to establish the regionalisation of that Assembly and the regionalisation of the agencies – be they training, be they economic development – because it is only when you get that regionalisation in place, that

> you can start overcoming the tendency which has existed, which is to concentrate on the easy bits first.
>
> (Jenkins, quoted in Committee on Welsh Affairs, 1998, p. 133)

However, there is no necessary reason why proper representation for regions within Wales under an Assembly will result in a more equitable distribution of economic development in general and inward investment in particular. Indeed, there is some concern that already advantaged areas of Wales may benefit further:

> What the Assembly as a whole must ensure is that the competition which will exist between regions is something which has a constructive outcome and does not result in, shall we say, the South East, just because it happens to be the biggest region, managing to gobble up all the benefits.
>
> (Jenkins, quoted in Committee on Welsh Affairs, 1998, p. 138)

Furthermore, there is every prospect that 'top-down' elected representation for regions within Wales, coupled with existing attempts at regionalization of activities by major bodies like the WDA, will adversely affect the overall performance of Wales in attracting inward investment. Such top-down processes may sit uncomfortably with new policy discourses emanating from the 'bottom up'.

CONCLUSION

In this chapter the authors have explored the evolution of territorially-focused institutional capacity in Wales and its impact upon the attraction and development of inward investment in Wales. The picture that emerges is that this institutional machinery – at the apex of which stands the Welsh Office and the WDA – has been relatively successful in attracting inward investment, not least because it offers investors a single port of call which reduces the transaction costs associated with location decisions. Although this institutional machinery has been criticized for being both hierarchical and undemocratic, the fact remains that it has been relatively effective in discharging its inward investment responsibilities. The creation of a directly-elected Welsh Assembly is perceived, by its supporters at least, in wholly positive terms as a means of redressing the democratic deficit on the one hand, and as a more robust economic development mechanism on the other. What these supporters have failed to realize to date is that the Assembly, laudable though it may be as a democratic innovation, could actually threaten the ability of Wales to further attract and develop inward investment.

As we noted at the outset, while the Assembly could in principle give Wales an edge over English regions in competing for inward investment, by assembling more attractive incentives packages for example, much depends on how the new democratic processes will modify the existing institutional capacity. However, we have identified a number of potential problems with the newly-devolved system, two of which merit particular attention: namely, 'the end of hierarchy' and the growth of sub-regional competition.

For all the criticisms of the traditional institutional machinery, like its hierarchical and exclusive character, its lack of democratic legitimacy and so forth, it had the capacity to arrive at decisions very quickly since the constituencies which had to be consulted were internal to the Welsh Office and the WDA. The advent of the Assembly, however, is likely to subject the WDA and the inward-investment process generally to much greater political scrutiny, and it remains to be seen whether time-consuming democratic debate is compatible with the exigencies of rapid decision-making. In other words, 'the end of hierarchy' may carry costs which have yet to be appreciated by the proponents of democratic devolution.

This problem is further compounded by the fact that the devolution proposals provide a stronger institutional voice for the four subregions of Wales in the form of Regional Committees of the Assembly on the one hand, and Regional Economic Fora on the other. This creates much greater scope for inter-regional rivalry within Wales as to where inward investment projects should be located, and this is a profoundly sensitive political issue given the growing economic divide between the eastern half of the country, which has done relatively well, and the western half which has been largely bypassed by foreign investment (Morgan and Price, 1998). Again, only time will tell whether the Assembly will be able to provide the necessary strategic leadership to overcome this problem of competing claims on scarce resources.

These debates are not likely to be resolved in the near future, but the absence of tax-varying powers for the Assembly may prove to be the decisive factor in preventing the current institutional reforms from having a significant effect on the trajectory of economic development policy in Wales.

Notes

1. This chapter concerns itself with inward investment in general rather than foreign direct investment in particular. However, most of what we have to say concerns the attraction and development of manufacturing affiliates of overseas multinationals.
2. 'There is no doubt that the territorial agencies enjoy a number of structural advantages over the English Regional Development Organisations, the principal of which is that each can operate as a "one stop shop", offering an inward investor not only a swift indicative offer of financial assistance but also a range of non-financial incentives such as prepared sites, infrastructure, training and even housing' (Trade and Industry Select Committee, 1997, quoted in Bourn, 1998).
3. There is some evidence to suggest that this could be the product of the redirection of resources away from overseas prospecting to domestic after-care activities, since a recent internal briefing to the WDA's international division indicated that the WDA had fewer overseas staff (27) than, for example, Locate in Scotland (33), Northern Ireland Development Board (37) and the Industrial Development Authority (Ireland) (57).
4. For instance, it was only in 1997 that 'New teams were established by the International Division to promote Wales in key sectors . . . [This] strategy of focusing on these sectors enables the Agency to apply the expertise developed over many years to the current market place' (WDA, 1997, p. 18).

References

AMIN, A., D. BRADLEY, J. HOWELLS, J. TOMANEY and C. GENTLE (1994), 'Regional Incentives and the Quality of Mobile Investment in the Less Favoured Regions of the EC', *Progress in Planning*, vol. 41, pp. 1–112.

AMIN, A. and N. THRIFT (1995), 'Globalization, Institutional "Thickness" and the Local Economy', in P. Healey *et al.* (eds), *Managing Cities: The New Urban Context* (London: Wiley), pp. 91–108.

BIRKINSHAW, J. (1997), 'How Multinational Subsidiary Mandates are Gained and Lost', *Journal of International Business Studies*, vol. 27, pp. 467–96.

BOURN, SIR J. (1998), 'Inward Investment Assistance to LG', *Letter from the Comptroller and Auditor General to Mr. A. Campbell, MP*, 30 January.

BRADBURY, J. and J. MAWSON (1997), 'Conclusion: The Changing Politics and Governance of British Regionalism', in J. Bradbury and J. Mawson (eds), *British Regionalism and Devolution: The Challenges of State Reform and European Integration* (London: Jessica Kingsley), pp. 273–309.

COMMITTEE ON WELSH AFFAIRS (1998), *The Impact of the Government's Devolution Proposals on Economic Development and Local Government in Wales,* vol. I (London: HMSO).

COMMITTEE ON WELSH AFFAIRS (1987), *Inward Investment into Wales and its Interaction with Regional and EEC Policies*, vol. I (London: HMSO).

COOKE, P. (1998), 'Global Clustering and Regional Innovation: Systemic Integration in Wales', in H.-J. Braczyk, P. Cooke and M. Heidenreich (eds), *Regional Innovation Systems* (London: UCL Press), pp. 245–62.

COOKE, P. (1992), 'Regional Innovation Systems: Competitive Regulation in the New Europe', *Geoforum*, vol. 23, pp. 365–82.

COOKE, P. (1980), 'Discretionary Intervention and the Welsh Development Agency', *Area*, vol. 12, pp. 269–77.

COOKE, P. and K. MORGAN (1998), *The Associational Economy: Firms, Regions, and Innovation* (Oxford: Oxford University Press).

COOKE, P., A. PRICE and K. MORGAN (1995), 'Regulating Regional Economies: Wales and Badenwurtenberg in Transition', in M. Rhodes (ed.), *The Regions and the New Europe: Patterns in Core–Periphery Development* (Manchester: Manchester University Press), pp. 105–35.

COOKE, P., M.G. URANGA and G. ETXEBERRIA (1997), 'Regional Innovation Systems: Institutional and Organisational Dimensions', *Research Policy*, vol. 26, pp. 475–91.

COX, K. and A. MAIR (1991), 'From Localised Social Structures to Localities as Agents', *Environment and Planning A*, vol. 23, pp. 197–213.

DUNNING, J. (1997), 'A Business Analytical Approach to Governments and Globalization', in J. Dunning (ed.), *Governments, Globalization and International Business* (Oxford: Oxford University Press), pp. 114–31.

EVANS, R. and A. HARDING (1997), 'Regionalization, Regional Institutions and Economic Development', *Policy and Politics*, vol. 25, pp. 19–30.

HARDING, A. (1991), 'The Rise of Growth Coalitions UK-style', *Environment and Planning C, Government and Policy*, vol. 9, pp. 295–317.

HEALEY, P. (1997), *Collaborative Planning: Shaping Places in Fragmented Societies* (London: Macmillan).

HILL, S. and M. MUNDAY (1994), *The Regional Distribution of Foreign Manufacturing Investment in the UK* (London: Macmillan).

HM Government (1997), *A Voice for Wales: The Government's Proposals for a Welsh Assembly* (London: HMSO).

HOOD, N. and S. YOUNG (1987), 'Inward Investment and the EC: UK Evidence on Corporate Integration Strategies', *Journal of Common Market Studies*, vol. XXVI, no. 2, pp. 193–206.

HUGGINS, R. (1997), 'Regional Competitive Specialisation: Development Agency Sector Initiatives in Wales', *Area*, vol. 29, pp. 241–52.

JESSOP, R. (1997), 'The Future of the National State: Erosion or Reorganisation? General Reflections on the West European Case', mimeo, University of Lancaster, Department of Sociology.

JONES, B. (1997), 'Wales: A Developing Political Economy', in M. Keating and J. Loughlin (eds), *The Political Economy of Regionalism* (London: Frank Cass), pp. 388–405.

KEATING, M. (1997), 'The Invention of Regions: Political Restructuring and Territorial Government in Western Europe', *Environment and Planning C, Government and Policy*, vol. 15, pp. 383–98.

O'LEARY, P. (1998), 'Of Devolution, Maps and Divide Mentalities', *Planet*, vol. 127, pp. 7–12.

MACLEOD, G. (1997), ' "Institutional Thickness" and Industrial Governance in Lowland Scotland', *Area*, vol. 29, pp. 299–311.

MARKS, G., L. HOOGHE and K. BLANK (1996), 'European Integration in the 1980s: State-centric v. Multi-level Governance', *Journal of Common Market Studies*, vol. 34, pp. 341–78.

MORGAN, K. (1997a), 'The Regional Animateur: Taking Stock of the Welsh Development Agency', *Regional and Federal Studies*, vol. 7, pp. 70–94.

MORGAN, K. (1997b), 'The Learning Region: Institutions, Innovation and Regional Renewal', *Regional Studies*, vol. 31, pp. 491–504.

MORGAN, K. (1991), 'Competition and Collaboration in the Electronics Industry: What are the Prospects for Britain', *Environment and Planning A*, vol. 23, pp. 1459–82.

MORGAN, K. and D. HENDERSON (1997), 'The Fallible Servant: Evaluating the Welsh Development Agency', in R. MacDonald and H. Thomas (eds), *Nationality and Planning in Scotland and Wales* (Cardiff: University of Wales Press), pp. 77–97.

MORGAN, K.A. and A. PRICE (1998), *The Other Wales: The Case for Objective 1 Funding Post-1999* (Cardiff: Institute for Welsh Affairs).

OHMAE, K. (1993), 'The Rise of the Region State', *Foreign Affairs*, vol. 72, pp. 78–87.

PAINTER, J. and M. GOODWIN (1996), 'Local Governance, the Cries of Fordism and the Changing Geographies of Regulation', *Transactions of the Institute of British Geographers*, vol. NS 21, pp. 635–48.

PARKIN, D. (1997), 'Warning on Success of Land Quangos', *Western Mail*, 30 July, p. 1.

PECK, F. (1996), 'Regional Development and the Production of Space: The Role of Infrastructure in the Attraction of New Inward Investment', *Environment and Planning A*, vol. 28, pp. 327–39.

PHELPS, N.A. and M. TEWDWR-JONES (1998), 'Institutional Capacity Building in a Strategic Vacuum: The Case of the LG Investment in South Wales', *Environment and Planning C, Government and Policy*, vol. 16, pp. 735–55.

ROBERTS, R. (1995), 'Bridgend's Proven Track Record Wins Battle', *Western Mail*, 18 October.

ROTH, K. and A.J. MORRISON (1992), 'Implementing Global Strategy: Characteristics of Global Subsidiary Mandates', *Journal of International Business Studies*, vol. 23, pp. 715–35.

RUGMAN, A. and J. D'CRUZ (1997), 'Strategies of Multinational Enterprises and Governments: The Theory of the Flagship Firm', in G. Boyd and A. Rugman (eds), *Euro–Pacific Investment and Trade: Strategies and Structural Interdependencies* (Cheltenham: Edward Elgar), pp. 248–72.

SAFARIAN, A.E. (1993), *Multinational Enterprise and Public Policy: A Study of the Industrial Countries* (Cheltenham: Edward Elgar).

STORPER, M. (1995), 'The Resurgence of Regional Economies, Ten Years Later: The Region as a Nexus of Untraded Interdependencies', *European Urban and Regional Studies*, vol. 2, pp. 191–222.

TEAGUE, P. (1994), 'Governance Structures and Economic Performance: The Case of Northern Ireland', *International Journal of Urban and Regional Research*, vol. 18, pp. 275–92.

TEWDWR-JONES, M. (1997), 'Land-use Planning in Wales: The Conflict between State Centrality and Territorial Nationalism', in R. MacDonald and H. Thomas (eds), *Nationality and Planning in Scotland and Wales* (Cardiff: University of Wales Press), pp. 54–76.

TICKELL, A. and J. PECK (1995), 'Social Regulation After Fordism: Regulation Theory, Neo-liberalism and the Global–Local Nexus', *Economy and Society*, vol. 24, pp. 357–86.

WDA (1997), *Annual report 1996–97* (Cardiff: Welsh Development Agency).

WDA (1993), *Report and Accounts 1992–93* (Cardiff: Welsh Development Agency).

WDA (1987), *Report and Accounts 1986–87* (Cardiff: Welsh Development Agency).

YOUNG, S. and N. HOOD (1995), 'Attracting, Managing and Developing Inward Investment in the Single Market', in A. Amin and J. Tomaney (eds), *Behind the Myth of European Union* (London: Routledge), pp. 282–304.

Part V
Conclusions

16 Globalization and Economic Development: Overview and Conclusions

Stephen Young and Neil Hood

The object of this volume has been to explore the interrelationships between and among globalization, multinational enterprise activities and economic development, and to highlight the implications for policy-makers. Writings to date around the theme of globalization have been extensive and diverse and have encompassed perspectives which range from the liberal to the radical/critical. Nevertheless, many issues remain unresolved and both conceptual thinking and empirical studies are still in short supply.

The distinguished scholars writing in this volume have added greatly to our understanding of the subjects under study from a variety of corporate, country and policy perspectives. The ideas and evidence presented have come from a range of disciplines including economics, strategic management, political science and geography. The authors, and their discussants at the Workshop from which this volume emanated, represent orthodox opinion by and large. Notwithstanding this, the conclusions reached on a number of topics were significantly different. The purpose of this concluding chapter is thus to highlight some of the major findings of the volume, but also to portray the diversity of opinion on a number of issues which are critically important for the future of the world economy. Comments and conclusions drawn in this chapter correspond to the main themes of the volume, and incorporate the ideas and arguments of both chapter authors and Workshop discussants.

GLOBALIZATION

One issue which is quite fundamental to this volume but which continues to intrigue is the meaning and extent of globalization. As a broad definitional statement, that presented by the IMF (1997, p. 45) is commonly accepted, that is:

> Globalization refers to the growing economic interdependencies of countries worldwide through the increasing volume and variety of cross-border transactions in goods and services and of international capital flows and also through the rapid and widespread diffusion of technology.

At this Workshop, Ed Safarian drew attention to the relevance of Nelson and Rosenberg (1993) to the subject under review. 'There is good reason to believe that in recent years, just as the roles of national innovation systems has become widely accepted, technical communities have become transnational as never before' (p. 17). They go on to state that there continue to be important differences between governments attempting to develop national technological policies and firms going transnational in this and other respects. This is but one of the key policy debates which globalization stimulates.

Some writers have argued that the extent and, therefore, the consequences of globalization have been much exaggerated; and point to the fact that the openness of economies is no greater than it was pre-1914 and that, relative to world output, cross-border capital flows are still only close to pre-World War I levels. Such comparisons are misleading: in the earlier period most capital flows were of a non-controlling portfolio form, whereas today they are integrally bound-up with management, technology and trade through the operations of MNEs; 'International production has become a central structural characteristic of the world economy' (UNCTAD, 1993, p. 101). In addition, as Kobrin (1997) has pointed out, the world economy is significantly different from that of a century ago, being broader in terms of the number of national markets actively involved, and deeper in respect of trade and investment interactions. As an indicator of the former, Enright (Chapter 13) has pointed out that countries representing nearly one-half of the world's population have either entered the world economy or dramatically changed their relationship with it in the last 20 years.

Despite these qualitative and quantitative changes, it is clear from the chapters in the volume that the world is far from being globalized, an observation which applies to industries, firms and countries. Yet pinning this proposition down is far from straightforward given the continuing debate over appropriate measures. Peter Buckley pleaded for the application of scientific method to the subject of globalization, suggesting that the beginnings exist in recent articles such as those by Makhija *et al.* (1997). The latter attempted to measure industry globalization on the basis of the extent of an industry's international linkages, and the integration of value-added activities within the industry. And there have been other efforts, such as that by Sullivan (1994) to measure the degree of internationalization (rather than globalization) of the firm.

So what is different? Michael Enright spoke of issues such as the development of global finance and financial markets; the spread of knowledge facilitated by improved communications, the widespread availability and use of technology, the rise of electronic communities over the Internet, the decoupling and decentralization of economic activities within and between firms, the activities of MNEs, reductions in barriers to trade and investment, the increased power of supranational organizations such as the EU, and the emergence of regions and regional identities that transcend borders.

Lynn Mytelka distinguished between two dimensions of globalization in her chapter. The one relating to FDI flows and the resultant global market for investment sites and the locational tournaments which take place across them; the other concerning the globalization of an innovation-based mode of competition. The latter invariably receives less attention than the former. In this case attention is drawn to a possible linkage between new opportunities for learning and the threat of increased turbulence stemming from the globalization process, thus reminding us of winner and loser countries and regions. In his interesting comments as discussant, Ed Safarian challenged some of the tests used by Mytelka to support the negative relationship between FDI and national innovation systems. On the specific question of capping the net incentives involved in locational tournaments, he acknowledged that such competition did reduce the public returns from private investment and handicapped the income of countries or regions, but drew attention to the need to balance the costs involved against those of better feasible alternatives in terms of reduction in employment, increased tax base, and so on.

Stephen Kobrin in this volume (Chapter 6) focused most strongly on the cost, risk and complexity of technology. He believes that the information revolution effectively eliminates the boundaries between manufacturing and services; and, particularly important for his argument, 'information technology facilitates the integration of geographically dispersed operations and allows networked coordination to replace ownership and hierarchy as the primary mode of control'. Certainly information technology was the factor which permitted the integration of the Indian software industry into the world economy, and there are similar examples elsewhere. Young, Slow and Hood (Chapter 5) suggest that IT could be one of the mechanisms to exploit the potential benefits from closer coordination of companies' international operations; this could be particularly important among smaller and non-dominant firms and those which operated on a multi-domestic basis because of the specific requirements of national markets.

What is interesting is to speculate on the limits of information technology as a driving force in integration. There is much debate in the field of services' activities and regional development concerning the factors which influence the balance between agglomeration and dispersion (paralleling in many ways the discussion by Enright on globalization versus localization in respect of regional clusters). As Buckley observed at the Workshop: 'Why are we here? Why aren't we all sitting at terminals communicating with one another? . . . There's obviously something very important about face-to-face dealings'. The 'glue' of agglomerative economies, at least in 1960s and 1970s studies, was regarded as being face-to-face contacts. And even in more recent work, emphasis is placed on the links between corporate complexes in and around key metropolitan centres with government, financial institutions and specialist business services. The functioning of these links requires face-to-face contacts, sociability and spatial proximity.

An important theme developed by Hafiz Mirza (Chapter 9) concerned the relationship between regionalization and globalization. This was discussed in the context of the emergence of East Asian MNEs; and the significance of government policies to promote regionalization, regionally-focused corporate strategies and the emergence of regional growth zones associated with regional spillovers. For many companies seeking to exploit liberalization of markets, and for countries attempting to promote outward-oriented development strategies, adjacent regional markets represent the obvious initial focus. Such company and country strategies are supported by the rapid growth in the number of regional integration agreements in the 1990s. As discussant to Mirza's paper, Michael McDermott highlighted the strong philosophy of cooperation within large industrial groupings in Asia and compared this to the Birkinshaw work on internal markets (Chapter 3). This was equally evident in their business activity within the wider region. The appropriate 'region' is not always obvious, admittedly. This is apparent in the long-standing ambiguities in the relationship of the UK and UK companies to the European Union as compared with the United States. In any event, questions concerning convergence or divergence in regionalism and globalism are of major significance for the continuation of favourable trends in cross-border integration. In respect of FDI, at least, Brewer and Young (1998) have predicted that problems in multilateral negotiations will promote regionalism into the twenty-first century, with inevitable fears of discriminatory trade and investment provisions in regional agreements.

GLOBAL FIRMS AND GLOBAL STRATEGIES

As with the concept of globalization itself, definitions of global industries and global firms and global strategies are proving problematic. In empirical work, Roth (1992) defined the following industries as global, namely, aircraft and parts, measuring and controlling devices, agricultural chemicals, construction machinery, ethical drugs, communications equipment, household auto and video equipment, electronic components and accessories, and medical instruments and supplies. Morrison and Roth (1992) added in watches, textile machinery, mining machinery, oilfield machinery, sewing machines, and insecticides and fungicides. This is a very wide range and illustrates the point that the criteria employed, whether at industry, firm or strategy level, are still imprecise.

Young *et al.* in this volume suggested the need to move away from the global/non-global dichotomy to develop instead a continuum from domestic to global, which is in line with other recent thinking. Kobrin proposed that the criteria for globalization (geographical spread, market servicing methods, value activities outside the home country, managerial vision and perspective and coordination) should be weighted on the grounds that global spread or even global spread using sales subsidiaries would not be indicative of a global company. However, a company with a global spread of *coordinated* sales subsidiaries probably would classify as 'global', since coordination facilitates a worldwide approach, worldwide interchange and worldwide learning. Certainly, different constituents of the value chain may reveal very different degrees of globalization/localization, which suggests that managerial attitudes, vision and perspective are critically important. The distinction in the early literature between global integration strategies and local responsiveness or multi-domestic strategies may no longer be very useful.

A number of important issues pertaining to MNEs' strategies emerge from the chapters in this volume (and associated Workshop discussion). The first concerns the necessity to distinguish between global competition and global firms. Globalization may be regarded as a ubiquitous process which will impact upon all companies. But this does not suggest that a global strategy is the appropriate response to maximize the economic value of the organization for shareholders. The case of the British bank in Young, Slow and Hood's chapter illustrates the point exactly: while the company views its strategy as being open to ideas and products from global markets, its priority has been to internalize these within its UK operations. Of course, the banking industry is still subject to regulation in many countries, and competitive pressures in the domestic market may not yet be sufficient to require an outward-oriented response. On the other hand, Hood and Peters (Chapter 4) provide some illustrations of the rapid globalization of professional service companies where global customers, market access and management ambitions made integrated strategies on a world scale the most appropriate response.

The Hood and Peters chapter addresses some of the drivers of development in business services, a diverse and ill-defined sector in which there is much evidence of 'global for global and local for local' strategic combinations. One element of this is shown to be the interaction between the outsourcing of services and the consolidation of functions in international companies. As Peter Buckley observed in his comments on the paper, the key issue is neither internalization nor externalization as companies respond to internationalization issues, but the balance between the two as multinational firms develop ever more flexible responses to the increasing volatility in the world economy.

Secondly, in general, international business scholars have perhaps paid insufficient attention to questions about domestic versus international expansion (although there has been significant debate in the export field). It may be (as Neil Kay implied as discussant to the presentation of John Dunning in Chapter 2) that internalization theory – the major theoretical paradigm in international business – has led to an emphasis on questions concerning choice of mode, for example, licensing versus foreign production. A resource-based perspective, by comparison, would ask why international expansion was preferred to domestic diversification in particular cases. To quote Neil Kay:

> If you look at expansion possibilities from the point of view of the firm, one of the features which tends to become apparent is the extent to which domestic diversification may often offer opportunities for resource sharing, synergies and economies of scope to a much greater extent than those afforded by multinational expansion.
>
> (Kay, 1997, pp. 153–76)

The potential opportunity costs of using Penrosian-style residual resources to pursue multinational expansion include the domestic expansion possibilities that may have been pursued instead.

Third and related is the question of the importance of the multinationals' home base. Hu (1992) was at the forefront of those refuting the notion of the 'stateless' MNE; he argued that most MNEs were national firms with international operations, based on measures such as domestic versus foreign sales and assets, ownership and control, nationality of people in the organization and legal nationality and taxation (see also Warhurst *et al.*, 1998); and compare Enright and Birkinshaw in Chapters 13 and 3 of this volume).

The importance of the home base – defined as the nation where the firm retains effective strategic, creative and technical control – is emphasised in Porter's (1990) work on the competitive advantage of nations; but has been refuted by Rugman and Verbeke (1997) in favour of a model involving multiple home bases and 'diamonds' of competitive advantage. This debate parallels that over the 'headquarters hierarchy syndrome' (Bartlett and Ghoshal, 1986, p. 88) as compared with the concept of heterarchy and global subsidiary mandates. In pushing back the frontiers with new concepts and research, it is still important to measure the importance of the phenomena. For example, Leong and Tan (1993) found that the transnational form of organization (Bartlett and Ghoshal, 1989) was little in evidence; and it would be interesting to explore the prevalence of regional, let alone global subsidiary mandates.

Fourth, despite the above point, Julian Birkinshaw's chapter on the internal market perspective on multinational corporate strategy provides a very significant contribution. The basic premise is that internal competition may take place for a 'Charter' which is the responsibility to perform certain activities for the MNE as a whole. This has implications not only for the management of the multinational, but also for country and regional economic development. In analysing and developing the concept, consideration undoubtedly needs to be given to sectoral and product characteristics. For example, within the electronics industry it may be appropriate for consumer electronics but not for semiconductors.

Finally, John Dunning in Chapter 2 draws attention to another major issue in the whole globalization debate, namely the expansion of cross-border strategic alliances and acquisitions and mergers (A&Ms) – so-called strategic asset-seeking FDI. Data are cited which indicate that three-fifths of the FDI between developed countries took the form of A&Ms, largely concentrated in the knowledge-intensive manufacturing and service sectors. From Dunning's perspective, interesting questions concern the implications of the globalizing economy of the 1990s for paradigms and theories: attention is drawn to the reduced significance of the 'push' factor, and the rising importance of knowledge incorporated in human and physical resources as a locational 'pull'. But the corporate strategy dimension of acquisitions and mergers is also of great significance and merits much greater attention than it has been given in research to date.

ECONOMIC DEVELOPMENT ISSUES

In a recent reconsideration of the benefits of FDI, Dunning (1994) proposed that the principal criteria by which national governments evaluate inward investment in the 1990s concern: 'Its perceived contribution to the improvement of the competitiveness or the productivity of the resources and asset-creating capabilities' (p. 30) within host countries. While the emphasis on competitiveness is recent, the measures of economic development contribution are little different; the exception concerns the greater attention being paid to sustainable development incorporating issues such as environmental quality. Otherwise the contributions of MNEs to capital formation, technology development and transfer, human-resource development and trade and the balance of payments are as significant today as in earlier periods.

The chapter by Buckley and Young (Chapter 7) provides an interesting insight into the formidable range of challenges facing a country like Egypt which is at a relatively early stage of positioning itself for foreign investment. They set out the conditions precedent to enhance the country's attractiveness as an investment location, recognizing that in the context of the themes of this volume Egypt has been a bystander on the world stage as globalization pressures have led to increasing integration of companies and countries elsewhere. This chapter raises some interesting questions about the holistic review of public policy which is so often necessary for a country to be a contender for the benefits of FDI. At the same time there is the central political question as to whether governments in developing country contexts may be comfortable with multinational companies as drivers of reform. In many ways globalization has set the entry price for such participation, not least because it has extended the options open to MNEs.

What is different is that in the efforts to attract FDI in an increasingly competitive marketplace, countries may have lost sight (or have had to lose sight) of the economic contributions. As Hamdani (1997) points out: 'Globalization is, therefore, triggering a process of systemic convergence in which all governments face pressures to pursue more or less similar policies to enhance their national (or regional) competitiveness' (p. 3). This presumption that inward FDI enhances competitiveness and economic development will undoubtedly be tested in the months and years ahead. With globalization, the anchoring of some types of FDI projects at national level will become increasingly problematic, with short product life-cycles, global performance measures and greater mobility of manufacturing and service projects. Globalization is also leading to a widening in sources of competition for inward FDI as certain types of projects will become globally as opposed to regionally mobile (linked to the internal market issue discussed above). Worldwide competition for such projects is leading to greater competitive bidding, both because of fewer constraints (the very limited scope of international rules at present) and more widely varying types and levels of incentives. The end result could be a 'race to the bottom' (see Mytelka, Chapter 12).

Daniel Chudnovsky in this volume (Chapter 8) comments that: 'Whereas the sectoral policies have been effective in attracting substantial FDI flows and in fastening some positive externalities to the host economy, they have been less successful in generating technological spillovers'. Moreover, most of the MNE affiliates surveyed in his research had not yet defined explicit strategies of integration with world or regional markets. In a sense, there is little new in this. A 1984/85 OECD report concerning the effects of incentives in the Republic of Ireland noted that: '. . . foreign-owned firms have developed few linkages with the indigenous economy, little in the way of local research or technological inputs, and depend heavily on imported raw materials and components' (cited in Thomsen, 1997, p.

224). Such states of affairs are the responsibility of the host country and its policies, not the MNE; nevertheless, there are legitimate concerns.

The debate over what constitutes 'economic development' emerged quite strongly in the presentation and discussion surrounding the paper of Stephen Kobrin. Reflecting a view that development theory has for the time being lost its way (Leys, 1996), Kobrin argues that the debate over enclaves, centre and periphery, and dualism takes a new meaning in the post-industrial era. Thus, as in the Indian software industry case, linkages to the national economy may be much weaker in the information age than hitherto. His view was that dualism is likely to be accentuated in the information age, with education and access to computers and communication networks being prerequisites for inclusion into the networked global economy and its associated prosperity. Lacking these attributes, the outcome is exclusion from global networks and associated poverty.

As discussant, Lynn Mytelka took issue with a number of these conclusions. She argued that while the electronics revolution would exacerbate the marginalization experience, the widening income gap (in evidence in advanced as well as developing countries) was a consequence of more fundamental changes such as the growing knowledge intensity of production. In addition she questioned what differentiated an enclave from a growth pole economy in a global era. Using the illustration of a classic enclave economy, such as a resource-producing state in colonial Africa, Mytelka argued that there was no comparison with the Indian software industry. In this latter case, the numbers of locally-educated software designers had grown substantially and numerous small indigenous firms had emerged; the software capabilities of the country were an important factor in the growth of the indigenous telecommunications industry, enabling local companies to play a full partnership role with multinationals in India.

While there is a clear need for more systematic study of this topic, there is much sympathy for the opinions of Ash Amin (speaking as discussant to Michael Enright). Accepting that globalization may generate only a limited set of gains in many parts of the world, he observed that 'a much greater threat for places is to be by-passed by globalization completely – to be simply left out in the cold . . .'. The case of Egypt is a telling illustration of a failure to integrate with the global economy.

Several of the contributions in this volume illuminate one of the foundational issues of economic development, namely the interface between what is happening within the company and the objectives of governments. For economic development practitioners (and many others) understanding the strategies of MNEs is difficult. Julian Birkinshaw's analysis of the three different internal markets (for products and services, for charters and for capabilities and practices) is a most insightful way of interpreting some of the dynamics of strategy as they affect subsidiaries of multinational companies. Clearly these markets are broadened, deepened and become ever more competitive in a globalizing world economy. But in terms of the Dunning comments earlier in this section, they require governments to take a close interest in competitiveness at the micro level, namely within the subsidiaries in their country.

Economic development is also about pursuing the 'art of the possible'. The Hood and Peters chapter examines some of the ubiquitous aspects of business service expansion which have made it such a widespread target for investment attraction. In developing different scenarios of virtuous and vicious circles in the light of the internationalization of services, a cautionary note is struck as to the contribution which might be made to economic development from some of this activity. The policy-maker is again encouraged in, for example, the case of call centres, to understand the options open for their medium-term development and not be overwhelmed by their short-term employment impact.

Still within this broad theme of corporate strategies and economic development, Terutomo Ozawa's chapter gives a significant perspective on the ways in which geography and company development have evolved in Japan. Tracing the origins of agglomeration back to Adam Smith, Ozawa categorizes both industries and industrial districts relating these to the internationalization process and its impact on the domestic economy. While the Japanese context has many unique and distinctive features, there are insights given here which both advise and caution those promoting clusters. Neil Hood, as commentator in this chapter, observed how many Japanese MNEs had shown propensities to create the characteristics of clusters (whether real or virtual) as part of the internationalization of their manufacturing sector – not least in order to preserve the competitiveness rooted in their domestic base. This poses the interesting question of the degree to which some types of globalization require the replication of home-base conditions.

Ewen Peters' contribution (Chapter 14) brings a specific and under-researched issue of economic development to the forefront of the debate on globalization, namely the question of plant upgrading. Central to this is whether plant upgrading is contestable from the host-country viewpoint. Julian Birkinshaw, as discussant, commented on the dearth of process level of analysis in this area and welcomed the presentation of a useful categorization of types of upgrade in the electronics industry cases which were considered. What is stark, however, is that this study draws attention to the scarcity of such upgrading examples among the world's top-500 electronics corporations. This serves as a reminder that globalization of strategic options for MNEs may well put such desirable upgrades beyond the reach of most governments and thereby limit the contribution of their subsidiaries to cluster development.

In concluding these brief remarks on economic development issues, the significance of outward investment as well as inward FDI must be acknowledged. In re-evaluating the benefits of inward FDI, it is equally important to reassess the contribution of outward FDI. Young, Slow and Hood argue the case for outward internationalization/globalization as necessary and desirable for home-country competitiveness. An economy which comprises dynamic, knowledge-intensive, export-oriented foreign multinationals alongside traditional, domestically-oriented indigenous enterprises is not only vulnerable to the whims of the global marketplace but is failing to capitalize upon global opportunities.

Stephen Kobrin queried this view that the Scottish and UK economies would be strengthened by the creation of indigenous global companies. Citing Robert Reich's (1990) 'Who is us?' article, he queried whether location matters. In a sense, however, the point at issue is not the choice between foreign and UK MNEs, but rather one of encouraging both.

Kobrin also suggested an inherent contradiction in the arguments presented in Chapter 5: on the one hand, it is suggested that the creation of UK global companies is desirable from an economic development perspective; while, on the other, it is proposed that policy measures are devised to encourage what is called a 'developmental headquarters corporation', meaning a strengthening of the home base of UK global enterprises. In a completely free market for international capital (the UK, interestingly, being the closest to this among the major economies), companies would allocate resources unhindered to locations where they achieve the greatest return. But in a situation where there is fierce competitive bidding for inward FDI, a 'hands-off' approach to outward investment runs the risk of effectively promoting a dual economy. The appropriate policy measures for outward investment do, of course, require careful consideration.

ECONOMIC POLICY

Questions of economic policy – at local, national, regional and global levels – were raised in many of the contributions to this volume. A number of the most important ones are reviewed in this section.

At the global policy level, Brewer and Young (Chapter 11) start from what appears to be a fairly orthodox view in which multilateral investment liberalization is to be encouraged to facilitate the gains from investment; these parallel the undoubted gains from multilateral trade liberalization. But in their work is the cautionary note that specific consideration should be given to the developmental needs of the emerging economies; they also argue the case for research to prove the benefits from multilateral investment liberalization which might otherwise be rejected at the individual country level.

The caution is necessary. In recent populist and much publicized work, Elliott and Atkinson (1998, pp. 269–70) argue that:

> Multilateral organisations are certainly needed, but they should be multilateral organisations that are part of the solution rather than part of the problem. A good start would be to follow the suggestion of abolishing the WTO and setting up a General Agreement for Sustainable Trade . . . Multilateral organisations should be there to control globalization, not to control it.

In a similar polemic, Gray (1998, p. 199) argues that:

> A regime of global governance is needed in which world markets are managed so as to promote the cohesion of societies and the integrating of States. Only the formation of global regulation – of commerce, capital movements, trade and environmental conservation – can enable the creativity of the world economy to be harnessed in the service of human needs.

In such works are indications of a mood shift in a number of quarters, which may lead to a backlash against globalization and a withdrawal into protectionism. This sobering theme is picked up by Kobrin in this volume, but from another angle. He counsels governments and global institutions against perpetuating systems within which education and access to the fruits of the information revolution are prerequisites to being in the global network. As he observes, 'a system in which large segments of the population are marginalised is not stable'. This is a challenge of the highest order to the formulators of economic policy in all areas.

A number of other economic policy questions are relevant at regional, national or local levels, depending on the context. For example, and with reference towards specific policies of investment targeting and subsequent reinvestment, Hood and Peters strike a cautionary note. Policy-makers are advised to look carefully at the types of business service centres which their cities and regions are attracting, with a view to investing in the appropriate infrastructure for their development if they demonstrate potential for higher added value. The assumption here is that service globalization may promise more than can be delivered with many countries attempting to attract high value added activities from the same few global players.

One specific and neglected policy area is that of the role of government and its agencies in supporting outward investment. Young, Slow and Hood ask if public policy has a role in this area, or are governments correct in large measure when they have schemes for exporting but not for other modes of international operations. The reader might well query whether or not this is business of government, given that the market has many established ways of achieving these ends. At the same time, it is suggested that in the case of young, small high-technology firms which face early and rapid pressures for internationalization at an immature stage of their development, such support might be justified. One part of this rationale is the scope for home-country benefit from spawning specialist small MNEs.

Both the Enright and Peters chapters raise interesting practical and process-related questions about clusters and partnerships respectively. Enright, in observing that many cluster development programmes are remarkably similar, advises against 'one size fits all' policies where all regions follow the same policies in pursuit of the same industries. This is in itself a reflection of the global spread of economic development philosophies and the transfer of the technology of supporting business development. As Enright observes, there is irony in a process which is directed to the embeddedness of economic activity into local society, yet attempts to do so with a set of disembodied policies regardless of the local context. Clearly this can only be offset by cluster-development programmes being tailored to both local economic and social reality. Regrettably this is a message that many policy-makers and politicians do not always want to hear. Part of the remedy for this may lie, as Peters suggests, in a new approach to partnership in areas of strategic plant upgrading within clusters whereby the local economic development bodies work in a proactive way with the actual MNE resource base within this area. By this approach local collaboration may be more firmly rooted in reality and founded on more attainable goals.

This volume directs relatively little attention to the detail of the national or local institutional frameworks designed to cope with the globalizing process. Sound development advice with intertwined institutional comment is proffered for Egypt by Buckley and Young. In a rather different way, Phelps, Morgan and Fuller (Chapter 15) chart the evolution of investment attraction mechanisms in Wales at a time of constitutional change in the country. One aspect which it emphasises and which rings true in other contexts is the necessity for integrative, but executive, structures at local level to match the decision processes of MNEs. They point to a trade-off between hierarchical and democratic structures, an issue of even more relevance in the ever more competitive world of investment attraction and development. It is to this world which Mytelka directs her policy advice as regards both linkages and bidding wars. The effects of the globalization of sourcing policies on the potential for local linkages are emphasised in the automobile and electronics industries. The principles outlined are, however, generic ones and the expected benefits in this activity have to be weighed against the costs of attracting or sustaining an investment. A plea is made on the bidding issue within Europe, for measures to convert the wide variety of incentives into comparable and quantifiable indicators which can more easily be related to the longer-term costs and benefits of locational tournaments. This is a challenging and controversial area, where modern and ever more innovative versions of a 'beggar thy neighbour' policies are a reflection of the globalization process.

FINAL NOTE

As will be evident, there is still much to be done to advance our understanding on the topic of globalization and economic development; and there is ample scope for healthy debate on many of its aspects. This can be amply illustrated by two statements in the volume. Stephen

Kobrin asserts in his chapter, 'Geography is increasingly irrelevant as a basis for the defining of markets and the organizing of economic activity'; while Michael Enright opines 'although distance might be less important for certain industries or activities to-day, geography in the sense of "place" is not'. In many aspects both are true, yet implying opposing positions. There is at the same time widespread interest in the role of agglomeration in both corporate competitiveness and in economic development, while simultaneously announcing the death of geography for many of the world's most rapidly-growing industries. We did not seek to arrive at a consensus on such issues within the Workshop, but we all learned from it and offer this volume as a contribution to the large outstanding research agenda in this important field.

While we had much debate, we avoided the charge which Queen Elizabeth (1533–1603) lodged against Mary, Queen of Scots, whom she described as 'The daughter of debate, that eke discord doth sow'.[1] Hopefully we sowed no discord as the participants returned to their home bases and many continued their careers, the better to contribute to further analysis and to policy formulation on globalization and economic development.

Note

1. Chamberlain, 'Sayings of Queen Elizabeth', p. 301, quoted in *Oxford Dictionary of Quotations* 3rd edn (1979) (Oxford: Oxford University Press).

References

BARTLETT, C. and S. GHOSHAL (1989), *Managing Across Borders: The Transnational Solution* (Boston, Mass.; Harvard Business School Press).

BARTLETT, C. and S. GHOSHAL (1986), 'Tap Your Subsidiaries for Global Reach', *Harvard Business Review*, November–December, pp. 87–94.

BREWER, T.L. and S. YOUNG (1998), *The Multilateral Investment System and Multinational Enterprises* (Oxford: Oxford University Press).

DUNNING, J.H. (1994), 'Re-evaluating the Benefits of Foreign Direct Investment', *Transnational Corporations*, vol. 3, no. 1, pp. 23–51.

ELLIOTT, L. and D. ATKINSON (1998), *The Age of Insecurity* (London: Verso).

GRAY, J. (1998), *False Dawn. The Delusions of Global Capitalism* (London: Grata Books).

HAMDANI, K.A. (1997), 'Introduction', in J.H. Dunning and K.A. Hamdani (eds), *The New Globalism and Developing Countries* (New York: United Nations University Press), pp. 1–10.

HU, Y. (1992), 'Global or Stateless Corporations are National Firms with International Operations', *California Management Review*, Winter, pp. 107–26.

INTERNATIONAL MONETARY FUND (1997), *World Economic Outlook, May 1997: Globalization – Opportunities and Challenges* (Washington, DC: IMF).

KAY, N. (1997), *Pattern in Corporate Evolution* (Oxford: Oxford University Press).

KOBRIN, S.J. (1997), 'The Architecture of Globalization: State Sovereignty in a Nationalised Global Economy', in J.H. Dunning (ed.), *Governments, Globalization and International Business* (Oxford: Oxford University Press), pp. 146–71.

LEONG, S.M. and C.T. TAN (1993), 'Managing Across Borders: An Empirical Test of the Bartlett and Ghoshal (1989) Organizational Typology', *Journal of International Business Studies*, vol. 24, no. 3, pp. 449–64.

LEYS, C. (1996), *The Rise and Fall of Development Theory* (Oxford: James Currey).

MAKHIJA, M.V., K. KIM and S.D. WILLIAMSON (1997), 'Measuring Globalization of Industries Using a National Industry Approach: Empirical Evidence Across Five Countries and Over Time', *Journal of International Business Studies*, vol. 28, no. 4, pp. 679–710.

MORRISON, A.J. and K. ROTH (1992), 'A Taxonomy of Business-Level Strategies in Global Industries', *Strategic Management Journal*, vol. 13, pp. 399–418.

NELSON, R.R. and N. ROSENBERG, 'Technical Innovation and National Innovation Systems', in R.R. Nelson (ed.), *National Innovation Systems: A Comparative Analysis* (New York and Oxford: Oxford University Press), pp. 3–21.

PORTER, M.E. (1990), *The Competitive Advantage of Nations* (London: Macmillan).

REICH, R. (1990), 'Who is Us?', *Harvard Business Review*, January–February, pp. 53–64.

ROTH, K. (1992), 'International Configuration and Co-ordination Archetypes for Medium-Sized Firms in Global Industries', *Journal of International Business Studies*, vol. 23, no. 3, pp. 533–49.

RUGMAN, A. and A. VERBEKE (1997), 'Global Strategies for Multinational Enterprises', in I. Islam and W. Shepherd (eds), *Current Issues in International Business* (Cheltenham, UK: Edward Elgar), pp. 132–50.

SULLIVAN, D. (1994), 'Measuring the Degree of Internationalization of a Firm', *Journal of International Business Studies*, vol. 25, no. 2, pp. 325–42.

THOMSEN, S. (1997), 'Attracting Investment in an Integrating World Economy', in J.H. DUNNING and K.A. HAMDANI (eds), *The New Globalism and Developing Countries* (New York: United Nations University Press), pp. 214–30.

UNCTAD (1993), *World Investment Report 1993: Transnational Corporations and Integrated International Production* (New York: UN).

WARHURST, C., D. NICKSON and E. SHAW (1998), 'A Future for Globalization? International Business Organisation in the Next Century', in T.A. Scandux and M.G.S. Serajio (eds), *Research in International Business and International Relations*, vol. 7 (Greenwich, Conn.: JAI Press).

Index

Note: page references in **bold** type indicate authorship.